W9-BTD-913

COLLEGIUM

CHRISTI REGIS

FROM THE COLLECTION OF

GEORGE SCHNER, S.J.
1946 - 2000

LECTURES
on the
HISTORY
of
PHILOSOPHY

GEORG WILHELM FRIEDRICH HEGEL

LECTURES ON THE HISTORY OF PHILOSOPHY
The Lectures of 1825–1826

VOLUME III

MEDIEVAL AND MODERN PHILOSOPHY

Edited by
ROBERT F. BROWN

Translated by
R. F. BROWN and J. M. STEWART
with the assistance of
H. S. HARRIS

B
2936
E5
B76
1990
v.3

Regis College Library
15 ST. MARY STREET
TORONTO, ONTARIO, CANADA
M4Y 2R5

WITHDRAWN

101407

UNIVERSITY OF CALIFORNIA PRESS
Berkeley, Los Angeles, Oxford

University of California Press
Berkeley and Los Angeles, California

University of California Press, Ltd.
Oxford, England

This volume is a translation of G. W. F. Hegel: *Vorlesungen über die Geschichte der Philosophie, Teil 4, Philosophie des Mittelalters und der neueren Zeit* (vol. 9 of G. W. F. Hegel: *Vorlesungen: Ausgewählte Nachschriften und Manuskripte*), edited by Pierre Garniron and Walter Jaeschke, copyright © 1986 by Felix Meiner Verlag GmbH, Hamburg.

The English edition has been prepared with financial support from the Division of Research Programs of the National Endowment for the Humanities, the generosity of which is greatly appreciated.

Copyright © 1990 by
The Regents of the University of California

Library of Congress Cataloging-in-Publication Data

Hegel, Georg Wilhelm Friedrich, 1770–1831.
  [Vorlesungen über die Geschichte der Philosophie. English]
  Lectures on the history of philosophy: the lectures of 1825–26 / Georg Wilhelm Friedrich Hegel: edited by Robert F. Brown: translated by R. F. Brown and J. M. Stewart with the assistance of H. S. Harris.
    p. cm.
  Translation of: Vorlesungen über die Geschichte der Philosophie.
  Includes bibliographical references.
  Contents: — v. 3. Medieval and modern philosophy.
  ISBN 0–520–06812–2 (v. 3: alk. paper)
  1. Philosophy—History. I. Brown, Robert F., 1941– . II. Stewart, J. M. (J. Michael) 1920– . III. Harris, H. S. (Henry Silton), 1926– . IV. Title.
B2936.H4B76   1990
109—dc20   89–38214
                                                                      CIP

Printed in the United States of America
1 2 3 4 5 6 7 8 9

The paper used in this publication meets the minimum requirements of American National Standard for Information Sciences—Permanence of Paper for Printed Library Materials, ANSI Z39.48–1984 ∞

CONTENTS

PREFACE   ix

ABBREVIATIONS, SIGNS, AND SYMBOLS   xiii

FREQUENTLY CITED WORKS BY HEGEL   xv

EDITORIAL INTRODUCTION   1

    1. The Importance of Hegel's *Lectures on the History of Philosophy*   1

    2. Previous Editions of the Lectures   3

    3. The New German Edition   4

      a. Nature and Origins   4

      b. Sources   7

      c. Establishment of the Text   8

    4. This English Edition   10

THE SECOND PERIOD: MEDIEVAL PHILOSOPHY   15

    A. Introduction: The Idea of Christianity   17

    B. The Church Fathers   27

    C. Arabic Philosophy   35

    D. The Scholastics   40

      1. General Character of Scholastic Philosophy   40

      2. Principal Moments of Scholastic Philosophy   51

        a. Beginnings   52

        b. Philosophical Consideration of Church Doctrine   53

        c. Further Development of Theology by the Scholastics   57

        d. Realism and Nominalism   62

e. Doctrinal System and Formalism 65
f. Mystics 67
E. Renaissance and Reformation .68
1. Transition to the Renaissance 68
2. Interest in Ancient Philosophy 71
3. Individual Renaissance Philosophers 74
4. The Reformation 94

THE THIRD PERIOD: MODERN PHILOSOPHY 105
A. Beginnings of Modern Philosophy: Bacon and
Boehme 107
1. Transition to the Modern Era 107
2. Francis Bacon 110
3. Jacob Boehme 117
B. First Period of Metaphysics: Descartes, Spinoza,
Malebranche 131
1. Nature and Periods of Modern Philosophy 131
2. René Descartes 135
3. Benedict Spinoza 151
4. Nicolas Malebranche 165

C. Critique and Second Period of Metaphysics: Locke,
Leibniz, and Others 170
1. John Locke 170
2. Hugo Grotius 178
3. Thomas Hobbes 180
4. Gottfried Wilhelm Leibniz 185
5. Christian Wolff 198
6. Metaphysical and Popular Philosophy 203
7. David Hume 213
D. Recent Philosophy: Kant, Fichte, Jacobi, Schelling 217
1. Immanuel Kant: Transcendental Aesthetic and
Analytic 217
2. Johann Gottlieb Fichte: *Wissenschaftslehre* 229
3. Kant: Transcendental Dialectic 236
4. Friedrich Heinrich Jacobi: General Orientation 240

5. Kant and Fichte: Practical Philosophy   244
6. Kant and Jacobi: Teleology, Faith, and
    Knowledge of God   246
7. Friedrich Wilhelm Joseph Schelling: Identity
    Philosophy   259
8. Conclusion   271

APPENDIXES

GLOSSARY   275
BIBLIOGRAPHY OF HEGEL'S SOURCES FOR MEDIEVAL AND
    MODERN PHILOSOPHY   285
INDEX   299

PREFACE

This, the first volume to appear of the English translation of Hegel's *Lectures on the History of Philosophy* in a new edition, is less a beginning than it is a stage in an ongoing project. Its predecessor and model is the recently completed *Lectures on the Philosophy of Religion*. Dr. Walter Jaeschke of the Hegel-Archiv staff (Ruhr-Universität, Bochum, West Germany) prepared a new and much more critical German edition of the *Philosophie der Religion*, working in collaboration with Professor Peter C. Hodgson (The Divinity School, Vanderbilt University), who edited the English edition and translation of it, and with Professor Ricardo Ferrara (Conicet, Argentina), who produced a Spanish edition. As work on the German edition progressed, the decision was made to produce as well new editions of other Hegel works also based on lecture manuscripts and transcripts, and to issue them in a ten-volume series (*G. W. F. Hegel: Vorlesungen: Ausgewählte Nachschriften und Manuskripte*). The University of California Press, under an agreement with the German publisher, Felix Meiner Verlag of Hamburg, is publishing all ten of the new volumes in English translation. Since the *Vorlesungen über die Geschichte der Philosophie* are included in that German series, this background is part of the story of how our enterprise came about.

In his work on the *Lectures on the Philosophy of Religion*, Hodgson developed and refined the editorial principles that will serve all subsequent volumes in the English-language editions. This translation of the *Lectures on the History of Philosophy* is the beneficiary of that prior labor, as it is of the experience gained by others who shared the work of translating the *Philosophy of Religion*: Professor Robert F. Brown (Philosophy, University of Delaware) and Mr. J. Michael Stewart (retired translator for UNESCO, Paris; now of Farnham, Surrey, England). Hodgson has shifted from the role of editor and translator of individual works to that of general editor of the series. Brown and Stewart are doing the translation of these *Lectures on the History of Philosophy*, and Brown has assumed the editorial responsibilities. In addition, we are very fortunate to be able to carry over from the former project to the present one our translation consultant, the eminent Hegel authority Professor H. S. Harris (York University, Ontario, Canada), whose advice and criticism greatly enhance the quality of our work. Walter Jaeschke, coeditor with Pierre Garniron of the German edition of this volume (*Vorlesungen über die Geschichte der Philosophie, Teil 4, Philosophie des Mittelalters und der neueren Zeit,* Hamburg, 1986), has been invariably helpful in the preparation of this English edition, both by freely offering advice and assistance and by providing us first with typescripts and then with page proofs from which to work, prior to the appearance of the German volume.

Two larger projects form the context or background for the German edition. One involves the preparations for publishing Hegel's Heidelberg and Berlin lecture manuscripts, as well as the lecture transcripts, within the framework of the *Gesammelte Werke* being produced by the Academy of Sciences of Rhineland-Westphalia. In the other, the Centre National de la Recherche Scientifique, Paris, is making the history-of-philosophy lectures accessible through a combination of philosophical, translational, and editorial work. Six volumes have already been published of Pierre Garniron's planned seven-volume French translation of, and commentary on, the first edition (*Hegel: Leçons sur l'histoire de la philosophie: Traduction, annotation, reconstitution du cours de 1825–1826,* Paris, 1971–1985). The Deutsche Forschungsgemeinschaft has supported his work, under the German-French academic exchange arrangement.

The editors and publisher of the German edition decided to issue first the final volume of these lectures, that on Medieval and Modern Philosophy. The treatment of Greek Philosophy will follow, with the first volume, on the Introduction and Oriental Philosophy, to come last in the order of publication. In this way an extensive editorial introduction explaining the whole in detail can, to best advantage, be written last. Since the English volumes are following on the heels of their German counterparts, the same publication sequence is imposed on us. As this Preface is being written, the editorial work for the German volumes on Greek Philosophy is still in progress, and that on the first volume is in its early stages. Hence the Editorial Introduction is not a full-dress explanation of all editorial procedures but only provides information sufficient to make this volume usable on its own.

We are indebted to the following institutions, which made the German edition possible in its present form by granting permission to use, and to publish the contents of, the five lecture transcripts for 1825–26: the Manuscripts Division of the Staatsbibliothek Preussischer Kulturbesitz, Berlin; the Hegel-Archiv of the Ruhr-Universität, Bochum; the Library of the Polish Academy of Sciences, Cracow Division.

The editors of the German edition received assistance from Gudrun Sikora and Dora Braun in transcribing the transcripts, in checking the final version with annotations, and in proofreading.

The National Endowment for the Humanities, Division of Research Programs, provided generous financial support for the work on this English edition. The University of Delaware granted the editor some released time from teaching duties. Without these forms of support this timely translation would not have been possible.

Finally, many words of appreciation are due to Mary Imperatore and Dorothy Milsom, for typing our seemingly endless versions and revisions on the computer with unfailing patience and good cheer.

Robert F. Brown

ABBREVIATIONS, SIGNS, AND SYMBOLS

SIGNS AND SYMBOLS

[. . .]   = Editorial insertions in the text

ˇ . . . ˇ   = Passages in the main text that correspond to footnoted variant readings. These symbols are used only in the case of textual variants, which offer a different version of the designated passage, usually from a different source, not textual additions, which occur at the point marked by the note number in the main text. Normally the note number for the variant is placed at the end of the parallel in the main text; exceptions are noted.

^{1} ^{2} ^{3} etc.   = Footnotes containing textual variants, additions, or editorial annotations. The type of note is designated by an initial italicized editorial phrase in each instance. Notes are at the bottom of the page, and there is a separate series of notes, numbered consecutively, for each Period (Medieval and Modern) into which the text is divided.

[*Ed.*]   = Editorial annotations in the footnotes; materials following this symbol are editorial.

34 | = Page numbers of the German edition, on the outer margins with page breaks marked by vertical slashes in the text. The German edition is *G. W. F. Hegel: Vorlesungen: Ausgewählte Nachschriften und Manuskripte,* vol. 9, *Vorlesungen über die Geschichte der*

Philosophie, Teil 4, Philosophie des Mittelalters und der neueren Zeit. Edited by Pierre Garniron and Walter Jaeschke. Hamburg, 1986.

(Ms?)   = Indication that a passage cited in W (= *Hegel: Werke*) may derive from Hegel's own lecture manuscript.

PUBLISHED SOURCES

GW   = *G. W. F. Hegel: Gesammelte Werke.* Edited by the Academy of Sciences of Rhineland-Westphalia in association with the Deutsche Forschungsgemeinschaft. 40 vols. projected. Hamburg, 1968 ff.

W   = *Hegel: Werke.* Complete edition edited by an Association of Friends. 18 vols. Berlin, 1832 ff. Some volumes issued in second editions. Vols. 13–15 contain *Vorlesungen über die Geschichte der Philosophie,* edited by Karl Ludwig Michelet. 1st ed., Berlin, 1833–1836. (2d ed., Berlin, 1840–1844.) In this volume W always refers to the first edition.

UNPUBLISHED SOURCES OF THE 1825–26 LECTURES

An   = Anonymous transcript (Cracow)
Gr   = Griesheim transcript
Lw   = Löwe transcript
Pn   = Pinder transcript
Sv   = Stieve transcript

FREQUENTLY CITED WORKS
BY HEGEL

GW = *Gesammelte Werke*. (See above under Published Sources.)

W = *Werke*. (See above under Published Sources.)

Berliner Schriften = *Berliner Schriften 1818–1831*. Edited by Johannes Hoffmeister. Hamburg, 1956.

Briefe = *Briefe von und an Hegel*. Vols. 1–3 edited by Johannes Hoffmeister. 3d ed., Hamburg, 1969. Vol. 4, parts 1 and 2, edited by Friedhelm Nicolin. Hamburg, 1977–1981.

Encyclopedia = *Encyclopedia of the Philosophical Sciences*. Translated from the 3d German ed., with additions based on student transcripts and lecture manuscripts, by W. Wallace and A. V. Miller. 3 vols. Oxford, 1892 (reprint, 1975), 1970, 1971. *Enzyklopädie der philosophischen Wissenschaften im Grundrisse*. 1st ed., Heidelberg, 1817: forthcoming in *GW*, vol. 13. 2d ed., Berlin, 1827: *GW*, vol. 19 (edited by W. Bonsiepen and H.-Ch. Lucas). 3d ed., Berlin, 1830: *Werke*, vols. 6–7 (containing additions based on student transcripts and lecture manuscripts). 6th ed., based on the 3d ed. without additions, edited by Friedhelm Nicolin and Otto Pöggeler, Hamburg, 1959.

Letters = *Hegel, The Letters*. Translated by Clark Butler and Christiane Seiler, with commentary by Clark Butler. Bloomington, 1984.

Phenomen- = *Phenomenology of Spirit*. Translated by A. V.
ology   Miller. Oxford, 1977. *Phänomenologie des Geistes*. Bamberg and Würzburg, 1807. *GW*, vol. 9 (edited by W. Bonsiepen and R. Heede, 1980).

Philosophy of = *Lectures on the Philosophy of Religion*. Edited
Religion   by Peter C. Hodgson. 3 vols. Berkeley and Los Angeles, 1984–1987. (English translation/edition of: *Vorlesungen über die Philosophie der Religion*. Edited by Walter Jaeschke. 1983–1985. Vols. 3–5 of *Vorlesungen: Ausgewählte Nachschriften und Manuskripte*. 10 vols. Hamburg, 1983 ff.)

Philosophy of = *Lectures on the Philosophy of World History*.
World
History
Sibree ed. = *The Philosophy of History*. Translated from the 2d German ed. (1840) by J. Sibree. Revised edition. New York, 1900.

Nisbet ed. = *Lectures on the Philosophy of World History: Introduction: Reason in History*. Translated from vol. 1 of *Vorlesungen über die Philosophie der Weltgeschichte* (ed. Hoffmeister) by H. B. Nisbet, with an Introduction by Duncan Forbes. Cambridge, 1975.

Vorlesungen über die Philosophie der Weltgeschichte.

Hoffmeister = Vol. 1, *Die Vernunft in der Geschichte*. Edited by
ed.   Johannes Hoffmeister. Hamburg, 1955.
Lasson ed. = Vol. 2, *Die orientalische Welt*. Vol. 3, *Die griechische und die römische Welt*. Vol. 4, *Die germanische Welt*. Edited by Georg Lasson. 2d ed.

Hamburg, 1923. Vols. 1–4 are paginated cumulatively. Since vols. 2–4 have not been translated, corresponding references from the Sibree translation of the 1840 ed. are cited when possible.

Science of = *Science of Logic*. Translated by A. V. Miller.
Logic   London, 1969. *Wissenschaft der Logik*. Vol. 1, *Die objektive Logik*. Nuremberg, 1812–1813. *GW*, vol. 11 (edited by Friedrich Hogemann and Walter Jaeschke, 1978). Vol. 2, *Die subjektive Logik*. Nuremberg, 1816. *GW*, vol. 12 (edited by Friedrich Hogemann and Walter Jaeschke, 1981). 2d ed. of vol. 1, book 1, *Die Lehre vom Sein*. Berlin, 1832. *GW*, vol. 21 (edited by Friedrich Hogemann and Walter Jaeschke, 1984). The English translation uses the 2d ed. of vol. 1, book 1, hence there is not an exact correspondence between it and *GW*, vol. 11, book 1.

(Frequently cited works by other authors are included in the Bibliography of Sources at the back of the volume.)

EDITORIAL
INTRODUCTION[1]

1. The Importance of Hegel's *Lectures on the History of Philosophy*

Hegel's interpretation of the history of philosophy clearly played a central role not only in shaping his own thought but also in fostering greater emphasis on historical thinking generally among his contemporaries and successors. Nevertheless, the relation of these lectures to his philosophical system as such is today a matter of dispute. Some doubt that they form a part of the system at all, whereas others, in agreement with some of his students, view them as the system's crowning achievement or culmination. What is indubitable in any event is that Hegel himself attached great significance to these lectures, no matter how he may have viewed their relation to his system. In his view the study of the history of philosophy is the study of philosophy itself. Had he not thought so, he would scarcely have lectured on the history of philosophy so regularly and at such length—as early as at Jena (1805–6), where he spoke from a full manuscript; subsequently twice at Heidelberg (1816–17, 1817–18), where he used an outline; and finally six times at Berlin (in the summer term of 1819, the winter term of 1820–21, and then at two-year intervals: 1823–24, 1825–26, 1827–28, 1829–30),

---

1. This Editorial Introduction, and the Preface as well, combine explanations composed for this English volume with those contained in the *Vorbemerkung* and the *Anhang: Zur Konstitution des Textes* of the German volume. Most of the materials in this Introduction that are taken from the German appear as the first parts of sections 1 and 2 respectively, and as virtually all of section 3. The rest has been written for this volume.

1

where he drew upon the Jena manuscript and the Heidelberg outline, with additions both written and extemporaneous. He began yet another series in November of 1831, although his sudden death on the fourteenth of that month cut that series short even before he could complete the Introduction.

Hegel's own students apparently shared his views on the importance of the history of philosophy. No other topic of his lectures has come down to us today in a larger number of auditor's transcripts than has this one, and no other comprises as many pages in the first edition of the *Werke,* prepared by the Association of Friends of the philosopher. So a few words are appropriate here about the general significance of this material.

First, these lectures constitute the very first comprehensive history of philosophy that treats philosophy itself as undergoing genuinely historical development. (Schelling made a similar attempt in 1827 but with less success and influence.) They depict philosophy as an integral intellectual activity that, despite its apparent diversity of contents and methods, has a distinctive unity and telos emergent precisely from its successive historical forms and schools. Hegel situates the varied philosophers and movements of the past within this progression, as at once conservers of previous insights and also critics and innovators. Thus the whole has movement and direction; the process is going somewhere. Philosophical thinking is historically produced and conditioned, it is an organic development over time, and the grasp of its history is itself a philosophical activity. It is easy to forget that Hegel's immediate predecessors as historians of philosophy treated the philosophical past mainly as a catalog of "timeless" systems or else as a temporal sequence of largely unrelated positions. It is a tribute to the power of Hegel's new perspective on this history that we (non-Hegelians included) have come to take so many of its elements for granted.

Second, these lectures are valuable for understanding Hegel's own systematic works such as the *Phenomenology,* the *Logic,* and the *Encyclopedia.* Central to his thought is the theme of spirit as engaged in self-realization through the processes of historical change. These lectures give a concrete account of the historical pilgrimage of Absolute Spirit in its highest expression as philosophical thought. They also enhance our understanding of his conception of his own place in the history of philosophy, as the beneficiary and culmination of his predecessors' work.

Third, these lectures are indispensable for a proper understanding and appreciation of the new consciousness of human life, culture, and intellect as clearly historical in nature, which profoundly altered the nineteenth-century mind—indispensable because they are a principal cause of that very transformation. Although earlier and simpler expressions of it appeared in the thought of Vico, Herder, and others, the new historical consciousness entered the European mind in full force through Hegel's thought, especially through these lectures and also those on the philosophy of history. Owing significantly to them, subsequent nineteenth- and twentieth-century intellectual life can in large measure be seen as the continuing effort to come to terms with this new historical consciousness.

2. Previous Editions of the Lectures

Karl Ludwig Michelet edited the lectures as they appear in volumes 13–15 of Hegel's *Werke* (Berlin, first edition 1833–1836, second edition 1840–1844). Michelet used the Jena manuscript together with transcripts and notes from the other series, and he took the tripartite arrangement of the 1823–24 series as the framework into which to fit the materials belonging to "Modern Philosophy." Michelet deployed various sources spanning a twenty-five year period, but he did so in an artificial construct not truly reflective of any given version. It is not known whether or not he used all the materials available to him; in his foreword (W 13:vii–viii) he actually mentions by name only a few transcripts, as ones he has "chiefly drawn upon." Although Hegel's lectures on other topics have been edited and published anew in their entirety subsequently to the *Werke,* Michelet's German editions have not to this day been superseded. That is probably due not so much to lack of interest in the topic as it is to the exigencies of history itself. Michelet's first edition is the one reprinted in volumes 17–19 of the *Sämtliche Werke,* edited by Hermann Glockner (Stuttgart, 1959). The second edition is quite different and less satisfactory; it is considerably abbreviated, is much less useful in its notes and apparatus, and gives a decidedly flat impression because it does not reflect with as much authenticity the spirit of Hegel's lectures.

Johannes Hoffmeister began a new edition with his *Hegel: System und Geschichte der Philosophie* (Leipzig, 1940), covering only the Introduction and Oriental Philosophy, which in Hegel's view precedes the actual history of philosophy. No further volumes appeared. The part of his edition containing the Introduction is still obtainable under the title *Hegel: Einleitung in die Geschichte der Philosophie,* prepared by Friedhelm Nicolin (Hamburg, 1959; reprint, Hamburg, 1966). Hoffmeister's work is the only previous effort that is critical in its treatment of the lecture transcripts.

E. S. Haldane and Frances H. Simson made their three-volume English translation, *Hegel's Lectures on the History of Philosophy* (London, 1892–1896; reprint, London and New York, 1955, 1963), from Michelet's second edition, an unfortunate choice, as explained above. Their work is generally fluent and reliable, although not always as precise as it might be in rendering certain technical terms; we have made use of it to the limited extent to which our text corresponds to the one they used. The present translation will not render theirs obsolete for the reason that theirs includes important materials that Hegel did not bring within the framework of the 1825–26 lectures.

Quentin T. Lauer made an English translation of the 1825–26 Introduction from Hoffmeister for his book *Hegel's Idea of Philosophy* (New York, 1971). Sir T. Malcolm Knox prepared a more extensive English version of Hoffmeister's Introduction, one completed by A. V. Miller and published as *Hegel's Introduction to the Lectures on the History of Philosophy* (Oxford, 1985). But the work of Lauer and that of Knox and Miller do not bear directly on the parts of the lectures presented in this book.

3. The New German Edition

a. Nature and Origins

The new German edition is not meant to be a continuation of Hoffmeister's work, nor a replacement for the older edition of the

Association of Friends. Michelet had at his disposal not only a number of student transcripts but also, in Hegel's own hand, his lecture notebook going back to the first series in Jena, with subsequent additions written on it. These materials are all lost today with the exception of the manuscripts for the Introduction from the Heidelberg and Berlin series. Nevertheless, it would have been possible from other surviving materials to distinguish and edit all six of the Berlin series and the beginning of the seventh, by a method similar to that of the new *Philosophy of Religion* edition. In successive versions of our lectures too, Hegel never merely repeated himself without variations in wording as well as in the arrangement of the figures in the history of philosophy. These separate lectures exhibit markedly less mutual diversity, however, than do those on other topics—such as the philosophy of religion—which Hegel brought to a systematic form only after lecturing on each several times. On our topic Hegel does frequently strike a new note, vary the parts he chooses to expound more fully, and even drop some old themes with new ones taking their place. But despite the frequent shifts in Hegel's ordering of individual philosophies—for instance, in the placement of the eighteenth-century Scottish and French philosophers relative to Hume—chronological factors prescribe his broader outline. For this reason, and not just to economize on space, it seemed best to forgo here the kind of sequential presentation of each lecture series in its entirety that was necessary for the *Philosophy of Religion,* since that would have vastly enlarged our volumes without commensurately enhancing their philosophical value.

This new edition consequently allows the whole to be represented by one of its parts—the lectures given in Berlin at the Friedrich Wilhelm University during the winter semester of 1825–26. This particular series is preferable to the others not by virtue of its philosophical content but on pragmatic grounds. We currently possess a much better stock of materials for reconstructing the 1825–26 lectures than we do for the rest, namely, five different transcripts. Also, this series is basically consonant with most of the others and so can, in a sense, serve to represent them—unlike, for instance, the lectures of 1823–24, which Michelet took as central for his arrangement of the materials for "Modern Philosophy" even though they have a number of peculiarities that set them apart.

Confined as it is to a single series, this new edition is not, to be sure, as rich in contents as Michelet's older editions. It does, however, let us see for the first time the actual form of presentation of this portion of Hegel's philosophy in the course of a single semester, whereas Michelet's compilation of the diverse contents of manuscripts and transcripts lumps together materials spanning more than twenty-five years. Furthermore, the text established here not only is an authentically reproduced conception of a single series but also is substantially more reliable than those components from 1825–26 that Michelet included in his volumes. While no edition based on transcripts can equal the authentic wording of Hegel's own manuscripts, this is of little significance for interpreting Hegel's portrayal of the history of philosophy because it is quite impossible to see from the older editions alone which passages come from Hegel's own hand. But now we can determine this approximately, by a very painstaking procedure of source criticism and with the help of the transcripts. On the one hand, we can identify passages in the *Werke* justifiably regarded as belonging to one or another of the Berlin series by reason of their concurrence with the transcripts. By this editorial method the attempted reconstruction of the wording of a series using the transcripts can provide pointers to the manuscripts underlying Michelet's edition and so help us determine their contents in approximate fashion. On the other hand, by a process of subtraction we can identify passages, some quite lengthy, that certainly do not concur with any of the Berlin transcripts. The passages in Michelet so identified as perhaps deriving from Hegel's manuscript are marked in the editorial footnotes by the symbol (Ms?).

The extensive annotations form another novel feature of the new edition. They permit a close comparison between the authors Hegel used and his own presentation—or rather, what the transcripts convey of his presentation. This comparison affords an insight into Hegel's method of working with primary and secondary sources.

The new German edition originated with a plan to publish just one of the 1825–26 transcripts. When its editors compared the different transcripts from this series (and from other series as well) with one another, however, they saw that a text based on a single transcript, no matter which one chosen, would be too riddled with mistakes to serve by itself as a defensible representative of Hegel's actual presentation. To follow their original plan but also to make the extensive corrections needed would require references to the other transcripts in order to justify corrections based on these comparisons. Therefore the editors of the German edition extended their original plan considerably, by constructing a text based on all five transcripts.

b. Sources

Five transcripts of the 1825–26 lecture series are presently available. Hoffmeister used three of them in his construction of the Introduction.

1. Griesheim (*Gr*): *Geschichte der Philosophie. Gr* is in the Staatsbibliothek Preussischer Kulturbesitz, Berlin. It is a very full fair copy (some 50 percent longer than *An* or *Pn*), on the whole reliable, but in places given to stylistic revision and even expansion of what Hegel said.

2. Anonymous (*An*): *Geschichte der Philosophie von Hegel.* It is in the Library of the Polish Academy of Sciences, Cracow Division. *An* is a very full source too, but in the form taken down during the actual lectures and so rougher in style than *Gr*, although sometimes more faithful. On the whole *An* broadly corroborates *Gr*, while in part correcting and supplementing it.

3. Stieve (*Sv*): *Geschichte der Philosophie. Vortrag von Herrn Prof. Hegel. Berlin den 31ten [Oktober] 1825. Sv* is in the Staatsbibliothek Preussischer Kulturbesitz, Berlin. A fair copy (in Hoffmeister's view, a direct transcription), it clearly condenses the text and is inferior to the other sources also in its reproduction of the wording.

In addition to these three, two new sources have come to light.

4. Löwe (*Lw*): *Geschichte der Philosophie nach Hegel.* (Added in another hand: *W[inter] S[emester] 1825–26.) J. C. Löwe.* *Lw* is in the Staatsbibliothek Preussischer Kulturbesitz, Berlin. A full fair copy, it is on the one hand related to *Gr* and on the other hand inferior in many respects to the text transmitted by *Gr. Lw* cannot therefore serve to corroborate *Gr*, although in a few passages it can supplement and correct it.

5. Pinder (*Pn*): *Geschichte der Philosophie von Prof. Hegel. Berlin. Winterhalbjahr 1825/26. Moritz Pinder. Pn* is in the Hegel Archiv, Ruhr-Universität, Bochum. A very full source, although in its wording prone to pregnant brevity, *Pn* is probably in a form taken down during the actual lectures. *Pn* is very similar to *Gr* and more particularly to *An*, but without being related to them. As such it serves to corroborate and to correct *Gr*, and occasionally also to supplement it.

c. Establishment of the Text

The text of this edition has been established by integrating the five transcript sources. Each source taken by itself exhibits a multitude of the sorts of defects mentioned above. But four of the transcripts (*Gr, An, Lw, Pn*), taken together, afford a quite extensively parallel transmission of the text. For this reason the errors hidden in them can be spotted from a collation of all five sources, and thus rectified by checking questionable passages against the other sources. Erroneous transmission in the broadest sense is any departure from the wording of the lecture series as it can be reconstructed with a high degree of probability. The edited text generally follows *Gr*, although the difference between the role of *Gr* as leading text and that of *An* and *Pn* as supplementary texts is comparatively slight. Our text follows *An* and *Pn* when they agree over against *Gr*, and it also follows one or the other of them in cases where there are grounds for assuming that the transmission of *Gr* is incorrect. Only infrequently is *Lw* incorporated into the text, at those few places where the other transcripts offer an unsatisfactory text and their relationship to *Lw* supports the supposition that *Lw* is authentically reproducing the original wording of the passage or at least its correct sense. Even more seldom is the wording of *Sv* chosen for the text, although that transcript does provide valuable hints for the attempt to establish the authentic transmission.

The transcripts are not mutually consistent with respect to their scant paragraph divisions, and they have only a few section headings. The fair copies show that these headings result from a subsequent organization of the text by the notetaker. Evidently it was not Hegel's general practice to indicate section headings himself, either in these lectures on the history of philosophy or in those on other topics given from handwritten notes. For this reason the editors of the German edition themselves established uniform headings and paragraph divisions, taking their cues wherever possible from indications in the transcripts and from the schema outlined at the end of Hegel's remarks introducing "The Third Period: Modern Philosophy." The headings in the transcripts for what we have called "The Second Period: Medieval Philosophy" are, respectively:

Gr: Medieval Philosophy.
An: The Second Period. 500–1500.
Sv: IInd Period
Lw: B. History of Philosophy. II. Part Two. Medieval Philosophy.
Pn: (no heading given)

The headings for "The Third Period: Modern Philosophy" read:

Gr: Modern Philosophy
An: Third Period
Sv: Third Period
Lw: B. History of Philosophy. III. Part Three. Philosophy of the Modern Era.
Pn: (no heading given)

After the section on Bacon and Boehme, *Sv* adds the further heading: Modern Philosophy.

The German edition employs for the fourth main section under "Modern Philosophy" the heading on which the transcripts concur, namely, "Kant, Fichte, and Schelling," even though it does not correspond well to either the scope or the structure of that section. A major part of this section is devoted to Jacobi, whose name is missing from the heading. Also, Hegel does not treat the philosophies of Kant and Fichte sequentially or as wholes, as we might have expected. His actual sequence of topics, prior to taking up Schelling, is: Kant's Transcendental Aesthetic and his Transcendental Analytic; the theoretical part of Fichte's *Wissenschaftslehre*; Kant's Transcendental Dialectic; Jacobi's general orientation; Kant's practical philosophy, with reference to Fichte; the teleological part of Kant's *Critique of Judgement* and his doctrine of postulates from the *Critique of Practical Reason* or the moral proof for God from the *Critique of Judgement,* again in conjunction with Jacobi's concept of faith and the concept of immediate knowing in general. This interweaving of his presentations of Kant and Fichte in particular does not occur in the other lecture series, even though Hegel always looked to Fichte's *Wissenschaftslehre* for a more consistent elaboration of the Kantian beginnings. (This English edition employs additional subheadings to highlight this sequence of topics.)

The text has been standardized according to the general principles employed for the *Philosophy of Religion*. By far the greater part of our text is attested by several transcripts. We may justifiably assume that the reconstruction of that part successfully recaptures the original wording from its refracted expression in the sources. There are, to be sure, additional sentences or sentence fragments transmitted only by a single transcript. When these come from a fair copy (*Gr, Lw,* or *Sv*), we cannot be certain that they actually belong to these lectures; when they come from *An* or *Pn,* we cannot be certain of the authenticity of the specific wording. The textual apparatus of the German edition gives information on these matters, although it contains only the more important variant readings. Its editors judged it impractical to provide in the apparatus detailed explanations as to how they constituted the text or how they reconstructed the lead text as a separate entity.

4. This English Edition
While the English text follows the German, it has been edited in a somewhat different format, comparable to that employed for the

Philosophy of Religion and other volumes in this series. The most obvious difference is that the German has two separate footnote systems while the English has but one. The German identifies all footnotes by a line-count system, leaving the text free of footnote numbers and editorial symbols but with the disadvantage of making it more difficult to locate the textual passages with which footnotes are associated. The German textual footnotes appear at the bottom of the page, keyed to the numbered lines to which they apply, whereas the editorial footnotes appear in a separate section at the back of the book and are keyed by page and line numbers to the appropriate passages. In contrast, the English edition combines both kinds of footnotes into an integrated series located at the bottom of the page, with footnote numbers that also appear in the text above. Each footnote starts with an italicized editorial notation or phrase indicating the type of note it is.

Most textual footnotes indicate variant readings for the corresponding passages enclosed within tilde marks (˜...˜) in the text, followed by the note number. Other variants consist simply of additional words or phrases to be supplied at the point in the text where the footnote number appears. The italicized notations commencing textual variants in the footnotes indicate the sources from which the variants derive and, where appropriate, also indicate the sources of the corresponding main text. For example, *"Thus Gr; Lw reads:"* means that the alternative wording following in the note is a variant (from *Lw*) to the text passage (enclosed within tildes), which comes from *Gr*. Examples of other locutions, appearing within more complex notations, are as follows: *"Thus Gr, similar in Lw"* means that *Lw*'s divergence from *Gr* is so slight that it need not be given as such in the apparatus. *"Gr, Lw"* indicates agreement between these two sources except for possible minor differences (such as spelling or inflection) of a sort that disappear in the standardized text in any event. *"Gr with Lw"* means that *Lw* has been used to enhance a passage based on *Gr*. The meaning of the several other kinds of italicized notation used should be clear from the context. The German edition has many textual notations containing no variant but just an indication of the transcript source for that portion of text. These mark passages for which the editors are less certain as to their reconstruction or their belonging to the original lectures. The English edition omits such notations, providing only those that contain variant readings or additions. A wholly editorial footnote begins with the bracketed sign [*Ed.*]. When editorial remarks are appended to textual footnotes, material following the [*Ed.*] sign in the note is editorial rather than a textual variant. In some instances we combine textual and editorial footnotes where they would otherwise coincide in the text. Editorial additions to the text, intended to help it read more smoothly or to provide missing terms, are enclosed within square brackets.

The editorial notes identify specific passages in the works of individual philosophers or in secondary sources that Hegel is quoting, paraphrasing, or clearly discussing, as well as other passages that likely form the background for a particular portion of text. The German edition quotes these passages extensively in the original languages, as well as furnishing German translations from other languages, either drawn from modern editions or, where necessary, made by the editors themselves. This practice adds greatly to the length of these editorial notes, which all together are appreciably longer than the text itself. The English edition identifies these passages but only occasionally quotes or paraphrases their contents. For the most part, however, we translate in full the remarks of the German editors themselves, which often disclose the general contents of the quotations in any event. Primary and secondary works are cited in the original editions or in the ones most likely used by Hegel, as well as in the best and most readily available modern editions. The full title and facts of publication for a work appear with its first citation in a given footnote series (except for certain works of classical authors and for "Frequently Cited Works by Hegel," which have their own abbreviations and listing in a table by that name at the front of the volume). Easily recognized abbreviated titles and references are used for subsequent citations. In the rare case where confusion between similar titles by the same author is possible, the abbreviated title we use is indicated at the end of the corresponding full entry in the Bibliography of Sources. This bibliography includes all the cited modern editions of works likely used by Hegel or related works by those same authors. They are listed in conjunction with the older editions. Other works cited appear only in the footnotes.

There is no direct correlation between individual editorial notes in the German and English volumes respectively, for we frequently combine into one footnote several German notes on adjacent or overlapping passages that are closely related in their contents. We also add (without identifying them as such) a few editorial notes of our own or supplementary remarks to the German notes, in cases where further background information is helpful to the English reader. We also correct a few errors detected in the German editorial notes and in several cases add what seem to us better citations than those provided there. Biblical citations and quotations are according to the Revised Standard Version.

Both editions modernize spelling and punctuation and standardize names and expressions in foreign languages. The English italicizes words and phrases for emphasis according to its own editorial needs, sometimes where the German does not and vice versa. The first occurrence of a philosopher's name not previously given in a section heading appears in small capitals, whereas the German uses wide spacing for that purpose. Apart from full bibliographical citation, books and essays are mentioned by the full or abbreviated title most familiar to the English reader, whether that be in the original language (Anselm, *Cur Deus homo*), a conventional designation (Schleiermacher, *Glaubenslehre*), or an accessible English version (Schelling, *Of Human Freedom*). Occasionally we add a subject heading of our own, or deviate from the paragraphing or punctuation of the German to form units of more manageable size. These are not in any event features of the lectures as spoken by Hegel but ones affected by the judgments and conventions of auditors or editors.

To facilitate comparison with the original, we give the page numbers of the German edition on the outer margins and indicate a page break by a vertical slash in the text. This translation strives to be faithful to the German without unduly sacrificing English style and without enforcing a one-to-one equivalence of English to German terms. Some technical or quasi-technical terms have several English equivalents each, and these are shown in the Glossary (in an appendix), which we used as a guide in our work and which was taken over and adapted from that developed in the course of work on the *Philosophy of Religion*. For German-speakers it will in most instances be possible to infer the German wording from the English; in a few cases, where for instance there is a play on words or an important nuance in the German that could not be captured well by the English, the German wording has been inserted in square brackets.

In keeping with the standard set by the English edition of the *Philosophy of Religion,* we eliminate unwarranted gender-specific language wherever possible when referring to God and to human beings. "God" can be repeated in place of "he" or "him," "God's" in place of "his." But since the important reflexive and intensive pronouns cannot suitably be avoided or made impersonal, "God himself" and the like occurs a number of times. *Mensch* is often "human being" or "one," and sometimes, where suitable, "we." For the sake of variety and to avoid the singular masculine pronoun we sometimes shift to plural forms. These choices are especially painful in passages about Adam, who is spoken of both as a male individual and as ungendered human nature itself (in theological resonance with the traditionally-rendered Platonic "Man"). Here we use our best judgment and a variety of expressions, without assurance of hitting on the happiest solution.

We began this work with Stewart as the primary translator for the text and footnotes for all of "Medieval Philosophy," as well as for the sections from Descartes through Hobbes, and with Brown as primary translator for "Bacon and Boehme" and the sections from Leibniz through Schelling. But we reviewed and criticized each other's work so extensively that each part of the ensuing translation is more accurately described as a product of our joint labors, which at the penultimate stage benefited greatly from thorough scrutiny by Harris. The general editor of the series, Peter Hodgson, guided the formation of this edition from the outset and suggested a number of improvements at the final stage of our work.

THE SECOND PERIOD
MEDIEVAL PHILOSOPHY

A. INTRODUCTION:
THE IDEA OF CHRISTIANITY

The first period covered some one thousand years, from Thales (550 B.C.) to Proclus, who died in A.D. 485, and down to the closure of the [Athenian] schools of pagan philosophy in A.D. 529. The second period extends from then on into the sixteenth century and so again covers one thousand years, which we intend to get through by putting on seven-league boots.[1]

In this second period, philosophy has its locus in the Christian world; we need refer to Arabs and Jews only in an external way, for the historical background. A new religion has arisen in the world, namely, Christianity. We have already become acquainted with its idea through the Neoplatonic philosophy. For the essential principle of it is that what has being in and for itself, God, is *spirit*. In that principle there is at the same time a quite definite statement of what spirit is: that it is not an empty word, not just a representation pure and simple, but that God is defined *concretely* as spirit. Only the concrete is what is true; the abstract is not true, for although the abstract is thinking too, still it must be concrete within itself in order to be true. The concrete is the absolute and so spirit that has being in and for itself. We have seen this concrete [the concrete absolute] in the forms that we considered previously. The shape that it takes in the Christian religion is, more precisely, that what God genuinely is has entered human consciousness, has become manifest. Or, to define it more exactly, the unity of divine and human nature, this unity that has being in and for itself, the being-in-self of the unity of divine and human nature, has come to

---

1. [*Ed.*] The precise date for the closure of the Athenian schools is given by only two of the historians of philosophy Hegel drew upon extensively: Thaddä Anselm Rixner, *Handbuch der Geschichte der Philosophie zum Gebrauche seiner Vorlesungen,* 3 vols. (Sulzbach, 1822–1823), 1:361; and Amadeus Wendt's expanded fourth edition of Wilhelm Gottlieb Tennemann's *Grundriss der Geschichte der Philosophie für den akademischen Unterricht* (Leipzig, 1825), p. 207. Cf. Jacob Brucker, *Historia critica philosophiae,* 4 vols. (Leipzig, 1742–1744), 2:347, 349. Hegel's reference to "seven-league boots" acknowledges that his coverage of the second thousand years will be much briefer (less than two-fifths of the present volume) than that of the first.

consciousness. [We shall consider] this implicit truth [*dies Ansich*] first.

Well then, the cultus or the Christian life consists in the individual or the subject itself being called upon or thought fit | to attain for itself this unity, to make itself fit for this spirit of God, the grace [of God] as it is called, to dwell in it. This is the doctrine of reconciliation.[2] God is now known as reconciling himself with the world. That God reconciles himself means, as we saw in Neoplatonic philosophy, that God is not the abstract, ¯but the particular, and to God¯[3] belongs the sphere of particularity, or what we call the world. This includes not merely external nature but, in particular, human individuality. The interest of the subject is of prime moment here: that God is a spirit, that God is realized and that God realizes himself in the consciousness of those individuals who have [this] consciousness, who are implicitly spiritual. It is typical of this [divine] realization within them that, because they are spirit and implicitly free, they accomplish this reconciliation through an inner process. They actualize what they are—spirit implicitly free—as their own freedom; that is, they attain to the consciousness of the grace of God, to the consciousness that the spirit or the grace of God is within them. By this means they reconcile themselves [with God].

What is concrete with regard to God, the absolute idea, is precisely the seeing of the worldly within God, seeing and knowing God's own other within him, not immediately of course, but in a spiritual way. In the older religions too the divine is united with the natural and the human, but it is not reconciled, it is only united in a natural way. In them the unity of God with the natural or with a human being is an immediate, and thus a spiritless, unity precisely because it is only natural. There is spiritual unity only insofar as spirit is concrete and living, only when the process [of reconciling] first brings forth this unity and freedom within itself. Spirit is not natural; it only is that into which it makes itself. The unity that is

2. [*Ed.*] See 2 Cor. 5:19.
3. *Thus Lw, similar in An, Pn; Gr reads*: that God particularizes himself, and to the particular

18

natural and has not been brought forth is a spiritless unity, for only the unity that is brought forth is spiritual. The negation of the natural belongs to this bringing forth of unity. The natural | must   3 be negated because it is the immediate, or what is devoid of spirit. The natural—what theologians call "the flesh"[4]—is what ought not to be; the natural state is that state in which human beings ought not to be or to remain. Nature is evil from the outset, so the natural or the spiritless is what ought not to be. Humanity is implicitly the image of God in existence, only it is natural. What is implicit ought to be made explicit, it ought to be brought forth; the first immediacy should be sublated, [the implicit image] should be brought forth.[5] This is in general the idea of Christianity.

In order to grasp or to recognize the idea of Christianity, one must have known the idea on its own account and arrived at the knowledge that the idea alone is what is true. In the work of the Neoplatonists we saw the idea in its universality. But they did not show that three-in-oneness or trinity [Dreieinigkeit] is what is true—and one must become conscious that this alone is what is true. [The Neoplatonists present] οὐσία [being] as unity of the infinite with πέρας [limit]; the second principle goes forth from the οὐσία, but the [procession] is itself an immediate mode ¯and that is the wearisome feature in Plotinus, Proclus, and the others.¯[6] A dialectical mode comes into play too, since the antitheses, which are taken as absolute, are brought back to their unity. But this method is only sporadically dialectical. In order to know the principle of Christianity as truth, the truth of the idea—of the concrete,

4. [Ed.] Hegel is referring to the concept of σάρξ (flesh), which Pauline theology regards as the power that dominates natural human beings and compels them to sin (see Rom. 8:7) but for Christians is overcome (see Rom. 8:3–4).

5. [Ed.] On the image of God, see Gen. 1:27. Where the German editors add "the immediacy" in brackets, we prefer "the implicit image," to connect this discussion of the image of God with that of the implicitly spiritual individual in the preceding paragraph.

6. Thus Gr; Lw reads: and it continues in this formal fashion.

[Ed.] For details about the dialectical trinity of the Neoplatonists, see Vol. 2. For Proclus the first principle (itself a trinity) is being as unity of the infinite and the limit. The second principle is the procession (πρόοδος) of this content out of itself. The third (not mentioned here) is the return (ἐπιστροφή).

of spirit as spirit—must be known, and this is the characteristic form that we encounter in the church fathers.[7]

What this amounts to, then, is that the worldly or the particular is no longer to be left in its immediacy, but it is to be considered as universal, as intellectual, as having its roots or its truth in God. In this way God is thought of as concrete. Among the worldly things that are thus taken up into God is humanity, which ought to *know* itself in God. (The world is taken up into God only in its truth and not in its immediacy, | which is why this position is not what we call pantheism, where the earthly shape is grasped according to its immediate naturalness.) So the determinate aspect of God is grasped as the initial humanity, the Firstborn Son.[8] This unity [of God and humanity] is an implicit unity; it is the concrete idea, but the concrete idea only implicitly.

The second thing to be noted in this regard is that what we call natural things remain simply in their implicit being; in other words, their truth does not enter into their vitality. Their vitality is their natural singularity, for natural things exist as singular, as individuals. But this very singularity of theirs is an immediate singularity, it is just something transitory. Singularity does not involve a turning about or looking back to its essence, to what it is in itself. This

7. [*Ed.*] Here, and in the next section, Hegel refers to the church fathers in very broad terms. Since he is discussing the formulation of the dogma of the Trinity, Hegel could have referred in particular to Tertullian, to the Cappadocians (Basil, Gregory of Nazianzus, and Gregory of Nyssa), and to Augustine. But there is no definite evidence that he had read these authors (apart from Tertullian's *Apology,* which is not relevant here). There is also no clear proof that he was familiar with Augustine's *On the Trinity,* although Hegel's own trinitarian doctrine is very similar in some of its formulations to Augustine's endeavor to comprehend the Trinity on the basis of the essential nature of spirit.

8. [*Ed.*] With "Firstborn Son" Hegel alludes to the designation of Jesus as μονογενὴς υἱός in the Gospel of John (1:14, 18; 3:16, 18) and the First Epistle of John (4:9). The correct translation of the Greek, however, would be "only-begotten Son," since that expresses the unique relationship of the (one and only) Son, whereas, strictly speaking, "Firstborn Son" calls for the complement of at least one other born subsequently. Hegel's rendition of the Greek phrase here may be deliberately fusing it with "initial humanity," therefore the "primordial humanity" of Gnostic myth, or at least positing a functional analogy between the two. This interpretation of the term is in dispute even today; it is most readily supported by John 1:14. Or the conflation may be influenced by Jacob Boehme; see *Philosophy of Religion* 1:382 and 3:99–100, 200, 293–294; cf. below, pp. 000–000.

is the ill fortune of natural things. That there is no truth for natural things is precisely why they do not attain freedom but remain simply in necessity. In other words, single things depend upon something other or alien that exerts control over them, so that when this other element unites itself with the natural things they only perish; they cannot endure the contradiction. But, as the consciousness that the true is for it and that in the truth it has the vocation to freedom, humanity is capable of *knowing* the eternal or what has being in and for itself, and it can set itself in a *relationship with* the eternal. To have this knowledge as a purpose, as its own purpose, is the liberation of spirit. In this knowing, consciousness does not remain as natural consciousness but abides as spiritual. That is, [humanity knows] that the eternal or the truth is *for* it. Therefore consciousness is essentially this process—not a remaining static in the immediate natural state but a passage through a process in which what is eternal or true, as its essence, becomes its object or purpose.

This, then, is the idea of Christianity. ⌐God is grasped as self-differentiating, as concrete,⌐[9] and the mediation or coherence with what we have termed "consciousness" consists in | humanity seeing its own root within God. But it is only the root, so that one still has to accomplish this process inwardly and for oneself in order to reach one's source and truth in God.

This is[10] the basic idea of Christianity. There are various ways of viewing this issue nowadays. One involves the historical question of whether this actually is the idea of Christianity, since the idea of Christianity had been grasped differently at different times. To answer that this is the historic idea of Christianity would involve a discussion confined to the historical evidence. But in a sense this historical discussion is not our present concern. We can accept the historical thesis as a lemma or proposition borrowed from the philosophy of world history.[11] But to the extent that ⌐Chris-

5

9. *Thus An; Lw reads:* In what is true, in God, since God is self-differentiating and holds fast the moments of the distinction,

10. *Thus An, Lw; Gr adds:* indicated or affirmed as *Pn adds:* supposed to be

11. [*Ed.*] See Hegel's *Philosophy of World History*, Sibree ed., pp. 323–326; Lasson ed., pp. 733–743.

tianity~[12] falls within the history of philosophy as well, the idea of Christianity has a different status here from what it would have in an external, historical treatment. In ~philosophical history~[13] the shape of this affirmation must be that this idea emerged in the world *necessarily* and, to be sure, as the idea of God. In other words, this idea has become the content of universal consciousness or of the consciousness of the nations, this idea has become the universal religion of the nations. In philosophical history the content is this: that the concept of spirit is laid down as the foundation, so that history is the process of spirit itself in raising itself to this standpoint of its own self-consciousness. History is the pathway of spirit as it casts off the mask of its primitive, superficial, veiled consciousness and arrives at the standpoint of its free self-consciousness, so that the absolute command of spirit, "Know thyself!," may be fulfilled.[14]

That this idea of Christianity had to emerge has been made plain in connection with the previous configurations [of consciousness]. That it emerged as a world religion pertains more to history. But it has already become clear from what we said that its emergence was logically connected with philosophy as such. | This necessity of the idea of Christianity is what has to be presented in more detail in the philosophy of history. Sometimes the knowing of this necessity has been called the a priori construction of history and decried as inadmissible and presumptuous.[15] Then Christianity is repre-

---

12. *Thus An; Pn reads:* it *Lw reads:* this *Gr, Sv read:* this question

13. *Thus Gr, Pn, An; Lw reads:* the history of philosophy

14. [*Ed.*] Hegel is alluding to the famous injunction that, according to Plato's *Charmides* 164d, was inscribed over the entrance to the temple in Delphi.

15. [*Ed.*] Hegel's contemporaries applied the concept of construction principally to the domain of mathematics and natural science. Since Hegel speaks here of a construction of history a priori, he is alluding rather to F. W. J. Schelling's use of the conception in *On University Studies* (1803) [trans. E. S. Morgan (Athens, Ohio, 1966)], Lecture Eight: "The Historical Construction of Christianity." We read there (p. 88) that "what is true of history in general is especially true of the history of religion, namely, it is founded upon an eternal necessity, and consequently it is possible to construct it. By means of such a construction history becomes closely bound up with the science of religion." See Schelling's *Sämmtliche Werke*, ed. K. F. A. Schelling, 14 vols. (Stuttgart and Augsburg, 1856–1861), 5:292. Friedrich Schlegel made a similar use of the concept of construction in *Die Entwicklung der*

sented as pure contingency. Alternatively, those who take God's providence and world governance seriously represent it as being all prepared in God's head, in which case the apparent contingency is that only now is it projected into the world. One can even say that it was God's eternal decree to have it enter the world at this juncture.

But then we want to discern what is rational and hence necessary in this divine decree. This approach can be called a theodicy, a justification of God; it is a demonstration that what has happened in the world has been rational. But more specifically it is a justification of our idea and our views. What this theodicy tells us is that the history and emergence of spirit belongs to that process whereby spirit comes to its knowledge or its consciousness concerning itself, in part as the history of the spirit that has to reflect itself inwardly to attain self-consciousness, as we have seen above. And it displays itself in history as a process ongoing in time. Since that presupposes that this idea has had to become universal consciousness or a universal religion, we have here the source of one characteristic shape that this idea takes for the particular consciousness. Tertullian says: "Now even the children have a knowledge of God that the greatest sages of antiquity did not have."[16] This idea was therefore destined to become universal religion. It does not merely receive and sustain the form of universal thought, but it emerges in the form of out-

---

Philosophie (Cologne, 1804–1805), where he concludes that "the essential element in true construction consists in the uniting of the philosophical and the historical." See the *Kritische Friedrich-Schlegel-Ausgabe,* ed. Ernst Behler with Jean-Jacques Anstatt and Hans Eichner, 35 vols. (Paderborn, Munich, Vienna, 1958 ff.), 13, pt. 2:323.

16. [*Ed.*] Hegel here combines a statement from the poem "Der Christ," by Christian Fürchtegott Gellert (1715–1769), with one from Tertullian's *Apology* 46. The text is closer to Gellert; what Tertullian actually states is that a Christian artisan readily understands things about the Creator that Plato says are difficult to discover and to make known. In the early fragments entitled *Volksreligion und Christentum* Hegel had compared these two statements, in remarking on the presumptuousness of Christian apologists; see *Hegels theologische Jugendschriften,* ed. Herman Nohl (Tübingen, 1907), p. 11. Here, however, his citation serves to emphasize the knowability of God. This juxtaposition of texts shows that the insistence upon God's unknowability that was current in Hegel's time reverts from a Christian to a pagan basis.

ward consciousness too—else it would be a philosophy. For the standpoint of philosophy is ⁻[to express] the idea in the form of thinking, not [as with religion] the way the idea is for the subject or is directed at the subject.⁻[17] The characteristic form through which this idea occurs as religion | belongs to the history of religion, that is, to religion's development and form, and here we have to leave that to one side.

We will, however, give just one example. The doctrine of original sin is well known. According to this doctrine our first parents sinned or became evil, and this evil state has permeated throughout all humanity as a hereditary disease. It has passed down to the most recent generation as something inherited or innate that does not belong to the freedom of spirit, that is not grounded in freedom, for it accrues only externally, coming upon them through heredity. Humanity deserves punishment for this hereditary sin; it draws God's wrath down upon itself. But this entire content has been rejected, no doubt because of [its presentation in] this form.[18] For this form deals chiefly with our first parents, with what is prior not in the order of thought but in time. The thought of what comes first is none other than humanity in and for itself (Adam). And what is predicated of humanity as such is represented here in the form of the first man, and evil is even represented as something contingent for this first man, in that he let himself be led astray and ate of the apple. We are not simply told that Adam picked the fruit of some tree; the story adds that it was the tree of the knowledge of good and evil.[19] Human beings must pick the fruit from this tree, other-

17. *Thus Gr, similar in Lw; An reads:* that the forms of universal thinking emerge.

18. [*Ed.*] In the second half of the eighteenth century the Augustinian doctrine of original sin had been either directly attacked or passed over in silence by a number of Protestant theologians, including Johann Joachim Spalding (1714–1804) and Johann Gottlieb Töllner (1724–1774), and by the philosopher Johann August Eberhard (1739–1809). Hegel's statement that the "entire content" was rejected because of its form might be understood as criticism of the Enlightenment, which, in rejecting the traditional form of the doctrine, also abandoned the view that humanity is evil by nature. In the *Philosophy of Religion* (1:288 with n. 47) Hegel characteristically names Kant in particular as representative of the new outlook.

19. [*Ed.*] See Gen. 2:9, 17.

wise they are not human but animal. Here the basic character of humanity ˉis declared in the distinction between good and evil.ˉ²⁰ We are also told that the serpent led Adam astray by telling him he would become like God. But in this instance the serpent was not lying. To the contrary, God himself subsequently confirmed it, saying: "See, Adam has become like one of us, knowing good and evil."²¹ It is quite simply in virtue of the fact that humans are thinking beings that they distinguish between good and evil. This implies that human thought alone is the root of good and evil. But they must make this distinction if they are not to remain animals. Because it does not think, an animal is ˉnot evil.ˉ²² | Thinking, 8 however, also contains the remedy for the ill to which thinking gives rise.

It is also said that a human being is evil by nature—the human as such.²³ That seems a hard saying, that humanity is intrinsically or by nature evil. But even if we discard this harsh saying about divine punishment and the like and use milder words for it, we still must say that, as it is by nature or immediately, humanity is what it ought not to be, and that, as spirit, humanity has instead the vocation to become explicitly what in its natural state it still is only implicitly. This representation of original sin tells us that, as natural, human beings are not what they ought to be. Natural being is the negative of the human vocation—it is the fact that the way human beings are immediately is not the way they ought to be. Heredity represents this as the characteristic of humanity generally and not just of Adam. The sublation of mere natural life is familiar to us primarily in our education. We know that it is through education that we are tamed, that through education we are brought into conformity with what is good. This bringing into conformity

20. *Thus An, similar in Pn; Gr reads:* whereby we distinguish ourselves from the animal realm, is that we know what good and evil are.

21. [*Ed.*] See Gen. 3:4–5, 22.

22. *Thus An; Lw reads:* neither good nor evil.

23. [*Ed.*] Hegel is referring to the doctrine of original sin, which found its authoritative dogmatic form in Augustine's controversy with Pelagianism at the beginning of the fifth century. See in particular Augustine's *On Original Sin* and his *On the Grace of Christ*. It cannot be proved, however, that Hegel knew these texts or the many others written in the course of the Pelagian controversy.

seems just to take place easily and of its own accord. It is of infinite importance that this reconciliation of the world with the self, this making the self good, is brought about by the simple means of education. These forms therefore must not lead us to misconstrue the content [of this doctrine] and to discard what lies in the thought itself; instead we should penetrate through the forms to the content, which is the thought itself. But on the other [side] we must not cling to them as absolute forms, in the way that a sterile orthodoxy wishes to recognize and hold fast the content in these forms alone.

What we are now concerned with is the making of the principle of Christianity (which we have already discussed at length) into the principle of the world. It is the world's task to introduce this absolute idea into itself, to actualize it inwardly, with a view to being reconciled with God. The first stage of this is the dissemination of the Christian religion, its establishment in human hearts. This, however, lies outside the scope of our discussion here. By the

9   "heart" we mean | the human subject as *this* man or woman who, by virtue of this principle, has a different status from what human subjects had heretofore. The subject is object of divine grace and has an infinite value, for it is the vocation of the subject, of the human being qua human, that the divine spirit should dwell within it, that its spirit should be united with the divine spirit; and this divine spirit is God. The vocation of humanity is for freedom, and in the Christian principle humanity is recognized as implicitly free. This principle of subjective freedom is initially a formal principle, and as such it is subjectivity.

The second stage is for the principle of the Christian religion to be developed for thought, to be appropriated and actualized in thoughtful cognition in such a way that this cognition achieves reconciliation and has[24] the divine idea within itself, and so that all the riches of the cultivation of thought, and especially the riches of the philosophical idea, are united with the Christian principle. For the philosophical idea is the idea of God. This further development of thoughtful cognition must be united with the Christian principle

---

24. *Thus Gr, Pn, Sv; An adds:* nature or

because thinking has the absolute right to be reconciled; the Christian idea must correspond to thought.

The third stage is for the idea to be implanted in actuality, to become immanent in it, so that there is not only a multitude of believing hearts but also the establishment of a kingdom, so that God's reconciliation with himself is accomplished within the world, not as a heavenly kingdom lying in the beyond (as was proclaimed at the time of the first appearance: "My kingdom is not of this world").[25] For the idea must be realized in actuality, because only then does it exist for spirit, for subjective consciousness. It must therefore be consummated not just in the heart but in a realm of actual consciousness. In other words, the laws, customs, and political constitutions, and whatever generally belongs to the actuality of subjective consciousness, have to be rational.

Such are the three tasks. The first, propagation [of the Gospel] in the heart, lies outside our consideration. The second, the development of the Christian religion for | thoughtful cognition, was   10
the task of the church fathers, a task that they accomplished. We do not have to consider in detail their reworking of the Christian principle, the reconciliation of the Christian idea with thoughtful cognition, for that likewise belongs to church history. All we have to do here is to indicate quite generally the standpoint of the church fathers in relation to philosophy.

B. THE CHURCH FATHERS

We know that the church fathers were very cultivated men philosophically and that they introduced philosophy, in particular Neoplatonic philosophy, into the church. They conformed the Christian principle to the philosophical idea and built the philosophical idea into it, and in doing that they developed a Christian system of doctrine [Lehrbegriff]. In that endeavor they went beyond the mode in which Christianity first appeared in the world, for the

25. [Ed.] See John 18:36.

27

doctrinal system as the church fathers developed it philosophically was not present in the initial appearance of Christianity. They dealt with all the questions concerning the nature of God (as what subsists in and for itself), questions concerning human freedom and the relationship of humanity to God (who is what is objective), questions concerning the origin of evil, and so on. They introduced and adopted into Christian doctrine what thought determined for them about these matters. The nature of spirit generally, the plan of salvation, the stages of the subject's spiritualization—the whole process of finite spirit with respect to its outward manifestation—this they recognized and presented in its profundity and in its particular moments. That is how we can define philosophically the relationship of the church fathers [to our topic].

It is just this philosophical development of the Christian principle by the church fathers that has been made into their crime. We all know that | Luther defined the purpose of his Reformation as leading the church back to its initial purity, back to the shape of Christianity in the first centuries. But the first centuries themselves already give evidence of this [philosophical] edifice, an extensively developed fabric of doctrine about what God is and the relationship of humanity to God. A specific dogmatics or a specific doctrinal edifice has not been comparably produced in the modern era since the Reformation; on the contrary, dogmatics has been either neglected or merely purified of later accretions. Hence this [doctrinal system] has become indeed ˉa tangled webˉ[26] in which the most complicated things are found. In modern times this stocking has been unraveled, because of the wish to lead Christianity back to the plain strand of God's Word as it is present in the New Testament Scriptures. The unraveling was to undo the ˉexpansion of the doctrinal system,ˉ[27] the doctrine of Christianity determined by means of the idea and according to the idea. We have gone back not only to the first centuries but to the initial appearance, so that

26. *Thus Pn, Lw; An, Gr read:* a complicated structure *Sv reads:* a complicated system
27. *Thus Gr, An; Pn reads:* philosophies, *Lw reads:* philosophy, this doctrinal edifice,

now only what has been reported about the initial appearance is regarded as the primary foundation of Christianity.

With reference to the justification of philosophy and of the church fathers, who gave philosophy validity within Christianity, the following remarks need to be made. Our modern view declares that the [biblical] words should be taken as the basis. The whole matter of properly representing and thinking [their meaning] is then just exegetical. The words are supposed to be set forth, and religion is supposed to be treated as positive, as given. ⁻Revelation is a given, something posited quite | externally, something positive.⁻[28] Such a given is supposed to be set forth literally. But on the other side we have, by the same token, the validity of the biblical saying: "The letter kills but the Spirit gives life."[29] This has to be granted in any case. ⁻But we should observe more carefully what it means to say⁻[30] that "the Spirit gives life." For "spirit" means none other than the very power dwelling in those who apply themselves to these letters, who grasp them and bring them to life. But what dwells in the subject and gives life are the [subject's own] accompanying representations and thoughts. These have to make themselves effective in the letter, and that is what we mean by bringing it to life, by comprehending it "in the Spirit." This happens now, in our own time. So we claim the right to bring spirit to bear on the letter while denying the same right to the church fathers, although they too brought spirit to bear on the letter. Yet it is specified expressly that the Spirit indwells the church, that it defines, interprets, and teaches. Hence the church fathers had the same right to deal "in the Spirit" with what is positive, with what is posited by sensibility. The issue turns only on how this spirit is constituted in and for itself, for there are very different spirits. Accordingly, the relation is established that "the Spirit gives life," meaning that the accompanying thoughts can be quite ordinary, healthy human understanding and, as has even been sug-

28. *Thus An with Pn; Gr, similar in Lw, reads:* Thus there is a given, something posited in a quite external way, from which a beginning is made.

29. [*Ed.*] 2 Cor. 3:6 says: ". . . the written code kills, but the Spirit gives life."

30. *Thus Lw; Gr, similar in Sv, reads:* The mere letter kills, but we are told

gested in recent times, that dogmatics must be made popular, that dogmatics should be suitable for the broad highway of ordinary consciousness.

β

The view that spirit has to make the mere letters come alive is then advanced in the more precise sense that spirit should just elucidate the given, that is, it should let stand the meaning of what is immediately contained in the letters. But we cannot have gone very far with our reflection if we fail to see through the deception

13 that lies in this attitude. Elucidating [*Erklären*] means | nothing else than making clear [*klar machen*], and that means making clear *to me*. But nothing can become clear to me that is not indeed within me. It has to answer to the needs of my knowing, my heart, my consciousness. Only insofar as it answers to ˉmy needsˉ[31] is it [truly] for me, and precisely when I make it clear to myself do I make it for me, that is, I make my own representation and thought count in it. Otherwise it is something lifeless and external for me, something not present to me. Therefore it is difficult to make clear to ourselves religions that are wholly alien, religions that are quite inadequate to our spiritual needs although they still do touch us somehow, even though only on an obscure, sensory, and subordinate side. So when we speak of "making clear," we are concealing the real situation behind a term. When we make this term itself clear, then all it means is that the inward spirit of a person seeks to know itself in the words to be elucidated, and can know nothing other than what lies within itself. It can be said, therefore, that the Bible has been made into a wax nose;[32] one person finds this in it,

31. *Thus Lw; Pn reads:* this [knowing]
32. [*Ed.*] Hegel also uses this expression in the *Philosophy of Religion* (1:123). He was probably familiar with it through Lessing. See in particular Lessing's *Axiomata, wenn es deren in dergleichen Dingen gibt: Wider den Herrn Pastor Goeze, in Hamburg* (Braunschweig, 1778): "The inner truth is no wax nose that every rascal can shape in conformity to his own face as he wishes." See Lessing's *Sämtliche Schriften*, ed. K. Lachmann and F. Muncker, 23 vols., 3d ed. (Leipzig, 1886–1924), 13:128; cf. his *Eine Duplik*, in *Sämtliche Schriften* 13:38, 62. The expression "wax nose" itself, however, may be traced back to the twelfth century—for instance, to Alain de Lille, *De fide catholica* I, 30 (Migne, *Patrologia Latina* 210.333). In the fifteenth century Geiler von Kaisersberg applied it specifically to Scripture; see M. D. Chenu, *La théologie au douzième siècle* (Paris, 1957), p. 361.

another finds that, and something firmly established shows itself equally to be not so, since it is treated by the subjective spirit.

In this connection we must comment a bit further on the character of the [biblical] text. It expresses only the way in which Christianity first appeared; that is what it describes, and what the principle of Christianity involves can only be embodied in that first appearance in a way that is not yet very explicit. In fact that appearance can give only an inkling of what the principle contains. And this is expressly declared in the text itself. Christ says: "When I am gone from you I will send you the Comforter, which is the Holy Spirit. He will lead you into all truth."[33] This is a doctrine about what the text means. So, according to the text itself, it is only after Christ and his teaching that the Spirit will come upon the apostles, that they will first be filled with the Spirit.[34] It can almost be said that if our intention is to lead Christianity back to its first appearance, then | we are leading it back to the standpoint of spiritlessness, for Christ himself said, "The Spirit will only come after me, when I am gone."[35] So the narrative of the first appearance contains in fact only the first inkling of what spirit is and what it will know as true, since the Spirit will only come later.

The other aspect is that even in that first appearance Christ appears as teacher and messiah who has more far-reaching characteristics than those of a mere teacher. As teacher, he was a man tangibly present for his friends, followers, the apostles, and others. But if he is supposed to be God for us humans, if he is supposed to be God in our human hearts, then he cannot have a sensible, immediate presence for us. God is present in this [immediate] way in the Dalai Lama, who is god for ˉthose peoples.ˉ[36] But according

14

33. [Ed.] See John 16:7–14.
34. [Ed.] A reference to Acts 2:4.
35. [Ed.] John 16:7 is explicit on this point: ". . . it is to your advantage that I go away, for if I do not go away, the Counselor will not come to you; but if I go, I will send him to you." The fulfillment of this saying occurs with the descent of the Holy Spirit on the day of Pentecost (Acts 2).
36. *Thus Gr, Pn; Lw reads:* the Hindus [*die Inder*].
[Ed.] Hegel may have said "Hindus," but it is Tibetan Buddhists who revere the Dalai Lama. In the *Philosophy of Religion* (2:579) Hegel depicts Lamaism as the

to the principle that God enters into human hearts, God cannot remain there before them as a sensible presence.

The second moment, therefore, is just that this sensible shape must disappear, so that it enters into recollection, so that it is taken up into Mnemosyne [memory]; it moves from the sensible present into the far-off realm of representation. Only then can the spiritual consciousness or relationship emerge. Christ has come to be only *far off*; but whither has he betaken himself? Now, for the first time, there comes the definitive statement that he has taken his seat at the right hand of God.[37] Now God has become known as concrete: God the One and, second, God's Son—just what we have met as Logos, Sophia, and so on.[38] Only through its removal from the sensible realm could the other moment be known *in God,* and only in this way could God be known as concrete.[39] In this context there first emerged the view that what is abstractly divine inwardly breaks up and is broken up. In this way the other within God or the distinct aspect within the divine, namely, God's Son, is on the one hand a moment within the divine, though not merely in the mode of an intelligible world or (as we have it in our imagination) a heavenly realm with many angels who also are finite and limited, | more like human beings. It is not enough that the concrete

15

---

religion whose spiritual efficacy is substance that "has its existence in one human being in particular" and "is present to and for other people in a sensible, external manner." This substance is somewhat spiritual and subjective, but only in a way that is bound to immediate, sensible existence. It is distinguishable from the outward existence of, for instance, the present Dalai Lama only insofar as it can also be at the same time the sensible presence of other lamas, or insofar as it can be the successive sensible reincarnations of this Dalai Lama in future lives. The devotee in this religion thus cannot get beyond focusing on this sensible presentation, cannot attain genuinely spiritual consciousness of its content.

37. [*Ed.*] See Luke 22:69, Acts 2:32–36 and 7:55.

38. [*Ed.*] See the discussion of Stoicism and Gnosticism in Vol. 2, as well as the *Philosophy of Religion* (3:84 with n. 71).

39. [*Ed.*] In contrast with the Dalai Lama (mentioned above), Christ's sensible presence had to be withdrawn from his community; cf. Hegel's 1824 explanation (*Philosophy of Religion* 3:219–223) of why Christ's sensible presence had to disappear and pass over into a spiritual shape for the Christian community. A sensible appearance is inherently ephemeral. So Christ's sensible appearance is destined to be spiritualized, to pass over into the sphere of representation, since only by its removal can God become known as concrete.

moment in God should be known, for it is also necessary that this representation of God should be known as tied to humanity, it should be known that Christ was an actual man. That is the tie with humanity in its *thisness*.[40] The moment of being *this one* is the great moment of shock in the Christian religion; it is the binding together of the most shocking antithesis. This higher view could not, however, be immediately present in the text or in the initial appearance. Instead, ˜the greatness˜[41] of the idea could only emerge after the initial appearance, the Spirit could only come after that appearance, and it was this Spirit that first developed the idea—a development that the church fathers carried out.

So the early Christian church's general relationship to philosophy is as follows. On the one hand the philosophical idea was implanted in this religion by the church fathers, while on the other hand there was joined onto it the moment within the idea by which it determines or particularizes itself inwardly—the Logos or Son of God and so forth, the singularity of a human individual. Thus [already in the philosophical idea] there is this particularization—the [divine] wisdom, activity, or reason, which abides still within universality. This particularization was further developed [by Christianity] into the immediacy of sensuous singularity, into the presence of the single individual. The particular progresses all the way to the singular. Subjectivity was determined to the point of the immediate singularity of an individual appearing in space and time, since the particular always determines itself to the point of the singular, of subjectivity, of individuality. ˜In Christian dogmatics these two elements have essentially permeated the idea, in the shape in which the idea presents itself by being conjoined with a singular, present individual who appears in space and time.˜[42] This therefore is the general form [of the idea]. | 16

---

40. [*Ed.*] Literally: "as This One [*als Diesen*]." In the 1821 Ms. of the *Philosophy of Religion* (3:114), Hegel refers to Christ as *NUR EIN solcher Dieser* ("only *one* such individual—'this' individual"), in a context stressing the uniqueness of Christ as the one realization of the idea for humanity and explicitly contrasting this with the Hindu notion of multiple incarnations of deity.

41. *Thus An; Gr reads:* the major part *Pn, Lw read:* the spirit

42. *Thus Gr; Pn reads:* These [are the] two moments therefore, the idea and the [moment] imbued with singular individuality.

On the one side the church fathers were opposed to the Gnostics just as Plotinus, among the Neoplatonists, also opposed them.[43] For the Gnostics the immediate presence (or the determination of the individual as This One) disappears, the immediate existence is etherealized into the form of the spiritual, whereas they [the church fathers] affirmed the immediate presence of the individual.[44] On the other side the church and the church fathers were opposed to the Arians, who also acknowledged the individual who had appeared but did not link him with the divine idea, with the moment of the particularization or self-determining of the divine idea, ˉwith the Logos.ˉ[45] The Arians took Christ to be a mere human being. Admittedly they exalted him as being of a higher nature, but they did not set him within the moment of God, of spirit itself. The Socinians view Christ wholly as a mere human being, a teacher like Socrates.[46] This was not at all accepted within the church; those

SAS

43. [*Ed.*] See Plotinus, *Enneads* 2.9.

44. [*Ed.*] Hegel is referring to the Docetism that in differing shapes was a nearly universal feature of Christian Gnosticism. In W 15:31 he cites August Neander, *Genetische Entwickelung der vornehmsten gnostischen Systeme* (Berlin, 1818), who discussed Basilides as one denying that the heavenly savior, who is distinct from the man Jesus, could have undergone bodily suffering (pp. 43–44, 49–50). Valentinus and Marcion might also be cited as prominent Docetists who held that Christ's body, which was crucified, was only a phantom body. Notable patristic opponents of Docetism include Tertullian (*Against the Valentinians*) and Irenaeus (*Against Heresies*). There is, however, no firm evidence that Hegel had read these texts himself, although he had certainly read Schelling's master's thesis, *De Marcione Paullinarum epistolarum emendatore* (1795), which dealt with Marcion's supposed misrepresentations of the Pauline writings (Schelling, *Sämmtliche Werke* 1.113–148); cf. Hegel's letter of 30 August 1795 to Schelling (*Letters*, p. 43; *Briefe*, Letter 14).

45. *Thus An; Gr reads:* with the breaking open of the divine idea.

[*Ed.*] Hegel is referring to the Arian controversies concerning Christology, which broke out at the beginning of the fourth century and were resolved at the Council of Nicaea (325) in favor of Athanasius, Alexander of Alexandria, and others opposed to Arius. They focused on whether Christ is of the same individual being or substance as the Father (ὁμοούσιος), or is only of a being or substance similar to that of the Father (ὁμοιούσιος). Hegel's formulation that the Arians "did not link him with the divine idea" does not do them full justice. Arius regarded Christ as the Logos, albeit as of an intermediate substance that is not one and the same as that of the Father.

46. [*Ed.*] The Socinians were a widely influential, unitarian religious community founded in sixteenth-century Poland, whose beliefs were mainly drawn from the Italian Protestant theologians Lelio Sozzini (1525–1562) and Franco Sozzini (1539–

who accepted it were pagans. So the church was opposed to the Arians and to all who, like them, did not conjoin the person of Christ with the moment of particularization in the divine idea. The person of Christ had to have its higher aspect. Exalting him as being of a superhuman nature is not enough, it goes only halfway. The church fathers maintained the unity of divine and human nature, a unity that has, in this individual, entered the consciousness of the church, and in this consciousness [they] stood opposed to the Arians. ˉThis is the principal determination [of Christian orthodoxy].ˉ[47]

At the time when the Germanic peoples in the West had taken possession of what had previously been the Roman Empire and were beginning to take shape and establish themselves, the East saw the outbreak of another revolution, the Islamic religion, whose adherents, the Arabs, turned to philosophy. | 17

C. ARABIC PHILOSOPHY

The Arabs soon developed an interest in culture, and their philosophy should therefore be mentioned in the history of philosophy. As we have said, they quite soon turned their attention to the arts, the sciences, and philosophy, and they became familiar with Greek philosophy, most notably through the Syrians. In Syria—in Antioch, and especially in Edessa—there were learned institutions. Once the Syrians came under the Arabs' sovereign power, they were the point of contact between Greek philosophy and the Arabs. The Syrians translated into Syriac many Greek works, especially those of Aristotle, and these were then translated in turn [by the Arabs]

1604). The Socinians rejected the dogmas of Incarnation and Trinity. Sources for Hegel's knowledge of Socinianism cannot be given with certainty, although the fact that he links them with Arians suggests that his information came from Johann Lorenz Mosheim, *Institutionum historiae ecclesiasticae antiquae et recentioris . . .* (Helmstedt, 1755). In addition, Hegel was probably familiar with Lessing's essay on the controversy between Leibniz and Andreas Wissowatius concerning the Trinity (Braunschweig, 1773); see Lessing's *Sämtliche Schriften* 12:71–99.

47. *Thus Gr; Sv reads:* Such was the relationship in which philosophy stood to the church.

from Syriac into Arabic.[48] Moses Maimonides, who was a Jew, gives more details about this, saying that the books of the philosophers reached the Arabs, who seized and adopted whatever Greek texts they could lay their hands on. He also states that they used Greek [philosophical] science especially for the defense of their dogmas, since there was a pressing need to defend Islam against the Christians who made up a large part of the peoples they had subdued. He adds that they were not, however, guided by the nature of this material itself but only looked to how it had to be deployed in order to support their assertions.[49]

We cannot say that Arabic philosophy involves its own proper principle and stage in the development of philosophy. In the main the Arabs took up and translated Aristotle's logical writings in particular. But they also translated his *Metaphysics,* among other works, and devoted numerous commentaries to it. Some of these commentaries were also translated into Latin and printed, and they are still extant, but nothing much is to be gained from them. The fact that the Arabs studied Aristotle is historically important. Aristotle's | works were translated from Arabic into Hebrew (in particular by the Jews in Spain and Portugal, who were closely associated with the Arabs), and from these [Hebrew] versions they were retranslated into Latin, or they were even directly translated from Arabic into Latin. So translation from Arabic is one of the main channels through which the writings and philosophy of Aristotle became known in the West. Aristotle's works passed from Greek into Syriac, thence into Arabic, then into Hebrew, and finally into Latin.[50]

18

48. [*Ed.*] Hegel's source on this two-stage translation process is Wilhelm Gottlieb Tennemann's *Geschichte der Philosophie,* 11 vols. (Leipzig, 1798–1819), 8, pt. 1:366. Cf. Johann Gottlieb Buhle, *Lehrbuch der Geschichte der Philosophie,* 8 vols. (Göttingen, 1796–1804), 5:36–37.

49. [*Ed.*] See Moses Maimonides, *The Guide of the Perplexed* 1.71. According to Maimonides, however, it was the Greek and Syrian Christians who began the science of Kalām (the adoption from the philosophers of premises that served their religious interests while rejecting those that did not); the Muslim Arabs only imitated it.

50. [*Ed.*] This brief summary of Arabic philosophy and its role as one channel for the transmission of Aristotle's philosophy is based on Tennemann (*Geschichte* 8, pt. 1:367–440). Tennemann's accounts of the great Arab philosophers—al-Kindī

Maimonides does mention by name one outstanding philosophical school or sect among the Arabs, which he calls the *medabberim,* or "speakers."[51] They accepted the atoms and the void [as absolute], so that creation is nothing but the joining of atoms and perishing is nothing but their separation.[52] In this way (through a more developed thought-structure) they brought the standpoint of the Orient, the basic standpoint of the one substance, to [the level of] determinate consciousness for thought too. (Pantheism ˉorˉ[53] Spinozism is the standpoint or general outlook of Oriental, Turkish, Persian, and Arabic writers, historians, or philosophers.)

Maimonides reports that this philosophical sect of the *medabberim* says that substance has many accidents but that no accident can endure for two moments; as soon as it arises it perishes too, and the substance (God) always creates another in its place.[54] So we cannot ascribe any being to the sensible or the natural, such that it substantially "is." Nothing sensible exists by nature. The nature

---

(c. 800–870), al-Farabī (c. 870–950), Ibn Sina (Avicenna, 980–1037), Ibn Rushd (Averroes, 1126–1198)—stress the predominance of Aristotelian thought in their works. Tennemann also discusses the intermediary role of Arabs and Jews (*Geschichte* 8, pt. 1:357–358). He does not speak of Hebrew translations himself but does refer to Buhle (*Lehrbuch* 5:250) on translations of Aristotle into Arabic and Hebrew. See also Rixner, *Handbuch* 2:60–61. None of these sources mentions Portugal as a site of translation. On this issue Michelet (in *W* 15:177) cites Amable Jourdain, *Geschichte der Aristotelischen Schriften im Mittelalter,* in the German translation by Ad. Stahr (Halle, 1831); Hegel might have been familiar with the French original (Paris, 1819). On translations of Aristotle, see also below, p. 000 and n. 112.

51. [*Ed.*] Hegel follows Maimonides in using the Hebrew term *medabberim,* which in Latin is rendered *loquentes* ("speakers"). In the West this school of speculative theologians is now more commonly known by the Islamic term *Mutakallimūn* ("dialecticians"), from *Kalām* (speculative theology). For the *Mutakallimūn* position, see Maimonides, *Guide,* author's preface, and 1.71–76. Hegel possessed the Latin translation of Maimonides by Johannes Buxtorf (Basel, 1629). The latter does not use the term *medabberim,* which Hegel got not from a Hebrew edition of Maimonides but from Tennemann (*Geschichte* 8, pt. 1:440–446).

52. [*Ed.*] See Maimonides, *Guide* 1.71, 73. Cf. *W* 15:126 (Ms?).

53. *Thus Pn; Gr reads:* or, if we like,

54. [*Ed.*] See *Guide* 1.73, discussion of the fourth, fifth, and sixth premises of the *Mutakallimūn.* But Maimonides' account does not equate God and substance as Hegel appears to do in this summary. On the contrary, "substances" are "atoms" (each term renders the same Arabic word in Maimonides' text), and God provides the accidents that the atoms must have. Cf. *W* 15:127 (Ms?).

of this or that body does not entail that it has these accidents; on the contrary, God creates all accidents instantaneously, without [causal] mediation or assistance. The abiding [*das Beharren*]—that which abides quite universally—is the substance [God]. Everything else is devoid of necessity; it is absolutely changeable, and it is changed and thus posited at every instant by the substance. Another accident emerges. According to this axiom they say, for instance, that we have not at all really | dyed a dress red when we believe we have colored it with red dye; on the contrary, at that instant God has ˉmade the red color a property of the dress.ˉ[55] The first red color does not persist but disappears in the first instant, and there appears another that is created in its turn. Scientific knowledge is also an accident of this kind, for we do not know today what we knew yesterday, and so on. The writer does not move the pen, for the movement is an accident created by God at that instant.[56] All we can discern here is the complete dissolution of all interdependence, of everything that pertains to rationality. God is inwardly what is completely indeterminate (the substance), and God's activity is the creation of accidents, which in turn disappear and are replaced by others. This activity is wholly abstract, and that is why the differentiating that has been posited by means of it is totally contingent. Or it is "necessary," but then that is an empty ˉword. Why substance posits what it doesˉ[57] is said to be in no way conceived, nor must any attempt be made to conceive it. Thus God is the substance of the activity, but as portrayed wholly irrationally.

This abstract negativity and complete dissolution, coupled with the abiding of the one [substance], is the basic characteristic of the

55. *Thus Pn; Lw reads:* added the red color to the dress.

56. [*Ed.*] See *Guide* 1.73. Cf. *W* 15:127–128 (Ms?). The first in this series of examples, that of the dress dyed red, conveys two points: that God directly creates the accident of redness in the dress as well as in the dye, so that the dye cannot be said to cause the color of the dress; that the redness instantly perishes (as does any accident) and is replaced by another created redness, and so on, because God's creative activity is continual.

57. *Thus Pn; An reads:* word, because he [God] posits the substance, but the fact that he posits the *physis* [actual nature]

Oriental mode of representation. Oriental writers are, above all, pantheists. Spinozism is their most general and most customary mode of intuition.[58] The Arabs developed the sciences and philosophy in this way, without defining the concrete idea as anything more than caprice. What is ultimate is rather the dissolution of everything concrete, or of determinacy, ⌐in substance.¬[59] There is bound up with this substance only changeableness as an abstract moment of negativity. | 20

Certain Jews, and especially Moses Maimonides, should also be mentioned at this point. Maimonides was a Jew who was born in Egypt and lived in Córdoba, Spain in the twelfth century. His work *Moreh Nebukim* (*Doctor perplexorum*, or *The Guide of the Perplexed*)[60] is still extant; it has been translated into Latin. Like the church fathers and Philo, he takes the historical configuration as fundamental and treats it metaphysically.[61]

58. [*Ed.*] On the concept of Spinozism, see below, pp. 000–000. On Hegel's view of the Oriental mode of intuition as Spinozism, see the *Philosophy of Religion* 2:95 n. 8, 266 with n. 90. In referring to Oriental writers as mainly pantheists, Hegel has in mind Jalāl al-Dīn Rūmī, with whom he became familiar in 1821 through Friedrich Rückert's paraphrases of his poetry. On Rūmī, see *Philosophy of Religion* 2:100 n. 22, as well as § 573 of the second (1827) and third (1830) editions of the *Encyclopedia*.

59. *Thus Lw; Gr reads:* in this substance. *Pn reads:* into substance. *An reads:* in the One. *Sv reads:* in the unity of substance.

60. [*Ed.*] Alternative German titles given (by *Lw, An*) are variants on *Guide to What Is Complicated.*

61. [*Ed.*] The source of these biographical details could be Brucker (*Historia* 2:857) or Tennemann (*Geschichte* 8, pt. 1:446–447), although both correctly give Córdoba as Maimonides' birthplace and Egypt as the place where he mainly worked, not vice versa as Hegel has it. Maimonides wrote the *Guide* in Arabic; Buxtorf's Latin translation of 1629, which Hegel used (see above, n. 51), goes back to the Hebrew translation made by Samuel ibn Tibbon at the beginning of the thirteenth century. Hegel apparently did not know the earlier Latin editions of 1240 and 1520. Hegel's concluding remark about Maimonides' method is valid, insofar as the *Guide* does not present thoughts as unfolding methodically but proceeds by explaining biblical expressions and passages. Although Maimonides distinguishes exoteric and esoteric biblical meanings, the allegorical method is less prominent here than in some of the church fathers or in Philo. Maimonides instead draws extensively upon the rabbinic corpus.

D. THE SCHOLASTICS

1. General Character of Scholastic Philosophy

The third division ˉin this period consists ofˉ[62] the Scholastics. It is European philosophy in the European Middle Ages. In contrast, those who are properly called the church fathers belong principally to the Roman world. The Christian church or community had of course spread within the Roman world, though it did so—particularly in the beginning—only by forming a self-enclosed communion of its own that had abandoned the world, that made no claim to carry weight or to rule within it. The [saved] individuals renounced the world and became martyrs in it. But in this same period the church did attain to a ruling position as well, for the Eastern and Western Emperors became Christians, and in this way the church became a public authority. It achieved a public existence, free of persecution, and so also acquired a great deal of influence over the secular realm. But then the political world fell into the hands of the Germanic peoples, and with them a new world arose in the West, the one to which Scholastic philosophy principally belongs. This revolution is known to us as a migration of peoples. New and different tribes poured over the old Roman world and established themselves within it, building their dominion on the ruins of the old. This new world was founded through conflagration and destruction—as we can still see from the present-day aspect of Rome, where the splendors of Christian temples are in part the remains of ancient ones, and the new churches stand upon and among ruins.

21 The primary element of the Middle Ages is | this duality, this cleavage. We see peoples who before were the rulers, peoples who built up the world that went before, who constructed their own languages, laws, constitution, arts, and science, their [universal] right; and the new nations imposed themselves on this world that was foreign to them. So this history does not present us with the development of a nation from within itself but with the development of a nation insofar as it emerges from the antithesis. It is and con-

62. *Thus Pn; Gr reads:* consists of the principal figures in this period,

tinues to be afflicted with this antithesis, it takes the antithesis up into itself and has to overcome it.

This is how these peoples displayed the nature of the spiritual process in them. Spirit consists in making a presupposition for itself, in giving to itself the natural domain as its ˉfoundation,ˉ[63] in separating itself from the natural and making the natural into spirit's object, its presupposition, something that spirit then has to work upon or mold and so to bring forth or produce from itself, to reconstruct from itself. That is why, although Christianity became triumphant and dominant in the Roman and Byzantine worlds, neither the Roman nor the Byzantine world was capable of genuinely activating the new religion within itself and of bringing its own world forth from the Christian principle. For in both those peoples everything was already complete—customs, laws, legal system, constitution, political order, art, science, the whole spiritual culture—everything was already in place. In contrast, it is alone concordant with the nature of spirit for this fully formed world to be generated *from out of spirit* and that this generation shall occur through reaction against something that has preceded and that is assimilated by this process.

So these conquerors established themselves in an alien territory and ruled over it. But at the same time they came under the authority of a new and alien spirit, which was imposed on them. On the one hand they exercised worldly sovereignty, but on the other hand they adopted a passive attitude toward the spiritual principle [of the older world]. The spiritual idea or spirituality, the spiritual itself, was implanted in them. Appearing on the scene as crude barbarians, dull in mind and spirit, they received the spiritual [seed] into that dullness. Their heart was as though pierced by it. | Thus   22 the idea became immanent in their crude and dull nature as something infinitely opposed [to it]; in other words, the infinite torment was kindled within them, so that they themselves can be portrayed as a crucified Christ. They had to endure the great inner struggle involved in this monstrous antithesis, and the philosophy that sub-

63. *Thus Pn; Gr, Lw read:* counterpart,

sequently established itself among them and was at first received as a given is one aspect of this struggle. These peoples were still uncivilized, but in all their barbaric dullness they were profound in heart and mind. The principle of the spiritual has been sown within them, and with it is necessarily posited this torment, this battle of spirit with the natural. Cultural development begins here from the most monstrous contradiction, and this contradiction has to resolve itself. Its two sides are essentially so related to each other that the spiritual is what is supposed to rule, to be master.

The genuine dominion of spirit, however, cannot be dominion in the sense that what stands over against it is something in subjection to it. The universal spirit cannot have the subjective spirit, to which it is related, standing before it as something outwardly obedient or servile, for this subject is spirit too. The dominion of spirit means that the spirit unites itself with itself within subjective spirit. This position of harmony or reconciliation appears at first as a contradictory relationship of the universal spirit to the subjective spirit, a relationship in which the one can have power only by subjugating the other. But this first appearance is only an outward show. All of the history that follows is a development toward reconciliation. What reconciliation involves is (on the one side) that subjective consciousness, worldly dominion, worldly being, laws, constitution, and the like, shall become rational. We have already seen how Plato advanced the idea of a Republic where philosophers were to rule.[64] Now we are in the age when it is expressly declared that what is spiritual should rule. This proposition has acquired

23 the | particular sense that the spiritual order, meaning the clergy, should rule, in other words, the spiritual in the particular shape of individuals. But its true sense is that the spiritual should be the determining factor, and this sense has come right down to our own day. Thus we see in the French Revolution how thought, abstract thought alone, is supposed to be the sovereign ruler of the world; constitution and laws are to be determined according to abstract thought, and thought is to constitute the bond between human

64. [Ed.] See Vol. 2 of this edition, as well as the corresponding passage in W 14:191–196.

beings. People are to be conscious that what counts among them is freedom and equality as abstract thoughts. These abstractions should be all that counts, and it is in them that the [individual] subject as well places its true value in relation to actuality.

It is worth drawing attention to one [other and more recent] form of this ultimate reconciliation, a form in which the subject is inwardly contented with itself just as it is, contented with its thoughts, its volition, its spiritual state, so that the subject, its own knowing, thinking, and conviction, has become the summum—has the character of the divine, of what has validity in and for itself. This reconciliation, something universally spiritual, is thus posited within my subjective spirit and is identical with me, so that I myself am what is universally spiritual, so that I subsist within my immediate spirit and that my immediate knowing is the sole criterion of validity. This is the most recent form of reconciliation. But it is one-sided, since what is spiritual is not grasped as subsisting objectively in and for itself but only as it is within my subjectivity as such, in my conscience. My conviction as such is taken to be what is ultimate.[65]

Once reconciliation has attained this latter shape, the position of the Christian religion that we set forth earlier[66] holds no further interest; it is only something past, a matter of history. What *we* know or are convinced of, the way things reveal themselves immediately in each subject's inwardness, that is what is true, what subsists in and for itself. All of the modes and processes by which the true, as what subsists in and for itself or as God, gets mediated with the human being, no longer hold any but a historical interest. That is all something | we no longer need or care about. And in like fashion the teachings and system of doctrine of the Christian religion have the status of something strange, something belonging only to a particular time that the people of that time took seriously.

24

65. [Ed.] In this paragraph and the one that follows, Hegel is referring to a "post-Christian" form of reconciliation, which he associates with the Enlightenment and its aftermath. He probably has in mind here such figures as Fichte, Jacobi, and Novalis. Cf. *Philosophy of Religion* 3:241–244, 343–347.

66. [Ed.] See the discussion of God's concrete manifestation in the world, according to Christianity, pp. 00–00 above.

The idea in and for itself—that the idea is concrete, is spirit, and that the subject itself must enter into this idea—all this has vanished and appears only as something in the past. Thus all that I have said about the principle of the Christian system of doctrine, and what I shall still have to say about the philosophy of the Scholastics, is of interest only from the [earlier] standpoint we have stated, that is, where the idea has validity in its concrete determinateness, but not ˉfrom the standpoint of the subject's immediate reconciliation with itself.ˉ67 The universal, therefore, is this antithesis containing within itself the principle of resolution, namely, that the spiritual is what should govern but does so only insofar as it is reconciling.

The only thing we have to consider more closely is the character of the antithesis as compared with philosophy. We must recall briefly in this regard the historical aspect, though just in its principal moments. The shape of the antithesis as it appears in history is from one side the spirituality that, as such, is supposed to be the spirituality of the [individual] heart. But spirit is one. Thus we have [one] association [*Gemeinschaft*] of those who stand within this spirituality, and there arises a community [*Gemeinde*]—insofar as the community has an outward shape and order by which it expands into a church. Insofar as the spiritual is the principle, the spiritual is immediately universal; for to be devoid of spirit is to be isolated with one's own sentiment and opinion. In this way the church gets organized. But the church itself goes on to enter into worldly existence, gaining wealth and possessions and becoming worldly itself, with all the passions of barbarity, since at first only the principle is present, the spiritual as principle of the heart. What belongs to the actuality of [individual] existence (including those same inclinations and desires | of the heart), and to the whole sphere of human relationships, is still determined according to these inclinations and passions, according to this barbarity.

Just as the church only contains the spiritual principle within itself but does not yet genuinely realize it, so that its [internal] relationships are not yet rational, the same thing is true of all

25

---

67. *Thus Gr; An reads:* where the universal interest rules immediately and always.

the other [human social] relationships as well, prior to the development or realization of the spiritual principle within the world. For the worldly element is present, it is there or exists, before it conforms with the spiritual, and this prior worldly being is the immediate world of natural [relations]. Consequently the church will have implicit in it the worldly ⌐principle in its immediacy⌐[68]—deception, avarice, deeds of violence, robbery, murder, envy, hatred, passion. All these vices of barbarism it will have in itself, and they typify its own governance as much as they do the world it governs. So its sovereignty is indeed a sovereignty of passion, when it ought to be a sovereignty of the spiritual. The two spheres, the spiritual and the secular, interlock, so that for the most part (even if not completely) this church is in the right according to its spiritual principle, but in the wrong according to its worldly principle of passionate determination.

Standing against this spiritual-secular realm there is the secular realm on its own account. So pope and emperor, church and empire, stand mutually opposed. This secular imperium is supposed to be subject to the spiritual order or the clergy (which has itself become worldly); the emperor becomes no more than *advocatus ecclesiae,* protector of the church.[69] This secular realm on the one hand stands on its own, yet it is in union with the other realm, so that it at the same time recognizes the spiritual as sovereign. A struggle between the two is inevitable, however, precisely because of both the worldly aspect within the church itself and the *bad* worldly element in the secular authority, its violence and barbarity, the way it is on its own account. This ongoing struggle with the spiritual must be at first a losing battle for the secular power, because it not only stands on its own but also acknowledges the other power; it must submit to the | spiritual realm and its passions. The   26
bravest, noblest emperors were excommunicated, sometimes by popes, sometimes even by cardinals and bishops. They had in some

68. *Thus Pn; An reads:* principle, this immediacy of the world
69. [*Ed.*] The office of protector of the church was not limited to the emperor. In the High Middle Ages, protectors of the church had the task of representing churches or monasteries in their secular affairs. As chief patron of the church in general the emperor was, as it were, its supreme protector.

measure to crawl to the Cross and could do nothing against it. They could not rely on their outward power because they were inwardly broken and thus always the vanquished. They had to yield.

When we turn in the second place to social practices, what we see on the one hand is the spiritual having unlimited weight within the heart of individuals, and on the other hand its antithesis in their barbarity, unruliness, passions, and desire. So we see individuals falling from one extreme into the other, from the one extreme of the crudest violence into the opposite extreme of the most complete renunciation of everything, the conquest of all inclinations, passions, and the like. The supreme example of this is furnished by the Crusades.[70] Off they go bent on their sacred purpose. On the way, however, they fall into all manner of passions, with their leaders in the forefront, letting themselves go altogether in individual acts of violence, savagery, and brutality. After making their journey in the most stupid and heedless manner, and having lost thousands on the way, they arrive at the gates of Jerusalem. Here they all fall on their knees, pray, are penitent and contrite. At that moment they are filled with courage, and so they capture Jerusalem. But then right away they lapse into the same brutality and passion as before. They wallow in blood and are extremely cruel, but then are contrite and penitent again, after which they revert to the pettiest passions, brutality, ˜greed, and avarice.˜[71] By their passions they corrupt the prize they have won for themselves through their bravery. This happened because it is only as an abstract principle that the [Christian] principle is within them or in their innermost selves, and their human actuality | in itself has not yet been spiritually developed. This is the way the antithesis presents itself in that actuality.

Although this very antithesis has many shapes in religion, at this point we need only recall their innermost core. On the one hand we have the idea of God and on the other what is known or cognized of him, that God is the Trinity. Another form of the antithesis is found in the cultus, in the process whereby individuals draw near to this idea, so as to belong to the kingdom of God and to have

70. [*Ed.*] The following passage refers to accounts of the conquest of Jerusalem under the leadership of Godfrey de Bouillon in 1099, during the First Crusade.

71. *Thus An; Gr reads:* of self-seeking and envy.

the certainty of this mediation. In the cultus this mediation is present or accomplished (that is, accomplished in the individual) only in its crowning point, known as the mass. In the mass individuals are related to the mediating element as something objective, and they are to partake of it in such a way as to acquire the certainty that they are sharing in the Spirit, that the divine is within them. This objective element is the host, which is on the one hand the divine as objective, and on the other an outward thing as far as its shape is concerned, but a thing that, in its complete externality, is supposed to be worshiped. Luther changed this practice. He fully retained the mystical element in what is termed the Lord's Supper, the fact that the subject receives into itself the divine, but [he added] that the sacrament is only divine insofar as it is consumed in faith, that is, insofar as in faith and in the partaking the divine ceases to be an outward thing. This faith and partaking is the beginning of subjective spirituality; and the sacrament is ˉspiritualˉ[72] to the extent that it takes place with faith and participation and does not remain an outward thing. In the medieval church and in the Catholic church generally, the host is venerated even as an outward thing, so that if it has been eaten by a mouse, both the mouse and its excrement are to be venerated.[73] Here the divine is taken in the sense of complete externality. This is the central point, the shocking antithesis that on the one hand is resolved but on the other hand remains a complete contradiction, so that, for example, one should hold steadfastly to the host even as a merely outward thing ˉand should venerate it.ˉ[74]

Tied to this externality is the other aspect, consciousness about the relationship. One's consciousness of the spiritual, | of what is 28 the truth, has been placed in the keeping of single individuals, it is in the possession of a priesthood that is separate from other people,

72. *Thus Gr; Pn reads:* valid
73. [*Ed.*] Hegel is here inveighing against the doctrine of transubstantiation, according to which the eucharistic bread and wine are in substance transformed into the body and blood of Christ. One of Hegel's auditors, the chaplain of St. Hedwig's Church, reported him to the government ministry for publicly vilifying the Catholic religion by this remark; see *Berliner Schriften 1818–1831*, pp. 572–575.
74. *Thus Lw, Sv; Gr reads:* and yet it is supposed to be this lofty thing, this absolute.

who are the laity. Exclusively in the hands of this priesthood are both the doctrinal definitions and the means of grace, that is, the procedures whereby the individual within the cultus is religious and attains certainty of partaking of the divine. And just as the spiritual orders have control of the cultus, so too they have control over the moral appraisal of the actions of individuals. They control the conscience of individuals, so that the inner sanctum of humanity, the conscience (in virtue of which an action can be ascribed to the single agent), the human capacity for accountability, is handed over to another person, and as a result the subjects are devoid of self even in their inmost being. These are the principal relationships of that externality in the religion itself, upon which all its further characteristics depend.

The relationship to philosophy, what we are concerned with here, is determined by this externality too. If we may state it in a theological form, the relationship can in general be expressed in this way: that the period of the Middle Ages was the lordship of the Son, not of the Spirit.[75] The Son is what distinguishes itself from the Father and, as Son, is comprehended solely as remaining in distinction—implicitly the idea, what the Father is, but still distinct. It is only with the Spirit that we have love, the uniting of both, of what the Son is and what the Father is. When we say that the Son is love, we thereby also say he is the Spirit and identify him with the Father. The Son is implicitly the concrete idea, but still not so in its distinction. Thus in the Middle Ages we have the divine idea standing fast in its unresolved distinction, in its externality.

If for a moment we dwell improperly on the difference without at the same time positing the identity, then the Son is the *other,* and this is what defines the Middle Ages. When we turn to the character of philosophy, we find a philosophy in the Middle Ages, | a thinking or conceiving, but it is a conceiving with a presupposition; we have the thinking idea not in its freedom but always as afflicted with the form of an externality or a presup-

75. [*Ed.*] This reference is to the periodization of history by the Calabrian monk Joachim of Fiore (1130–1202). Hegel distances himself philosophically from this position by the expression, "If we may state it in a theological form."

position. So there is in this philosophy quite the same character as in the general condition of things. That is why I have already called to mind the concrete [medieval] character, since in any age there is always *one* determining characteristic that is present in it.

˜The Christian principle contains within itself˜[76] the highest summons to thinking, because in it the idea has a wholly speculative content. On the one hand the idea is to be grasped with the heart; "heart" is what we are calling the single human being. The identity of the individual with the idea lies in the fact that the middle term of the idea, the Son, as the mediating agent itself, is represented in the form of immediate singularity, as *this* man. This is the identity of ˜the spirit˜[77] with God, the identity for the heart as such. But since it is at the same time a cohering with God and in God, this coherence itself, and so the object of the entire idea, is mystical and speculative, and that very point involves a summons to thinking that the church fathers earlier, and now the Scholastic philosophers, have answered.[78] In this way Scholastic philosophy is essentially theology and this theology is immediately philosophy. Apart from philosophy the content of theology is only the content that is to be found in religion generally, namely, the representation of the system of doctrine. But it [this dogmatic theology] is also scientific knowledge, [there is also] a thought-content in it. Its scientific aspect includes the historical element—the existence of a certain number of New Testament codices, and the history of popes, councils, bishops, and church fathers—none of which, however, pertains to God's nature and its relationship to humankind. As doctrine of God, theology has for its essential object the nature of God, and this content is by its nature essentially

76. *Thus Pn, similar in An; Gr reads:* Medieval philosophy therefore contains the Christian principle, which is *Lw reads:* Implicit in medieval philosophy is that the Christian principle is

77. *Thus Gr; An reads:* the heart

78. [*Ed.*] See above, pp. 000–000. As answer to the "summons to thinking," Hegel probably is referring in particular to the elaboration of trinitarian doctrine from the second half of the second century down to Augustine. Neither here nor in the *Philosophy of Religion,* however, is there evidence of a detailed knowledge of these doctrinal disputes.

speculative. And since the content is a summons to thought, this true theology can only be a philosophy. |

We now have to discuss in more detail the way in which the Scholastics worked. As we said already, their philosophizing or thinking was burdened with an absolute presupposition, namely, the teaching of the church, which was, to be sure, itself speculative, implicitly what is true. But this teaching still ˉwas in the mode of representation.ˉ[79] So their thinking does not appear as issuing freely from itself or as inwardly self-moving but as depending on a given content, one that is speculative but still contains ˉwithin itself the mode of immediate existence.ˉ[80] The consequence is that with this presupposition thinking will be essentially inferential. Inference is the mode of formal logical procedure: a finitely particular determination is presupposed, from which one proceeds to another. As particular, such determinations are altogether finite; they function externally, they do not return unto themselves in cyclical fashion, they do not reunite integrally.

Bound up with this finite form is an immediate, finite content too; on the whole there is a finite form of the content. In similar fashion the thinking is not free, for the absence of self constitutes an essential determination in the content of thinking. If we are to express and treat thinking more concretely, by appealing more directly to what is human, then we speak of humanity, of healthy human understanding, of natural intuition. We speak of the concrete human disposition as, for example, in Greek humanity. "Concrete" here implies that we, as thinking or feeling human beings, have a living presence [*präsente Gegenwart*], that this concrete content has its roots in our thought and constitutes the material for the consciousness that is essential to us. It is our object, and by it formal thinking directs its course. In this essential consciousness the aberrations of abstract reflection have an end that sets a limit for them and brings them back to what is humanly concrete, to natural intuition and right thinking. |

The mode of philosophizing current in the Middle Ages lacks a

---

79. *Thus Pn; Gr reads:* consisted of external objects.
80. *Thus Gr; An reads:* a [merely] historical truth.

content of this kind. On the one side there is the teaching of the church, while on the other side the natural human being has not yet attained to rationality or even worked its way out of barbarism to humanity. Savagery or barbarism consists of the very antithesis that we have depicted, and is all the more frightful the more it has this monstrous antithesis in what is spiritual. ˉIt is barbarism rather than lack of development,ˉ⁸¹ but it is all the more frightful the more it is burdened by the antithesis of the spiritual.

Since this opposition generally prevails, since human beings in themselves, in what is called healthy human understanding, have not yet penetrated to the point of rationality, the thinker does not yet have any concrete content of that sort to direct the course of formal thinking. Whatever the thinker may reflect about the content hangs unsteadily upon the determinations of reflection, of formal thought, of inference. Whatever emerges by way of treatments of nature, by way of definitions of natural relationships, laws of nature, and the like, is not yet supported in experience, and the same is true of reflections on what is particular or on the human domain; they are not yet grounded or determined by sound human understanding. In this regard the content as well within this sphere is still devoid of spirit. And these spiritless relationships are [simply] inverted when it is time to pass over to the defining of what is higher or spiritual: they are carried over into the spiritual realm.

2. Principal Moments of Scholastic Philosophy

These features constitute the general character of philosophizing in this period. The field is very broad, and we shall leave its breadth to literary history. In briefly going on to details, we want to highlight the principal moments of the external procedure [of philosophy]. The first | indications of philosophy that we find in the Middle Ages, when independent states ˉwere beginning to be formed,ˉ⁸² are no more than surviving scraps from the Roman world, the collapse of which had been followed by decline in every respect. So

81. *Thus An; Pn reads:* So it is not naive or undeveloped,

82. *Thus Gr; An reads:* and culture were in their infancy, *Lw reads:* and scientific interest were in their infancy,

the West knew little more than ˉthe compendium of Boethiusˉ[83] on Aristotelian logic, Porphyry's *Isagoge,* an unsatisfactory treatise *De dialectica* by Augustine, and *De categoriis,* which is a bad paraphrase of Aristotle's *Categories.* This quite external and highly formal material was ˉall that was known at that time.ˉ[84]

a. Beginnings

ˉPhilosophy properly speaking began in the ninth century with JOHN SCOTUS ERIGENA.ˉ[85] We do not know whether he was born in Ireland or Scotland. He had some acquaintance with Greek and Arabic. He read Greek writings by [Pseudo-] Dionysius the Areopagite and translated them into Latin. In 824 the Greek Emperor Michael Balbus made a present of this text to Emperor Louis the Pious, and Charles the Bald had it translated by this Irish Scot, John Scotus. In this way something of Alexandrine philosophy became known in the West. The pope upbraided him somewhat for not sending the text to him in advance and for not seeking official approval. Scotus also wrote a number of works himself, on nature, *De naturae divisione,* in which a degree of profundity and acumen is unmistakable.[86] A selection of Erigena's writings has been pub-

83. *Thus Pn, similar in An; Gr reads:* texts by Boethius and Cassiodorus
84. *Thus An; Pn reads:* the inception.
[*Ed.*] Hegel's source is obviously Tennemann (*Geschichte* 8, pt. 1:49). Cf. W 15:159 (Ms?), where Hegel adheres more closely to his source by indicating doubt about Augustine's authorship of the treatises on dialectic and on the categories, and correctly attributes to Cassiodorus the "compendium" of extracts from Aristotelian logical writings.
85. *Thus An, similar in Pn, Lw; Gr reads:* John Erigena from Eryng in the county of Wales was the first, in the ninth century.
[*Ed.*] The brief biographical account that follows is based on Tennemann and Brucker. The statement that Erigena did not seek papal approval for his translation of Pseudo-Dionysius depends on a quotation from Bulaeus [C. D. du Boulaye], *Historia universitatis Parisiensis* 1:184, as transmitted by Tennemann (*Geschichte* 8, pt. 1:68). The statement about the presentation of the text by Michael Balbus is not in Tennemann but in Brucker (*Historia* 3:616). Cf. also Dieterich Tiedemann, *Geist der spekulativen Philosophie,* 6 vols. (Marburg, 1791–1797), 4:182.
86. [*Ed.*] Scotus's main work is *On the Division of Nature,* in five books; an edition was published at Oxford in 1681. Tennemann also mentions his treatise *On Divine Predestination,* as well as works no longer extant that dealt with mystical theology, Aristotle's moral philosophy, dogmatic philosophy, and education (*Geschichte* 8, pt. 1:75). Presumably Hegel gives Erigena little attention because he regards his philosophy as a mere echo of Neoplatonism; cf. W 15:160–161.

lished by Dr. Hjort in Copenhagen.[87] Scotus Erigena was also reproached by a church council for not supporting his position by
the Holy Scriptures and the *auctoritates patrum*, | but founding   33
his propositions on human and philosophical arguments.[88] So this
was the beginning.

b. Philosophical Consideration of Church Doctrine

Among subsequent philosophers Anselm and Abelard gained re-
nown.

ANSELM[89] was a learned monk who lived from 1034 to 1109.
He was highly honored, and in later life he was elevated to the
office of archbishop of Canterbury. His chief endeavor was to treat
church doctrine in a philosophical manner, to give proofs for it. He
especially is even said to have laid the foundation for Scholastic
philosophy and to have proved philosophically the basis of church
doctrine. In this regard he states that Christians must come to reflective cognition [*denkende Erkennen*] through faith, not come to
faith through the intellect. If they succeed in winning through to
reflective cognition, they will rejoice at proving to themselves by
thought what they already believe. If they do not succeed in proving
the faith of the church by thought, then they must stay with the
teaching of the church, not abandon it.[90] Very noteworthy is the
following passage, which captures the whole of his meaning. In his
treatise *Cur Deus sit homo,* which is rich in ˜speculations,˜[91] he
says that it seems negligence to him—*negligentia mihi videtur*—
if, after having been established in faith, we do not seek to un-

87. [*Ed.*] Peder Hjort's *Johan Scotus Erigena* . . . (Copenhagen, 1823) locates
his philosophy in the context of medieval and modern Christian speculation, and
in this connection briefly mentions Hegel's *Science of Logic.* Hjort gives no lengthy
extracts from Erigena, just quotations in the footnotes.

88. [*Ed.*] Here again the source is Bulaeus (*Historia* 1:182) as transmitted by
Tennemann (*Geschichte* 8, pt. 1:72n).

89. [*Ed.*] The following brief biographical account is drawn from Tennemann
(*Geschichte* 8, pt. 1:115 ff.), who in turn relies on Eadmer's Latin *Life of St. Anselm,*
which is commonly appended to editions of his collected works. Tennemann states
(p. 121) that "Anselm laid the first formal foundation of Scholastic philosophy."

90. [*Ed.*] The three preceding sentences paraphrase a passage from Anselm's
Letter 41, which is cited in Tennemann (*Geschichte* 8, pt. 1:160n); cf. W 15:163,
n. 1 (Ms?).

91. *Thus Gr; An reads:* acumen,

derstand, *intelligere*, what we believe.[92] *Intelligere* is reflective cognition. Nowadays, however, that is declared to be pride or presumptuousness, and immediate knowledge or belief is held to be superior to cognition. But Anselm, the learned Scholastic of the Middle Ages, and the [other] Scholastics, have proclaimed the contrary view.

34   He is famous in particular for the so-called ontological | proof of the existence of God, which he formulated to prove by a simple argument that God is. In the preface to that treatise he says that this quest gave him no peace by day or by night and that for a long time he took the thought for a temptation of the Devil. But finally he succeeded.[93] The simple content of this proof embodies the antithesis of thinking and being. It is striking for us to see that only now, and not at some earlier time, do thinking (or the universal) and being come to be mutually opposed in this abstraction—and in this way the highest antithesis enters consciousness. Bringing the highest antithesis to consciousness is the greatest depth of profundity. But Anselm's proof has the defect of being formulated in the mode of formal logic. More specifically, it runs as follows: "We think something, we have a thought; this thought is on the one hand subjective, but the content of the thought is what is wholly universal. This universal is at first only universal as thought. Being is distinct from it. Now if we think something and even if, for example, we think God (the content does not matter), what we think perhaps may not even be. But we regard as most perfect what is not only thought but at the same time exists. Consequently God,

92. [*Ed.*] See *Cur Deus homo*, bk. 1, chap. 2. Tennemann reproduces (*Geschichte* 8, pt. 1:118, n. 69) the passage that Hegel paraphrases; cf. *W* 15:163 with n. 2. For Hegel this treatise, *Why God Became Man*, is "rich in speculations" because it seeks to exhibit from rational grounds the necessity of the Incarnation as the remedy for human sin. Cf. the use Hegel makes of this same passage in *Philosophy of Religion* 1:154.

93. [*Ed.*] This account of the circumstances of Anselm's discovery of the "ontological proof" (Kant's term) derives from Tennemann (*Geschichte* 8, pt. 1:116–117), whose account in turn comes not from Anselm's *Proslogion* itself but rather from Eadmer's biography. However, the *Proslogion*'s preface does speak of the genesis of the treatise, although Hegel's secondary sources do not mention the fact; therefore Hegel may have consulted Anselm's works themselves.

who is what is most perfect, would be imperfect if he were only in thought and the attribute of being did not belong to him. Consequently we must ascribe being to God."[94] The content of the proof is of the highest kind. It expresses this identity of thinking, that is, of the thought of God or of the purely universal and absolute thought, with being. We grant that what is true is not what is mere thinking, but what also *is*. But here we must not take thinking to be merely subjective, for by "thought" we mean here the absolute, pure thought.

The proof has been attacked from the formal, logical side. Kant too has attacked and refuted it for this reason,[95] and the whole world afterward hastened to agree with him that the proof is untenable. The formal defect is the presupposition—that the unity of thinking and being, as what is most perfect, as God, is presupposed. The authentic proof | would be the demonstration that thinking by itself, thinking taken by itself, is something untrue, that thinking negates itself and by that negation determines itself as that which is. Just as on the other side too it must be shown, in regard to being, that the dialectic proper to being is its self-sublation, its self-positing as the universal and *eo ipso* as thought.

This proof was already criticized in Anselm's day by a monk, GAUNILO, in a text to which he gave the name *Liber pro insipiente*. Anselm replied to him, [in his] *Liber apologeticus contra insipientem*.[96] [Gaunilo] showed the same thing as Kant, that being and thinking are distinct. The objection is that when we think of something this is by no means to say that it exists. For example, when

94. [*Ed.*] The quotation is a free rendering of a passage in chapter 2 of the *Proslogion*. Again Hegel is probably drawing it from Tennemann (*Geschichte* 8, pt. 1:137n); cf. *W* 15:165–166 (Ms?). Hegel's reference to "what is most perfect" shows that he views the proof in light of the subsequent Cartesian proof from the concept of a most perfect being; see below, nn. 104 and 106, pp. 000–000. The various designations for God in the *Proslogion* are not adequately captured by "what is most perfect."

95. [*Ed.*] See Immanuel Kant, *Critik der reinen Vernunft*, 2d ed. (Riga, 1787), pp. 621–631; English translation by Norman Kemp Smith, *Critique of Pure Reason* (London, 1929, 1933), B 620–631. Also see below, pp. 000–000 with n. 428.

96. [*Ed.*] These titles are: *On Behalf of the Fool* and *Apology Directed against the Fool*. Hegel draws his versions of them from Tennemann (*Geschichte* 8, pt. 1:139, 145).

we think of one hundred dollars.[97] But what we are speaking of here is pure thought as such. The unity of these different orders is the very thing at issue. It is in no way a novelty to point out that they are different; Anselm was equally well aware of that. Plato says that God is what is infinitely living, whereby soul and body, being and thought, are eternally united.[98] That is the ˉabsoluteˉ[99] definition of God.

Anselm therefore laid the foundation for Scholastic philosophy by introducing philosophy into ˉthe treatment of church doctrine,ˉ[100] which therefore stands in this respect on a much higher level than does the doctrine of today. God is the content of religion, a content that only with the spirit truly *is* and only through thought can be truly comprehended. That is one point about Anselm that has to be stressed. The other is that ˉhe set up the antithesis of thinking and being in its most acute form.ˉ[101] In the ensuing philosophy, with Descartes, we shall again find thinking and being at their extreme point [of antithesis].[102] |

36 ABELARD lived from 1097 to 1142 and won great esteem after Anselm's day. He too philosophized about the doctrines of the church, in particular the Trinity. His lectures were attended by audiences of several thousands.[103] Just as Bologna was then the center for legal studies, so Paris was for the theologians the center for their

97. [*Ed.*] Hegel draws this formulation of the objection from Tennemann's citation (*Geschichte* 8, pt. 1:140n), and the example of one hundred talers from Kant's *Critique of Pure Reason*, B 627, an example that originated with Johann Bering, *Prüfung der Beweise für das Dasein Gottes* . . . (Giessen, 1780), p. 79.

98. [*Ed.*] See Plato, *Phaedrus* 246b-d. Cf. the translation of this passage in W 14:209–210 (Ms?), where Hegel also remarks: "That is a great definition of God."

99. *Thus Pn; Gr reads, similar in Lw:* speculative, authentic

100. *Thus An; Gr, Lw read:* medieval theology, *Pn reads:* religion,

101. *Thus Lw; Pn reads:* thinking started out from the highest point.

102. [*Ed.*] See below, pp. 000–000.

103. [*Ed.*] Abelard was born in 1079. Only *Gr* gives 1097, probably on the basis of Rixner (*Handbuch* 2:27). Since Griesheim used Rixner to supplement his lecture notes on other occasions (see, for example, pp. 000 and 000 below) we may assume the error here is not Hegel's. The brevity of the biographical data makes it impossible to identify Hegel's source here with certainty. The fuller version in W 15:170 echoes Brucker (*Historia* 3:734–735). Stress on Abelard's attention to trinitarian doctrine reflects Tennemann (*Geschichte* 8, pt. 1:173–175); so do references to his audiences and to the preeminence of Paris (p. 202).

science, the seat of philosophical theology. Anselm and Abelard were the founders of Scholastic philosophy. In fact we still have many works by Scholastics in this sense, but they are very long-winded, in many folios, and ˉthe later they come in time the more formal they are.ˉ[104]

c. Further Development of Theology by the Scholastics

We have next to consider in more detail the specific form that Scholastic theology took. In the general education of the clergy, theology was studied by collating passages or "sentences" on doctrinal matters from the church fathers, from Augustine in particular, and others. This procedure was made the basis for the teaching of ˉtheology.ˉ[105] The next step was presenting the doctrinal system of the church in methodical form and at the same time coupling the metaphysical basis with it, so as to fashion theology into a scientific system. Most notable among those particularly responsible for this are the following persons.

PETER OF NOVARA in Lombardy is commonly called Peter Lombard. He wrote *Four Books of Sentences* and was therefore also called *Magister sententiarum.* Any Schoolman who distinguished himself generally has a sobriquet of this kind, such as *doctor invincibilis, sententiosus, angelicus, divinus, deus inter philosophos,* and the like. Peter Lombard died in 1164.[106] He collected the main definitions of church doctrine and then joined | questions and answers about particular matters to them. But in his *Sentences* the answers usually were only appended in a problematic format. ˉThus the questions were not, properly speaking, answered decisively.ˉ[107] He used for this purpose a large number of proof texts

37

104. *Thus Gr, similar in Lw; Pn reads:* are wholly formal.
105. *Thus An; Gr reads:* the church.
106. [*Ed.*] The brevity of the account of the "Master of the Sentences" makes difficult the identification of Hegel's sources. Tennemann (*Geschichte* 8, pt. 1:233–234) discusses the method of question and answer; Brucker (*Historia* 3:767) gives the year of his death but Tennemann does not. The honorific titles Hegel cites are "doctor invincible," "rich in meaning," "angelic," "divine," and "god among philosophers."
107. *Thus Gr, similar in An; Pn reads:* [There were] still diverse suppositions concerning the meanings of words.

from the church fathers. The other writer who is famous in this regard was Aquinas.

THOMAS AQUINAS was born near Naples in 1224, of noble parentage, and he died in 1274 while traveling to the Council of Lyons. He was a Dominican. He composed commentaries on Aristotle and Peter Lombard and wrote his own *Summa theologiae.* *Summa* means "system of doctrine." Aquinas was known as *doctor angelicus* or even *doctor universalis.* His *Summa* contains profound philosophical thoughts covering the entire scope of theology and philosophy. He too juxtaposes questions, remarks, and objections, and he indicates as well the point on which the resolution of the issue depends. The main business of Scholastic theology was to elucidate and comment on the *Summa* of Thomas Aquinas.[108] Countless commentaries were also written on Peter Lombard's *Four Books of Sentences.* There are many other less important figures as well. The main thing was to make theology philosophical and more systematic; Peter Lombard and Thomas Aquinas are the most renowned in this respect, and for many years their work was the foundation for all subsequent scholarly compilations.

JOHN DUNS SCOTUS, *doctor subtilis,* a Franciscan, was a well-known figure in the formal development of philosophical theology. He was born at Dunston in the county of Northumberland. He too wrote a commentary on the *Magister sententiarum.* He was even called *deus inter philosophos.* One writer says of him that, from the way he improved philosophy, he could have been its inventor had he not found it in existence already. He knew the mysteries | of the faith as if he had not [merely] held them on faith; he knew the properties of angels as if he were himself an angel. In a few years' time he wrote so much that one person can hardly manage to read

38

108. [*Ed.*] Hegel's main source is again Tennemann (*Geschichte* 8, pt. 2:551–552), on whom he draws selectively, not mentioning, for instance, what Tennemann says about the *Summa contra gentiles.* The brief statement about the dissertational method of the *Summa theologiae* is not taken from any of Hegel's main sources. The correct Latin honorific titles for Aquinas are found in Brucker (*Historia* 3:802): *doctor communis* ("common doctor"—Albert the Great and Alan of Lille each bore the title "universal doctor") and *doctor angelicus* ("angelic doctor"). Tennemann gives his title as "universal and English doctor," possibly misreading *Angelicus* (capitalized in Brucker) as *Anglicus.*

it or to understand it. There are twelve folios of his in print. In 1304 he came to Paris and then in 1308 to Cologne, where the Dominicans, who at that particular time occupied the chairs of theology, gave him a very proper welcome; but he died there soon afterward. He wrote a commentary on Peter Lombard's *Sententiae,* then expounded *quaestiones* on that text and indicated the argument for each side. He raised the Scholastic method of disputation and its material to the highest level, to its pinnacle. He propounded a host of theses, developed many distinctions, coined many new words, and stabilized the terminology.[109] Scholastic terminology is, to be sure, barbaric Latin; it is not the fault of the Scholastics, however, but of the Latin culture [of the time], that the categories of the new intellectual culture were not available in the Latin language. Scotus is also regarded as the originator of the quodlibetal method[110]—the eristic treatment of individual topics that speaks of everything but without a systematic ordering of the whole.

By the middle of the twelfth century, Scholasticism had become quite generally [accepted]. The *doctores theologiae dogmaticae* were the guardians of public instruction who criticized books, declared them heretical, and so on. They were to a certain extent a kind of church consistory, "fathers" of a sort in regard to the Christian system of doctrine. The Sorbonne in Paris belonged to this movement. Later on the Aristotelian texts became ˉbetterˉ[111]

109. [*Ed.*] These biographical data and assessments of Scotus's work largely derive from Hegel's main sources: Tennemann, *Geschichte* 8, pt. 2:700–712; Brucker, *Historia* 3:827–828; Tiedemann, *Geist* 4:607 ff.; Rixner, *Handbuch* 2:110–111. Sancrucius is the "writer" who praised Scotus so highly, in his preface to the latter's collected works (London, 1672), p. 8. Brucker cites this (3:828) as an example of misplaced admiration of Scotus in England even after the work of Bacon and Hobbes; Hegel does not explicitly associate himself with Brucker's view. Tennemann explains that jealousy of Scotus's fame and disputational skill led to his removal from Paris to Cologne in 1308. Hegel does not draw his account of Scotus's method of argument directly from his sources, nor does he endorse Tennemann's view (*Geschichte* 8, pt. 2:705) that Scotus "occasioned renewed and vain disputes by a mass of empty or useless neologisms, often expressed in a barbaric way."

110. [*Ed.*] This probably refers to the view of Carl Fridrich Stäudlin that Scotus originated this "skeptical" method: *Geschichte und Geist des Skepticismus . . . ,* 2 vols. (Leipzig, 1794–1795), 1:552. Tennemann challenges this view (*Geschichte* 8, pt. 2:713n) by pointing to Henry of Ghent.

111. *Thus An; Gr reads:* generally

known, the object of more commentary and interpretation, and Aristotle came to be greatly admired. We have already shown how the Aristotelian corpus became known in the West; Emperor Frederick II had Aristotle's books translated from Arabic and Syriac into Latin.[112] Some church bodies also got involved with 39 them, and | a synod held in Paris initially prohibited the reading of the *Metaphysics,* the *Physics,* and the *Summae* prepared from them. In 1231 Pope Gregory issued a bull directed against [the University of] Paris, which forbade the reading of Aristotle's *Physics* until it had been inspected and purged of errors. Later, however, it was decreed that no one in Paris was to become Master of Philosophy who had not studied and expounded the prescribed works by Aristotle, the metaphysical books and some of the physical ones.[113]

ALBERT THE GREAT deserves our special attention, among those who excelled in their commentary on the Aristotelian corpus. Al-

---

112. [*Ed.*] See above, pp. 000 with n. 50, for one way in which the Aristotelian corpus become known. A second way, via the role of Emperor Frederick II, was made the basis of a controversy aroused by A. H. L. Heeren, *Geschichte des Studium's der classischen Litteratur . . . ,* 2 vols. (Göttingen, 1797). Heeren argued for a direct translation from Greek to Latin, in response to the order of Frederick II (1:183); Buhle defended the traditional view of an intermediate Arabic stage in the process (*Lehrbuch* 5:245–252). According to Heeren there was not even an intermediate Syriac stage (as *Gr* and *Lw* indicate); moreover, there had been direct translations as early as the twelfth and early thirteenth centuries. Hegel may have been misled here by the role of Arabic intermediaries in the earlier period, or perhaps by Buhle's reference (*Lehrbuch* 5:258–259) to the translation of Aristotle's *Historia animalium* from Arabic by Michael Scotus (c. 1175–1236). Buhle cannot have been well informed about Michael Scotus, since he misstates his year of death as 1190, four years before Frederick II was born.

113. [*Ed.*] Tennemann speaks of a severe interdict pronounced by a church synod in 1209 (*Geschichte* 8, pt. 1:359). The three texts Hegel mentions were actually cited by his sources in connection with a less severe interdict of 1215, in statutes for the University of Paris issued by the papal legate, Robert de Courçon. In the second half of the twelfth century David of Dinant and Amaury of Bène had expounded Aristotelian texts in a Neoplatonic-pantheistic and heterodox way; *W* 15:177 (Ms?) gives an excerpt about this from Brucker (*Historia* 3:697), who in turn drew upon Bulaeus. Tennemann discusses the papal bull of 1231 (*Geschichte* 8, pt. 1:359), also drawing upon Bulaeus; cf. *W* 15:177 (Ms?). He also states (p. 361) that the much later decree of 1366, stipulating the study of Aristotle, was issued by two cardinals.

bert was a German. Twenty-one folio-volumes of his writings are still extant. He [wrote] on [Pseudo-]Dionysius the Areopagite and on Aristotle's *Physics,* as well as a commentary on Peter Lombard's *Sententiae.* A Dominican, he was born in Lauingen in Swabia, and his family name was von Bollstedt. He studied in Padua, where his study room is still on display. He died in 1280. He is said to have been weak-minded and dull-witted in his youth. But then, so the story goes, the Virgin Mary appeared to him with three beautiful women, commended philosophy to him, and bestowed wisdom upon him. [She] liberated him from his feebleness of mind, promising him that he would give light to the church and would die a true believer despite his scientific knowledge. So he devoted himself to philosophy. Magical arts were attributed to him; he is supposed to have invented a talking machine that so frightened Thomas Aquinas he nearly fainted when he saw it. But five years before his death Albert again forgot all his philosophy just as quickly as he had learned it, relapsed into his previous dullness of wit, [and, so we are told,] died an orthodox believer. An adage about him states that "Albertus repente ex asino factus est philosophus et ex philosopho asinus" ["Albert was suddenly made a philosopher from an ass, and suddenly an ass from a philosopher"].[114]

At that time information about the history of philosophy was very scanty. This is clear from a few of Albert's pronouncements about it. He says the Epicureans got their name from lying indolently upon their backsides (*quod supra | cutem iacebant*), and because those would have been *supra curantes* who troubled themselves about unnecessary things. He represents the Stoics as being like our choirboys, putting their philosophy into song (*facientes cantilenas*) and ˉwandering about the porticoes and colonnades.ˉ[115] In his view the *Currendejungen* are possibly a surviving remnant

40

114. [*Ed.*] In his brief account of Albert's life, Hegel combines information derived from Tennemann (*Geschichte* 8, pt. 2:486–487), Tiedemann (*Geist* 4:369), and Brucker (*Historia* 3:789–798).

115. *Thus Lw with An, similar in Sv; Gr reads:* chanting it in the porticoes.
[*Ed.*] For Albert's dicta on the Stoics and the Epicureans, as reported by Hegel, see Tennemann (*Geschichte* 8, pt. 2:489, n. 115); cf. Tiedemann (*Geist* 4:372). W 15:179 cites the same passage, but with ἐπί *cutem*; Hegel's source for the corresponding Latin phrase in our text is not known.

of their school.[116] In Gassendi's *Life of Epicurus*[117] Albert is cited as saying that the earliest Epicureans were Hesiod, then Achalius (who he was is not stated), Cicero's friend Caecina, whom others called Tetinnus, and even [the Israelite philosopher] Isaac. The earliest Stoics he gives as Speusippus, Plato, Socrates, and Pythagoras.

These anecdotes give a picture of the state of culture at that time. The main thing in this period, however, is familiarity with Aristotle and particularly with his logic, with what has survived from most ancient times.

d. Realism and Nominalism

A third point to which attention must be drawn is a central perspective still of interest to us today, a feature that persisted throughout the entire Middle Ages. It is the distinction between realist and nominalist philosophy. This distinction was drawn throughout the entire Scholastic period, and the controversy was conducted with the utmost vehemence and Scholastic subtlety. We distinguish between earlier and later nominalists and realists. Listed among the earlier are ROSCELIN and ABELARD.[118]

Prominent among the later [nominalists] is WILLIAM OF OCKHAM, an English Franciscan also known as *doctor invincibilis,* 41 who | died in 1347 in Munich. [He] restored this question to the [philosophical] agenda.[119] The Franciscans were Ockhamites, for

116. [*Ed.*] These are schoolboy choristers who sing before people's houses at the time of a funeral or during the Advent season, in return for receiving small gifts.

117. [*Ed.*] See Pierre Gassendi, *De vita et moribus Epicuri libri octo* (The Hague, 1656), bk. 2, chap. 6, pp. 51–52. Gassendi cites these pronouncements contained in a work on the immortality of the soul and attributed to Albert, as evidence of Albert's ignorance of classical times. Cf. W 15:179–180 (Ms?); cf. Gassendi's *Miscellanea* (Lyons, 1658), 5:191.

118. [*Ed.*] In coupling Roscelin of Compiègne (c. 1050–c. 1120) and Abelard, Hegel follows Brucker (*Historia* 3:674), who in turn cites John of Salisbury's *Metalogicon* (bk. 2, chap. 17) to the effect that Abelard was Roscelin's pupil. Tennemann, however, stresses the differences between the two and doubts John's contention (*Geschichte* 8, pt. 1:170n, 337). In fact Abelard studied with Roscelin at Loches, although he also had other teachers such as the realist William of Champeaux (1070–1120).

119. [*Ed.*] The "invincible doctor" was born about 1285. Today his death is put in 1349, or else within the period 1347–1350. Tennemann (*Geschichte* 8, pt.

Ockham himself was a Franciscan, whereas the Dominicans were Thomists, after Thomas Aquinas. This distinction [in labels] persisted, and the interests of the religious orders became involved. Ockham and the Franciscans are also noteworthy from a political angle. Ockham was a supporter of Emperor Ludwig of Bavaria and sought to uphold Germanic freedom against the pretensions of the Roman see with his pen, as the emperor did with his sword.[120] This point of controversy had political ramifications; for example, Louis XI of France had the books of the nominalists confiscated or impounded, but in 1481 he in turn released them.[121]

The general distinction between realists and nominalists relates to the antithesis between universal and singular. At issue is the universalia, the universal, the Platonic Idea, the genus as such, the essence of things. The main question was whether this universal exists *realiter* or whether it is only nominal, that is, a subjective representation or a thought-object. For us today the expression "realism" has quite the opposite sense, for the issue for us is whether sensible things, as they are in their immediate existence, are something genuine and substantial, so that a proper being can be ascribed to them. Idealism stands opposed to realism and is, abstractly, the view that the sensible, as it shows itself to the senses immediately in its singularity, is not something genuine. But in the Middle Ages it was the reverse. Scholastic realism maintained that the universal, the universalia or genera, the essence of things or the idea, was something independent and having being on its own account, was something existing. Over against this the nominalists said that it

---

2:841–843) is Hegel's source for the date 1347, as well as for the view that Ockham reawakened the old nominalist-realist debate.

120. [*Ed.*] Ockham not only sought to uphold "Germanic freedom" (including that of the Franks), but also—while in France—defended the rights of secular authority in general. Tiedemann (*Geist* 5:164) speaks of "the pretensions of the Roman see," but with reference to the interests of Emperor Philip the Fair. Ludwig of Bavaria did, however, give Ockham refuge in 1330 when he was under the proscription of Pope John XXII for his views on evangelical poverty, and Ockham in turn supported him in a series of polemical writings. Hegel's reference to the pen and the sword comes from a statement by Ockham, given in German by Tiedemann (*Geist* 5:165) and in Latin by Tennemann and Brucker.

121. [*Ed.*] See Tennemann (*Geschichte* 8, pt. 2:945–947), who bases his account on Bulaeus (*Historia* 5:706, 739–740).

was only a matter of representation or subjective generalization, that when we form genera and the like these are names or representations we make for ourselves. This is the issue, and it is of great interest. The antithesis here is on a much higher plane than the ancients knew it. For the nominalists, | therefore, the universalia were mere abstractions that in themselves have no reality. Their subsistent being is only in the individual [mind or creature], and [universal] life or being as such has no distinctive reality of its own.[122]

A multitude of definitions and distinctions enter into this debate. In another of Ockham's texts the standpoint of the realists is presented as follows.[123] Some are of the opinion that each universal, whatever names things of the same kind, is *realiter* a thing existing apart from the soul; that the essence of any singular is distinct from any singular [as such], but also from any [other] universal, so that the universal human being is a true thing [*eine wahre Sache*] apart from the soul, which exists *realiter* within the universal. This universal human being is distinct from everything singular and from all [other] genera, [for instance,] from universal life or from ˉnatural substance.ˉ[124] So each genus possesses real existence on its own account. Ockham declared to the contrary that the universal is not something possessing *esse subiectivum*, whether within or apart from the soul, but is an *esse obiectivum* within the soul. The universal is a depiction within the soul that has objective reality in the way the representation has reality in the thing: it is for us a sign

42

122. [*Ed.*] Hegel's formulation of the nominalist position at the end of this paragraph echoes a passage in which Rixner (*Handbuch* 2:26) criticizes Roscelin for failing to recognize the "vitality of ideas," for taking them to be mere abstractions, "mere generic names that are nothing real in themselves." See W 15:182 (Ms?).

123. [*Ed.*] The fact that Hegel speaks of "another of Ockham's texts" shows that he erroneously attributes to Ockham the nominalist position as just described, whereas W 15:182 (Ms?) correctly ascribes it to Roscelin. His ensuing statement, however, does reflect Ockham's account of the realist position (*In librum primum sententiarum*, dist. 2, quaest. 4), as given by Tennemann (*Geschichte* 8, pt. 2:846, n. 3); cf. Hegel's excerpt and translation in W 15:185–186 (Ms?).

124. *Thus An; Lw reads:* universal existence. *Gr reads:* existence.

of what exists in nature.[125] This is the main question for the Scholastics, and it is of itself a sufficiently weighty question.

e. Doctrinal System and Formalism

The last thing to be noted about the Scholastics is that they not only introduced all possible formal conditions of the understanding into the church's system of doctrine but also treated these objects, which are intelligible in themselves, according to sensible and wholly external relationships. So it can be said, on the one hand, that their treatment of the church's doctrinal system was profound, and on the other hand that they made the doctrine mundane, through wholly inappropriate external relationships, so that what we have here is the | worst sense of worldliness that one can adopt. The church's system of doctrine does of itself involve a historical moment, a specification of external, sensible relationships. The Christian principle contains within itself this connection [with the external world]. The Scholastics grasped this aspect and treated it with infinite acuteness in their ⁻finite, formal⁻[126] dialectic. Let me give a few examples.

With JULIAN, ARCHBISHOP OF TOLEDO, we find this kind of treatment of *quaestiones*.[127] The system of doctrine, properly speaking, was beyond dispute. But various side issues were investigated or attached to it, and these were regarded as matters on which the

43

~

---

125. [*Ed.*] This statement of the position is based on Ockham's *In librum primum sententiarum*, dist. 2, quaest. 8, although it is taken by Hegel from two footnotes in Tennemann (*Geschichte* 8, pt. 2:859, 862); cf. the full excerpts with free and highly abridged German translation, in *W* 15:187–188. That translation speaks of "a depiction that has objective reality in the soul" and leaves out of account Ockham's "adequation" between the thing (*res*) and the mind (*intellectus*). The transcripts for our text lack "within the soul," thus giving to "objective reality" a modern connotation; they also misrepresent the ending of the passage, which actually says the representation is the "sign" of a thing outside the soul (and not itself something that "has reality in the thing").

126. *Gr reads:* finite *Pn, Lw read:* formal *An reads:* infinitely acute

127. [*Ed.*] Julian of Toledo lived in the Kingdom of the West Goths, in Spain; he died in 690. Taking him up after Ockham is a far greater departure from chronological treatment than, for instance, discussing Albert the Great after Aquinas.

church took no stand. So the proofs given for the content of the doctrinal system could be disputed, but not the content itself. Apart from the dogmatic content, however, there was a great deal of additional content discovered by sharp-witted people that was open to debate. For instance, an inquiry of this kind arises concerning the dead. Human beings shall rise again and be clothed with bodies. This is a doctrine of the church. But in the case of the body we enter the sensible sphere and so open the issue to debate. Out of the wish to define this resurrected body, the following questions emerged. In what time of life will the dead arise? As children, in youth, as adults, in old age? And in what shape, with what bodily constitution? If they had been thin [will they be again] thin, if fat then fat again? Will there still be different sexes? And will people get back the nails and hair they have lost?[128]

Another question of prime concern was the birth of Christ, whether it had been natural or supernatural. The topic was treated with a precision befitting an obstetrician, in an early treatise entitled *De partu Beatae Virginis*.[129] In Peter Lombard we find *quaestiones* on the creation, ˉthe fall, the | Trinity, the angels,ˉ[130] and on such issues as whether there could have been divine providence and predetermination if there had been no creatures. Or, where was God before the Creation? Thomas of Strasbourg answered: "Tunc ubi nunc, in se, quoniam sibi sufficit ipse" ["Then as now, within himself, because he is self-sufficient"]. This question relates to a trivial attribute of spatial location not pertinent to God. Also, can God know more than he does know? For possible knowledge can be distinguished from actual knowledge. Can God do at all times

128. [*Ed.*] These questions originally come from Julian's *Prognosticon futuri saeculi,* although Hegel quotes them from Tennemann (*Geschichte* 8, pt. 1:61); cf. W 15:192 (Ms?). Tennemann himself drew them from Cramer's sequel to Jacques-Bénigne Bossuet's *Discours sur l'histoire universelle,* which is: *Jacob Benignus Bossuet: Einleitung in die Geschichte der Welt und der Religion, fortgesetzt von Johann Andreas Cramer* (Leipzig, 1772), pt. 5, vol. 2, p. 84.

129. [*Ed.*] Paschasius Radbertus (786–860), a monk of Corbie during the Carolingian Renaissance, wrote two volumes *De partu Beatae Mariae Virginis* ("On the Birth by the Blessed Virgin Mary"). Hegel draws upon Tennemann (*Geschichte* 8, pt. 1:61), who in turn draws upon Bulaeus (*Historia* 1:169); Tennemann lacks the remark, "a precision befitting an obstetrician." Cf. W 15:192 (Ms?).

130. *Lw reads:* the fall, *An reads:* the angels, on the fallen,

what he can do at one time, for instance, can he at all times create King Solomon? Where were the angels after their creation? Have there always been angels? How old was Adam when he was created? Why was Eve taken from Adam's rib and not from some other part of his body, and why was she created when Adam was asleep? Why did the first human beings not mate in Paradise? How would the human race have been perpetuated if they had not sinned? Why did the Son become incarnate, not the Father or the Holy Spirit? Could not God also have adopted or have assumed (*suppositare*) human form as a woman? [Could] God also have entered the Devil? Could not God also have appeared in the shape of an ass or a pumpkin? ("Num Deus potuerit suppositare mulierem? Num diabolum? Num asinum? Num cucurbitam?") And in that event how could a pumpkin have preached, or been crucified? In this way the Scholastics introduced these wholly external forms of sensibility into this purely spiritual domain, and by doing so they made it mundane.[131]

⁻These then are the principal moments to be taken into account in the case of Scholastic philosophy, including the mundane aspect we have just noted, this introduction of distinctions from the understanding and sensible relationships into what, in and for itself and according to its own nature, is spiritual, absolute, and infinite.⁻[132] |

f. Mystics

But with respect to the latter tendency we must nevertheless note that, alongside that finitization and degeneration, there were also

131. [*Ed.*] Hegel derives much of this paragraph from Tennemann (*Geschichte* 8, pt. 1:236–237). Thomas of Strasbourg's answer is not found in Tennemann but in Rixner (*Handbuch* 2:153). The question about King Solomon appears neither in Tennemann nor in W 15; nor does the Latin term *suppositare*, which Hegel apparently transposed from the extended Latin quotation, derived from Erasmus of Rotterdam, *Encomium moriae* ("The Praise of Folly"). Erasmus asks (§ 28) whether God could have been incarnate in the Devil, and so forth. Hegel, however, takes the quotation from Brucker (*Historia* 3:878); cf. W 15:193–194, which shows that he realized these questions were intended as a caricature of the Scholastic method.

132. *Thus Gr, similar in Lw; Pn reads:* The finite is thus introduced into what is infinite and absolute.

many great Scholastics who were known as mystics. They kept themselves pure both on the side of the church's doctrine and on the side of the philosophical mode of its treatment. They even fashioned their morality, religious feeling, and love for God from their ˉauthentic sensibilityˉ[133] and gave us their treatises and precepts concerning philosophy in this sense.

JEAN CHARLIER, also known as John Gerson, wrote a *theologia mystica* in the fourteenth century.[134]

Among others was RAYMOND OF SABUNDE, who in 1437 wrote a *theologia naturalis,* a topic he grasped in a speculative spirit.[135] This approach should therefore be set in contrast to that [mundane] one. In order to do justice to the Scholastic theologians, these mystics must be taken into account as well.

E. RENAISSANCE AND REFORMATION

1. Transition to the Renaissance

After these special topics we must now speak of the general progress of spirit.[136] On the one hand we have seen how the doctrinal system was treated in a philosophical manner. But we have also seen a development of formal logic, and we have seen the highest content, or what has being in and for itself, made into something mundane. The existing church also made itself mundane in the very same way; it assimilated every sort of passion, ambition, avarice, and vice. It established and maintained a relationship of dominance

133. *Thus An, Lw, similar in Gr; Pn reads:* inner [life]

134. [*Ed.*] This brief reference to Gerson (d. 1429) stems from Tennemann (*Geschichte* 8, pt. 2:955–986), who cites his work as *Considerationes de mystica theologia* and also links him with Raymond of Sabunde. Hegel does not endorse Tennemann's highly critical assessment of these two mystics.

135. [*Ed.*] Hegel's information about Raymond (c. 1385–c. 1436) derives from Rixner (*Handbuch* 2:157), who says he sought to demonstrate Christian dogmas to unbelievers by rational arguments. None of the sources mentions the great influence on Raymond of the thought of Ramon Lull (1235–1315).

136. [*Ed.*] In the introductory pages of this section Hegel is reviewing the general progress of spirit in the preceding period, the Middle Ages. In doing so, however, he is stressing those features, such as freedom and the increasing inwardness of thinking, that point forward to the Renaissance and the Reformation.

over the inner sanctum of humanity, and of priests over the laity. On the other hand, the secular order | spiritualized itself inwardly 46 or established itself inwardly, and it did so in a manner legitimated by spirit.

About the general circumstances of the age we should note that, while we see on the one side the principle of human selflessness [*Selbstlosigkeit*]—the state in which spirit is not at home with itself, the internal cleavage of humanity—we also see on the other side that the legal or political condition has become generally more rigid, which leads to the formation of a selfishness [*Selbstischkeit*] that is not only more barbaric [but also] self-seeking. Contained in this ˉselfishnessˉ[137] is an element of barbarity that must [be made to] fear the punishment of the church if it is to be kept within bounds. But now we see the right of ownership or the legal order emerging. It is, of course, the feudal system or serfdom that is the prevalent order, but it all now becomes something legally fixed, that is, fixed in its connection with freedom. "Legal right" [*Recht*] means that the freedom of all individuals should come into existence and be treated by the law as strictly valid. ˉLegal right is established in this way, even though [social] relations that, properly speaking, pertain to the state are made into private property.ˉ[138] Thus the validity of that human selfishness which is connected with human freedom is firmly established over against the principle of the church, the principle of selflessness. Although they rest upon birth, the [social] structures of feudal monarchy are not, however, caste-dependent as well, in the way they are with the Egyptians and the Hindus. Someone of the lowliest estate can attain to the very highest positions in the ecclesiastical hierarchy. In Italy towns and citizen organizations asserted their freedoms and got their rights recognized ˉvis-à-visˉ[139] both the secular and the spiritual authorities. The freedom of these towns became established. The Capitani in Italy moved out of the feudal system, and even within the feudal system | right was established and recognized at least 47 in a formal way. Bit by bit the civic and legal order with its free-

137. *Gr reads:* independence
138. *Thus Gr; Lw reads:* The right of property has become valid.
139. *Thus An; Gr reads:* by

doms emerges, with business, commerce, and the arts all playing their parts. It is through the arts that humanity brings forth from itself the divine and portrays it. Though the artists were still so pious as to have selflessness as their inner principle, it was nevertheless as artists that they were pious, and it was from their subjective capacities that these portrayals and representations of religious subjects emerged.

Connected with this is the fact that humanity or the worldly domain thus knew itself to be inwardly justified, and it held fast to [categorial] determinations based upon subjective freedom. In business too individuals are essentially concerned with their own free activity; they themselves are the activating and productive element. People have reached the point of knowing themselves to be free and of getting their freedom recognized; they have reached the point of seeing that it lies in their own hands, that they have the strength to act in their own interests and for their own purposes. So now the time came when the arts and sciences flourished again, and in such a way that, in the sciences especially, people turned to the works of the ancients. These works became the object of studies that, in contrast [with theology], were called the *studia humaniora* ["more humane studies"], that is, studies in which humanity gains recognition in its own activities and pursuits. The fact that human beings themselves count for something interested them in those who, simply qua human, count for something too [namely, the great pagans]. Tied to this is the more specific feature that the formal cultivation of the Scholastic spirit became more universal. As a result, in this cultivation thought discovered itself inwardly, and from this discovery sprang the antithesis between understanding and the teaching or the faith of the church. This antithesis was generally represented to the effect that something affirmed by the church could be known by the understanding to be false.[140] It was

140. [*Ed.*] On the doctrine of double truth, see below, pp. 000 with no. 143 (on Pomponazzi), p. 000 with n. 198 (on Vanini), and p. 000 (on Bayle). Hegel's brief reference to the doctrine of double truth here does not indicate the conditions of its emergence in the history of ideas. Its inception was in connection with the Averroistic interpretation of Aristotle current in Paris in the second half of the thirteenth century—in particular by Siger of Brabant—in opposition to the Christian

important that understanding or thinking generally did apprehend itself in this way, albeit on the whole in opposition to the positive [namely, to religion]. |

48

2. Interest in Ancient Philosophy

The most direct way in which they looked back to humane values in the domain of the sciences was through the arising in the West of an interest in the works of antiquity, and in particular the West's acquaintance with Greek philosophy. The ancient philosophies were revived. Free philosophy or systems that would have begun from thinking [itself, namely, the forms of rationalism], had not yet emerged; there were just the renewal and rebirth of ancient philosophical systems.

The West's acquaintance with the Greek originals involved external political events, in that the Turks invaded Greece and conquered Constantinople. In this emergency the Greek Empire sent envoys to the West to implore the help of Christendom. For the most part these envoys were Greek scholars, men of scientific culture such as Chrysoloras. These envoys, and the scholars who fled to the West later, brought about a closer acquaintance with the [ancient] Greeks.[141] Petrarch learned Greek from a Greek monk in a monastery in Calabria, where many of the exiles who had fled from Greece were living.[142] In this way especially the ancient phi-

---

Aristotelianism of Albert the Great and Thomas Aquinas. If one wanted to recognize Averroistic Aristotelianism as logically consistent, but not to give up the doctrine of the church, then the doctrine of double truth seemed to afford the only way out of their irreconcilability. Here, however, Hegel makes use of the doctrine in elucidating the spiritual upheaval of the early modern era.

141. [*Ed.*] Buhle (*Lehrbuch* 6, pt. 1:127) tells of the mission of Manuel Chrysoloras from Constantinople to Italy in 1387, and of his second journey in 1395 to reside permanently in Italy; cf. Tennemann, *Geschichte* 9:23. Of course Hegel stated above (p. 000) that the texts of Aristotle's logical writings had been known for a long time in the West and that his *Metaphysics* and other works had been known since the end of the twelfth century.

142. [*Ed.*] Buhle states clearly (*Lehrbuch* 6, pt. 1:125–126) that the monk Barlaam learned his Greek in Calabria (in the monastery of St. Basil), went to the East, and subsequently was sent as an envoy from Constantinople to the papal court at Avignon, the actual place where he became Petrarch's teacher. See also Buhle, *Geschichte der neuern Philosophie seit der Epoche der Wiederherstellung der Wissen-*

losophies were reawakened, and we still have from this period a mass of texts that elaborate one or another ancient philosophy.

All of the Greek schools found adherents. There were, for example, Aristotelians, Platonists, and others, but now in a quite different sense from that in which the Scholastics called themselves by these names. Pomponazzi was particularly well known. There were Averroists who contended so violently about the immortality of the soul that a church council had to settle the question. These [Italian] Aristotelians draw upon the [original] texts | themselves.[143] There were also Platonists. Cardinal Bessarion, who had been patriarch in Constantinople and had come there from Trebizond, made Plato better known in the West.[144] Ficino in Florence then translated

schaften, 6 vols. (Göttingen, 1800–1804), 2, pt. 1:32–33, 41–42; Tennemann, Geschichte 9:22.

143. [Ed.] Tennemann (Geschichte 9:64) and Buhle (Geschichte 2, pt. 2:528) note the fame of Pietro Pomponazzi (1462–1525). Hegel's statements about the Averroists, as transmitted, reflect a misunderstanding; cf. W 15:215, where the facts are correctly presented, following Tennemann (Geschichte 9:63–72), although Buhle also covers this issue amply (Geschichte 2, pt. 2:534 ff.). The controversy concerned the view of Thomas Aquinas that Aristotle's De anima, chap. 3, teaches the independent existence of the individual human intellect. The Averroists—Alexander Achillini (1463–1512), Marcus Antonius Zimara (1460–1532), and Andreas Caesalpinus (1519–1603)—held that there is one immortal and universal rational soul for the whole human species, whereas their opponents, the followers of Alexander of Aphrodisias (fl. A.D. 220), held that there are individual rational souls and that they are mortal. Both parties opposed the church's teaching on the soul, and the Fifth Lateran Council (Session 8, 19 December 1513) condemned the views of these "Neo-Aristotelians." The Averroists were also opposed by the pure Aristotelians, including Pomponazzi and Julius Caesar Scaliger (1484–1558). Pomponazzi held that the soul's immortality cannot be shown on Aristotelian grounds, and that the church's doctrine should be believed but cannot be demonstrated philosophically; cf. his Tractatus de immortalitate animae (Bologna, 1516), especially chap. 15 (Tennemann cites chap. 12.) On the subordination of reason to the faith of the church, see below, p. 000, also p. 000 with n. 198 (on Vanini), and p. 000 (on Bayle).

144. [Ed.] For information on Basilius Cardinal Bessarion (1403–1472), Hegel draws upon Brucker (Historia 4, pt. 1:1–45), although Buhle has the fuller account (Geschichte 2, pt. 1:67–70, 129 ff.). Bessarion, born in Trebizond, was an envoy to Italy in the interest of reuniting the Greek and Roman churches, and took part in church councils at Ferrara (1437) and Rome (1443)—both subsidiary to the Council of Florence (1439–1445). Upon his return to Constantinople the emperor appointed him patriarch, but representatives of the Greek church, who regarded his efforts at church union as treason, kept him from the post. He was named a cardinal

Plato. The Medici were patrons of the arts and sciences, and attracted Greek scholars to their court; one of them founded a Platonic Academy headed by Ficino.[145] [Nor should we forget] Count Pico della Mirandola.[146] Epicurean philosophy was made known later by Gassendi. Stoic philosophy found its adherents too.[147] Cabalistic philosophy and the Pythagorean philosophy

---

after returning to Italy. Brucker correctly describes Bessarion as a pupil of the Byzantine philosopher George Gemistos Plethon (1355–1450), who was regarded as a *Plato redivivus*. Bessarion, however, sought to combine the Platonic and Aristotelian philosophies; cf. Buhle, *Lehrbuch* 6, pt. 2:143.

145. [*Ed.*] Buhle (*Geschichte* 2, pt. 1:75–77), Tennemann (*Geschichte* 9:131), and Rixner (*Handbuch* 2:188) all refer to the Plato and Plotinus translations by Marsilio Ficino (1433–1499). Hegel owned copies of these editions of Plato (Lyons, 1590) and Plotinus (Basel, 1615); see the Bibliography of Sources. Hegel's sources differ as to which Medici founded the Platonic Academy: Tennemann names Lorenzo, whereas Rixner correctly credits Cosimo (cf. Buhle, *Geschichte* 2, pt. 1:72–74). Brucker (*Historia* 4, pt. 1:48) cites Ficino's introduction to his Plotinus translation, which attributes the inspiration for the Academy to speeches by Plethon at the Council of Florence that were heard by Cosimo the Elder (not Cosimo II, as W 15:216 erroneously states).

146. [*Ed.*] Hegel means Giovanni Pico (1463–1494), who was the elder and more important of the two Counts of Mirandola. He and his nephew, Giovanni Francisco, are discussed in Brucker (*Historia* 4, pt. 1:55–61), Rixner (*Handbuch* 2:191–193), Buhle (*Geschichte* 2, pt. 1:381–401), and Tennemann (*Geschichte* 9:146–156). Pico sought to combine Platonic and Cabalistic thought with biblical revelation, and in opposition to astrology. See below, p. 000 with n. 157.

147. [*Ed.*] Here and in the rest of this paragraph Hegel juxtaposes, in a highly condensed form, references to the revival of the ancient philosophical schools, in the manner of Brucker (*Historia* 4, pt. 1), who treats successively the revivals of the Aristotelian, "Pythagorean-Platonic-Cabalistic," Parmenidean, Ionic, Stoic, "Democritean-Epicurean," and Skeptical philosophies (pp. 117–609). Brucker deals explicitly with Gassendi's efforts on behalf of Stoicism (pp. 510–535), as also does Rixner (*Handbuch* 2:268–269), who links him with the renewal of Stoic philosophy by Justus Lipsius (1547–1606); see also n. 115 above, and Buhle (*Lehrbuch* 6, pt. 2:288 ff.). In his juxtaposition of the Pythagorean and Cabalistic philosophies (pp. 353–448), Brucker devotes no less than seventeen pages (357–374) to the influence of Johann Reuchlin (1455–1522); cf. Tennemann (*Geschichte* 9:164–167) and Tiedemann (*Geist* 5:483–485). Hegel's brief account of Reuchlin, as transmitted by *Pn*, jumbles the reports in Brucker, who states (pp. 358–363) that Reuchlin learned Greek in Paris, began the study of Hebrew in Basel with Johann Wessel—a relationship reported by the Protestant theologian Philipp Melancthon (1497–1560)—and continued it with a Jewish physician (Jacob Loans) of the Emperor Frederick III when he was sent to Vienna as ambassador to the imperial court; cf. Buhle (*Geschichte* 2, pt. 1:402–403; *Lehrbuch* 6, pt. 1:189) and Tiedemann (*Geist* 5:484).

proper (all very obscurely mixed together) were also elaborated anew, and propagated particularly by a certain Reuchlin. The enthusiasm for Greek culture was so great that Reuchlin learned the language from a Greek in Vienna. Reuchlin also deserves credit for having prevented the Imperial Diet from decreeing that all books in Hebrew should be burned. Stoicism [was brought to life again] by ˜Lipsius.˜[148] The Ciceronian form of philosophy became widespread too—a rather popular philosophy, but one that deals with everything that takes place in the human soul and feelings. ˜That is its merit, which is all the greater in view of the prevalent [religious] selflessness.˜[149]

3. Individual Renaissance Philosophers

Alongside this peaceable emergence of ancient philosophy there were some particularly striking and noteworthy figures whose impulse for cognition, for speculating and knowing, manifested itself in a vigorous and stimulating fashion. Among them we find many great individuals, great owing to the energy of their character and | their spirit, or great owing to their love for the sciences. But they are also marked by an equally great mental and emotional confusion of their spirit and character. The age was rich in individuals of this kind who exhibited in their thoughts, disposition, and outward circumstances a wild alternation between extreme genius and extreme perversity.

In this respect GIROLAMO CARDANO (1501–1576) is particularly notable.[150] We still have ten folio-volumes of his works, including

50

The call for all books in Hebrew to be burned was addressed to the emperor Maximilian by an author of Jewish descent, Johann Pfefferkorn, a few years after his baptism as a Christian. The archbishop of Mainz had the task of scrutinizing the books, and Reuchlin defended their preservation. By doing so he incurred the hostility of the Dominicans of Cologne, at whose instigation he was condemned for heresy in 1520; see Brucker's account (p. 366), as well as Buhle (*Geschichte* 2, pt. 1:404–405). Brucker also reports on the rebirth of Ciceronian philosophy (p. 90—citing Marius Nizolius, 1498–1576) as does Buhle (*Lehrbuch* 6, pt. 1:286–287; *Geschichte* 2, pt. 2:665–666).

148. *An reads:* Leibniz.

149. *Thus An; Gr, with Lw, reads:* Human feelings and the like had been found noteworthy, in contrast with the church's principle of selflessness.

150. [*Ed.*] Buhle, Hegel's principal source on Cardano, gives incorrect dates, as

his autobiography, *De vita propria,*[151] in which he could not speak about himself more harshly. The following examples will serve to give a picture of the contradictions [in his character].[152] He speaks first of his lot prior to birth, when his mother swallowed potions intended to cause a miscarriage. His wet nurse died of the plague. His father was very hard on him. Later he took up the sciences, became a doctor of medicine, and traveled a great deal, going everywhere. He first became professor of mathematics [in Milan] and then professor of medicine in Bologna. He went to Scotland several times. His life as a whole was spent in constant inner and outer turmoil. He says that he experienced the utmost torments of heart and mind, and he found the greatest bliss in torturing himself and others. He flogged himself severely, and bit his fingers and lips till the tears came; in this way he freed himself from his agony of spirit and gained some relief. In his habits, outer life, and conduct he went in similar fashion from one extreme to the other; at one moment he was calm, at another like a madman or lunatic, now industrious and studious, now dissolute and squandering all his goods. Naturally in these circumstances he brought up his children very badly. He had one of his sons' ears cut off for his dissolute ways. Another son killed his own wife and was executed by the sword. Cardano himself was famed far and wide as a profound astrologer; he foretold the birth of many kings and princes, and hence he traveled even to Scotland. He was a sound mathematician too; the solution for cubic equations is still called Cardano's rule, named after him.[153] About himself he says: "I have a spirit that is trained

---

does Tiedemann. The correct dates, given in our text, are reported only by Griesheim, who possibly inserted them after referring to Rixner (*Handbuch* 2:26).

151. [*Ed.*] Cardano's works were published in a ten-volume folio edition by Carolus Sponius (Lyons, 1663). His autobiography, *The Book of My Life*, was published in Lyons in 1557 (English translation by Jean Stoner, London, 1930).

152. [*Ed.*] Hegel's source for the biographical details that follow was probably Buhle (*Lehrbuch* 6, pt. 1:360–364; *Geschichte* 2, pt. 1:856–860). But the report that Cardano's wet nurse died of the plague is transmitted only by Brucker (*Historia* 4, pt. 2:64). The sources speak of only one journey to Scotland, on which see Brucker (pp. 67–68), who also covers his reputation as an astrologer (pp. 74 ff.).

153. [*Ed.*] See Cardano's *Ars magna; sive, De regulis algebraicis . . . , XI: De cubo et rebus aequalibus numero* (Nuremberg, 1545), in his *Opera*, 10 vols. (Lyons, 1663), 4:249–251. Hegel does not mention here that Cardano was not the inventor

51 in the sciences, I am sensitive, elegant, | honorable, high-spirited, wily, beneficent, loyal, inventive, good-natured, self-educated, desirous of miracles, artful, shy, hardworking, pious, garrulous, scornful of religion, spiteful, treacherous, a magician, unhappy, ill-disposed to the masses, jealous, given to obscenity, obsequious, fickle, and so forth. These are the contradictions of my nature and the habits that are in me." This is what he says himself in his book *De vita propria.*[154]

In the same way TOMMASO CAMPANELLA is a mixture of all possible characteristics. He was born in Stilo in Calabria in 1568 and he died in Paris in 1639. We still have several folio-volumes of his work. Among other things, he spent twenty-seven years in harsh imprisonment in Naples. Most of his works that we still have were written under this external duress. He suffered much inner and outer turmoil.[155]

Other figures in this intellectual ferment who deserve particular mention are Giordano Bruno and Vanini.

---

of the method named for him, but was given it by Tartaglia in 1539; its inventor may have been either Niccolo Tartaglia (1506–1559) or Lodovico Ferrari (1522–1565).

154. [*Ed.*] For this quotation, see Buhle (*Lehrbuch* 6, pt. 1:364–365; *Geschichte* 2:859–860). Hegel's abridged version follows both Buhle's choice of words and his erroneous attribution (p. 858) of the passage to the autobiography. Brucker's Latin version (*Historia* 4, pt. 2:69) assigns it to another work in Cardano's *Opera* (5:523): *De animi qualitatibus.* In two places, for each of which *Gr* is our sole authority, the reconstructed text is defective: "beneficent" (*wohltätig*) should read "cheerful" (*wohllustig*), and "ill-disposed to the masses" (*der Menge gram*) should read "ill-disposed to my own" (*den Meinigen gram*); in each case the error is probably not Hegel's, nor due to an error in hearing on Griesheim's part, but to his mistake in deciphering his notes from the lecture.

155. [*Ed.*] Hegel's account of Campanella is based on Brucker (*Historia* 4, pt. 2:108–126), although the assertion that he was "a mixture of all possible characteristics" could derive from a remark in Rixner (*Handbuch* 2:275–276) that refers to his combination of "scientific observation of nature with religious enthusiasm and genial piety"; cf. Tennemann (*Geschichte* 9:295 ff.). Hegel probably omits the reasons for Campanella's imprisonment because his sources give little credence to the religious charges against him, namely, that he was an atheist who held Democritus's views, or to the political charges, namely, that he sought, in collaboration with the Turks, to foment a revolution in Calabria. He was absolved of the charge of treason in 1626 and of the charge of heresy three years later. Neither Hegel nor his sources mention the work for which Campanella is best known today, *The City of the Sun* (Frankfurt am Main, 1623; original ms. version, 1602).

GIORDANO BRUNO was born at Nola, near Naples, in the sixteenth century.[156] He traveled widely in most European countries. In Naples he at first became a Dominican, but he said bitter things about a number of doctrines—transubstantiation and the Immaculate Conception—and against the crass ignorance of the monks and their iniquitous life. Afterward he lived in many states, in Geneva in the time of Calvin, and later in Lyons and Paris, where he posted up theses for public disputation—a favorite procedure at that time. (The Count della Mirandola circulated some nine hundred theses in Europe and issued invitations to attend the disputation about them in Rome, promising to defray from his own pocket the travel costs of those who had farthest to come.) Bruno's theses were directed against the Aristotelians, that is, the Scholastics.[157] He also spent time in London and in numerous German universities; he taught in Wittenberg and in Prague. Finally he returned to Italy and lived for a while undisturbed in Padua. But he was seized in Venice by the Inquisition, brought to Rome, and, because he would not | recant, was burned for heresy in Rome in 1600. He met death steadfastly.

His writings are very seldom found together because he had them printed all over the place; most of them are to be found in

52

156. [*Ed.*] Bruno was born in 1548. The following somewhat incomplete account of his life follows very closely that of Buhle (*Geschichte* 2, pt. 2:704–712), as does the account in *W* 15:224–225.

157. [*Ed.*] On Count Giovanni Pico della Mirandola, see above, p. 000 with n. 146. Hegel's reference to his theses and the disputation echoes Tennemann (*Geschichte* 9:149). Buhle states (*Geschichte* 2, pt. 1:383) that these theses came from diverse sources, fifty-five of them from Proclus, *In Platonis theologiam*—an edition of which (Hamburg, 1618) Hegel possessed. Hegel omits mention that the disputation did not take place, owing to opposition from the clergy (so Tennemann) or from the pope (so Buhle). Here Hegel seems to identify the Aristotelians with the Scholastics, although elsewhere (*W* 15:215) he knows to distinguish between them; see n. 143 above, for further differentiation among the Aristotelians. The probable explanation is that whereas Bruno's theses were originally directed against the Scholastics, their title when published subsequently in Wittenberg (1588) described them as directed against the Peripatetics, that is, the Aristotelians; cf. Buhle (*Geschichte* 2, pt. 2:707, 709n) and Tennemann (*Geschichte* 9:381). Actually three of the theses are directed against Aristotelians; see Bruno, *Opera latine conscripta*, ed. F. Fiorentino et al., 3 vols. in 8 (Naples, 1879–1891; reprint, Stuttgart, 1962), 1, pt. 1:72–81 (articles 26, 51, and 53). Hegel's equation of Aristotelians with Scholastics diminishes the force of Bruno's critique of Aristotelianism.

the Göttingen University library.[158] Jacobi in particular drew attention to him.[159] The fullest information about him is to be found in ˉBuhle's history of philosophy.ˉ[160]

Two aspects of Bruno's work have to be considered: his philosophical thought and his so-called "Lullian art."[161] Bruno's writings especially display a most lively inspiration of thought. Generally speaking, his philosophy is Spinozism. The separation of God from the world, and all the relationships of externality, are cast aside in Bruno's living idea of the unity of everything.[162] In more detail, the

158. *An adds, in the margin:* There is only one of his writings in the library here.

[*Ed.*] Tennemann refers (*Geschichte* 9:375, n. 90) to the "careful, critical use that Herr Buhle makes of most of Bruno's writings . . . thanks to the abundant resources of the Göttingen library." This refers principally to Bruno's books on the "Lullian art," of which Buhle states (*Geschichte* 2:715) that only very few copies still exist.

159. [*Ed.*] In the first appendix to Jacobi's *Letters on the Philosophy of Spinoza,* he presents an extract from Bruno's dialogues, *Cause, Principle, and Unity* (Venice, 1584); see Friedrich Heinrich Jacobi, *Ueber die Lehre des Spinoza in Briefen an den Herrn Moses Mendelssohn,* 2d ed. (Breslau, 1789), pp. 261–306; reprinted in Jacobi's *Werke,* 6 vols. (Leipzig, 1812–1815), 4, pt. 2:5–46. In the preface to the second edition of his *Spinoza-Briefe,* Jacobi discusses briefly Bruno's life and his alleged obscurity of presentation, a charge that he contests at least so far as the extracted passage is concerned. He also explains that his main purpose in drawing attention to Bruno is to set him alongside Spinoza and so to "present as it were the summa" of pantheistic philosophy. On the question of whether Bruno's thought could be described as "Spinozistic" (although he lived before Spinoza!), see Brucker (*Historia* 4, pt. 2:55 ff.).

160. *Thus Gr; Lw reads:* the history of philosophy by Buhle, a professor at Göttingen.

[*Ed.*] Buhle devotes far more space to Bruno (*Geschichte* 2, pt. 2:703–856) than does Brucker (*Historia* 4, pt. 2:12–62), Tennemann (*Geschichte* 9:372–420), or Tiedemann (*Geist* 5:570–582).

161. [*Ed.*] Whereas Tennemann (*Geschichte* 9:388–389) and Buhle (*Geschichte* 2, pt. 2:752–753) regard the "Lullian art" as extraneous and nonessential to Bruno's own thought-world, Hegel affirms its connection with Bruno's "universal ideas"; see below, pp. 000 and 000 (with n. 180).

162. [*Ed.*] The "most lively inspiration" of Bruno's style, as seen in his *Cause, Principle, and Unity,* Hegel knew at least from Jacobi's extract (see n. 159 above) and from the presentation in Buhle et al. The characterization of his philosophy as Spinozism appears in Jacobi. Hegel finds that Bruno and Spinoza agree in that each of them undoes both the separation of God from the world and all of the relationships of externality. But while "[these relationships] are cast aside in Bruno's living idea of the unity of everything," Spinoza "casts all this [finite being] into the abyss of the One Identity," and he makes no attempt "to grasp how the One is organized

chief aspects of his view are as follows. He puts matter on one side as one determination, and form on the other side as the second determination.[163] Form is the universal understanding, the universal form of the world as totality, which has the same relationship to the production of natural things as the human understanding has to the formation of the concept; it is the inner artist that fashions the shape from within. The trunk springs from the innermost part, out of the root or the seed; from the trunk spring the branches and from the branches the blossoms. Everything is inwardly arranged. This [inner] understanding is the effective understanding or cause, not mere *causa efficiens* but also formal understanding, and it has then the characteristic of the final cause. Final cause is determination in terms of purpose. We shall have occasion to refer to this categorial determination in greater detail when we come to the Kantian philosophy. The living organism whose principle is vitality, the formative principle that in its efficacy brings forth only itself, that abides with itself and preserves itself—that is purpose in general. "Purpose" should not call to mind the external image of an understanding that frames a purpose for itself, and forms matter outwardly according to this [prior] specification. "Purpose" is thus inwardly determined activity, | which does not function as mere cause in relation to others but returns into itself and preserves itself.[164] This is the *form*.

53

---

within itself, as Bruno did" (see pp. 000 below). This "Spinozism" in Bruno's position does not, as in Spinoza himself (see p. 000 below), have the meaning of acosmism. As a system of differentiated being, as an infinite unity of finite determinations, the universe for Bruno is itself divine, living, and beautiful.

163. [*Ed.*] This is based on a passage in the third dialogue of Bruno's *Cause, Principle, and Unity* that recognizes two kinds of natural substance, form and matter; English translation by Jack Lindsay (New York, 1962), p. 100. Hegel, however, takes the reference from Tennemann (*Geschichte* 9:394); it also appears in Jacobi, *Spinoza-Briefe*, p. 278 (cf. *Werke* 4, pt. 2:19).

164. [*Ed.*] The extended treatment of form as "the universal understanding" adapts and abridges several passages from Tennemann (*Geschichte* 9:391–392) excerpted from the second dialogue of Bruno's *Cause, Principle, and Unity* (pp. 81–82); a slightly different version appears in Jacobi, *Spinoza-Briefe*, pp. 263–265 (cf. *Werke* 4, pt. 2:7–9). For Kant's concept of final cause or determination in terms of purpose, see pp. 000 below. Hegel elsewhere lays great stress on the concept of inner purposiveness or the vitality of organic life, for instance, in the *Encyclopedia* §§ 153

We have already said that matter is one of the determinations. But the main point in Bruno is that he affirms the unity of form and matter, that matter in itself is alive. "Matter" presents only what is abiding [or permanent], and to the extent that the abiding is the abstract it is the formless that, however, is capable of any form. The form is not imposed on it from without but is on the contrary immanent in it, identical with it, so that [matter] posits and produces these modifications and transformations itself. It is thus the prerequisite of all corporeality, it is itself intelligible, the universal, what is understandable, the final cause.[165] In this connection Bruno has recourse to the Aristotelian forms of *dynamis,* or of potency (possibility) and actuality. He says it is impossible to attribute existence to a thing that lacks the force to exist. And this [force] immediately entails the active mode; the one presupposes the other, passivity and activity are inseparable. If an efficacy was present all along, then there must also have been present all along a capacity to be acted on, to be created. The complete possibility

---

ff. and the *Philosophy of Religion* 1:428–429. The stress here on the activity's returning into itself may involve a reference to an ensuing sentence in the same Bruno text (p. 82), as cited by Tennemann (*Geschichte* 9:392), about how the sap in plants returns to the roots, and how something comparable happens in animals and in the whole. The concept of the universal understanding as what returns (ἐπιστρέφον) appears in a translation from Proclus in W 15:85; cf. p. 000 below, on the Spinozistic *causa sui* as return into self in the other.

165. [*Ed.*] This paragraph resumes discussion of the matter-form distinction introduced in the preceding paragraph. Beginning with the second sentence, it presents a highly condensed summary of passages that Tennemann (*Geschichte* 9:393–399) bases loosely upon the third and fourth dialogues of *Cause, Principle, and Unity.* These passages from Tennemann deal with: the inseparable union of form and matter in one substance; matter as what abides; the formlessness and simplicity of matter as such; the immanence of form in matter; matter as the prerequisite of corporeality. Buhle and Jacobi also cite elements of this kind from the dialogues, as well as a long extract from the teachings of the Peripatetics and Plotinus; cf. Jacobi, *Spinoza-Briefe,* pp. 278–291 (cf. *Werke* 4, pt. 2:19–32). On the last point, Bruno himself stresses that matter is the prerequisite of the incorporeal domain as well. Neither Bruno nor any of Hegel's sources expressly defines matter as "the universal, what is understandable, the final cause," at least not in this general fashion. Hegel is here drawing his own conclusions from the passages cited. His designation of matter as final cause may refer to a passage in Tennemann (p. 393) stating that the purpose of final causality is the perfection of the whole, which consists in the fact that in the various divisions of matter all forms achieve actual existence.

of the existence of things cannot precede their actual existing, nor can it be left over after they have existed. Everything can exist and everything is. The first principle is possibility and actuality both; for Bruno the two are one indivisible principle.[166] This involves a very important categorial determination, for in the capacity to be effective or to exert force there lies equally the characteristic of being effected or produced, of matter. But without force or efficacy this matter is nothing—an empty abstraction. The universal whole [*Universum*] is uncreated nature—everything that nature can be. Uncreated nature contains all matter under the immutable form of its changing shape.[167]

This is Bruno's main idea. What reason strives for is to recognize this unity of form and matter in everything. To penetrate to this | unity, to fathom the secrets of nature, we must investigate the opposed and conflicting uttermost ends of things, and these extremes he called "maximum" and "minimum." We must investigate these uttermost ends, these extremes. It is in these extremes that [the things] become intelligible in particular; [the extremes] are what have to be thought of as united, and this union is infinite nature. To develop what is opposed from this one [nature], to unfold its antitheses from that opposition ⁻and to present these extremes as null⁻[168] is, says Bruno, the peculiar and profoundest

---

166. [*Ed.*] Hegel does not point out that although Bruno uses the Aristotelian concepts, he does so in a perspective that is different from Aristotle's, indeed opposed to it. Bruno also uses the (Scholastic) distinction between passive and active capacities in a sense counter to its intended use, since he stresses their unity and ascribes to matter the same attributes as he does to the divine nature. As is clear in particular from W 15:232 (Ms?), the statements in the preceding seven sentences of our reconstituted text attributed to Bruno come not from Tennemann's version (*Geschichte* 9:396) but, with condensation and distortion, from Jacobi (*Spinoza-Briefe*, pp. 283–284; cf. *Werke* 4, pt. 2:24–25). Hegel substitutes "force" (*Kraft*) for "capacity" and identifies this force with "the active mode." More especially, the statement that "Everything can exist . . . ," transmitted only by An, misrepresents Bruno's actual contention, confined to the first principle alone, that it can be everything and also is everything.

167. [*Ed.*] In the preceding three sentences Hegel is again loosely following Jacobi (*Spinoza-Briefe*, pp. 291, 285; cf. *Werke* 4, pt. 2:32, 26), in passages drawn from the fourth and third dialogues of *Cause, Principle, and Unity*. Once again he substitutes "force" for "capacity," and makes other minor changes.

168. *Thus An; Lw reads:* and not only recognize this unity

secret of the [philosophical] art.[169] This is a pregnant saying, that the development of the idea is to be displayed and known as being *necessary*—a necessity of distinctions and determinations that brings it back at once to unity. Here we have the primordial principle, or what is elsewhere called the form. Bruno locates it under the determination of the minimum, the smallest, but in such a way that it is at the same time the greatest—the One, which is at the same time the All.[170] In the universal whole, he says, the body is not distinct from the point, nor the center from the periphery, nor the greatest from the smallest; there is nothing but midpoint, the midpoint is everywhere. The ancients said this about the father of the gods, that he has his seat in every point of the universe.[171] This is the basic idea that Bruno elaborated. In these investigations there emerges the inspiration of a noble soul, a thinking that is profound.

The second point connects with this general idea; it is Bruno's "Lullian art." The name comes from RAYMON LULL, *doctor illu-*

---

169. [*Ed.*] Up to this point in the paragraph Hegel combines two passages from the fourth and fifth dialogues of *Cause, Principle, and Unity* (pp. 129–149) that occur in separate contexts there and in Jacobi's presentation (*Spinoza-Briefe*, pp. 292, 305; cf. *Werke* 4, pt. 2:32, 45). In the first, Bruno himself speaks not of the unity of form and matter but of the world-soul, which is and does all in everything, and through which all individual things constitute one single being. Hegel's discussion of maximum and minimum, however, follows Bruno more closely here, and even more closely in W 15:233.

170. [*Ed.*] Hegel refers here to Buhle's comment (*Geschichte* 2, pt. 2:808–809) on Bruno's *De triplici minimo et mensura* (Frankfurt am Main, 1591). In saying that Bruno's primordial principle "is elsewhere called the form," Hegel probably is alluding to previous references to the concept of form, which is prominent in the second dialogue of *Cause, Principle, and Unity*; see above, pp. 000 and n. 164. Hegel could not see clearly from his sources, and the Bruno excerpts they present, that in the last three dialogues of that work the concept of form becomes less important than the concept of matter. Nor did he take into account the difference between the two treatises, in the later of which philosophical atomism acquires a new content and greater significance. Hegel's own chief interest is in the principle of the unity of the universe as a "coincidence of opposites" (which, incidentally, is a key theme in the thought of Nicholas Cusanus—1401–1464—a predecessor of Bruno and a major figure in his own right, whom Hegel does not discuss in these lectures).

171. [*Ed.*] This is another reference to the fifth dialogue of *Cause, Principle, and Unity* (p. 137), to a passage transmitted by Jacobi (*Spinoza-Briefe*, pp. 297–298; cf. *Werke* 4, pt. 2:37–38). This theme also appears in Cusanus, *On Learned Ignorance* (1440), bk. 2, chap. 12.

minatus, who devised an *Ars magna Lulliana.*[172] Lull lived in the thirteenth century and came from Majorca, where he was born in 1235. He is one of those tempestuous natures continually tossed about by circumstances. As a | young man he reveled in a life of 55 pleasure. Then he lived as a hermit in a desolate place, where he had many visions. These awakened in his violent, fiery nature an irresistible urge to spread Christianity among the Muslims in Asia and Africa. ¯There he was imprisoned and ill-treated,¯[173] and he died in 1315 as a result of the ill-treatment in Africa. He spent many years in Milan and Paris, and learned Arabic in order to be able to carry out his work of conversion among the Muslims. He sought support from all the crowned heads of Europe and from the pope. Along with his principal aim of spreading Christianity, Lull

---

172. [*Ed.*] Rixner (*Handbuch* 2:126) gives Lull's honorific title, which expresses the supposition that he received his philosophical art from a heavenly inspiration; cf. Tennemann (*Geschichte* 8, pt. 2:830). The term *ars magna* ("great art") usually designates the art of alchemy, but we cannot infer from this that Lull's method was deemed a type of alchemy. The title of the work in which Lull presented the final version of his method was *Ars generalis ultima venerabilis magistri, ac doctoris illuminati Raymundi Lulli Maioricensis* . . . (1305–1308); in 1307 Lull also wrote a shorter version, the so-called *Ars brevis,* and *Ars magna* probably denotes the longer work. The biographical data that follow in our text are based mainly on Tennemann (*Geschichte* 8, pt. 2:830–833), and occasionally on Rixner (*Handbuch* 2:127); cf. Brucker (*Historia* 4, pt. 1:10–21). Today Lull's year of birth is reckoned as 1232, or perhaps 1233. Tennemann and Rixner both speak of journeys to Asia and Africa, although Lull's Asian journey was in fact limited to a short stay in Cyprus, Asia Minor, and Jerusalem (1301–1302). Tennemann mentions three missionary journeys to North Africa; on the first Lull fell into mortal danger in Tunis, during the second he suffered harsh imprisonment, and on the third he was so ill-treated that he died, as result of his injuries, while returning to Spain. Scholars today think Lull made four such journeys, and they question the accuracy of the foregoing account of his death, which they date sometime between December 1315 and March 1316. Hegel's historical sources give Montpellier as the location of Lull's extended stay, whereas the transcripts (*An, Gr, Lw, Pn*) give Milan; perhaps Hegel had Montpellier in his notes but said "Milan" instead. Tennemann says (p. 832) only that Lull turned in vain to Rome, Genoa, and Majorca for support (he might have added the French court as well); there is no basis for Hegel's "all the crowned heads of Europe." The Council of Vienna (1311–1312) did adopt several of his proposals, in particular a plan to establish institutes for the study of Arabic, as well as Syriac and Hebrew; cf. Rixner (*Handbuch* 2:1–29).

173. *Thus An; Lw* reads: He endeavored to accomplish this with burning zeal, despite all the tribulations that befell him,

devoted himself at the same time to his "art," which is connected with the art of thinking, or more precisely with an enumeration and ordering of the conceptual determinations or the pure categories—the sort of ordering that encompasses all objects, so that they can be defined according to it.[174] He established nine classes of things, which he then depicted within nine circles. Each circle is portrayed graphically. Some of the circles are fixed and some are movable; through the rules of rotation, whereby the predicates intersect, universal science and all concrete [knowledge] were supposed to be exhaustively generated in accordance with his categories. For each class he had in turn nine predicates or determinations. First there were nine absolute predicates (wisdom, goodness, magnitude, unity, might, will, virtue, truth, eternity, majesty); second, nine relative predicates (difference, similarity, opposition, beginning, middle, end, being greater, being lesser); third, nine further categories (where, what, whence, why, on account of what, how great, and so on); and fourth, nine substances (God, humankind, angels, heaven, the elementarium, the instrumentarium, and so forth). As we have said, he plotted these on circles in the belief that concrete objects, in fact the totality of science and knowledge, would be defined by the combination of such predicates.[175] This, then, is what 56 was called the "Lullian art." |

174. [Ed.] The statement that Lull devoted himself to his art "along with" his missionary activity conceals the inner unity of these two seemingly unconnected interests. For Lull, his art stands in the service of the knowledge of the truth of Christianity, and of a philosophy compatible with biblical teaching. This is evident from its strictly anti-Averroistic character, stemming from his acquaintance with the reception given to Aristotelianism in Paris in the late thirteenth century.

175. [Ed.] Whereas the detailed presentation of Lull's art in W 15:197 also draws on Rixner (Handbuch 2:126), here Hegel relies exclusively on Tennemann (Geschichte 8, pt. 2:834–836). Hegel erroneously deviates from Tennemann on certain points, and Tennemann himself is guilty of some errors; there are also errors of hearing on the part of the auditors—"Elementarium, Instrumentarium" replacing "Elementativum, Instrumentativum." Actually Lull has six classes of concepts: (1) absolute principles; (2) relative principles; (3) rules of discovery, or basic questions; (4) subjects (not substances, as Hegel has here and in W 15:198); (5) virtues; (6) vices. Each of the six classes has nine subdivisions. Hegel and Tennemann speak instead of nine classes, and Hegel says they are inscribed within nine circles; whereas Lull's Ars generalis ultima and his Ars inventiva, which alone contain this enumer-

Bruno now did something similar and further refined this art.[176]
In the *Topics* Aristotle offers a summary of all categories, all universal representations and determinations, and mnemonics depends
upon this too. Mnemonics also figures in the *Auctor ad Herennium*

---

ation of principles—the earlier works do not—distinguish but four figures. The first
circle has as its center the letter A, designating the origin of all actual being, and
has a circumference divided into nine parts (letters B through I, plus K) representing
the nine absolute principles (our text substitutes "wisdom" and "unity" for "duration"). The second circle, with the letter T at its center, rearranges the same nine
letters on the divisions of its circumference, to represent the relative predicates
("equality" is missing in our text, and "unity" has been misplaced to the set of absolute predicates, which accounts for the numerical discrepancies). Ternary groups
of these predicates (BCD, EFG, HIK) define three triangles inscribed in the second
circle, which represent the totality of relations of all created beings: each being is
distinct from another, or in agreement with it, or in opposition to it. The third figure
is not a circle but a graduated table with 36 positions defined in the horizontal and
vertical directions that furnish various combinations of letters from the first two
figures. The fourth figure, consisting of three concentric circular pieces laid atop one
another, is the figure Hegel mentions. The bottommost and largest circle is fixed,
whereas the two upper and smaller circles can be rotated. Each of the three has the
same nine letters (B . . . K) on its circumference. With the letters on the circles capable of representing relative as well as absolute predicates, the various possible
alignments of the three circles yield a total of 1,680 combinations. With this apparatus Lull formulated correct syllogisms through the discovery of various combinations of premises, middle terms, and conclusions. Hegel's mention of six circles
in *W* 15:197 shows that his description has in view the accounts given by Rixner
(*Handbuch* 2, appendix, pp. 86–90) and by Brucker (*Historia* 4, pt. 2:18a—table),
which do not, however, derive from Lull's *Ars generalis ultima*. Rixner cites instead
Johann Heinrich Alstedt's study, *Clavis artis Lullianae* . . . (Strasbourg, 1609).

176. [*Ed.*] This statement echoes a commonplace of the contemporary histories
of philosophy, such as Rixner (*Handbuch* 2, appendix, p. 90); editor Johann Jakob
Wagner said something similar in his *Journal für Wissenschaft und Kunst* (Leipzig),
1 (1805): 67–68. Bruno's refinement consists in part in better use of the combinatory
possibilities of Lull's figures. For example, by transposing and doubling the letters
of the third figure (see n. 175 above), Bruno increases the binary combinations from
36 to 81, and by further rotation of the circles he obtains more than 200 columns
with 96 entries each (instead of 84 columns with 20 entries each); cf. Bruno's *De
lampade combinatoria Lulliana* (Wittenberg, 1587), in the *Opera latine conscripta*
2, pt. 2. Bruno's own interest runs less to the combinations themselves and more
to the formal possibilities of the system, and thus he shares in the Renaissance approach to Lullianism, in particular that of Agrippa of Nettesheim (1487–1535).
Bruno, however, puts the formal element in the service of a new, naturalistic ontology. The importance he attaches to mnemonics can also be understood in relation
to this formal development of the Lullian art, as well as to Renaissance Lullianism
in general.

(ascribed to Cicero).[177] It is just a matter of definite images in the imagination. One fixes these images firmly and transfers to them all the individual representations of all particular contents and objects one seeks to know by heart. Say, for example, we want to remember a speech or a tale. Each representation in it is incorporated into these images, in the order in which they follow one another. The first image, for instance, Hercules, can be ordered in this way according to the letters: of Aaron, then (2) Abimelech, (3) Achilles, and so on. For instance, in the case of Aaron the high priest, a superficial wit must combine the content that one has to retain with the image, namely, the letters; and when I affix the content to the image, it is as if I no longer have it in my memory but merely read it off, as from a picture [*Tableau*].[178] The difficulty lies only in forming a conjunction between the content and the images. This too is an inferior art. Anyone practiced in it can certainly learn something by heart with great ease.

Both the "Lullian art" and Bruno's efforts are connected with this mnemonics. In Bruno's case, however, the tableau is not sim-

177. [*Ed.*] While it cannot be proved that modern mnemonics originates in the Lullian art, several major sixteenth-century philosophers, particularly Bruno and Campanella, attributed their exceptional memory to practice of the Lullian art. Bruno, for example, sought to facilitate his mastery of the numerous terms resulting from the combinatory possibilities, by linking the nine letters of the Lullian alphabet with the names of well-known personalities (B with Brutus, C with Caesar, and so on), then with nine attributes predicable of such subjects, then with nine relations affecting them, and so forth. In associating Lullian art with Aristotle's *Topics*, Hegel may have in mind a comparable remark by Buhle (*Geschichte* 2, pt. 2:716); in W 14:408–409, in a discussion of the *Topics*, Hegel states that Cicero and Bruno worked out the Aristotelian categories more fully. The *Auctor ad Herennium*, a pseudo-Ciceronian treatise on rhetoric addressed to C. Herennius, was written about 86–82 B.C.; bk. 3, chap. 17, § 30, briefly discusses mnemonics. Hegel knew it from Johannes Augustus Ernesti's edition of Cicero's *Opera omnia* (Leipzig, 1737).

178. [*Ed.*] This example occurs neither in Bruno's writings nor in the *Auctor ad Herennium*. Since pre-Christian classical authors are unlikely to have used "Aaron" or "Abimelech," Hegel is probably citing a medieval or modern source that it has not been possible to identify. Hegel concerned himself with mnemonics on several occasions, and as editor of the *Bamberger Zeitung* he published newspaper reports about French disputes concerning mnemonics; see *GW* 5:391–394.

ply a picture of external images as they stand, but a system of ideas, thought-determinations or universal representations.[179] Bruno passes over to this art from his universal ideas, which we have already touched on; in fact the understanding in general, the infinite form, the active understanding, is what is first, it is the foundation, and it develops itself.[180] This understanding takes the form it had for the Neoplatonists. The light of substance emanates from | the 57 first primordial light, from the *primus actus lucis,* but the numerous substances and accidents cannot receive the full light, they are only contained in the shadow of the light. The development of infinite nature proceeds through a succession of moments. Its single parts, the created things, are no longer what infinite nature is in and for itself but are only a shadow of the original ideas, of the first *actus* of the light.[181]

179. [*Ed.*] This declaration is confusing insofar as it seems to point to an opposition between the original Lullian art and "Bruno's efforts," although Hegel uses much the same terms to characterize Bruno's Lullian art as Buhle applies to Lull himself. Buhle states (*Geschichte* 2, pt. 2:716) that ancient logicians and rhetoricians formed their topical and mnemonic principles from everyday concepts and psychological rules, whereas the Lullian art is based on systematic tables of basic concepts in which all other concepts were contained or from which they could be derived, together with figurative presentations of these tables. Hegel's sources could not in any event have enabled him to distinguish between the original Lullian art and the form it took with Bruno. The expression "as they stand" could refer to Lull, but ought to refer to ancient mnemonics.

180. [*Ed.*] This remark could refer either to the chronological development of Bruno's thought or to the systematic connection of his writings; in neither case, however, would it be correct. More likely Hegel has in mind a passage in Buhle (*Geschichte* 2, pt. 2:734), which states that the mnemonics follows upon the discussion of metaphysical principles—not, however, those Hegel has expounded. In our text "already" actually refers to the sequence in Buhle, who prefaced his treatment of mnemonics with an overview of the Lullian art, as seen in Bruno's *De compendiosa architectura et complemento artis Lullii* (Paris, 1582); cf. *Opera latine conscripta* 2, pt. 2:6–8; see also Bruno's *De umbris idearum* (Paris, 1582). Buhle (pp. 719a–732) speaks of an active understanding or agent intellect that brings forth from itself a wealth of new ideas; what in the primordial understanding is one light, life, spirit, and so on, in nature becomes contrast and distinction.

181. [*Ed.*] The Neoplatonists Hegel refers to are probably Plotinus and Proclus; see his account of them in W 15:53, 85. On their importance for Hegel's interpretation of Bruno, see n. 184, p. 000 below. The rest of this passage, beginning with "the light of substance," is based on Buhle's account (*Geschichte* 2, pt. 2:724) of

Bruno also wrote a book entitled *De umbris idearum* ["The shadows of the ideas"]. The progression from the first principle or the primordial light, from the superessential, from this ὑπερουσία, is to the essences and from them to what actually exists. What actually exists contains traces, images, or shadows of the superessential, which are partly to be found as material, natural things. In the other aspect ˉthey ˉ[182] enter within the sphere of sensation and perception, so as to become known ˉin these modes.ˉ[183] Things move away from the primordial light into darkness. But since all things cohere closely within the universe, the material with the spiritual and the whole with the single part, so that one principle is both first and last, the lowest can, by following the tone of the universal Apollo's lyre (an expression of Heraclitus, [denoting] universal harmony, universal form), be brought back step by step to the highest, since the All is one being. The [outward] procession is the same as the return. On the one side nature, within its bounds, brings forth all from all, and so the understanding too [from its side] can be cognizant of all from all.[184] The first understanding radiates its light

---

Bruno's *De umbris idearum*, except that Buhle speaks of "the substance and its accidents"; cf. Bruno, *Opera latine conscripta* 2, pt. 1:21–22; cf. W 15:238.

182. *Thus Gr, Lw, Pn; An, Sv read:* the shadows

183. *Thus Gr, Lw, Pn; An reads:* by subjective reason. *Sv reads:* within the subjective.

184. [*Ed.*] Hegel's exposition in this paragraph of Bruno's *De umbris idearum* (*Intentiones* V, VII, and IX) is based on Buhle (*Geschichte* 2, pt. 2:724–726), who describes this progression from the superessential to its traces in the motion and diversity of natural things, and the correlative cognitive return from the plurality of objects to the unity and stillness of truth; all things cohere in this one universe, one principle, one system; cf. Bruno, *Opera latine conscripta* 2, pt. 1:23–26. However, whereas Buhle mentions "the universal Apollo's lyre," Hegel takes the mention of Heraclitus from Plato (*Symposium* 187a), who paraphrases him (fragment 51, Diels-Kranz) as saying: "The One, divided within itself, unites with itself like the harmony of a lyre or a bow." Bruno's *De umbris idearum* is his earliest extant work. Part 1, which provides a philosophical foundation for the mnemonics (*Ars memoriae*) of part 2, is strongly Neoplatonic in tone, in particular in the parallel it draws between the progress of knowing and the hierarchy of shadow and light (without basing this hierarchy on a geocentric worldview). But since Hegel disregards the chronology of Bruno's writings, he uses this work to describe an attitude to Neoplatonism (see n. 181 above) that does not hold for Bruno's later works. Hegel stresses this affinity by interpreting Bruno's concept of the "superessential" through that of Proclus's ὑπερουσία, to which Buhle refers only at a later point (p. 745); cf. W 15:81, 85.

from the innermost to the outermost, and then takes its light back again from the outermost. Each particular can, according to its capacity, grasp something of the light. What is here contrast is in the primordial understanding harmony. These stages or this order of progression ought to be investigated. "Try then," he exclaims, "to see if you can identify the images contained [in the ideas]—for then your memory will not grow weary, and you will be cognizant of this universal order, this universal rhythm."[185] | 58

Bruno tried, therefore, to develop this understanding. He portrayed the general system of development and noted more specifically that the determinations of natural things correspond to the determinations that appear within the subjective understanding.[186] He indicates there the moments of the primordial form. The ὑπερουσία is being, goodness, and unity. This derives mainly from what we have already seen in Proclus. Goodness is life, and unity is what turns [us] back and leads [us] back. Bruno treats the metaphysical and physical world, systematizes these determinations, and shows how what appears as natural is, in the other mode as thought, something understandable.[187] Thinking is activity,

185. [Ed.] These last five sentences are taken almost word for word from Buhle (*Geschichte* 2, pt. 2:731–732), who is in turn citing two passages from Bruno's *De umbris idearum,* Concepts X and XIII; cf. Bruno, *Opera latine conscripta* 2, pt. 1:45–46. The last two sentences evidence Hegel's own embellishment; cf. the more faithful version in *W* 15:240 (Ms?).

186. [Ed.] Hegel is probably referring to another passage in *De umbris idearum* (Concept XXVI), again as transmitted by Buhle (*Geschichte* 2, pt. 2:733–734), which states that we conceive something better from its idea, which is in the understanding, than from its form in the natural (material) thing itself, and even better from its idea in the divine mind; cf. Bruno, *Opera latine conscripta* 2, pt. 1:51.

187. [Ed.] The preceding five sentences are based on Buhle (*Geschichte* 2, pt. 2:745), who is citing Bruno's *Sigillus sigillorum* (London, 1583), 11; cf. Bruno, *Opera latine conscripta* 2, pt. 2:203–204. Here Bruno draws a threefold distinction concerning form: (1) the primordial form or ὑπερουσία, which in the metaphysical world is a thing, a principle of plurality; (2) the form of the physical world, which comprises traces of the ideas expressed in matter and revealed in things, goods, and individuals; (3) the form of the rational world, which comprises shadows of the ideas, now elevated from their individual expression for the senses, into universal concepts. Hegel's mention of Proclus suggests he is drawing a parallel with the highest levels of Proclus's ontology, with the unity of superessential being and life; cf. *W* 15:81, 85, which, however, calls the moment of return "understanding," not "unity." Of the transcripts, *Gr* alone expresses the difficulties of paralleling Bruno and Proclus: "we have seen approximately these [moments] in the case of Proclus."

and in his view it portrays inwardly, by means of an inner script, what nature portrays outwardly, by means of an outer script. The ˘understanding˘[188] takes the outer script of nature up within itself, and the inner script is also imaged in the outer; there is one form that develops [in both]. ˘It is one and the same principle—what the understanding organizes outside itself, and what thinks within the human mind.˘[189] Bruno seeks to define these different types of script, and in this effort he has twelve basic forms, which serve as his starting point: *species, simulacra, imagines,* and so forth.[190] He wrote a number of essays about them: *De simulacris, De imaginibus, De sigillis,*[191] [demonstrating] that the appearing of things therefore constitutes signs or letters, which then correspond to a thought-determination.

There is then in Bruno a great beginning at thinking the concrete, absolute unity. The other great thing is his attempt to grasp and exhibit the universe in its development, in the system of its [progressive] determination, to show how the outward realm is a sign of the ideas. These are the two aspects that were grasped by Bruno.

Like Bruno, Vanini too was a martyr for philosophy. LUCILIO CESARE VANINI[192] was born in 1583 at Taurozano near Naples, and

188. *Thus Pn; An reads:* inner script

189. *Thus Pn; Gr reads:* It is a world-principle, what expresses itself throughout the world.

190. [*Ed.*] The preceding four sentences are loosely based on Buhle's abbreviated summary (*Geschichte* 2, pt. 2:734) of the first twelve paragraphs of Bruno's *Ars memoriae;* cf. Bruno, *Opera latine conscripta* 2, pt. 1:56–62. Buhle's list of Bruno's twelve "types of script of the soul" includes the three that Hegel mentions.

191. [*Ed.*] *De simulacris,* transmitted only by *Lw,* is probably a mistaken inference from the mention of *simulacra* in the preceding sentence. *De imaginibus* is an abbreviation of Bruno's *De imaginum, signorum, et idearum compositione* (Frankfurt am Main, 1591), and *De sigillis* either of *Explicatio triginta sigillorum* (London, 1583) or of *Sigillus sigillorum.*

192. [*Ed.*] This biography of Vanini is based on Buhle (*Geschichte* 2, pt. 2:866–869; cf. *Lehrbuch* 6, pt. 1:406–410). Rixner (*Handbuch* 2:262) correctly gives the year of Vanini's birth as 1585; Buhle and Brucker (*Historia* 4, pt. 2:671–672) have 1586. Rixner and Brucker give Taurozano as the place of birth, as does *Gr* alone of the transcripts; Griesheim probably consulted Rixner to supplement his notes on this point. Buhle correctly locates Vanini's trial in Toulouse, not in Paris as our text reads, following *Gr.*

he was burned at the stake in Toulouse in 1619. He traveled a great deal and | was particularly excited by his reading of Cardano. He spent time in Geneva and Lyons, and once he had to flee to England; he journeyed widely. He was put on trial in Paris. One accuser testified that Vanini had committed blasphemy. In reply to the charge of atheism Vanini held up a straw in court and said that even this single straw sufficed to convince him ˉof the existence of God.ˉ¹⁹³ In Toulouse his tongue was torn out and then he was burned. In any event the whole proceeding is very obscure, and mainly the product of personal animosity. Art flourished in the Catholic church, but when freethinking came on the scene the church was quite unable to accommodate it and parted company with it. In the cases of Bruno and Vanini it took its revenge on freethinking. To this extent free thought parted company with the Catholic church and has remained opposed to it.

Two works by Vanini are still extant. One of them, entitled *Amphitheatrum aeternae providentiae divino-magicum, christiano-physicum, nec non ˉastrologo-catholicum,ˉ*¹⁹⁴ *adversus veteres Philosophos, Atheos, Epicureos, Peripateticos et Stoicos* (1615), is a refutation of the ancient philosophers, atheists, Epicureans, and the like, in which he presents their philosophies and the reasons for them with great eloquence, whereas the refutations come off feebly.¹⁹⁵ The second work, entitled *De admirandis naturae reginae deaeque mortalium arcanis dialogorum inter Alexandrum et Jul. Caesarem [libri]* (1616), consists of investigations into physical and other matters, in dialogue form, but in such a way that ˉthe com-

193. *Thus Gr, Lw; Pn reads:* of the Trinity.

194. *Gr reads: astronomico-catholicum,*

195. [*Ed.*] Only *Gr* gives the full title of this work (Lyons, 1615), which is evidently taken from Rixner (*Handbuch* 2:262)—who erroneously substitutes *astronomico* for *astrologico*; Brucker (*Historia* 4, pt. 2:678) and Buhle (*Geschichte* 2, pt. 2:873–875) get it right. Buhle is the source for the statement that the expositions of ancient philosophies are more convincing than the refutations. For instance, Vanini persuasively expounds the view of modern atheists that human souls vanish at death as do the souls of animals, and he presents only weak arguments against the Epicurean denial of the immortality of the soul. The title of Vanini's treatise is somewhat misleading, for it deals with recent philosophies as well, such as those of Cardano, Pomponazzi, and the Averroists.

piler does not seem to come down in favor of [either] view.‾[196] Its main thrust is that nature is the deity and that everything arises mechanically, that nature or the universe in its interconnectedness can be conceived [as stemming] from mechanical causes.[197] |

60

Vanini also speaks repeatedly about the opposition of this doctrine to the church, about opposition on the part of what reason recognizes. He repeatedly affirms that reason has indeed come upon this thought that it can find no grounds for refuting, but that since reason contradicts the church the Christian must submit to the faith, and that he himself submitted, since reason cannot have insight into everything.[198] In this way he formulates objections to Providence and adduces reasons and argumentation to show that nature is God.[199] Then he proves, through one of his interlocutors, that the Devil is mightier than God and that he, not God, rules the world. Vanini gives the following reasons. One example is that Adam and Eve sinned contrary to God's will and so brought ruin

196. *Thus An, similar somewhat further on in Gr, Lw; Gr at this point reads:* it is not indicated in which personage Vanini presents his own opinions.

197. [*Ed.*] Here again the full title of Vanini's work is cited only by *Gr*, who evidently took it from Rixner (*Handbuch* 2:262); actually in Rixner the title ends with *arcanis,* and the ensuing subtitle includes *libri IV* as the needed antecedent to the genitive *dialogorum*. It was published in Paris in 1616 and consists of sixty dialogues between Alexander and Julius Caesar. Hegel's description of the contents derives from Buhle (*Lehrbuch* 6, pt. 1:414; *Geschichte* 2, pt. 2:876–877); cf. *W* 15:246 (Ms?). Vanini's pretense of not endorsing one or another of the positions he presents misled the theologians of the Sorbonne into approving the work, even though they are ridiculed in Dialogue Thirty-seven. The explanation of the universe as a whole from merely mechanical causes appears in Dialogue Four.

198. [*Ed.*] Buhle states (*Geschichte* 2, pt. 2:873) that Vanini followed the example of Pomponazzi, who, when his philosophy ran counter to the teaching of the church, affirmed that he, as a submissive son of the church, nonetheless believed the contrary to what reason dictated. A number of passages in Vanini's *Amphitheatrum* and other works support this assessment.

199. [*Ed.*] The full title of the *De admirandis* describes nature as "queen and goddess of mortals." Buhle's account (*Geschichte* 2, pt. 2:875) is probably responsible for Hegel's statement that Vanini "formulates objections to Providence"; Vanini's own account in the *Amphitheatrum* (Exercise 4) is different. There he says that the world, not being eternal, must have an incorporeal and intelligent first cause. After giving the philosophical objections to creation and providence, Vanini then appears to wish to refute these objections—although the refutation ends up after all with a pantheistic conception of God as all things, and of the eternity of the world.

and unhappiness on the entire human race. Also, Christ himself was crucified by the power of darkness. On these grounds Vanini proves the Devil's supremacy over God. God wills that all human beings should be blessed, to which Vanini objects that the Jews have fallen away from God, that Catholics are a minority of the human race, and that by subtracting those of the Catholics who are heretics, atheists, adulterers, prostitutes, drunkards, and the like, then even fewer are left. This clearly demonstrates the supremacy of the Devil.[200] Such are the grounds held by the understanding, by reason; they cannot be refuted, yet one should submit to the faith—and Vanini claims to do so even though reason views things as it does.[201] But they did not believe Vanini. [His critics] assumed that if reason has some definite insight and this insight is not countered by reason, then the rational person cannot be serious in failing to adopt such an opinion, cannot believe the opposite. It was not credible that such a person's faith could be stronger than this insight.

There are many other remarkable men who belong to this period and who are also usually referred to in the history of philosophy, such as Michel de Montaigne, Charron, and Machiavelli.[202] Men like this are mentioned, although they properly belong not to philosophy but rather to general culture. | Their endeavors and writings are then classified as philosophical insofar as they have drawn upon themselves, have drawn upon their own consciousness, their

61

200. [*Ed.*] This summary of Vanini's arguments for the superiority of the Devil probably comes not directly from *De admirandis* but from Buhle (*Geschichte* 2, pt. 2:877–878), who cites them as an example of Vanini's insolence and criminal blasphemy; cf. *W* 15:247 (Ms?). Here again Vanini claims to be presenting these blasphemous views only in order to refute them from the standpoint of the traditional doctrines of the fall and redemption. His argument alludes to 1 Tim. 2:3–4: " . . . God our Savior, who desires all men to be saved and to come to the knowledge of the truth."

201. [*Ed.*] On the problem of "double truth," see n. 198 above. Hegel seems to assume that Vanini poses the issue in much the same way as Pomponazzi (see n. 143 above). Probably because he had not read Vanini himself, Hegel overlooks the fact that for Vanini this theory became a tool of agitation, a vehicle for the propagation of heterodox views.

202. [*Ed.*] This juxtaposition of Montaigne (1533–1592), Pierre Charron (1541–1603), and Niccolò Machiavelli (1469–1527) shows that Hegel here follows Buhle (*Geschichte* 2, pt. 2, sec. 5), who treats them (pp. 908–934) along with Justus Lipsius, Jean Bodin, Francis Bacon, and others.

own experience and observation, their own life. This kind of reasoning or cognition is quite antithetical to the Scholastic cognition that we have discussed. In their writings we find sound, perceptive, highly spiritual thoughts about human life, about what is right and good. They offer us a philosophy of life from the sphere of human experience, from the way that things happen in the world, in the human heart and spirit. They grasped and imparted experiences of this kind, and the result is partly entertaining, partly instructive. Moreover, by the principle that governed their creative activity they diverged completely from the sources and methods of the cognitive mode that had prevailed hitherto. But since they do not take the highest inquiry of philosophy as the topic of their investigation, and since they have not reasoned from thought as such, they do not properly belong to the history of philosophy. Owing to their contribution, however, humanity has acquired a greater interest in what is its own, in its own experience, consciousness, and the like, gaining the self-confidence that all this has value and validity for it. This is the principal merit of these authors. Their contribution is more to cultivation in general and to philosophical cultivation in particular [than it is to philosophy proper].

4. The Reformation

We now have to mention a transition that concerns us because of the universal principle that gets recognized in it at a higher level, and recognized in its justification. Giordano Bruno, Vanini, and others belong to the time of the Reformation and later. The Reformation therefore plays a part in this period.

We have already remarked upon the first manifestations of this
62 principle, the principle of our own human thought, | our own knowing, its activity, its right, its trust in itself.[203] It is the principle of finding satisfaction in our own activity, reason, imagination, and so forth, of taking pleasure in our products and our work and deeming it permissible and justifiable to do so, indeed regarding our own work as something in which we may and should essentially invest our interest. This, therefore, is the beginning of humanity's

203. [Ed.] See pp. 000 above.

reconciliation with itself. This validation of the subjective domain now needed a higher—indeed, the highest—confirmation in order to be completely legitimated and to become even the absolute duty. To attain to this level it had to be grasped in its purest shape.

The highest confirmation of this principle is the religious confirmation, when this principle of our own spirituality and our own autonomy is recognized in our relation with God and to God. Then this principle is sanctified by religion. Sheer human subjectivity, sheer human freedom—this fact that we have a will and we do this or that with it—is not yet justified on its own account but is on the contrary a barbaric self-will, one that finds its satisfaction only in subjective purposes having no rational substantiation and that is not justified. Nor [is it justified] even if the will has purposes, and determinations in its purpose that are congruent with the form of rationality, such as right or my freedom—not freedom of this particular subject but human freedom in general, legal right, the right that belongs to the other as well as to me. Even when self-will contains the form of universality, that directly involves only a "being permitted." It is indeed no small matter if what is permissible is recognized as such and not merely as something subjective, not as sinful in and of itself. Industry, art, and the like uphold the principle of my own activity too, insofar as my activity accords with what is right.

But so far as its content is concerned, the principle is limited in this way primarily to particular spheres of objects. Only when this principle of activity is established and recognized in relation to the object that has being in and for itself, namely, in relation to God— | only when it is thus grasped in its perfect purity ˉfreed from impulses andˉ[204] finite ends—only then does it receive its confirmation. Only then do human beings acquire the inner certainty of their worth in relation to God. The Lutheran faith is then that a human being stands in relationship with God, appears in it as *this* person only, and must exist in this relationship exclusively. In other words, our piety and hope of blessedness, and all that that entails,

---

204. *Thus Gr* (frei von Trieben); *An reads:* and not together with various dreary [*trüben*],

require the involvement of our heart, our inmost being, our sensations, convictions, and disposition—in a word, everything of our own is involved. Human subjectivity is ˉthe soil [of the relationship]ˉ²⁰⁵ along with this inmost self-certainty—and only it can genuinely come into consideration in relation to God. The person must himself or herself feel penitence and remorse, the heart must be filled with a genuinely holy spirit. Here therefore the principle of subjectivity, of pure self-relation, of true freedom, upon which all else rests, is not just recognized; what is plainly demanded is that everything in the cultic activity and in the religion should depend upon it alone. That only this counts in God's eyes is the highest confirmation of this principle; *faith* alone, our own heart alone, the subduing of our own heart and the inspiration of it, is the principle of Christian freedom.

In this way, then, the principle of Christian freedom was first established and brought to consciousness, to genuine consciousness. Within the inmost aspect of the human being, therefore, a place was posited that is all that matters and where a person is present only with self and with God; and one can only be with God when one is at home with self. I must be at home in my conscience; this right of mine as the householder is not to be disturbed, no one else shall presume to have a say in it. There all externality with reference to me is banished, ˉincluding the externality that was present in the sacramental host.ˉ²⁰⁶ Only in communion and in faith am I connected with something divine. The distinction between laity and priests is annulled. There are no longer any laity, | for all lay persons are admonished to stand on their own with regard to their own faith. Imputation falls within the domain of individual right, for no one else can take my place, no authority can absolve me of my accountability. Good works are something external. Good works are nothing without conviction, without the presence to self of the spirit that is at home with itself. But the way that the heart is inwardly for itself is the way that it relates itself to God,

205. *Thus Pn; Gr and Lw read:* requisite
206. *Thus Lw with Gr; Pn reads:* [for] the sacramental host involves the inmost aspect of the heart.

without mediation, without the Blessed Virgin, and without the saints—that is what is demanded.

⌐This, then, is the great principle [of the Reformation], that all externality disappears at the point of the absolute relationship to God. All⌐²⁰⁷ self-estrangement, with its consequent dependence and servitude, therefore disappears. Praying in a foreign tongue or having [divine] science in a foreign tongue is proscribed. It is in language that we are conceptually productive. The first outward expression that humanity gives to itself is by means of language; ⌐whatever we represent to ourselves we represent⌐²⁰⁸ to ourselves, even in the inmost self, as something spoken. This is the first and simplest form of production and of existence, through which what lies within comes to consciousness. This first [outward] form becomes something fragmented and alien if we have to receive and express in a foreign tongue what affects our highest interest. This breach with the human being's first emergence from self and into consciousness gets annulled by that [Reformation] principle. To be here at home with self and in our own domain, to speak, think, and represent in our own language, likewise belongs to the form of liberation. This is of the utmost importance. Without his translation of the Bible into German Luther would not have consummated his Reformation. There would not have been a general Reformation without it; subjective freedom would not have been fostered without this form that consists in thinking in one's own language. |

This principle of subjectivity became a moment of religion itself and thereby attained to its absolute recognition; it was grasped, by and large, in the only form in which it can be a moment of religion. Fulfilled now for the first time is the commandment of the Christian religion, to worship God in spirit.²⁰⁹ God, a spirit, is [for us] only under this condition of the free spirituality of the subject,

65

---

207. *Thus Lw with Gr; An reads:* Every external circumstance, all *Sv reads:* All externality, all

208. *Thus Gr (a little further on); Lw reads:* when we will something, then we represent it

209. [*Ed.*] Hegel is referring to John 4:24, which reads: "God is spirit, and those who worship him must worship in spirit and truth."

for it is only free spirituality that can relate to spirit; a subject in which there is some lack of freedom does not function spiritually, does not worship God in spirit. This is the universal aspect of this principle.

We should note that this is how the first enunciation of this principle was grasped in religion and how it received its absolute justification. But it first appeared as posited simply in connection with religious objects; it did not yet extend to the broader development of this subjective principle itself in its vitality. Human beings became aware of being implicitly reconciled, and of being able to reconcile themselves explicitly. To that extent they acquired another shape in their actuality, for a strong mind [*Mut*] and [inner] certainty are permitted to maintain a clear conscience. A pious life of one's own, soundly lived and even enjoyed, was no longer regarded as something to be renounced; monastic renunciation was renounced instead. But at first this principle did not yet extend to any wider content [beyond piety itself].

Furthermore, the religious content was grasped mainly as it is for representation and for the memory, that is, in its historical shape. That is how the beginning or the possibility of an unspiritual mode entered into this spiritual freedom. The ancient belief of the church, the creed, was left as it had been before. So this content, which is essentially a speculative content that has a historical side, was accepted and left in this arid form. It is to be believed in this form, albeit accepted within the subject's conscience [*Gewissen*] as 66 a conscientious certainty [*das Gewisse*], | and it is to be treated as what is true, as the highest truth.

One immediate consequence was that speculative knowledge— the dogmatic content speculatively elaborated—got entirely set aside. What a person needed is the inward assurance of reconciliation, the assurance of salvation and of blessedness, that is, the relationship of subjective spirit to absolute spirit. Thus the form of subjectivity—as faith, longing, repentance, conversion—became established as the preponderant element. What is plainly important is the content of truth, ˉor the essence of God, but the doctrinal system hasˉ²¹⁰ the shape of the truth's initial appearance for rep-

210. *Thus Pn with An; Gr, similar in Lw, reads:* but the doctrinal system of the divine nature and process is grasped in

resentation. The Reformers not only rejected all of the finitude, externality, and cleavage, all of the formalism that Scholastic philosophers stressed—and they were right to reject it—but on the other side they also set aside the philosophical development of church doctrine, and they did this [precisely] on the grounds that the subject has delved deeply within itself, within its ˉown heart.ˉ[211] This delving deeply within the self, its penitence, contrition, and conversion, this preoccupation of the subject with itself, was the moment that was said principally to have been legitimated. The subject did not delve more deeply into the content but cast away the mundane version of the universal content, though with it cast away as well the earlier plumbing of the depths of spirit; speculative elaboration was left to one side and abandoned.

To this very day we find in the dogmatics of the Catholic church the echoes and, as it were, the heritage of the philosophemes of the School of Alexandria, for the philosophical or speculative element is much greater in Catholic dogmatics. In the Protestant doctrinal system or in Protestant dogmatics—to the extent that it does still include an objective element and has not been made wholly | empty—the content is, on the contrary, more historical in kind or more vested in a historical form, with the result that the doctrine becomes arid. In the Catholic church the linkage of theology with philosophy has in substance always been preserved. In the Protestant church, by contrast, the subjective religious principle parted company with philosophy. But in philosophy that principle was later authentically brought back to life.

In this principle of the Reformation the religious content of the Christian church is on the whole preserved. But it is preserved in such a way that this content receives its authentication from the witness of spirit, that it is to be valid for me to the extent that it asserts its validity within my conscience or my heart. This is what Christ said: "If you keep my commandments, it will come home to you that my word is true."[212] The criterion of truth is the way

67

211. *Thus Gr; Pn reads:* sensibilities.
212. [*Ed.*] The saying is not biblical in this form. Hegel is probably referring to passages such as John 15:10 and more especially John 14:21, which reads: "He who has my commandments and keeps them, he it is who loves me; and he who loves me will be loved by my Father, and I will love him and manifest myself to him."

that what is true authenticates and evidences itself in my heart. Whether it be the truth is something that must make itself evident in my heart. My own spirit is rightly in the truth only when in this way it is within this content. The way that the content is in my heart is the way it is [the truth].

So far the content does not have within itself the confirmation that it acquired through philosophical theology, through speculative thinking—through the fact that the speculative idea makes itself valid in the content. Nor does it have the historical confirmation that is conferred on a content with a historical, outer aspect, by the hearing of historical testimony and subsequent determination of its accuracy. Instead the doctrine has to confirm itself as authentic through my spirit, through my own heart, through the ~repentance, conversion,~[213] and rejoicing of the mind or soul[214] in God. Of course we must begin with doctrine, with the outward content; to this extent the doctrine is an outward starting point, and it is indeed necessary. But taken in this way, without reference to me, to the ~attitude of my spirit or my heart toward it,~[215] doctrine is, properly speaking, | meaningless. ~As Christian baptism and Christian education or as the cultivation of a pious disposition, however, this outward starting point is at the same time bound up with outward attestation.~[216] The truth of the gospel, of Christian doctrine, exists only in an authentic attitude toward it. And this is just what is said: that the soul reconstitutes itself inwardly, sanctifies itself inwardly, becomes sanctified, and that the criterion of the content lies only in this sanctification. Only for ~this sanctification~[217] is the content a true content. No use is to be made of the

68

213. *Thus Gr; Lw reads:* remorse
214. [*Ed.*] In this paragraph *Gemüt* ("mind" or "soul") refers to the whole or organic personality, which is susceptible to "cultivation" or "formation." In contrast, *Herz* ("heart") refers to a more limited aspect of the person, one that is "awakened" in specific response to the witness of the spirit.
215. *Thus An; Gr reads:* inward attitude of my spirit or my heart,
216. *Thus Gr with Pn, similar in Lw; An reads:* But in this starting point . . . there lies already the basis for the authentic knowledge that ensues.
217. *Added in conformity with Gr and Pn; Lw reads:* the spirit that is holy.

content except that it should ⁻become edifying,⁻[218] and [serve] to awaken the inner process of the soul.

To take this content in an external fashion is quite a different way of doing things and quite wrong. The modern principle that the content of the New Testament should be treated like the ancient Greek and Latin authors, ⁻with the methods of philological and historical criticism,⁻[219] follows that path. But the content ought to function essentially for spirit and for spirit alone. It is a perverse approach to seek to prove the truth of the Christian religion in this external, historical way, ⁻as orthodoxy has done,⁻[220] where the content is taken in the form of something devoid of spirit.

This, then, is the first attitude of spirit toward this [divine] content: that the content as such is certainly essential, but it is equally essential for the holy and sanctifying spirit to relate itself to the content. [In the second place,] however, this spirit is essentially a thinking spirit too. Thinking as such must also develop in it, must indeed be developed essentially as the form of spirit's inmost unity with itself. Thinking must come to the point of differentiating and examining this content, and must pass over into the form of spirit's purest unity | with itself. This thinking is initially abstract thinking. As abstract, it discloses itself immediately, and this abstract thinking also involves more specifically a relationship to religion, to theology. Even when the content of which we are here speaking is taken only in historical, external fashion, it is still said at the same time to be religious, to contain in it the manifestation of the nature of God. This entails the more specific postulate that this very thought directed to the inner nature of God also posits itself in connection with this content. But insofar as this thought is initially understanding, and metaphysics of the understanding, it will eliminate speculation and the rational idea from the content and make the content something empty, without absolute significance—so

218. *Thus Pn, similar in An; Gr reads:* edify the soul, should awaken it to confidence, rejoicing, repentance, and conversion,
219. *Thus Lw, similar in Gr; Sv reads:* critically and exegetically,
220. *Thus Gr; Lw reads:* for which orthodoxy has been attacked,

that all that remains is an outer history, which can be of little interest with regard to the absolute content.

The third attitude is that of rational, concrete, speculative thinking. In accordance with the previously mentioned standpoint as to how the religious content and its form are determined, religion has in the main set aside the speculative content as such and its further elucidation, it has for the most part forgotten how this content was enriched by the treasures of ancient philosophy, the profound ideas of all the earlier Eastern religions, and so on. So the content has objectivity, but this means only that the objective content is said to be no more than the beginning—it should subsist not ¯on its own account¯[221] as outer history, but only as a beginning from which the soul is supposed to cultivate and sanctify itself inwardly and spiritually. Hence all that enrichment of the content, by virtue of which it became philosophical, has been set aside. What follows afterward is only that spirit, as thinking, once again delves deeply within itself in order to be concrete and rational.

The principle of the Reformation then was the moment of spirit's being-within-self, of its being free, its coming to itself. That is just what freedom means: to relate oneself to oneself, in the determinate

70 content. The vitality of spirit consists in | being returned into itself in what is determinate or other than itself. What remains [simply] as an other within spirit is what is unassimilated or dead. Insofar as it is related to something other, and the other continues to subsist as alien to spirit, ¯and [yet] is supposed to be wholly its essence,¯[222] spirit is unfree. Hence this abstract moment, this specification that spirit should essentially be free within itself, should be at home with itself, constitutes its basic definition. And to the extent that spirit advances to cognitive knowing, to spiritual categories, so far as it looks about itself and goes forth into a *content*, it will, in doing so, operate as within its own property,[223] it will affirm the content essentially in that property and will want to have it as its own. The

221. *Thus Pn, An; Lw reads:* as internally grounded content,
222. *Thus Pn; Lw reads:* as something destructive of its essence,
223. [*Ed.*] Hegel is probably anticipating here a turn of phrase in Boehme's *Aurora*; see p. 000 below.

content subsists in and for itself, yet it is spirit's own. Moving within its own property, its own content, and advancing to cognitive knowing, there spirit will for the first time be in motion concretely, for spirit is concrete being. This property determines itself on the one hand as outer, worldly property, as finite, natural, worldly being; and it determines itself on the other hand as inner possession, ˉdivine knowing and striving.ˉ[224] |

71

224. *Thus An; Gr reads:* as the mystical, divine, Christian being and life. *Lw reads:* and only as the Christian's divine life and being.

[Ed.] As indicated by "for the first time" (in the preceding sentence), Hegel here anticipates the first section in "Modern Philosophy." When the property within which spirit moves is understood as outer, worldly property, Hegel is thinking of the philosophy of Francis Bacon; when it is understood as inner possession, he is thinking of Jacob Boehme.

THE THIRD PERIOD
MODERN PHILOSOPHY

A. BEGINNINGS OF MODERN PHILOSOPHY: BACON AND BOEHME

1. Transition to the Modern Era

First of all we must consider this concrete shape of cognitive know-ing, and in doing so we enter into the third period. Next after the concrete shape we must deal with the emergence of thinking on its own account.[1] With the reflection of its being-within-itself, thinking at this stage arises essentially as something subjective in such a way that it has an antithesis in [outwardly] subsistent being. The exclu-sive concern is then to reconcile this opposition, to conceive the reconciliation at ˉits ultimate extreme,ˉ[2] ˉto grasp the most ab-stract and the ultimate cleavage of being and thinking.ˉ[3] From this point onward all philosophy concerns itself with this unity.

Since independently abstract thinking proceeds from philosophy itself, we first of all leave behind thinking's unity with theology. Thinking separates itself from theology, just as in Greek culture too it separated itself from the mythology of the folk religion and only at the end, in the Alexandrian philosophy, did it again seek out this form for thinking and reconcile the mythological representations with it.[4] Here too, therefore, we leave behind the unity of ˉtheol-ogyˉ[5] with philosophy. The bond nevertheless remains plainly im-plicit, for theology continues to be through and through the same thing as philosophy and it cannot separate itself from philosophy.

1. [Ed.] "This concrete shape of cognitive knowing" picks up the reference, at the end of the preceding section, to the twofold form of spirit's new property, as "outer, worldly property" (for Bacon) and "inner possession" (for Boehme). "The emergence of thinking on its own account" anticipates Hegel's presentation of Descartes.

2. Thus Pn, An, Lw; Gr reads: its ultimate existence, namely, in the most abstract extremes,

3. Thus An with Lw; similar in Pn; Gr reads: [for] this ultimate cleavage is the most abstract antithesis of thinking and being, and we have to grasp its reconciliation.

4. [Ed.] This interpretation of the development of Greek philosophy by means of the category of separation from, and reconciliation with, folk religion, reflects Hegel's treatment of Xenophanes, Anaxagoras, and Alexandrian philosophy; cf. W 13:284, 289-290, 388 ff., and W 15:5 ff., 32, 71 ff., 92.

5. Thus An; Lw reads: religion

Theology always has to do with the thoughts that it brings along with it, and these thoughts—[this] "private" metaphysics—are then universal reflections, the general opinions and the like of the time. Whenever theology has recourse to the everyday metaphysics of experience [*Hausmetaphysik*], what we have is an uncultivated understanding, an uncritical thinking that is, of course, bound

72 up with its own peculiar or special | conviction, ˉbut lacks [adequate] grounding. In it there are, to be sure, general laws.ˉ⁶ These thoughts are, however, only mental images [*Vorstellungen*], and they furnish the judgment, the criterion, what is decisive. These general images are no more than the sort of reflection found on every public street—the most superficial of all thoughts. When thinking emerges on its own account in this way, we are therefore cut off from theology. We shall, however, first consider one instance in which the two [philosophy and theology] are still united, namely, Jacob Boehme.

Spirit moves and finds itself now within its own property,⁷ which is partly the finite, outer world and partly the inner world (which means principally the Christian world). What we have to consider next is spirit, as it were, but spirit within its concrete world as its own property—hence the concrete mode of cognition.

The first two philosophers that we have to treat are Bacon and Boehme; the second group comprises Descartes and Spinoza, with Malebranche; the third, Locke, Leibniz, and Wolff; and the fourth, Kant, Fichte, and Schelling. It is with Descartes that the philosophy of the modern period, or abstract thinking, properly begins.⁸

6. *Thus Pn with An; Gr reads:* and this [conviction] is supposed to authenticate it [that thinking].

7. [*Ed.*] At this point "property" [*Eigentum*] indicates "possession," not "attribute." Hegel echoes (with some differences) the statement in Boehme's first work, the *Aurora*, chap. 9, § 41, that "all creatures in heaven and in this world are formed or imaged [*gebildet*] from the [seven] spirits [of God] and live therein as in their own property." See Jacob Böhme, *Theosophia revelata; Das ist, Alle göttliche Schriften des gottseligen und hocherleuchteten deutschen Theosophi*, ed. Johann Otto Glusing, 4 vols. (Hamburg, 1715), 1:103. See also the bibliographical comments at the end of n. 38 below.

8. [*Ed.*] This division of modern philosophy into four periods undergoes little alteration in each of the Berlin lectures, exclusive of 1823–24. The latter (cf. W 15:274–275) seek to distinguish three epochs: (1) Declaration of the union of think-

Baconian philosophy means in general a philosophizing that bases itself upon *experience,* upon the observation of outward or spiritual nature, of human beings in their inclinations and desires and in their rational and lawful character. Observations become the basis, conclusions are drawn from them, and by this means one discovers universal viewpoints, the laws of this domain. With Bacon, however, this type of philosophizing was not yet very well developed; he was but its originator, although he is cited as the principal figure in this approach whenever one needs to be named. | 73

The life circumstances of this commander in chief of the philosophy of experience follow below.[9] We can make a general remark about the lives of the modern philosophers, namely, that from this point on, their circumstances assume a shape quite different from that of the philosophers of antiquity. In the case of the ancient philosophers, one's philosophy determined one's [life] situation. An individual could actually *live* as a philosopher, and this often happened; that is to say, one's outward circumstances were determined in conformity with this purpose of one's inner life. There we were dealing with "plastic" individualities. And in the Middle Ages it was especially clerics or doctors of theology who pursued philosophy. In the [subsequent] transitional period philosophers showed themselves to be in a state of struggle—in an inner conflict with self and an outer conflict with circumstances, and so they were driven about wildly and restlessly in life.[10] In modern times the relation-

---

ing and being (Bacon and Boehme); (2) Metaphysical union, as (a) metaphysics proper (Descartes, Spinoza, et al.) and (b) the decline of metaphysics; (3) Union as the object of philosophy (Kant to Schelling). This division in the *Werke* may be derived from editor Michelet's no-longer-extant notebook of 1823–24; the notebooks of Hotho and Hube confirm it. Michelet attaches this threefold division to the fourfold one without remarking on their differences in conception and, moreover, makes the threefold division of 1823–24 the basis of the section on modern philosophy. See also below, p. 000 with n. 81.

9. [*Ed.*] Tennemann describes Bacon, Newton, and Locke as leaders [*Führer*] of the subsequent age, with Bacon and Locke giving direction to its philosophical spirit and method; see Wilhelm Gottlieb Tennemann, *Geschichte der Philosophie,* 11 vols. (Leipzig, 1798–1819), 11:68. It is thus probable, though not certain, that Hegel had Tennemann's description in mind when characterizing Bacon as "commander in chief" [*Heerführer*].

10. [*Ed.*] Earlier in this lecture series Hegel refers to "plastic" (that is, self-shap-

ship is different. Philosophers occupy no specific position in the state; they live in bourgeois circumstances or participate in public life, or in living their private lives they do so in such a way that their private status does not isolate them from other relationships. So the distinction lies in the nature [of society] as a whole. In the modern era the outer world has become calm and orderly; the social orders and their modes of life have been established and the worldly principle is reconciled with itself, so that worldly relationships have organized themselves in a way that is compatible with the nature of things, that is rational. This universal nexus, based on the understanding, is so powerful that every individual is part of it. Since we have constructed an inner world within ourselves, a religious or scientific world, and at the same time the outer world has become reconciled with itself, what is now the case is that inner and outer can coexist as autonomous and independent. The individual is now in a position to relegate the outer aspect of life to the external order, whereas in the case of those earlier plastic individuals the outer could only be determined wholly by the inner. Now, with the greater strength of the individual's inner aspect, a

74   person can leave the outer aspect | to contingent circumstances, just as we leave our clothing style to the contingency of fashion; we can relinquish the outer aspect to be determined by the conventions of the circle in which we find ourselves.

2. Francis Bacon

[Francis] Bacon, Baron Verulam, earl of Saint Albans, keeper of the great seal, and chancellor of England, was born in London in 1561. His father was keeper of the great seal under Queen Elizabeth. In his youth Bacon attached himself to the earl of Essex, the queen's favorite; through him Bacon rose in rank, but he is said to have displayed great ingratitude toward his patron. He is reproached for letting himself be induced by the earl's enemies, subsequent to his fall from power, to accuse him of high treason. Under James I

---

ing) individuals in the Socratic and Platonic dialogues (cf. W 14:65, 185); in this volume, pp. 000–000, he discusses the medieval and Renaissance philosophers. For a detailed treatment of this theme of the individual philosopher's relation to philosophy and to society, see W 15:275–277.

Bacon became lord chancellor of England, but in this position he became guilty of the grossest corruption, so that he was impeached and tried by Parliament, at which time he displayed the greatest weakness of character. He was ⁻condemned to prison⁻[11] and fined. After a while, however, he was released from prison because of [public] hatred of the current ministry rather than on account of his innocence. He then retired to private life and occupied himself for the rest of his days with the sciences alone, but he never regained the personal respect he had forfeited by his conduct, his intrigues, and his relationship to his wife. He died in 1626.[12]

Many cultivated persons have spoken and thought about matters of human interest—affairs of state, the mind, the heart, external nature, and so on—according to experience or a cultured knowledge of the world. Bacon was such a man of the world, who thrived on affairs of state and who dealt with actuality in a practical manner, observing human beings, their circumstances and relationships, and working effectively with and within them: he was a cultured and reflective man of the world. | After his career in the state had ended, he turned to scientific activity and treated the sciences in the same manner, according to concrete experience and insight, particularly in the way a practical man of the world considers their use. Value is accorded to what is present at hand. He repudiated the Scholastic method of reasoning or philosophizing from quite remote abstractions—the blindness for what lies before one's eyes. What constitutes the [philosophical] standpoint now is the sensible appearance as it comes to the cultivated person and as such a person reflects on it, on its utility and the like.

So what is noteworthy is that Bacon applied himself to the sciences in a practical manner, apprehending phenomena in a re-

75

---

11. *Thus An, similar in Pn, Sv; Gr, Lw read:* put in the Tower [of London]
12. [*Ed.*] Hegel's main source for these biographical details is Johann Gottlieb Buhle, *Geschichte der neuern Philosophie seit der Epoche der Wiederherstellung der Wissenschaften*, 6 vols. (Göttingen, 1800–1804), 2, pt. 2:950–954. He probably also drew upon Jacob Brucker, *Historia critica philosophiae*, 4 vols. (Leipzig, 1742–1744), 4, pt. 2:91–93. But the basis for Bacon's dismissal from office is not given in Buhle or Brucker, or in Tennemann (*Geschichte* 10:7 ff.), who omits all negative character traits. In W 15:279 Hegel explains Bacon's "relationship to his wife," namely, that he married a wealthy woman and then squandered her wealth.

flective fashion and considering first ⁻their utility.⁻¹³ He pursued this course methodically; he did not put forward mere opinions or sentiments and did not express his views on the sciences in the way a fine gentleman would, but proceeded meticulously and established a method for scientific cognition and general principles for cognitive procedure. The methodical character of the approach that he introduced is just what makes him noteworthy in the history of the sciences and of philosophy, and it was through this principle of methodical cognition that he had great influence [on others] too.

Bacon ranks as the commander in chief of the philosophy of experience; he will always be referred to in this sense. Speculative knowing, or knowing from the concept, stands opposed to knowing from experience or argumentation on the basis of experience. This opposition is indeed often grasped so harshly that cognition from the concept is ashamed of cognition from experience just as, on the other side, cognition from experience boasts of its own worth over against the concept. We can say about Bacon what Cicero said about Socrates: that he brought philosophy down into the mundane affairs and the homes of human beings.¹⁴ To that extent cognition from the concept or from the absolute can look down its nose on this [experiential] cognition. But it is necessary to the scientific idea for the particularity of the | content to be developed. The idea is concrete, it determines itself inwardly, it has its development, and complete cognition is always more developed cognition. When we say that the idea is still limited, we mean only that the working out of its development is not yet far advanced. What we are dealing with here is the working out of this development; and in order for this working out of the determination of the particular from the idea to take place, and for cognitive knowledge of the universe or of nature to develop, knowledge of the particular is necessary.

It is the special merit of the modern era to have produced and

76

13. *Thus An; Sv reads:* what is present at hand.

14. [*Ed.*] See Cicero, *Tusculanae disputationes* 1.10–11. Thaddä Anselm Rixner had already drawn this comparison between Bacon and Socrates, in his *Handbuch der Geschichte der Philosophie zum Gebrauche seiner Vorlesungen*, 3 vols. (Sulzbach, 1822–1823), 2:9. Cf. also Cicero, *Academicae quaestiones* 1.4.

fostered this cognitive knowledge of the particular. Empiricism is not sheer apprehension by the senses. To the contrary, it is essentially concerned to discover the universal, the laws or species; and in bringing them forth it begets the sort of thing that belongs to the region of the idea or of the concept, or that can be taken up into the region of the concept. When science is mature, it no longer begins from the empirical at all, although for it to come into existence science requires passage from what is singular, or what is particular, to the universal. Without the development of the sciences of experience on their own account, philosophy could not have advanced beyond the point that it reached among the ancients.

This passage of the idea into itself is something we must deal with; the other aspect is its beginning, the passage by which the idea comes to existence. In every science we begin from fundamental principles. At first, however, these abstract determinations themselves are results of the particular; it is when the science is mature that we begin from them. The same point applies to philosophy: the working out of the empirical aspect has been a necessary condition for the idea coming to existence and advancing toward more detailed development. For example, in order for the history of modern philosophy to occur, there had to be behind it the general history of philosophy, the course of philosophy through so many millennia; spirit had to have taken this long route in order to produce modern philosophy. Once it is mature, philosophy can burn its bridges behind it, but we must not overlook the fact that philosophy itself would not have come into existence without them. This then is the spirit of the Baconian philosophy.

Bacon is especially famous for two works. | *De augmentis scientiarum* is a classification or systematic encyclopedia of the sciences—an outline that must have excited much attention among his contemporaries. It classifies the sciences according to memory, imagination, and reason. Then it proceeds through the individual sciences (history, poetry, general science) in the style of the day; the interest that it held for its time lay in its ordering of knowledge in this intelligible way.[15] One of its principal features is that posi- 77

15. [*Ed.*] Bacon's *De dignitate et augmentis scientiarum* (1623) is a revised and expanded version of his earlier work, *The Advancement of Learning* (1606). It di-

tions are made plausible through examples, such as those from the Bible. When Bacon discusses kings, popes, and so on, then he brings up Ahab, Solomon, and the like.[16] It was, after all, the custom of the medieval and even later ages to employ the Bible as a means of proving points. For example, just as the Jewish forms were normative in the current laws (the marriage laws), so they were models of the same sort in philosophy.[17] Even ˉtheologyˉ[18] is brought into Bacon's presentation, and magic as well;[19] he speaks about alchemy, the transmutation of metals, the rejuvenation of the body, and the prolongation of life,[20] and he discusses all of this material

---

vides human teachings into history, poesy, and philosophy, according to the three intellectual faculties of memory, phantasy, and reason (bk. 2, chap. 1). Chapters 2–13 (of bk. 2) treat history and poesy. Books 3–9 treat theology, philosophy, natural science, medicine, and other topics. See *The Works of Francis Bacon,* ed. James Spedding, Robert Leslie Ellis, and Douglas Denon Heath, 7 vols. (London, 1857–1874), 1:425–426.

16. [*Ed.*] Examples of this sort abound in Bacon's writings, although they do not touch upon Ahab. One example translated by Hegel deals with the use of cosmetics by Jezebel, Ahab's wife; see 2 Kings 9:30, and *De augmentis,* bk. 4, chap. 2 (*Works* 1:602); cf. W 15:290 (Ms?). Mention of Solomon could refer to Bacon's dedication of his *Novum organum* (1620) to James I, whom it compares to Solomon (*Works* 1:124). Also on Solomon, cf. the beginning of the dedication of *De augmentis* (*Works* 1:431), as well as bk. 1, chap. 3 and bk. 8, chap. 2.

17. [*Ed.*] Hegel's sources for support of this contention are uncertain. Perhaps it derives from conversation with Eduard Gans, who later treated this topic thoroughly in *Das Erbrecht des Mittelalters* (pp. 70 ff.), which is vol. 3 of his *Das Erbrecht in weltgeschichtlicher Entwicklung,* 4 vols. (Stuttgart, 1829).

18. *Thus Gr, Pn, An; Lw reads:* theurgy
[*Ed.*] Bacon treats theology in *De augmentis,* bk. 3, chap. 2 and bk. 9, chap. 1.

19. [*Ed.*] Actually Bacon distinguishes three forms of magic and attributes a different value to each. Superstitious magic, as practiced in all religions and by all peoples, is scarcely worthy of attention (*Novum organum,* bk. 1, § 85; *Works* 1:193). Natural magic, closely associated with astrology and alchemy, has noble ends but is plagued with defective methodology, errors, and hoaxes (*De augmentis,* bk. 1; *Works* 1:456–457). For the more specific characteristics of the defective methods of natural magic and Bacon's repudiation of it, see *Novum organum,* bk. 1, § 85 (*Works* 1:193). Genuinely metaphysical magic, however, rests upon metaphysics and the investigation of forms, and so is fundamentally distinct from natural magic; see *De augmentis,* bk. 3, chap. 5 (*Works* 1:571, 573); see also the discussion of forms in the next paragraph of our text.

20. [*Ed.*] Here Hegel cites the essential functions Bacon ascribes to alchemy (*De augmentis,* bk. 1; *Works* 1:457). As in the case of magic, his citation does not reflect Bacon's critical stance in distinguishing different forms of alchemy, some of which

in an intellectually rational way. Bacon remains on the whole within the perspectives of his age.

More striking is the method that he expounded copiously in his second writing, his *Organon.*[21] He declares himself opposed to deduction, to the syllogistic method of deduction that proceeds from a presupposition or from some Scholastic abstraction, and he insists upon induction, which he sets in opposition to deduction.[22] But induction is a kind of deducing too, as Aristotle was well aware. Induction means making observations, performing experiments, and taking note of experience, and from this experience deriving general characteristics [of things].[23] He then calls these general characteristics *formae* and insists on the point that these forms are to be discovered and known; and these *formae* are none other than uni-

---

result in useful discoveries (*Novum organum,* bk. 1, § 85; *Works* 1:192–193). Genuine alchemy is not separated from genuine magic and indeed distinguishes itself from ordinary alchemy not by its purposes but by its means (*De augmentis,* bk. 3, chap. 5; *Works* 1:574). Although Bacon does refer in passing to the rejuvenation of the body and the prolongation of life, he makes it clear elsewhere that the proper place for those topics is in the discussion of medicine (*De augmentis,* bk. 4, chap. 2; *Works* 1:590).

21. [*Ed.*] Hegel confuses the temporal and topical sequences of Bacon's two principal works. The *Novum organum* (1620) appeared first, although in Bacon's overall plan it forms the second part of the *Instauratio magna;* the first part, *De augmentis,* appeared in 1623. A statement of Bacon's overall plan is prefaced to the *Novum organum* (see *Works* 1:134). Bacon never completed parts 3 through 6.

22. [*Ed.*] See *Novum organum,* bk. 1, §§ 11–34 (*Works* 1:158–162), especially §§ 13–14, which repudiate the syllogism. Bacon does not explicitly oppose the Scholastics in this context, but that opposition is implicit in his repeated polemic against the current sciences, relative to what they have discovered up to his day (§§ 11, 18). The contrast between syllogistic and inductive methods occurs in §§ 19–32; § 19 contrasts the method that flies straight from the sensible and particular to the most general theses with the true method, which ascends steadily and gradually from the sensible to the universal (*Works* 1:159). Bacon also distinguishes his concept of induction (as an instrument for the determination of concepts) from the usual ones (as a means solely for the discovery of theses), among which he also implicitly reckons Aristotelian induction (§ 105; *Works* 1:205–206). See also *De augmentis,* bk. 5, chap. 2; *Works* 1:621.

23. [*Ed.*] The *Novum organum* clearly expresses the fact that induction is also a deducing (for example, in bk. 1, § 105; *Works* 1:205–206); see also the preceding note. See Aristotle's *Prior Analytics* 1.23 for the relationship of induction and deduction via the mediating concept. Hegel mentions the Aristotelian distinction between dialectical (or demonstrative) and rhetorical syllogisms, in *W* 14:409.

versal characteristics, species, or laws.[24] He says, "Although in nature nothing truly exists but bodies, which of themselves produce individual acts, yet in science nature's law and the knowledge of that law is regarded as the foundation for | knowledge as well as for activity." This law and its articles or more precise specifications Bacon calls "forms." "Whoever is cognizant of the forms thoroughly grasps the unity of nature in what are seemingly the most dissimilar materials."[25] He goes over this point extensively and adduces many trivial examples of it. He says that the question arises whether the warmth of the sun, by which we see grapes ripen, is a specific warmth or a universal warmth. We must let grapes ripen by a wood fire and learn from this experiment that it is only a universal (and not a specific) warmth by which grapes ripen—a method that to us appears tedious.[26]

One chief characteristic of his method is that Bacon spoke out against treating nature teleologically, or considering things according to final causes, which contributes nothing to cognitive knowledge. For that knowledge we must stick to treatment according to *causae efficientes*.[27] Considering things in terms of final causes in-

24. [*Ed.*] On forms, see *Novum organum*, bk. 2, § 17 (*Works* 1:257–258), where Bacon cites examples such as warmth and light, and says, for instance, that the form of light and the law of light are one and the same thing. He concludes that "the power of the human being can free itself only through the uncovering and discovering of these forms, and can raise itself above the general course of nature, it can extend itself and soar in creating what is new, and new modes of operation." The earlier Berlin lectures do not deal with Bacon's concept of form. It is first found in the 1823–24 lectures, in connection with the treatment of a review by Dugald Stewart ("Dissertation prefixed to the supplemental volumes of the Encyclopaedia Britannica, exhibiting a General View of the Progress of Metaphysical, Moral and Political Philosophy in Europe, from the Revival of Letters," in *The Quarterly Review*, vol. 17 [April 1817]). Hegel refers to this review in connection with Bacon (*W* 15:290–296) as well as with Locke (*W* 15:422). The 1825–26 lectures develop the concept of form without express reference to this review. In the subsequent lectures of 1827–28 and 1829–30 this theme drops out.

25. [*Ed.*] These two quotations, and the substance of the intervening sentence, are paraphrases from a passage from *Novum organum*, bk. 2, §§ 2–3 (*Works* 1:228–229); cf. *W* 15:294 (Ms?).

26. [*Ed.*] See *Novum organum*, bk. 2, § 35 (*Works* 1:289–290); cited in part in *W* 15:294–295 (Ms?).

27. [*Ed.*] This statement is incorrect. Bacon not only repudiates the effort to know final causes ("the inquiry is fruitless and produces nothing, just as a virgin

cludes, for example, explaining the thick coat of animals as serving the purpose of warding off heat and cold, or hair on the head for the sake of warmth, or lightning as God's punishment, or leaves on the tree for the purpose of preventing harm to the fruit and sap. Bacon says that both ways of treating things can very well coexist.[28] Treatment in terms of final causes refers principally to outer purposiveness, as Kant's apt distinction has shown us;[29] whereas inner purposiveness constitutes the foundation ˉof the organic,ˉ[30] [it is an] end in itself. External ends, however, are heterogeneous to these [ends in themselves], they are not connected [directly] with the objects under consideration. This is the sum and substance of what we have to say about Bacon.

3. Jacob Boehme

In Bacon we had an English lord chancellor, in Boehme we have a German shoemaker; the former is commander in chief of external philosophizing, the latter stands in direct opposition to it. Boehme's style [of philosophizing] has been long forgotten. He was labeled an enthusiast, | and only in more recent times has he been restored to honor, although on the other side he has also been accorded too much honor.[31] He was born of poor parents in 1575 in Upper

79

consecrated to God gives birth to nothing") but also is very critical of knowledge of material and efficient causes; see *Novum organum*, bk. 2, § 2 (*Works* 1:228) and *De augmentis*, bk. 3, chap. 5 (*Works* 1:571); cf. *W* 15:291 (Ms?). According to Bacon, whereas earlier scientists had despaired of knowing formal causes, this kind of knowledge is the crucial thing; see *Novum organum*, bk. 2, § 3 (*Works* 1:228–229). In a different passage (*W* 15:293–294) Hegel seems to be clear that in this context Bacon's concern is with formal causes, that the issue is what Bacon understands these forms to be; cf. n. 24 above, on the *Quarterly Review* article.

28. [*Ed.*] See *De augmentis*, bk. 3, chap. 4 (*Works* 1:569–570). Bacon drew his examples of final causes in this passage from Galen's *De usu partium*. But Bacon himself says nothing about lightning as divine punishment. The statement that both kinds of explanation (final and efficient causality) can coexist probably refers to the latter part of this same passage in Bacon, which reads: "both causes can very well coexist, since one indicates the design or purpose but the other the sheer observed consequence."

29. [*Ed.*] See below, p. 000 with n. 450.

30. *Similar in Gr, Pn; An reads:* of everything,

31. [*Ed.*] The Enlightenment gave Boehme the label of "enthusiast" (*Schwärmer*). Tennemann (*Geschichte* 10:188), among others, evaluated him in this way.

Lusatia, in Altseidenberg near Görlitz, and as a peasant boy he tended livestock. In the course of his life he had a number of un-settling experiences [illuminations]. Thus while still a cowherd he saw a recess in a thicket from which gold or metal glistened in his direction, so that the greatest brilliance struck him and awakened his mind inwardly from its dull stupor. Subsequently he was ap-prenticed to a cobbler, and at his master's he had a second vision of this sort. His master had polished pewter vessels. The brilliant luster of this metal transported Boehme into the center of ˉthe hid-denˉ[32] nature and into a glorious sabbath of the soul; ˉhe was em-braced by the divine light and ˉ[33] remained for seven days in the highest contemplation of the realm of joy. He tells that in his twenty-fifth year, thus about 1600, he had gone outdoors ˉin order

---

Hegel is evidently referring to Tennemann's depiction of both Boehme's soul and his writings as *schwärmerisch,* and to his statement about the recent rehabilitation of Boehme's reputation. Tennemann says that *"Schwärmerei* is antithetical to philosophy because it is poetry and it despises reason as a source of knowledge," and that Boehme cannot be regarded as a philosopher. In support of that he cites Boehme's *Aurora* (see n. 36, p. 000 below) to the effect that "if one is to be a philosopher and is to investigate God's essence in nature, one has only to call on the Holy Ghost." Hegel's reference to "too much honor" probably has in mind Boehme disciples such as Louis Claude de Saint-Martin (1743–1803), Franz von Baader (1765–1841), who may have been his source for information about Saint-Martin, and perhaps also the literary figures Novalis (1772–1801) and Friedrich Schlegel (1772–1829). It cannot be ascertained whether Hegel knew of Boehme from other traditions prior to the "Boehme-renaissance" at the turn of the century, such as that associated with the biblical exegete and philosopher of nature Friedrich Christoph Oetinger (1702–1782). But he was, in all probability, aware of Schelling's interest in Boehme, which began as early as 1799. Hegel acquired a more detailed knowledge of Boehme's writings after receiving a gift of a Boehme edition in 1811 from his pupil and friend Peter Gabriel van Ghert; see *Briefe* 1:317, 324, 330, 350, 381–382 (cf. *Letters,* pp. 573–574, 590). The biographical details that follow in the text derive from Abraham von Frankenberg's biographical and bibliographical account, which was appended to the various editions of Boehme's collected works (published under the title *Theosophia revelata;* see above, n. 7, and p. 000, n. 38) and grandiosely entitled: "Historischer Bericht von dem Leben und Schriften des Deutschen Wunder-Mannes und Hocherleuchteten Theo-Philosophi Jacob Böh-mens"; see *Theosophia revelata,* vol. 2. Hegel's information comes from §§ 2–7 and 10–11 of this posthumous hagiography; its form here is a somewhat abridged and imprecise version of the biography in *W* 15:298–299. Von Frankenberg's credulous stories clearly align him with those who give Boehme "too much honor."

32. *Thus An, Lw; Gr, Pn read:* beautiful
33. *Thus Pn, similar in An; Gr reads:* his entreaty was answered and he

to drive this phantasy from his brain.‾³⁴ There in the green coun-
tryside a light dawned on him so that he could see through the features, figures, and colors ‾of the creatures and into their heart, he
could see all things in their innermost nature.‾³⁵ *De signatura rerum*
is the title of the work in which he seeks to describe the features
of all things and sees into their heart. After this he lived in Görlitz.
His first written work is the *Aurora*, or *Morgenröte im Aufgange*,
which was followed by many more; second came *Ueber die drei
Prinzipien*, third, *Ueber das dreifache Leben in Gott*, and then
others. He died in 1624 in Görlitz, as a master cobbler.³⁶ What
other sort of reading he did is not known, but he certainly did read
theosophical and alchemical writings, for the expressions in | his
works show as much; he speaks in barbaric fashion of "the divine
Salitter, Marcurius," and the like.³⁷ He was much persecuted by the
clergy, and yet caused less of a stir in Germany than he did ‾in Holland and in England, where his writings have been repeatedly published.‾³⁸ He became known as the *philosophus teutonicus,* and in

80

34. *Thus W; Gr reads:* and driven all thoughts from his head. *Pn reads:* filled
with thoughts of God. *Lw reads:* in a state of mental confusion.

35. *Sv reads:* of the creatures and into their heart. *Pn reads:* and into the innermost heart of the animals. *Gr reads:* of all things and into their innermost nature.
Lw reads: so that from the outward aspects of things he could discern their nature.

36. [*Ed.*] Boehme wrote the *Aurora* (English: *Dawn*) in 1612. In 1613 he sold
his cobbler's bench, and in subsequent years he engaged in trade involving, at various times, linen and woolen goods, and gloves; see the biographical account in
Theosophia revelata 2:62–63. The life of a merchant was more compatible with his
literary intentions. On the other books mentioned here, see n. 38 below.

37. [*Ed.*] *Salitter* stands for "sal niter," *Marcurius* for "mercury." The spelling
of *Marcurius* is deliberate, to suggest a connection with *das Mark,* meaning "core,"
"essence," or "vigor." On these concepts, see n. 47, p. 000.

38. *Thus Gr; Lw reads:* in England and Holland. There and in Hamburg his
works appeared in print.

[*Ed.*] Gregor Richter, the Lutheran *pastor primarius* of Görlitz, in 1613 forbade
Boehme to write any more, after seeing a manuscript version of his first book, the
Aurora; he denounced him from the pulpit and accused him of heresy. As a result
the Görlitz town council demanded that Boehme leave the city. Boehme did not actually absent himself from Görlitz (except on business trips), but he did honor the
ban on writing until, in 1619, he composed his second book, *Von den drei Principien
göttlichen Wesens* (English: *The Three Principles of the Divine Essence*). The correct
title of Boehme's third book, mentioned by Hegel, is *Vom Dreifachen Leben des
Menschen* (English: *The Threefold Life of Man*); it was written in 1619. The *De
signatura rerum* (English: *The Signature of All Things*) dates from 1622. Following

fact it is through him that philosophy of a distinctive character first emerged in Germany.[39]

Reading his works is a wondrous experience. One must be conversant with the [philosophical] idea in order to locate what is true in this extremely confused method. His form of presentation and of expression is barbaric, is a struggle of his ˉmind with the language,ˉ[40] and the content of the struggle is the profoundest idea, which exhibits the uniting of the most absolute antitheses. The main figure for him is Christ and the Trinity, and then come the chemical forms of mercury, *salitter* [sal niter], sulfur, the acrid, the sour, and so on. We can say that he wrestled to conceive or to grasp the negative, the evil, the devil within God. He deals a lot with the Devil, and often addresses him by saying: "Come here, you

---

the usual practice, the *Aurora,* the *De signatura,* the *Mysterium magnum* (English: *The Great Mystery*) of 1623, and the *Clavis* (English: *Key*) of 1624, are identified here by the Latin titles; English titles are used for the rest. Clerical persecution of Boehme continued for the remainder of his life, and on his deathbed he was interrogated extensively about his beliefs before being allowed to receive the sacrament. In the lectures of 1827–28 Hegel remarks on difficulties concerning Boehme's funeral. Despite the turmoil of the Thirty Years War, Abraham Wilhelmson von Bayerland got originals and copies of Boehme's works out of Germany and to Amsterdam and made Dutch translations of them. The first published editions appeared in Holland, beginning in 1634; the first complete edition appeared in Amsterdam in 1682. Translations were also made into Latin, French, and English. On these editions, see *Theosophia revelata* 2:80–100. In the seventeenth century English translations were made of most of the major works, by John Sparrow (reissued in this century by C. J. Barker and D. S. Hehner); but because their language is so archaic, they have not been utilized here in English renditions of Boehme's passages or Hegel's paraphrases of them. The standard German edition of Boehme is *Sämtliche Schriften,* ed. Will-Erich Peuckert, 11 vols. (Stuttgart, 1955–1961), being a facsimile reprint of *Theosophia revelata,* ed. Johann Wilhelm Ueberfeld, 8 vols. (Amsterdam, 1730). That in turn is an improved version of the 1715 *Theosophia revelata,* which Hegel owned and which is cited in the German edition of these lectures and in this translation. The chapter and paragraph numbers differ in the translations by Sparrow, who used older and less reliable editions and manuscript copies.

39. [*Ed.*] Von Frankenberg says Boehme was dubbed *philosophus teutonicus* by Balthasar Walter, who had spent many years in Arabia, Syria, and Egypt, researching the hidden wisdom of the East, and had then become Boehme's friend and disciple. See his "Historischer Bericht," no. 1, § 18 (in *Theosophia revelata* 2:11–12).

40. *Thus Lw, similar in Pn; Gr reads:* mind or consciousness with the language, *An reads:* mind and his consciousness (language),

blackguard."[41] To comprehend even the negative in the idea of God, to conceive God as absolute identity—this is the struggle that he had to endure; [it] has a frightful aspect, because Boehme is still at such an early stage in the process of thought-formation. One side of his thought is his quite crude and barbarous presentation; but on the other side we recognize his German and profound soul, which deals with what is most inward and in so doing exercises its power and energy. Nonetheless his principal views everywhere take on quite different forms, and it would be a delusion to undertake to give a consistent presentation and development of his views so far as concerns their particular expression.

We cannot say much about Jacob Boehme's thoughts without employing his own mode and form of expression. His principal thought, indeed we can say his sole thought, is the | Trinity   81 [Dreieinigkeit]: it is the universal principle in which and through which everything is, and it is indeed that principle in such a way that everything has this Trinity within it, not just as a Trinity of representation but as real. The rest [of his thought] is then the ex-plication of the Trinity, and the forms that he uses to designate the distinction that emerges in it are quite diverse. For him this trinity [Dreiheit] is the universal life, the wholly universal life in each and every individual; it is the absolute substance. He says: "All things in this world have come to be in the image of this trinity. You blind Jews, Turks, heathen and blasphemers, open your eyes, I must show you this trinity in unity within the whole of nature, that all things are created in the image of God, since nothing will be found nor may endure without energy, without sap, and without smell or taste. You say there is one single essence in God. Look to yourself, O Man! A human being is made according to the power of God and according to the image of this trinity. Look to the inner self and notice that you have your spirit in your heart, veins, and intel-lect; all the energy that moves within them and in which your life

41. [Ed.] Boehme addresses the Devil as "blackguard," and also as "detestable tormenter," in a passage of instruction on how to deal with him when he comes to assail the unfortunate soul. See his *Trost-Schrift von vier Complexionen* (English: *On the Four Complexions*) of 1621, §§ 44–45 (*Theosophia revelata* 1:1602–1603).

stands signifies God the Father; your light is aroused (or born) from this energy, for it is in that very power that you see, understand, and know what you ought to do." The same light shines within the whole body, for in its energy stirs your whole life and the whole of your knowledge; [this light] is the Son.[42]

This light, this seeing and understanding, is the second determination. It is relationship to itself: from the light proceed reason or understanding, and wisdom, and these two are one thing under the command of the soul—the energy and the beholding of energy, your spirit, and that signifies God the Holy Spirit, and this Holy Spirit is from God and rules also within this spirit, within you, if you are a child of light and not of darkness. "Now observe that in wood, stone, and herb nothing can yet be born and grow should one of the three be wanting. First is the energy, from which a body comes to be, and then the sap. The sap is the heart of a thing, its movement or vitality, and the third is a | welling up of energy, smell, and taste. That is the spirit of the thing. So when one of the three is lacking, no thing can endure."[43] Boehme therefore treats everything as this Trinity.

The first principle is therefore God the Father.[44] He is altogether the first, yet at the same time this first is essentially differentiated inwardly and is the unity of these two elements. God is everything, darkness and light, love and wrath, but he calls himself one

42. [*Ed.*] The quotation, and the sentence following, constitute an abridged paraphrase of *Aurora*, chap. 3, §§ 36–37 (*Theosophia revelata* 1:44–45). Hegel's other quotations from Boehme that follow are also paraphrased or are otherwise inexact. In this paragraph and the following one, as well as further on in this discussion of Boehme, *Kraft* is sometimes rendered as "power," although more often, in accord with our glossary, as "energy" or "force." For Boehme's position as presented here, *Kraft* is associated on the one hand with the (divine) "power" or "might" of the theological tradition, and (perhaps more importantly) on the other hand with the meaning of "energy" as source of vitality, as affirmed by the traditions of alchemy and natural philosophy.

43. [*Ed.*] For the quotation, see *Aurora*, chap. 3, § 47 (*Theosophia revelata* 1:46); cf. W 15:323–324 (Ms?). The sentence that precedes it draws upon *Aurora*, chap. 3, § 38 (*Theosophia revelata* 1:45).

44. [*Ed.*] See *Aurora*, chap. 3, § 14 (*Theosophia revelata* 1:39), which begins: "The Father is everything, and all power subsists in the Father: He is the beginning and the end of all things, and outside him there is nothing; all that has existed has done so from out of the Father."

God alone, in accordance with the light of his love. There is an eternal *contrarium* between darkness and light; neither of the two encompasses the other, and yet there is simply and solely one single essence. The principle of the concept was completely alive in Jacob Boehme, but he could not express it in the form of thought. "That one single [essence]," he says, "is differentiated by torment [*Qual*]." From this torment he derives "sources" or "springs" [*Quellen*], a good play on words. Torment is inward negativity; "springs" he calls vitality or activity, and he also correlates this term with "quality" [*Qualität*]—which he makes into *Quallität*—so that there are determinate distinctions. "[The one essence is differentiated] also by the will, and yet it is no disunited essence."[45] The absolute identity of distinctions is found throughout his works.

God the Father is therefore the first, but we must not expect a wholly determinate distinction here; when Boehme speaks of the first or of the One, it has at the same time very much a natural aspect, the aspect of the first natural being. He speaks of the simple essence, of the hidden God, as we have seen done before by the Neoplatonists. This first principle is also called the *temperamentum*, ⌐a neutralized [or harmonious] mode of being,⌐[46] as well as the great *Salitter*, which is the hidden one or the one not yet revealed.[47] He says: "But you must not think that God stands in

45. [*Ed.*] The account of God as the eternal *contrarium* of darkness and light, and so forth, is based on Boehme's 1622 treatise, *Von der Wahren Gelassenheit* (English: *Of True Resignation*), §§ 9–10 (*Theosophia revelata* 1:1673); cf. W 15:306 (Ms?). For Boehme's wordplay on *Qual-Quellen-Qualität*, see *Three Principles*, chap. 10, §§ 39–43 (*Theosophia revelata* 1:469–470).

46. *Thus Pn; An reads:* where what is distinct is moderated,

47. [*Ed.*] On the one simple essence, see Boehme's *Clavis* §§ 145–146 (*Theosophia revelata* 2:3696–3697). On God's hiddenness, see the 1623 essay, *Von der Gnadenwahl* (English: *On the Election of Grace*), chap. 2, §§ 19–20 (*Theosophia revelata* 2:2420), and n. 56, p. 000. On the Neoplatonists (Plotinus and Proclus), see W 15:48, 75. On *temperamentum*, again see n. 56. The fact that Hegel explains *temperamentum* as "a neutralized [or harmonious] mode of being" indicates that he is guided by the meaning of the verb *temperiren* ("to moderate"). On *Salitter* or *Salniter*, see W 15:307: "it is the shoemaker's mangling of the word *sal nitri* or saltpeter (which is still called *Salniter* in the Austrian dialect), therefore just the neutral, and in truth universal, essence." Hegel does not point out that Boehme characterizes the great *Salitter* in diverse ways. Here Hegel has in view the meaning given in the initial chapters of the *Aurora*, that the *Salitter* is one ele-

heaven or perhaps above the heavens, or that he seethes like an energy or a quality that has no reason and knowledge within it, like the sun, for instance, which takes its circular path and radiates warmth and light upon the earth and its creatures, whether for good or ill—No, God is not like that at all, but is an all-power-ful, | all-wise, all-knowing, all-seeing, all-hearing, all-smelling, all-tasting one who exists within himself as mild, cheerful, sweet, merciful, and joyful, indeed as joy itself."[48]

Boehme says that someone who considers the whole array [*curriculum*] of the stars readily recognizes it to be the source of nature. ˉSo all things areˉ[49] made from the same forces and are thus eternal.[50] The Father is what he calls all these forces, namely, the seven planets, the seven qualities such as the acrid, the bitter, the sweet, and so on. But here there is no determinate distinction by virtue of which there are precisely seven, ˉno thought-determination; with Boehme we find nothing fixed of that sort.ˉ[51] "But you must raise

ment of the heavenly *Pomp,* alongside which is the second, *Marcurius* or *Schall* ("sound"); see *Aurora,* chap. 4, §§ 13–14 and 9–10 (*Theosophia revelata* 1:50). Beginning with chapter 8, Boehme introduces the doctrine of the seven *Quellgeister* ("source-spirits"—including *Marcurius*), which are the dynamic attributes of the great *Salitter* that eternally both distinguish themselves from one another and beget one another. This *Salitter* has its consummation in the seventh *Quellgeist,* which is "body" or *Corpus* that is born from the other six. Boehme then calls this body or spirit the "*Salitter* of God" in the proper sense, but it is at the same time the *Salitter* of nature, since God's "body" is the source and ground for the powers and creatures of nature. See *Aurora,* chaps. 11, 15, and 16 (*Theosophia revelata* 1:118 ff.).

48. [*Ed.*] This slightly altered quotation from *Aurora,* chap. 3, § 11 (*Theosophia revelata* 1:38), transmitted by *Gr,* is not found in the other transcripts but is present in identical form in Rixner's *Handbuch* 2, appendix, p. 106 (§ 6). Griesheim doubt-less took this passage from Rixner rather than from Hegel's lectures, although Hegel may, in lecturing, have referred to it.

49. *An reads:* So they [the stars] are all *Pn reads:* Everything is *Lw reads:* All things are

50. [*Ed.*] On the stars as "mother of all things," see *Aurora,* chap. 2, § 15 (*Theosophia revelata* 1:30); cf. *W* 15:308 (Ms?).

51. *Thus Gr; Pn reads:* for they are not yet a thought-determination. *Lw reads:* for we are not to think of some exact thought-determination here.

[*Ed.*] This statement about the forces of the Father conjoins two distinct pas-sages: *Aurora,* chap. 4, § 6 (*Theosophia revelata* 1:48) refers to many different qual-ities that cohere in the Father as one force or energy and emanate from him; *Aurora,* chap. 3, § 18 (*Theosophia revelata* 1:40) discusses seven spirits of God that are

your mind up within spirit and consider the whole of nature, its breadth, depth, height, and so on—ˉall this isˉ⁵² the body of God, and the forces of the stars are the springs or veins [*Quell-Adern*] within the body of God in this world. It is not the whole triumphant, holy threefoldness of Son, Father, and Holy Spirit that is within the *corpus* of the stars, but rather power [*Kraft*] in general or the Father." Then he asks whence heaven acquires such energy. "Here you must look into the luminous, triumphant, divine energy and into the threefoldness. All the forces are within it, as they are within nature. This all, this heaven and earth, is the whole God who has thus made himself creaturely in such a multitude of beings." So when we consider nature we see God the Father, we behold in the stars God's strength and wisdom.⁵³

Boehme then proceeds to the second principle, that a separation must have taken place within this *temperamentum*.⁵⁴ "Without contrariety [*Widerwärtigkeit*] no thing can become manifest to itself. If it has nothing that stands against it, then it goes out and does not return into itself, and thus it knows nothing of its ˉoriginal condition [*Urstand*]."ˉ⁵⁵ He uses *Urstand* for "substance," and it

---

signified by the seven planets. These spirits are not yet explicitly designated as *Quellgeister*, as natural forces or qualities, but only as princes of the angels. The doctrine of seven *Quellgeister* or qualities in God is first developed in chaps. 8–11, whereas here Boehme speaks only of a simile wherein nature signifies the Father. The correspondence implied by Hegel, between the seven *Quellgeister* and the seven "planets" (actually, five planets plus sun and moon), only emerges explicitly in *Aurora*, chap. 26, § 37 (*Theosophia revelata* 1:352).

52. *Thus Pn; Lw reads:* everything is *Gr reads:* he says, heaven and stars are

53. [*Ed.*] These successive quotations are paraphrases from *Aurora*, chap. 2, §§ 16–17 and 31–33 (*Theosophia revelata* 1:16, 33–34). Hegel, however, is responsible for the statement that "power in general or the Father" is what is "within the *corpus* of the stars." Boehme himself writes (§ 17) of "the luminous-holy and eternal source of joy that is indivisible and unchangeable, that no creature can adequately grasp or express, and that is within itself, beyond the *corpus* of the stars." The last sentence is based on *Aurora*, chap. 3, § 8 (*Theosophia revelata* 1:37); cf. W 15:308–309 (Ms?).

54. *Thus Pn, An, similar in Gr; Lw adds:* Here he employs terminology that, regrettably, is not in ordinary use.

[*Ed.*] See n. 56 just below.

55. *Thus Gr; Pn reads:* original condition (understanding)." *An reads:* original condition (substance)."

[*Ed.*] See Boehme's incomplete 1622 essay, *Von göttlicher Beschaulichkeit* (En-

84 is a pity that we may not make use of this and so many | other striking expressions. Without contrariety life would have no sensible texture, no efficacy, no willing, no understanding and scientific knowledge. "Had the hidden God, who is one unified essence and will, not projected himself into divisibility of will, and had God not injected this divisibility into enclosedness or identity (return in the relation to self) so that this divisibility would not stand in conflict [with it]—how should God's will be manifest to him? How might there be a cognition in one unified will?"[56]

We see that Boehme is infinitely above that empty abstraction of the infinite, the eternal, the highest being, and the like.[57] He says: "The beginning of all beings is the Word as the breath of God, and God remains the One from all eternity. The Word is the beginning and eternally remains the eternal beginning—as revelation of the will of God." By the "Word" Boehme understands the revelation of the divine will. The Word is the emanation of the divine One and is yet God; what has emanated is the wisdom of all powers [Kräfte] (δύναμις). From such a revelation of all powers, in which the will of the eternal beholds itself, flow the understanding and ⁻scientific knowledge⁻[58] of the "something" or "selfhood" [Ichts], as opposed to the nothing [Nichts]—[this Ichts is] self-consciousness within the spirit, relation of vitality with itself. So the other [to God] is the image of God; Boehme calls this the Mysterium Magnum, the Separator, the creator of all creatures, the emanation of the will, which makes the One ⁻peaceably divided [schiedlich].⁻[59]

glish: Of Divine Contemplation), chap. 1, § 8 (Theosophia revelata 1:1739); cf. W 15:313 (Ms?).

56. [Ed.] See Of Divine Contemplation, chap. 1, §§ 9–10 (Theosophia revelata 1:1739); cf. W 15:313 (Ms?). The last quoted sentence in our text, however, should properly read (as does Boehme): "cognition of itself."

57. [Ed.] See below, p. 000.

58. Thus W; Lw reads: mode

59. Thus Boehme; An reads: definitive [schliesslich].

[Ed.] The German schiedlich, used by Boehme, means "peaceable," or "without strife." But it shares the same root with scheiden, which means "to divide or separate." What schiedlich suggests here is the peace that ensues when conflicting elements are parted in such a way that they can coexist harmoniously (hence, "peaceably divided"). For Boehme, the Separator or the Son converts the turmoil of powers in the Father into a stable structure of elements capable of mutual coexistence. There

The Son is the heart pulsating in the Father, the kernel in all energies, the cause of the burgeoning joy in all. From eternity the Son
of God is perpetually born from all the powers of his Father, he is
the brilliance that shines in the Father; if the Son did not thus shine
in the Father, then the Father would be a dark valley, the Father's
power would not ascend from eternity to eternity, and the divine
essence could not endure.[60]

So this *Ichts* is the Separator, what instigates, what draws dis-
tinctions. He also calls this *Ichts* Lucifer, the inborn Son | of God   85
and magistrate of nature. But this Lucifer has fallen, and this is the
origin of the evil in God and from God himself. Here we have Jacob
Boehme's greatest profundity. The *Ichts,* the self-knowing, the
egoity or selfhood, is what forms images of, or imagines, itself
within itself, it is the fire that consumes everything inwardly; this
[fire] is what is negative in the Separator, it is the wrath of God,
and it is hell and the Devil. The passing over of the *Ichts* (selfhood)
into nothing is the fact that the I, what has been distinguished,
imagines itself within itself.[61] In distinguishing, what has been dis-

---

follows in *Gr* at this point a long excerpt from Rixner's *Handbuch.* The themes in
this paragraph concerning the eternal beginning derive from *Of Divine Contemplation,* chap. 3, §§ 1–5 (*Theosophia revelata* 1:1755–1756); cf. *W* 15:313–316 (Ms?).
In both the lectures and *W* 15:314 Hegel erroneously has "the wisdom of all
powers," whereas Boehme has "wisdom, the beginning and cause of all powers."
The *Mysterium magnum* (1623), an exposition of the Book of Genesis, is a large
and more disciplined work of Boehme's maturity; Hegel might have gotten from it
a somewhat different picture of Boehme's thought, had he not instead concentrated
so much on the earlier and cruder formulations of the *Aurora.*

60. [*Ed.*] These points about the Son derive from *Aurora,* chap. 3, §§ 15, 20,
22 (*Theosophia revelata* 1:39–41).

61. [*Ed.*] In this paragraph of the text Hegel links various themes that Boehme
treats separately; he also makes a simple identification of selfhood (*Ichheit*) with
the *Ichts.* For Boehme the concept of the *Ichts* has its place in the consideration of
God apart from nature and creatures, in which God is designated as *Ungrund* (a
concept not found in Hegel's presentation) or as an "eternal nothing"; see *Mysterium magnum,* chap. 1, § 2 (*Theosophia revelata* 2:2717–2718). In the eternal
bringing-forth Boehme distinguishes: (1) an eternal will (Father); (2) an eternal heart
of the will; (3) an outgoing from these, which is a spirit of the will and heart. See
also n. 59 above. From Boehme's writings one cannot demonstrate an identification
of the *Ichts* with the Separator, or with Lucifer and with the "inborn" (thus *Gr,
Pn,* and *An*) or "firstborn" (thus *W* 15:316) Son. Hegel was probably led to make
these identifications by the fact that Boehme describes in somewhat similar terms

tinguished posits itself on its own account. Boehme says: "Heaven and Hell are as far from each other as are *Ichts* and nothing (*ens* and *non ens*), as day and night."[62]

He casts this theme into many forms, in order to grasp the *Ichts* or the Separator as it arouses itself within the Father, as it arises within him[63]—and Boehme finds this no easy matter. Here he takes up the qualities and energies within the Father, such as acridity, and then represents the going-forth of the *Ichts* as a contracting or sharpening, as a lightning bolt that breaks forth. The lightning bolt is the mother of the light, it gives birth to light and is the father of wrath [*Grimmigkeit*]. The lightning is what is absolutely fecund, the divine birth, the triumphing of all spirits as one spirit; all the energies are in one another. Each one of the seven spirits of God is totality. One gives birth to the others through itself. The divine birth is the arising of the lightning bolt that is the life of every quality.[64] Boehme says: "You must not think as though in heaven there is a particular *corpus* that one calls God; instead the divine power as a whole, [which is] heaven itself and the heaven of all heavens and from which all the angels of God, as well as the human spirit, are born, is called God the Father. This divine birth, this beginning

---

the functions of the Separator (in *Of Divine Contemplation*, chap. 3, § 12; *Theosophia revelata* 1:1757–1758) and Lucifer (*Aurora*, chap. 12, §§ 101–107 and chap. 13, §§ 31–34, 92–104). In treating Lucifer's fall, Boehme's intention is in fact to present it as Lucifer's own freely willed decision; see *Aurora*, chap. 13, §§ 31–35, 38–40, 46–48, and also *Mysterium magnum*, chap. 9, §§ 3–4 (*Theosophia revelata* 2:2754–2758). For Boehme's discussion of selfhood, see *Of Divine Contemplation*, chap. 1, §§ 18, 26 (*Theosophia revelata* 1:1741, 1743); for the link of God's wrath with hell, see *Aurora*, chap. 19, § 119.

62. [*Ed.*] See Boehme's 1622 dialogue, *Vom übersinnlichen Leben* (English: *Of the Supersensual Life*), § 42 (*Theosophia revelata* 1:1696). In W 15:317 Hegel refers to earlier forms of the comparison of *ens* and *non ens* with day and night; he probably has in mind Philo and Plotinus; cf. W 15:25, 62–63.

63. [*Ed.*] See nn. 59 and 61 above.

64. [*Ed.*] See *Aurora*, chap. 8, § 4, on the qualities in the Father, chap. 8, §§ 15–17, 19–20, on acridity, and chap. 10, §§ 33, 34, 38–40, 54, on the lightning in relation to the qualities and to wrath (*Theosophia revelata* 1:77 ff., and 111–115). The *Aurora* does not speak about the *Ichts*. Hegel connects Boehme's discussion of the origin of the qualities, and the breaking forth of the lightning bolt that is the life of all qualities (*Aurora*, chap. 10, § 33), with the theme of the divine birth (*Aurora*, chap. 11, §§ 5–13).

of heaven and earth, is everywhere. In God the Father there arises the lightning bolt or the Separator, and from the Separator the living God first is born. You can name no spot in heaven and earth where the divine birth of the threefoldness is not present; and all three Persons are born in your heart too." ˜The springing forth of the divine birth is everywhere.˜[65] | These are thus the fundamental determinations. The [divine] energy becomes also desirous and effectual, this energy is the original condition of sensuous life; eternally sensuous life originates within it, and the torment [*Quaal*] produces the ˜effective sensibility.˜[66]

In the *Quaestiones theosophicae* Boehme also employs, especially for the Separator, the antithesis or the forms of Yes and No.[67] In the *Aurora* he divides the sciences into philosophy, astrology, and theology; philosophy [deals] with the divine power, with what God is, and how everything is created; astrology, with forces of nature and of the stars; theology, with the kingdom of Christ, how it is opposed to the kingdom of Hell.[68] Boehme says: "You should know that all things consist of Yes and No, that the One as the Yes is energy and life—it is the energy of God and is God himself. But this truth would itself be unknowable without the No. The No is a counterstroke to the Yes, to the truth, so that the truth may be manifest, may be something, so that there may be a *contrarium* [to the No, namely], ˜the eternal love.˜[69] Nevertheless the Yes is not sundered from the No, they are not two things alongside one another, but only *one thing*. Of themselves, however, they separate into two beginnings, they constitute two centers. Without them

86

65. *Thus Pn; similar in An, Lw; Gr reads:* The Separator thus first bears the living God.
[*Ed.*] For the preceding quotation, and this sentence, see *Aurora*, chap. 10, §§ 55, 58, 60 (*Theosophia revelata* 1:115–116); cf. W 15:322–323 (Ms?).

66. *Thus An; Lw reads:* free sensibility. *Pn reads:* actual vitality.
[*Ed.*] On sensuous life, see *Of Divine Contemplation*, chap. 3, §§ 11–12 (*Theosophia revelata* 1:1757).

67. [*Ed.*] This treatise of 1624 is also called *Von 177 theosophischen Fragen* (English: *Theosophical Questions*). On the Yes and No, see n. 72 just below.

68. [*Ed.*] On this division of the sciences, see *Aurora*, preface, §§ 84–88 (*Theosophia revelata* 1:18–19); cf. W 15:305–306 (Ms?).

69. *Thus Pn; An reads:* for one to love. *Gr reads:* whereby to recognize what is true. *Lw reads:* that there may be something sensitive, the truth, a fountain of love.

both, all things would be nothing and would stand still. Without them there is no understanding, for understanding originates in distinctiveness within multiplicity. The will that has ⁻opened up [*aufgeschlossen*]⁻[70] develops dissimilarity in order to be something of its own, in order that there may be something that sees and senses the eternal ⁻seeing.⁻[71] The No originates from the eternal will. In the No the Yes has something that it can will, in the No the Yes becomes manifest. We call it No because it is an inward-turned desire, negatively closing in on itself. This will that withdraws within itself grasps itself; the grasping of self is the lightning bolt or *Schrack*. Therefore the light originates amidst the darkness, for the unity becomes a light. The receptivity of the desiring will becomes | a spirit. It has its torment in what is acrid. Accordingly, that is, according to the withdrawal, God is angry or jealous, and therein lies evil."[72] This is the main characteristic of the second principle.

87

The third principle of the threefoldness is the unity of the light, the Separator, and the energy; this, then, is the Spirit. "In the entire depths of the Father there is nothing besides the Son, and this unity of Father and Son in the depths is the Spirit—an all-knowing, all-seeing, all-smelling, all-hearing, all-feeling, all-tasting spirit."[73] The sensible itself, smell and taste, is also spirit. The abyss of nature is God himself. God is not something remote that has its own particular position or place; on the contrary, the divine birth is everywhere.[74]

These are Boehme's main thoughts. On the one hand their articulation is unmistakably barbarous, and in order to put his thought into words he employs powerful, sensuous images such as *Salitter*, Tincture, Essence, *Qual, Schrack,* and the like. On the

70. *Thus Pn; W and Boehme read:* flowed out [*ausgeflossen*]
71. *Thus W and Boehme; Pn reads:* being.
72. [*Ed.*] This long quotation derives from *Theosophical Questions*, question 3, §§ 2–5 and 10–13 (*Theosophia revelata* 2:3591–3594); cf. *W* 15:319–321 (Ms?).
73. [*Ed.*] The quotation is from *Aurora*, chap. 3, § 30 (*Theosophia revelata* 1:43).
74. [*Ed.*] On the abyss (*Abgrund*) and the divine omnipresence, see *Of Divine Contemplation*, chap. 3, § 13 (*Theosophia revelata* 1:1758).

other hand, however, there is here undeniably the ¯greatest¯[75] profundity, one that grapples with the forceful unification of the most absolute antitheses. Boehme grasps the antitheses in the harshest, crudest fashion, but he does not let their obstinacy deter him from positing their unity.

We have still to mention Boehme's pious nature, the edifying element or the journey of the soul in his writings.[76] This path is profound and inward to the highest degree, it is moving and full of sensibility, and someone familiar with Boehme's own forms will discover this depth and inwardness; but of course we cannot completely reconcile ourselves to the form his thought takes—¯especially not in its details.¯[77] With this comment we conclude our discussion of the preliminary period of modern philosophy and proceed to its first period proper, which we begin with Descartes. | 88

B. FIRST PERIOD OF METAPHYSICS: DESCARTES, SPINOZA, MALEBRANCHE

1. Nature and Periods of Modern Philosophy

Now we come for the first time to what is properly the philosophy of the modern world, and we begin it with Descartes. Here, we may say, we are at home and, like the sailor after a long voyage, we can at last shout "Land ho." Descartes made a fresh start in every respect. The thinking or philosophizing, the thought and the formation of reason in modern times, begins with him. The principle in this new era is thinking, the thinking that proceeds from itself. We have exhibited this inwardness above all with respect to Christianity; it is preeminently the Protestant principle. The universal princi-

75. *Thus Gr, Lw; Pn reads:* utmost *An reads:* most extreme
76. [*Ed.*] In addition to the biographical accounts, Hegel probably is referring to the three, more mystical than theosophical, writings of 1622 collectively entitled *Der Weg zu Christo* (English: *The Way to Christ*), which later were well known in pietist circles: *Von wahrer Busse* (English: *Of True Repentance*), together with two works already cited, *Of True Resignation* (n. 45), and *Of the Supersensual Life* (n. 62); see *Theosophia revelata* 1:1621–1704. The first publication of Boehme's writings, in 1624, also bore this title, *Der Weg zu Christo*.
77. *Thus Pn; Gr reads:* one that admits of no definite view about its details.

ple now is to hold fast to inwardness as such, to set dead externality and sheer authority aside and to look upon it as something not to be allowed. In accordance with this principle of inwardness it is now thinking, thinking on its own account, that is the purest pinnacle of this inwardness, the inmost core of inwardness—thinking is what now establishes itself on its own account.[78] This period begins with Descartes. What is deemed valid or what has to be acknowledged is thinking freely on its own account, and this can happen only through my thinking freely within myself; only in this way can it be authenticated for me. This means equally that this thinking is a universal occupation or principle for the world in general and for individuals. Human beings must acknowledge and scrutinize in their own thoughts whatever is said to be normative, whatever in the world is said to be authoritative; what is to rank as established must have authenticated itself by means of thought.

As a result we find ourselves once more in the properly philosophical domain for the first time since the ˉNeoplatonist and Neopythagorean school.ˉ[79] That is why in the older histories of

78. [Ed.] With the reference to a "pinnacle" of inwardness Hegel establishes a connection between, on the one hand, the philosophy of Descartes and modern philosophy as a whole and, on the other, Christianity and Neoplatonism, for in discussing Neoplatonism he used the phrase "pinnacle of actual being" (Spitze des Seyenden) to render Proclus's ἀκρότης τῶν ὄντων. This pinnacle of actual being is further defined, in W 15:84 (Ms?), as "what is centered on self [das Selbstische], what has being-for-self, the subjective, the point of individual unity." Hegel also sees (in W 15:114–115) a parallel development in Christianity: "For human beings there has dawned in their consciousness of the world the fact that the absolute has attained this ἀκρότης of concreteness—the pinnacle of immediate actuality; and this is the appearance of Christianity." Whereas this "pinnacle of immediate actuality" attained in Christianity bears the mark above all of the moment of spatial and temporal finitude, in both Neoplatonism and Cartesian philosophy the determinations of its content occur in terms of the subjective, of what has being-for-self. This shows that Hegel regards modern philosophy, beginning with Descartes, as taking up again or resuming the history of philosophy, a history interrupted by the Middle Ages. See also the following note.

79. Thus Pn; Gr, Lw read: Neoplatonist school and associated movements.

[Ed.] This view that modern philosophy follows upon the philosophy of late antiquity is based not only on the scant importance Hegel attached to the Middle Ages as far as the history of philosophy was concerned, as a period "which we intend to get through by putting on seven-league boots" (see p. 000 above), but also on his supposition of an agreement in content between the philosophers of late antiquity

philosophy too, dating from the seventeenth century, we find only Greek and Roman philosophy treated, and Christianity forms the conclusion, as if in Christianity and from then on there had been no more philosophy because it was no longer necessary; this is how Stanley, for instance, presents it in his history of philosophy.[80] The philosophical theology of the Middle Ages did not have as its principle the free thought that proceeds from itself. But now this thinking | is the principle, although we must not expect to find here 89 a philosophical system that develops from thought methodically. Thinking is the principle, and what is deemed valid is valid only through thinking. The ancient postulate is presupposed: in order to know truth we must attain it by meditative thinking alone. That is plainly the foundation.

This still does not, however, involve developing the concrete, the many, and our worldview, from thought itself; it does not involve demonstrating the definition of God and the determination of the phenomenal world as proceeding necessarily from thought. On the contrary we have only a thinking, the thinking of a content, that is *given* by representation, by observation, by experience. On the one hand we have a metaphysics, on the other the particular sciences. The elements that are joined together in this thought are thinking as such and the material of thought derived from consciousness or from experience. We shall, of course, encounter the antithesis between a priori thinking, in which the determinations that are to be valid for thinking are to be taken from thinking itself, and empiricism as the specification that we must take experience as our starting point, that it is from experience that we must draw our conclusions, do our thinking, and so on. We will con-

---

and those of modern times regarding the concept of the self-thinking thought; see, for example, W 15:13: "The fundamental idea of this Neopythagorean—also Neoplatonic or Alexandrian—philosophy was the thinking that thinks itself, the νοῦς, which has itself for object." This theme also links these two periods to Aristotelian metaphysics and to the Christian doctrine of the Trinity. See also the preceding note.

80. [Ed.] See Thomas Stanley's *Historia philosophiae* (Leipzig, 1711). Hegel's statement is probably not to be understood as a general assertion about all older histories of philosophy. Georg Horn's *Historiae philosophicae libri septem* ... (Leiden, 1655) is one example to which the criticism would not apply.

sider this antithesis again later on. Though it is the antithesis between rationalism and empiricism, it is but an antithesis of the second rank, because even the kind of philosophizing that wishes to grant validity only to immanent thought, even rationalism, does not develop its determinations methodically from the principle of thought [alone] but also takes its material from inner or outer experience.

The first form of philosophy that thinking generates is metaphysics, the form of the reflective understanding [*denkendes Verstand*]. The second form is skepticism and criticism directed against this reflective understanding. To metaphysics as the first form belong Descartes, Spinoza, Leibniz, and others, [as well as] the French materialists. The second attitude is negative toward the first; it is the critique of metaphysics, and it attempts to consider cognitive knowing on its own account, so that its determinations are deduced from cognition itself | and dealt with as determinations that develop out of cognition itself. ˉThe first period of metaphysicsˉ[81] includes Descartes, Spinoza, and Malebranche. The third stage, [which is] the second period of metaphysics, [includes] Leibniz,

90

81. *An reads:* In the first period of metaphysics [one] *Pn, Sv read:* The first period is (*Sv adds:* therefore) that of metaphysics [and it] *Lw reads:* The first period (first period of metaphysics)

[*Ed.*] The relationships between the stages and periods referred to here in the text of this paragraph are somewhat obscure, and this obscurity is evident in the incongruities among the sources. The distinction between a first form of philosophy generated by thought, and a second form marked by a skeptical, critical attitude toward the first, corresponds essentially to the subdivision of the second epoch of modern philosophy in the 1823–24 lectures (see W 15:274–275, section b: (α) Metaphysics, (β) Skepticism). But the way in which these 1825–26 lectures are articulated does not reflect this idea of a historical link between a metaphysical period and an ensuing skeptical period. What Hegel terms the "first period of metaphysics" is, in the structure of this series, in fact the second stage of modern philosophy, which treats Descartes, Spinoza, and Malebranche. If he sometimes, as here, also regards it as the initial stage in the history of modern philosophy proper, that is because the actual first stage, represented by Bacon and Boehme, does not yet belong to philosophy in the full sense of the term. This dual sense of Hegel's references to a "first period" is most clearly expressed by *Lw*, probably after subsequent reflection on Hegel's conception of these philosophical stages. The second—the skeptical or antimetaphysical—attitude probably comprises in the main Hobbes, Hume, and aspects of the Kantian philosophy (which Hegel discusses at various places in the third and fourth stages).

Locke, and Wolff; the fourth stage is the philosophy of Kant, Fichte, and Schelling.

René Descartes is the initiator of philosophy in the modern world insofar as it makes thought its principle. Here thinking on its own account is distinguished from philosophizing theology, which it puts on the other side. What we have here is an entirely new territory.

2. René Descartes

The biographical data on Descartes (in Latin, Cartesius) are as follows. He was born of old, noble stock in 1596 at La Haye, a small town in the province of Touraine, in Normandy.[82] He received the customary education in a Jesuit school where he made great progress, being of a lively and restless spirit, seizing upon everything and sampling all manner of systems and forms, studying in particular philosophy, mathematics, chemistry, physics, astronomy, and other subjects. When he was ˜seventeen˜[83] years of age he developed a dislike for bookish study but retained his zeal for the sciences. He went to Paris and threw himself into the whirl of Paris life for a considerable time. Then he returned to his studies, withdrawing to a Paris suburb where for two years he lived hidden from all his acquaintances and occupied himself uninterruptedly with the ˜study of mathematics.˜[84] Only after these two years did his friends redis-

82. [Ed.] The sources for Hegel's biographical data in this paragraph are Brucker (*Historia* 4, pt. 2:203–207), Buhle (*Geschichte* 3, pt. 1:4 ff.), and Tennemann (*Geschichte* 10:210 ff.). The belief that Descartes's family belonged to the old nobility goes back to an erroneous report in Adrien Baillet's two-volume biography, *La vie de Monsieur Des-Cartes* (Paris, 1691), 1:2. Baillet's error was repeated in most subsequent histories of philosophy, including Brucker's (*Historia* 4, pt. 2:20). Descartes's father belonged to the "nobility of the robe" (families recently ennobled for services to the Crown), and it was only in 1668, after the philosopher's death, that his family received the letters of nobility. Hegel's statement about Descartes's birthplace (confirmed by multiple transcripts) combines reports derived from Tennemann and others, which correctly give Descartes's birthplace as La Haye in Touraine, with Buhle's erroneous statement (*Geschichte* 3, pt. 1:4) that he was born at La Haye in Normandy (which fostered the misconception that Touraine is a part of Normandy).

83. *Thus An; Gr reads:* eighteen *Lw reads:* seventeen or eighteen *Sv reads:* twenty-eight

84. *Thus Lw; Gr reads:* sciences.

cover him, bring him out of his solitude, and introduce him once again into the larger world. Now he put his studies entirely aside and threw himself into actual life. He went to Holland and entered military service. Soon thereafter, in 1619, the first year of the Thirty

91 Years | War, he entered the service of Bavaria [as] a volunteer and served in several campaigns under [Count von] Tilly. For instance, he was present at the Battle of Prague, when Frederick of the Palatinate lost the crown.[85] In winter quarters he studied diligently and—for instance, in the imperial city of Ulm—made the acquaintance of townsfolk who were engaged in mathematics. At Neuburg on the Danube he was fired anew by the urge to reform philosophy. He vowed to the Virgin Mary that he would undertake a pilgrimage to Loretto if ⌐he succeeded in his design to accomplish great things in the field of knowledge.¬[86] In 1624 he left military service and made several journeys through Germany, Poland, Prussia, and other lands, and from 1629 to 1644 he lived in Holland, where he wrote and published most of his works.[87] ⌐His writings include many controversial pieces and essays defending himself against repeated attacks by the clergy.¬[88] Several members of the clergy

---

[Ed.] According to Baillet and Brucker, this first withdrawal into solitude in Paris lasted from 1614 to 1616. When, as the text continues, his friends did "introduce him once again into the larger world," he did not engage in a life of pleasure, as before; on the contrary, as the text indicates, he went to Holland and there entered military service. Hegel's account reflects that of Brucker (*Historia* 4, pt. 2:208), who speaks of Descartes being led back to his former pleasures, but adds that this did not divert him from the study of philosophy.

85. [Ed.] The report that Descartes was present at the Battle of Prague comes from Baillet (*La vie . . .* , 1:72–73); today it is questioned.

86. *Thus Lw; Gr reads:* he succeeded in penetrating to the core of philosophy. *Pn reads:* she would assist him.

87. [Ed.] In fact Descartes's military service ended in 1620; Hegel's error derives from Buhle (*Geschichte* 3, pt. 1:7). Descartes's residence in Holland began at the end of 1628; Hegel's error on this derives from Tennemann (*Geschichte* 10:210). Tennemann (pp. 210–216) is also Hegel's main source for the remainder of this paragraph, especially what is said about the intrigues and attacks by the clergy. Except for occasional trips to France, Descartes remained in Holland until 1649; possibly Hegel mentions 1644 because Descartes took an extended journey to France in that year.

88. *Thus Gr; Pn reads:* He had to defend himself against many attacks on the part of the clergy. *Sv reads:* He incurred the hostility of the clergy.

resorted to intrigue in their attacks on him. Finally Queen Christina of Sweden invited him to her court in Stockholm, which was at that time the gathering place for famous scholars, and here he died in 1650.

Descartes inaugurated a new period in mathematics as well as in philosophy. His method still constitutes the essential basis of present-day analytic geometry, for he was a pioneer [in this field] too.[89] He also cultivated physics, optics, astronomy, and other subjects. Within his philosophy we must distinguish what alone has primary interest for us from what does not; hence we leave aside his application of metaphysics to particular questions (including ecclesiastical matters and investigations). Our concern is to distinguish the very course of his thoughts and the way in which he deduced and demonstrated them. To do justice to his thoughts, we must for our part be familiar or conversant with the necessity in the progression of these determinations. The method by which his thoughts are deduced is not one we can find particularly satisfactory. |

92

Descartes began at the beginning, ˉfromˉ[90] the universal, from thinking as such, and this is a new and absolute beginning. His contention that the beginning must be made from thought alone he expressed by saying that we must doubt everything, *de omnibus est dubitandum*—but not in the skeptical sense that we must remain in this doubt, in this complete indecision of the mind [*Geist*] that finds its freedom there and so achieves peace of mind. Cartesian doubt means instead that we must renounce every presupposition and prejudice and commence from thinking just in order to proceed

---

[*Ed.*] See in particular Descartes's letter to Gisbert Voet, in *Œuvres de Descartes,* ed. Charles Adam and Paul Tannery, 13 vols., rev. ed. (Paris, 1964–1972), 8, pt. 2:1–194.

89. [*Ed.*] Hegel is referring to Descartes's *Geometry,* a work published at Leiden in 1637 as an example of the application of the method developed in the concurrently published *Discourse on Method.* Hegel had studied Descartes's *Geometry* in Victor Cousin's edition of Descartes's works (Paris, 1824), 5:309–428; he refers specifically to it (pp. 357 ff.) in his *Science of Logic,* pp. 289–290 (cf. GW 21:287–288).

90. *Pn reads:* in

from thinking to something firm, in order that we may attain a pure beginning. The skeptics do not have this same need to arrive at something firm, since for them doubt is the outcome.[91]

The first point, therefore, is that we must make no presuppositions; this is a very great and important principle. The reason why we must make no presuppositions Descartes gives in his own fashion as follows. We find that our senses are often mistaken about the sensible world, so we cannot presuppose that sense experience is certain and it is therefore imprudent to rely on it. Nor can we trust our representations. This is a matter of empirical experience. We know that in our dreams we suppose we have before us many things, or we admit of innumerable things, that at no time exist, and we can provide no sign nor any definite criterion by which we distinguish through observation what appears to us in ˜sleep˜[92] from our representations in the waking state. It is the same with mathematical propositions; these too may inspire us with doubt, for many people err in that which is held to be most certain, and many things are accepted as valid that subsequently appear to be false. We have been told that God created us[93]; but to take this as our starting point leaves open the possibility that God created us as liable to error. Were we | not created by God but by ourselves, it would be even more probable that we are so imperfect as to err.[94]

These are Descartes's reasons. Hence his requirement is that thinking should proceed from itself and that therefore no presupposition may be made, since every presupposition is something

93

---

91. [*Ed.*] In this exposition of the Cartesian principle of doubt, as presented in the *Discourse on Method* and the *Principles of Philosophy*, Hegel bases himself on Spinoza's statement in his treatise, *Descartes' "Principles of Philosophy"*: "he sought to call all things into doubt, not as a Skeptic would, who has no other end than doubting, but to free his mind from all prejudices, so that in the end he might discover firm and unshakable foundations of the sciences" (*The Collected Works of Spinoza*, ed. Curley, 1:231; see below, n. 146, for the full reference). See also the paraphrase of this passage in W 15:335 (Ms?).

92. *Thus Gr; Pn reads:* dreams

93. *Gr adds:* and in consequence we would have this representation

94. [*Ed.*] In this paragraph Hegel follows quite closely Descartes's presentation in the *Principles of Philosophy*, pt. 1, §§ 4–5. See *The Philosophical Writings of Descartes*, trans. John Cottingham, Robert Stoothoff, and Dugald Murdoch, 2 vols. (Cambridge, 1985), 1:193–194; *Œuvres* 8, pt. 1:5–6; cf. W 15:336–337 (Ms?).

found already there that thinking has not posited, something other than thinking; and thinking is not present to itself in the presupposition. The so-called immediate intuition or inward revelation of our modern period falls under this heading too.[95] Thinking is to be the point of departure; it is the interest of freedom that is the foundation. Whatever is recognized as true must present itself in such a way that our freedom is preserved in the fact that we think. In the Cartesian form [of this position] the stress is not on the principle of freedom as such, but instead on reasons more popular in tone, namely, that we must make no presuppositions because it is possible to be mistaken. The second proposition is that we must seek what is certain. What is certain is certainty [Gewissheit] itself, knowing [Wissen] as such, in its pure form as relating itself to itself—this is thinking. Once we have jettisoned in this way whatever we are able to doubt, this point is all we are left with.

This "I think" is then the starting point—it is what is utterly certain (just as Fichte too begins with immediate knowing), it presents itself within me.[96] The next to enter on the scene is the determination of being, and so Descartes says, "cogito ergo sum, I think therefore I am." About anything we can doubt that it is—God, corporeal things, the world, and so on—except that we cannot doubt that *we* are. We cannot think about ourselves that we do not exist. The determination of being is immediately [bound up] with the I; ˜the pure I or this cogito is immediately bound up with it.˜[97] "This is the first and most certain knowledge of all, and it presents itself to anyone who philosophizes in an orderly fashion."[98] This is the famous cogito ergo sum; in it thinking and being are thus inseparably bound together.

From one side we view this proposition as a syllogism: being is

95. [Ed.] Hegel's reference is to Jacobi. See pp. 000–000 below.

96. [Ed.] Here Hegel interprets the first proposition of Fichte's *Wissenschaftslehre* in the sense of immediate knowing; see pp. 000–000 below.

97. *Thus Lw; Gr reads:* the pure I is cogito. *An reads:* when I think, I have the being of my I.

98. [Ed.] Hegel's account, beginning with the final sentence of the preceding paragraph and ending at this point, is based fairly closely on Descartes's *Principles of Philosophy*, pt. 1, § 7 (*Writings* 1:194–195; *Œuvres*, 8, pt. 1:6–7); cf. W 15:339 (Ms?).

94   deduced from thinking. Against this logical connection Kant | objected that being is not contained in thinking, that it is distinct from thinking, and he is quite correct.[99] They are, however, inseparable, that is, they constitute an identity. What is inseparable [from another] is nonetheless distinct [from it], although the identity is not endangered by this difference; the two are a unity. All the same, this is not a syllogism, for a syllogism comprises three terms; [needed] here is a third term that would mediate between thinking and being. But that is not how it is. It is not "I think, therefore I am"—the "therefore" is not here the "therefore" of the syllogism, for it expresses only the correlation by which being is immediately linked with thinking.[100] In Descartes, therefore, we see expressed the identity of being and thinking.

Gassendi raised a second objection, namely, that I can equally well say, "*Ludificor, ergo sum*—I am tricked by my consciousness, therefore I exist." Descartes himself was very well aware that there is some force to this objection. He says, "I conceive 'thinking' as embracing whatever takes place in our consciousness, to the extent that we ourselves are conscious of it; willing, sensation, imagining, and so on—all this is also contained in it." If I say "I see, I go for a walk," the I is [implicit] in the determination of seeing or of going, but I am in it also as thinking. When I say "I," that *is* thinking. It is absurd to suppose that the soul has thinking in one particular pocket and sensation, seeing, wishing, and the like in another. Thinking is what is wholly universal. Thought represented as what is thinking *is* the I; it is the universal, which is also present in wishing, feeling, going, and so forth. Descartes says, "In seeing, walking, and the like there is involved at the same time something that occurs through a bodily function." Therefore the conclusion here is not absolutely certain, for in dreams it can often happen that

99. [*Ed.*] See below, n. 428.

100. [*Ed.*] In his "Reply to the Second Set of Objections" (to the *Meditations*), Descartes holds that we recognize the connection "by a simple intuition of the mind." If this recognition involved a syllogism, the "third term" needed would be the major premise: Everything that thinks is, or exists. But the recognition actually comes directly from our own experience: I cannot think without existing. See *Writings* 2:100; *Œuvres* 7:140–141; cf. the condensed translation in W 15:340 (Ms?).

we believe we are walking. Sensing and representing are no longer 95
universal thinking, and it is only with the universal that being is
immediately bound up.[101] |

To have insight into this identity is quite easy. Thinking is the
wholly universal, not the particular—seeing, walking, and the like.
In everything particular there is the universal too; thinking is reference to self, it is the universal, reference of self to self, pure being
at one with self. When we speak of "being," therefore, we must
not represent to ourselves something particular, the being of some
concrete content. If we do that, then "being" means nothing but
simple immediacy. Thinking is movement within self, but pure reference to self, pure identity with self. This is being too. Immediacy
is being. Thinking is this same immediacy, but it is at the same time
also mediation with itself—it is its *self-negating* mediation with
itself, and therefore it is immediacy too. "Immediacy" is a one-
sided determination; thinking contains it, but not it alone, for
thinking also contains the determination of mediating itself with
itself; and by virtue of the fact that the mediating is at the same
time the sublation of the mediating, it is also immediacy. In thinking there is certainly being. "Being" is a much poorer determination
than "thinking," it is what is abstracted from the concrete[ness] of
thinking. Next, then, we must consider Descartes's metaphysics,
where the unity of being and thinking is primary, and where thinking is taken as pure thinking.

Descartes offered no proof of this thesis of the unity of thinking
and being. Thinking and being are different determinations, so
the proof of their identity must be expressly furnished, and this
Descartes fails to do.

---

101. [*Ed.*] Gassendi's argument is in the "Fifth Set of Objections" to the *Meditations* (*Writings* 2:180; *Œuvres* 7:258–259). Descartes's direct reply is that
metaphysical certainty attaches to the act of thinking alone, not to walking or to
other kinds of acts, which can always be doubted (*Writings*, 2:243–244; *Œuvres*
7:352). Hegel's rebuttal in the text draws upon the *Principles of Philosophy*, where
the stress shifts to the sensory awareness (a kind of thinking) of walking and the
like, from which Descartes concludes that he exists even though it might be false
that he is walking (*Writings* 1:195; *Œuvres* 8, pt. 1:7–8). Statements about "having
thinking in one particular pocket" and about thinking as the universal are Hegel's
own embellishments and are not found in Descartes. Cf. *W* 15:341–342 (Ms?).

For the present, therefore, that is where we stand. This is on the whole the most interesting idea of modern philosophy, and Descartes was at any rate the first to formulate it.

Consciousness is certain of itself; with the "I think," being is posited. Consciousness now seeks to extend its cognitive knowledge and finds that it has within itself representations of many things. What matters here is the progression from abstract unity to greater concreteness. Descartes goes to work in an externally reflec-96 tive way. | We find within ourselves all manner of representations, and consciousness is not deceived about this so long as it does not insist that there is something similar and objective outside it.[102]

I am presenting this in the way Descartes does. Among the diverse representations that ˜we have˜[103] there is also one of a supremely intelligent, supremely powerful and absolutely perfect being, and this is the most excellent of all our representations. The question now arises, "Is this a merely contingent representation, or one that is necessary and eternal?" Descartes replies: "There is this one necessary representation, that the universal or what we call 'God' *is*."[104] For the universal is supposed to be just that in whose representation necessary existence is contained.

This had already been said by Anselm, that "God is what is most perfect." The question then arises, "But does this most perfect [being] also exist?" This is an illegitimate question. For what is most perfect is supposed to be just that in whose concept existence already lies. That is [the definition of] ˜what is most perfect˜[105]— existence and representation are bound up together in it. This idea is therefore a presupposition. We would say now that we find this idea within ourselves as the highest idea: that the One *is*. So it is

102. [*Ed.*] See *Principles of Philosophy*, pt. 1, § 13 (*Writings* 1:197; *Œuvres* 8, pt. 1:9); cf. W 15:345 (Ms?).
103. *Thus Lw; Pn reads:* Descartes takes up in a . . . [*illegible*] naive sequence
104. [*Ed.*] See *Principles of Philosophy*, pt. 1, § 14 (*Writings* 1:197–198; *Œuvres* 8, pt. 1:10); cf. W 15:346–347 (Ms?). Where Hegel speaks of "representation" here, Descartes has "idea." In the next paragraph of our text, which reintroduces Anselm, Hegel shifts to "idea" and speaks of "the idea of God" as "the shape of a representation that I have within me."
105. *An reads:* what is perfect
[*Ed.*] See n. 33, p. 000 above.

presupposed in this way, and if we ask whether this idea also exists, that is precisely what the idea is: that with it existence is posited too. Here in the form of God no other unity is expressed than the one found in *cogito ergo sum*—being and thinking inseparably linked. *Cogito* means consciousness as pure thinking. Here with the idea of God we have the shape of a representation that I have within me. The entire content of this representation—the Almighty, the All-wise, and so forth—consists in predicates that emerge only subsequently. The content itself, which is all that we are concerned with, is the content of *the idea,* of pure thought, of what is purely all-embracing, of the universal, bound up with existence, with actuality, with being.

Hence we see these determinations following upon one another in an empirical and naive manner, one that is therefore not philosophically or | metaphysically demonstrative. Descartes says: "This concept is not made by us. We do not find in ourselves the perfections that are contained in this representation; it is given to us as eternal truth."[106] The same thing is then said in a quite different form: we are absolutely certain that God is, and this absolute certainty is the *proof* that God *is.* Descartes continues: "We must believe what is revealed to us by God, although we do not directly conceive it. We must not be surprised that it surpasses our capability." Here he falls into a commonplace view. "˜On this account˜[107] we must not weary ourselves with investigations. [For instance,] freedom of will and divine foreknowledge are both certain, only we do not know how to unite them."

The first attribute of God is that God is truthful, that God is the

97

106. [*Ed.*] See *Principles of Philosophy,* pt. 1, §§ 15, 18 (*Writings* 1:198–199; *Œuvres* 8, pt. 1:10, 12). Descartes says the idea of a highest being or a sum of all perfections represents "a true and immutable nature"; here he does not call it "eternal truth" (Hegel's term). On Descartes's distinction between thing (*res*) and eternal truth, see n. 111 below. Cf. *W* 15:351 (Ms?). Hegel's restatement of the point in the text sentence that follows refers in particular to Jacobi; see pp. 000–000 below.

107. *Thus W and Descartes; An reads: Yet*
[*Ed.*] The preceding "quotation," on revelation, paraphrases *Principles of Philosophy,* pt. 1, § 25 (*Writings* 1:201; *Œuvres* 8, pt. 1:14). This one is loosely based on §§ 26 and 41 (*Writings* 1:201–202, 206; *Œuvres* 8, pt. 1:14, 20); cf. *W* 15:352 (Ms?).

giver of all light. So it is quite contrary to God's nature to deceive us. Hence what we can, by our cognitive capacities, discern as clear and distinct for us, is the case, is true; what is thought, what is rightly and clearly discerned, is the case because God has given us the capacity of thought.[108] What is asserted here then is that through thinking we experience how things are in fact; God's truthfulness is made into the absolute bond between subjective cognition and the actuality of what is thus known. We shall see this expressed even more definitely in Malebranche.[109]

We have here the antithesis between subjective cognition and actuality. At one moment we are told the two are inseparably linked, that thinking is being. The next moment they are regarded as different, so that the need to mediate them arises, and the proof of their unity rests on the mediating. Set forth here on one side is ˉour subjective cognition,ˉ[110] and on the other side actuality. What mediates between them is the | truthfulness of God or the truth of God. This truth itself is in its turn none other than the fact that the idea of God immediately contains actuality within itself as well. We call the concept and its reality "truth"; so these linkages of idea and actuality are for us only represented in different relations. These are the fundamental characteristics [of the Cartesian metaphysics].

Descartes continues as follows: "What comes under our consciousness we consider either as things or as their qualities, or else as eternal truths in us as inborn and innate ideas (*ideae innatae*) that we have not constructed."[111] The expression "eternal truths"

98

108. [*Ed.*] The first two sentences of this paragraph come directly from *Principles of Philosophy*, pt. 1, § 29; the third is a paraphrase from § 30 (*Writings* 1:203; *Œuvres* 8, pt. 1:16). Cf. W 15:352–353 (Ms?).

109. [*Ed.*] See below, pp. 000–000.

110. *Thus An, Lw; Gr reads:* our cognition, *Pn reads:* our cognition as subjective,

111. [*Ed.*] The "quotation" paraphrases the initial sentence of *Principles of Philosophy*, pt. 1, § 48 (*Writings* 1:208; *Œuvres* 8, pt. 1:22), but in such a way as to identify "eternal truths" with "innate ideas." Hegel is therefore disregarding Descartes's definition (in the Third Meditation) of "idea" as a thought that is an image of a thing, although he seems to refer to this same passage when he mentions "innate ideas that we have not constructed." Actually Descartes here distinguishes three kinds of ideas: innate, adventitious, and those "invented by me" (*Writings* 2:25–26; *Œuvres* 7:37–38). On innate ideas, see also the Fifth Meditation (*Writings* 2:44; *Œuvres* 7:64).

has remained in current usage down to the present time. It signifies universal, wholly universal, determinations or wholly universal [logical] connections, and these are here represented as innate with us.[112] The expression "innate" is misleading because it denotes a natural mode and is not suited to spirit; so it [the innateness of truth] is a content grounded in the nature of our spirit. Spirit is active, and in its activity it behaves in a determinate way that has no other ground than its own freedom.

As for the specific points to which Descartes directs his attention, the universal determinations of things are substance, duration, order, and others, and he now gives us their definitions.[113] He lays down as the basic principle that nothing must be assumed, and the differentiated content or the representations to which he passes on at this point he still takes to be something found within our consciousness. "Substance" he defines as an object that requires no other thing [Etwas] for its existence (this is Spinoza's definition too); the only such substance is God. We too can say that this is the genuine definition of substance, namely, the unity of the idea and reality, and that only God is such a substance. The other things that we call "substances" do not exist on their own account, they do not have their existence in their very concept; they can only exist through a divine concurrence [concursus Dei]. God is the absolute linkage between concept and actuality. | ⌐The others, the finite [substances],⌐[114] which have a limit and stand in a dependent rela-

99

112. [Ed.] When Hegel says the expression "eternal truths" remained in use, he could be referring to Spinoza, Malebranche, and Leibniz, although the theme of "eternal truths" receives his particular attention in regard to John Locke; see n. 215 below. An example of an eternal truth is the idea that "nothing comes from nothing." See Principles of Philosophy, pt. 1, § 49 (Writings 1:209; Œuvres 8, pt. 1:23–24); cf. W 15:357 (Ms?). On Hegel's identification of innate ideas and eternal truths, see the preceding note.

113. [Ed.] Descartes includes number in this list. See Principles of Philosophy, pt. 1, §§ 48, 51, 55 (Writings 1:208–211; Œuvres 8, pt. 1:22–24, 26); cf. W 15:357 (Ms?).

114. Gr reads: The others, the finite [things], Lw reads: The other, finite [order], An reads: The others are finite
[Ed.] The definition of substance in this paragraph is based on Principles of Philosophy, pt. 1, § 51 (Writings 1:210; Œuvres 8, pt. 1:24); cf. W 15:357–358 (Ms?). On Spinoza's definition of substance, which Hegel here equates with Descartes's, see below, pp. 000–000.

tion, require something else. The substances other than God cannot be termed "substances" *univoce,* that is, in one and the same sense.

˘He now goes on to distinction,˘[115] the [*distinctio*] *realis.* There are two species of things, in the first place thinking things, and secondly things that pertain to what is extended.[116] Here we have the distinction between thinking and what is extended, spatial, mutually external. Thought, concept, or what is spiritual, thinking and self-conscious, is what returns into itself, what is at home with itself. The opposite to thought is what is not at home with itself— what has being outside itself, what is extended, what is not free. These, then, are created substances, and these two [species of] substance can be grasped under the common category "created substances" because they are things that require only God's concurrence in order to exist.[117] Finite things need another finite thing for their existence, but the entire sphere of extended substance (the kingdom of nature), or that of spiritual substance, constitutes a totality within itself. Each of the two, the entirety of each aspect, can be grasped without the other; each is a totality on its own account. (Spinoza also [speaks in] this way.)[118] The other, *singular* things require still other singular things for their existence, but the realm of thinking and that of extension, as entire substances on their own account, are totalities, they do not need each other in order to exist; they require only the concurrence of God for that.

Substance has attributes and each [species] has several of them, although each has a distinctive attribute that constitutes its nature

---

115. *Lw reads:* But we now proceed to the distinction, *Sv reads:* He then distinguished

[*Ed.*] *Principles of Philosophy,* pt. 1, § 60, distinguishes real distinctions, modal distinctions, and conceptual distinctions; real distinctions between substances exist where we can clearly and distinctly understand the one substance without the other (*Writings* 1:213; *Œuvres* 8, pt. 1:28).

116. [*Ed.*] See *Principles of Philosophy,* pt. 1, § 48 (*Writings* 1:203; *Œuvres* 8, pt. 1:23); cf. W 15:358 (Ms?).

117. [*Ed.*] See *Principles of Philosophy,* pt. 1, § 52 (*Writings* 1:210; *Œuvres* 8, pt. 1:24–25); cf. W 15:358 (Ms?).

118. [*Ed.*] Here again Hegel's portrayal of the Cartesian viewpoint is clearly colored by his view of Spinoza; see below, pp. 000–000, especially Spinoza's definitions of the finite, and of thought and extension as two attributes each of which is, on its own account, the entire totality.

and essence. Thinking constitutes the attribute of spirit, thinking is its quality. Extension constitutes the essence or the quality of body, and a body is just extended. What the understanding grasps of body is its substance, its own | genuine nature, and this is just extension, which in turn has two defining characteristics, matter and motion.[119]

According to Descartes the nature of body is consummated in its being extended. All else that we count as the qualities of bodies are only secondary qualities, modes, and so forth—other aspects of the primary quality, extension.[120] Descartes says, in effect, "Give me matter and motion and I will create the world for you."[121] ˉThinking seeks the simple characterization of things that are distinguished.ˉ[122] This involves in addition the mechanical way of viewing nature: the Cartesian philosophy of nature is purely mech-

100

119. [Ed.] The first three sentences of this paragraph are rather loosely based on *Principles of Philosophy*, pt. 1, § 53 (*Writings* 1:210–211; *Œuvres* 8, pt. 1:25); cf. W 15:359 (Ms?). The statement that "what the understanding grasps of body is its substance" is reminiscent of the terms in which Hegel portrays Spinoza (see below, p. 000). Descartes does not say matter and motion are the defining characteristics, but instead he equates extension and matter, and distinguishes shape [*figura*] and motion as their defining characteristics. For Descartes's definitions, see *Principles of Philosophy*, pt. 2, § 4 (on matter) and § 24 (on motion) (*Writings* 1:224–225, 233; *Œuvres* 8, pt. 1:42, 53).

120. [Ed.] On extension as the nature of bodily substance, see the preceding note. It is Locke (see below, p. 000) and not Descartes who makes an explicit distinction between primary and secondary qualities. But the distinction, proposed earlier by Galileo Galilei (1564–1642), is, in the form enunciated by Locke, directly in the line of Cartesian thinking, for Locke took it from the scientist Robert Boyle (1626–1691). In a Cartesian spirit Boyle distinguishes geometrical or mechanical qualities, which we recognize adequately as such, from those that we perceive in a quite different manner even though they can be reduced to geometrical or mechanical qualities. The secondary qualities can therefore never be anything but modes of extended substance, whereas the primary qualities already encompass many modes. On Descartes's differentiation of modes, attributes, and qualities, see *Principles of Philosophy*, pt. 1, § 56 (*Writings* 1:211–212; *Œuvres* 8, pt. 1:26).

121. [Ed.] The probable source for this putative quotation is Buhle (*Geschichte* 3, pt. 1:9). Buhle applies Archimedes' famous aphorism to Descartes's philosophy of nature, whereas in his Second Meditation Descartes himself applies it to the *cogito* and the search for one firm and unshakable point (*Writings* 2:16; *Œuvres* 7:24). On the function of matter and motion in the creation, see *Principles of Philosophy*, pt. 3, § 46 (*Writings* 1:256–257; *Œuvres* 8, pt. 1:101).

122. *Thus Pn; An reads:* Descartes seeks the simple characterization of bodies in matter and motion.

anistic, since he reduces everything to conditions of rest and motion. The digestion, sight, and hearing of living things are all of them just mechanical effects of this kind, effects that have matter and motion as their principles. So we have the basis and origin of mechanistic philosophy before our eyes; it is then a further insight that matter and motion do not suffice to explain living beings.[123] The great point in all this, however, is that in its determinations thought does not just proceed in an external fashion and simply grasp itself, that it makes these thought-determinations into what is true in nature.

At this point Descartes passes over from metaphysics to mechanics, to the world system, the motion of the heavenly bodies, the vortices, ˉto the pores or particles that collide with one another;ˉ[124] and in this way he comes to speak of earth and sun and finally of saltpeter and gunpowder. This is how his metaphysics

123. [Ed.] In criticizing Descartes for a mechanistic view of life Hegel fails to take into account Descartes's description of the human capacity for feeling and desiring, especially his doctrine of the union of soul and body, as presented in the Sixth Meditation; see also n. 131 below.

124. An reads: to the pores or articles; Lw reads: The pores or particles move;

[Ed.] In this sentence Hegel gives a very sketchy survey of the further exposition of Descartes's Principles of Philosophy. The transition from metaphysics to mechanics occurs where Descartes passes from part 1 ("The Principles of Human Knowledge") to part 2 ("The Principles of Material Things"), that is, to the doctrine of extended substance and of mechanical or local motion. Descartes presents his "world system" in part 3 ("The Visible Universe"), which also deals with the motion of the heavenly bodies and of vortices, discussion of the latter being linked with that of pores and particles. Since matter and extension are identical, matter initially fills the whole space; but the vortical movement of the whole gives rise to particles, and since these are spherical in form, the existence of empty spaces between them must be assumed (pt. 3, §§ 49–50; Œuvres 8, pt. 1:104). "Pores" is the name given by Descartes to the empty spaces between particles (pt. 3, § 105; Œuvres 8, 1:153–154). For his exposition of the formation of the sun, see pt. 3, §§ 20–23, 32, 54, 72 ff. (Œuvres 8, pt. 1:86–88, 93, 107, 125 ff.). On the earth, see pt. 3, §§ 14–21, 26, 28–29, 33, 38–40, 150, and pt. 4, "The Earth" (Œuvres 8, pt. 1:84–86, 89–91, 93, 96–97, 198, 203 ff.). Saltpeter and gunpowder are discussed in pt. 4, §§ 109–115 (Œuvres 8, pt. 1:263–265). (The English edition, Writings, does not include the text of most of these sections dealing with cosmology and physics.)

125. [Ed.] This formulation, transmitted only by An, does not make clear whether Hegel takes not only the Cartesian tradition (Spinoza, Malebranche, Leibniz, and others) but also those whom he elsewhere terms empiricists (such as Locke and Newton) to be representatives of a "reflective mechanics."

proceeds. Initially, universal thoughts are the object of concern; after that comes a transition to the determinate, and this determinate or physical domain establishes a physics that is the result of observations and experience. In this way Descartes mingled a multitude of observations with this type of metaphysics, and hence his metaphysics is an obscure and confused thing for us. | 101

The reflective treatment [denkende Betrachtung] of the empirical is what predominates in this philosophy. The same mode of "reflective mechanics" [denkende Mechanik] is evidenced by philosophical schools from this time on.[125] Descartes's works have been newly published in French by Professor Cousin in Paris. So far nine octavo volumes have appeared, consisting for the most part of letters on physical and mechanical subjects of all kinds.[126] The first part [of Descartes's work] treats de principiis cognitionis humanae; the second, de principiis rerum naturalium, is a physics. It was Descartes's intention to compile a third part as well, dealing with ethics, but he did not accomplish that. In contrast, Spinoza's principal work is his Ethics, which in its first part likewise deals with general metaphysics, but which includes no second part on the philosophy of nature. Spinoza's correspondence does include observations on nature, but what he published is an ethics, a philosophy

126. [Ed.] Œuvres de Descartes, 11 vols., ed. Victor Cousin (Paris, 1824–1826); volumes 10 and 11 were published in 1825 and 1826, subsequent to the beginning of this lecture series. The following two sentences of the text confuse the structure of the Principles of Philosophy with that of Descartes's work as a whole. Descartes's system of physics includes not only the first two parts of the Principles, namely, "The Principles of Human Knowledge" and "The Principles of Material Things" (not, as Hegel has it, "of Natural Things"), but also the third and fourth parts, "The Visible Universe" and "The Earth." So the reference to "a third part dealing with ethics" must refer to Descartes's work as a whole as the author himself envisaged it, for instance in his letter to the French translator of the Principles, where he writes: "The whole of philosophy is therefore like a tree whose roots are metaphysics, whose stem is physics, and whose branches are all the other sciences, which can be reduced to three main ones, namely, medicine, mechanics, and ethics. By ethics I understand the highest, most perfect study of morals, which, since it presupposes the entire knowledge of the other sciences, is the ultimate, highest grade of wisdom." There he explains also why he feels unable to complete a comprehensive system of philosophy conceived as he envisages it, because he lacks the resources to carry out the necessary experiments to support and validate his reasoning (Œuvres 9, pt. 2:14, 17). Nevertheless, Descartes's 1649 treatise, The Passions of the Soul (which Hegel mentions in W 15:364), treats of the subject in schematic fashion.

of spirit.[127] There is nothing on ethics in Descartes, and what concerns cognitive knowing or the intelligent spirit is to be found in the first part, dealing with the principles of human knowledge.[128] These are the main aspects of Cartesian philosophy.

We must refer to a few other particular forms that are usually dealt with in metaphysics (by Wolff as well[129]), such as the relation of the soul to the body. We find many systematic views on this topic in metaphysics.[130] One is that of the *influxus physicus*, [the notion] that spirit functions in corporeal fashion, that external things have a mechanical relation to the soul in the way that one thing affects another by pressure or collision. This is a very crude notion, one that Descartes rejects.[131] He established the spiritual or intellectual sphere as free on its own account. ˉIn his *cogito* I am at first only certain of myself, since I can abstract from everything.ˉ[132] On this

127. [*Ed.*] On Spinoza's ethics, see below, p. 000. Here Hegel appears to disregard Spinoza's discussion of evil both in his correspondence (however, see below, p. 000), and also in the *Theologico-political Treatise* and the *Political Treatise*.

128. [*Ed.*] Part 1 of the *Principles of Philosophy* deals not only with questions of metaphysics—as mentioned previously by Hegel—but also with such principles of human knowledge as pertain to the philosophy of subjective spirit, according to Hegel's own system outline: doubt, error, free will, imagination, sensible nature, and so forth.

129. [*Ed.*] Hegel is probably referring particularly to Wolff's rational psychology. See Christian Wolff, *Psychologia rationalis methodo scientifica pertractata*, new rev. ed. (Frankfurt am Main and Leipzig, 1740), section III (reprinted in *Gesammelte Werke*, division II, 6:451–587), which deals with the interaction between mind and body.

130. [*Ed.*] Further on in these lectures Hegel distinguishes three such systems (see pp. 000 and 000 below; cf. *W* 15:456–457). But see also Hegel's criticism of the "thoughtless" representation of the soul-body relation in Epicurus (*W* 14:499–500).

131. [*Ed.*] Descartes does not reject the idea of a mechanical relationship between external things and the soul in quite the explicit fashion Hegel's wording suggests. But such rejection is implied by what Descartes says about the real difference between thinking substance and extended substance, which is probably what Hegel has in mind; see in particular *Principles of Philosophy*, pt. 1, § 60 (*Writings* 1:213; *Œuvres* 8, pt. 1:29) or, with direct reference to the relation between soul and body, the Sixth Meditation (*Writings* 2:52–53; *Œuvres* 7:76). The conjunction (*compositio, unio, permixtio*) of soul and body affirmed a few pages later in the Sixth Meditation (*Writings* 2:59–62; *Œuvres* 7:85–90) also precludes a purely mechanical relationship between them; see also n. 123, p. 000 above.

132. *Thus Gr; An reads:* I am conscious of myself and of my freedom, without anything external.

basis Descartes founds the subsistence of spirit on its own account. But then the middle term or the link between the abstract universal and the particular external [body] has to be identified. Descartes identifies it by saying that God is the intermediary, the middle term. This is what is called | the system of assistance, namely, that God is the metaphysical ground of the reciprocal changes. Changes occur in the soul as well as in the body. Bodily changes correspond to those in the soul. This correspondence is effected by God—this is the *systema assistentiae*.[133] Here we see the need for a mediating element between the two opposites. The unity of the idea, or of the concept, and what is real, is in God alone. In its further moments this point receives particular emphasis in Spinoza's system.

102

3. Benedict Spinoza

Spinozism is related to Cartesianism simply as a consistent carrying out or execution of Descartes's principle.

First, however, we must examine the circumstances of Spinoza's life.[134] He was born in Amsterdam in 1632, of a Portuguese-Jewish family. His given name was Baruch, but he changed it to Benedict. ˜At an early age he got into conflict with the rabbis in the synagogue,˜[135] and he stopped attending the synagogue. He was offered a great deal of money to return to the synagogue, and when the

---

133. [*Ed.*] The adoption of a *systema assistentiae* in its developed form is, owing to its agreement with Occasionalism, to be attributed to Malebranche rather than to Descartes, as Hegel himself confirms elsewhere (*W* 15:367). The passages in Descartes that go furthest in this direction occur in his *Treatise on Man* (1629–1633), which was to exert such a decisive influence on Malebranche (see p. 000 below). Hegel does not mention this treatise, although Rixner does (*Handbuch* 3:44–49).

134. [*Ed.*] Hegel's account of Spinoza's life and works is derived from the *Collectanea de vita B. de Spinoza*, appended to vol. 2 of H. E. G. Paulus's edition, *Benedicti de Spinoza Opera quae supersunt omnia*, 2 vols. (Jena, 1802–1803). Hegel had a small part in the work on this edition; see the editorial report by M. Baum and K.-R. Meist in *GW* 5. From the *Collectanea* Hegel relied mainly on the Spinoza biography by Johannes Colerus, a Lutheran clergyman in The Hague, with the additions of the Spinozist, Count Boulainvilliers. One departure is that this source does not expressly make the Jews responsible for the assassination attempt on Spinoza; in *W* 15:368 Hegel assigns responsibility to the rabbis.

135. *Thus An with Pn, similar in Lw, Sv; Gr reads:* In his youth he received instruction from the rabbis,

Jews sought to rid themselves of him by assassination, he narrowly escaped with his life. He then left the Jewish community, without, however, formally going over to the Christian church. He now applied himself particularly to the study of Latin. He studied Descartes's philosophy and published an exposition of it according to the geometrical method (subsequently included in his works). Later he achieved fame through his *Theologico-political Treatise,* which contains the doctrine of inspiration, an assessment of the Mosaic 103 scriptures particularly from the | standpoint that the Mosaic laws apply only to the Jews—a critical treatment of the Mosaic books. Most of what later Christian theologians have written in a critical spirit on inspiration and the limitation of the Mosaic Law to the Jewish nation, usually purporting to show that these books were not compiled until a later time—a principal topic for Protestant theologians—they found already in Spinoza.[136] In 1664 Spinoza went to Rijnsburg near Leiden, and from 1665 on he lived ⁻in a village near The Hague, and in The Hague itself,⁻[137] where he supported himself by grinding optical lenses, after declining several donations from his friends. The elector Palatine, Carl Ludwig, offered him a chair of philosophy at Heidelberg with freedom to teach and to write, because this prince believed that Spinoza "would not abuse this freedom by disturbing the public religion." Spinoza declined the offer because "he did not know within what limits philosophical freedom must be confined in order not to disturb the

136. [*Ed.*] For this discussion see the preface and chapters 5, 8–11 of Spinoza's *Theologico-political Treatise* (1670) in *Chief Works,* trans. R. H. M. Elwes, 2 vols. (London, 1883; reprint, New York, 1951), 1:8, 69, 114; *Opera,* ed. Paulus, 1:148–149, 219, 270–271; *Spinoza: Opera,* ed. Carl Gebhardt, 4 vols. (Heidelberg, 1926), 3:9–10, 69, 112–113. We do not know the extent of Hegel's acquaintance with the development of the historical criticism of the Bible. For instance, it is improbable that he knew the work of the Deist Johann Lorenz Schmidt (1702–1749) and not confirmed that he knew that of the "neologist" Johann Salomo Semler (1725–1791); undoubtedly he did know Lessing's 1777 publication of the "Fragments" of Hermann Samuel Reimarus (1694–1768), taken from the latter's *Apology for Rational Worshipers of God.* But whereas Spinoza's influence on the later views of Lessing and Herder concerning the relation of Scripture and history is evident, his impact on the initial historical-critical study of the Bible is not as clear as Hegel here suggests.

137. *Thus An, Lw; Pn reads:* in a village near The Hague, *Gr reads:* in The Hague or in Vorburg near The Hague,

public religion."¹³⁸ He remained in Holland with no ties of any kind, and died of consumption on 22 February 1677. Only after his death was his *Ethics* published, by his closest friend, the physician Ludwig Meyer. ˜The great hatred Spinoza aroused among the Jews was equaled by the hatred the Protestant clergy had for him.˜¹³⁹

His principal work is his *Ethics*. It consists of five parts. The first deals with God, and the second with the nature and origin of the mind [*Geist*]; so he does not deal with nature but passes straight over from God to mind. The third book | deals with [the nature   104 and origin of] our emotional states and passions, and the fourth with the forces of the emotions or, as its title puts it, with human bondage. Finally, the fifth book deals with the power of the understanding, of thinking, or with human freedom.¹⁴⁰

Spinoza's system itself is on the whole very simple. The difficulty of grasping it is due partly to the method, the closely woven method by which he presents his thoughts, and [partly] to his restricted viewpoint, which leaves one dissatisfied about [some of its] major aspects and lines of inquiry.

˜Spinoza's simple reality [*das Einfache*]˜¹⁴¹ is absolute substance; only absolute substance truly is, it alone is actual or is actuality. ˜It is˜¹⁴² the unity of thinking and being, or that whose

138. [*Ed.*] These two approximate quotations come from an exchange of letters between J. L. Fabricius (on behalf of the elector Palatine) and Spinoza. See Spinoza's *Letters* 53 and 54 (*Chief Works* 2:373–375; *Opera,* ed. Paulus, 1:639–640; *Opera,* ed. Gebhardt, 4:235–236 = Letters 47 and 48).

139. *Thus Gr; Pn reads:* The Jews and the Protestants hated him greatly. *An reads:* By his writings he incurred great hatred from the Jews and the Protestants. *Lw reads:* Hostility to Spinoza was even greater among the Christians than among the Jews.

[*Ed.*] Hegel knew about the circumstances of the publication of Spinoza's *Ethics* from Ludwig Meyer's preface to it in the *Opera* edited by Paulus (2:3 ff.), and about the hostility of the Protestant clergy from the Colerus biography in Paulus, which cites an attack on Spinoza by Johann Musaeus, a theology professor at Jena (2:650). Musaeus called him an impostor who, under the devil's influence, perverted human and divine laws.

140. [*Ed.*] Here Hegel gives the titles of the five parts of the *Ethics,* using *Geist* where Spinoza has "mind" (*mens*).

141. *Thus Gr; Lw reads:* The principal idea

142. *Thus Pn, Lw; An reads:* This substance is *Gr reads:* It is, as for Descartes, [*Ed.*] This sentence refers to the definition of *causa sui*; see n. 149 below.

concept contains its existence within itself. We have before us two determinations, the universal or what has being in and for itself, and secondly the determination of the particular and singular, that is, individuality. Now it is not hard to demonstrate that the particular or the singular is something altogether limited, that its concept altogether depends upon an other, that it is dependent, does not truly exist for itself, and so is not truly actual. With regard to the determinate, Spinoza established this thesis: *omnis determinatio*[143] *est negatio* [all determination is negation]. Hence only the non-particularized or the universal *is*. It alone is what is substantial and therefore truly actual. As a singular thing, the soul or the mind is something limited. It is by negation that ˉa singular thing is.ˉ[144] Therefore ˉit [the singular thing]ˉ[145] does not have genuine actuality. This on the whole is Spinoza's idea.

The general point to notice here is that thinking, or the spirit, has to place itself at the standpoint of Spinozism. This idea of Spinoza's must be acknowledged to be true and well-grounded. There is an absolute substance, and it is what is true. But it is not yet | the whole truth, for substance must also be thought of as inwardly active and alive, and in that way must determine itself as spirit. Spinoza's substance is the universal, and consequently the abstract, determination. We can call it the absolute foundation of spirit, not, however, as its absolutely fixed underlying ground, but as the abstract unity that spirit is within itself.

If thinking stops with this substance, there is then no develop-

105

---

143. *Thus Gr, Pn, Lw, Sv; An adds:* (particularization)

[*Ed.*] For this axiom, see Spinoza's Letter 50, to Jarig Jelles (*Chief Works* 2:369–370; *Opera*, ed. Paulus, 1:634; *Opera*, ed. Gebhardt, 4:240). There Spinoza states that, as perceived, figure or body is determined not in terms of its being (what it is) but in terms of its nonbeing (what it is not): "As therefore figure is none other than determination and determination is negation (*non aliud, quam determinatio et determinatio negatio est*), it can, as we have said, be none other than negation." Hegel's formulation shows, however, that his citation is probably not directly from Spinoza but from Jacobi: *Determinatio est negatio* (Jacobi, *Spinoza-Briefe*, pp. 31n, 182; *Werke* 4, pt. 1:62, 182). The first edition of Hegel's *Science of Logic* also quotes this axiom in Jacobi's version (*GW* 11:76). The generalized form with *omnis* first occurs in Hegel's 1817 review of vol. 3 of Jacobi's *Werke*, in the *Heidelbergische Jahrbücher der Litteratur* 1:6 (cf. *W* 17:8).

144. *Thus Pn; Gr reads:* it [mind] is a singular thing.

145. *Thus Lw, Pn; Gr, Sv read:* it [the mind]

ment, no life, no spirituality or activity. So we can say that with Spinozism everything goes into the abyss but nothing emerges from it. In Spinoza the particular is adopted from representation without being justified. For it to be justified he would have to deduce or derive it from his substance, but this is not what happens. What differentiates and forms the particular is said to be just a modification of the absolute substance and nothing actual in its own self.[146] The operation upon it is just the stripping away of its determination or particularity, so that it can be thrown back into the one absolute substance. This is what is unsatisfying in Spinoza. Leibniz takes individuality, the opposite mode, as his principle, and in that way outwardly integrates Spinoza's system.[147] The great merit of the Spinozist way of thinking in philosophy is its renunciation of everything determinate and particular, and its orientation solely to the One—heeding and honoring only the One, acknowledging it alone. This view [*Ansicht*] must be the foundation of every authentic view. But it [the One] is ˜something utterly fixed and immobile.˜[148] It is the universal.

We still have to mention a few characteristics of a more specific sort. To render his philosophy mathematically conclusive and consistent, Spinoza presented it according to a geometrical method, but one that is only appropriate for the finite sciences of the understanding. Hence he begins | with definitions. These definitions involve universal determinations, and they are adopted directly or presupposed, they are not deduced, for Spinoza does not know how he arrives at them. He says, "By that which is its own cause, *causa sui*, I understand that whose essence includes existence within itself, and which cannot be thought of otherwise than as existent."[149] This

106

146. [*Ed.*] See Spinoza's *Ethics* I, prop. 25, corol., in *The Collected Works of Spinoza*, ed. and trans. Edwin Curley, vol. 1 (Princeton, 1985), p. 431; *Opera*, ed. Paulus, 2:59; *Opera*, ed. Gebhardt, 2:68. Curley's second volume, to contain some of the other works by Spinoza discussed here, has not yet been published.

147. [*Ed.*] See the discussion of Leibniz below, pp. 000–000.

148. *Thus Pn, An; Gr reads:* an utterly fixed immobility, whose sole activity is to plunge everything into the abyss of substance. *Lw reads:* something utterly immobile; everything is plunged into the abyss of substance.

149. [*Ed.*] See *Ethics* I, def. 1 (*Collected Works* 1:408; *Opera*, ed. Paulus, 2:35; *Opera*, ed. Gebhardt, 2:45). The first six definitions and the explication of the sixth are quoted in German—as transmitted by Hegel himself—in *W* 15:379–382.

is a wholly speculative concept. A cause produces an effect that is something other than the cause. A cause of itself is a cause that produces an effect, but in this case the distinction is sublated, for a cause of itself produces only itself. This is a fundamental concept in all speculation—return into self within the other.

The second definition is that of the finite. "Finite" means what is bounded by something else of the same kind. In this other it finds an end in which *it* is not, for what is there is an other, and indeed an other of its own kind. For things that are said to limit one another must be of the same kind, they must stand in community and have a common soil. Thus a thought is limited by another thought, a body by another body, but not a body by a thought or vice versa.[150]

The third definition is that of substance. "Substance" is what is conceived within itself and through itself, that is, something the concept of which does not require for its conception the concept of any other thing, what has no need of an other[151]—else it would be finite, accidental. The second [moment] of substance is the attribute, which (according to definition 4) is what the understanding grasps of substance as constituting its essence. But ⁻where the substance passes over to the attribute⁻[152] is not stated. The third [moment] is the mode, namely, the affection of substance or that, in an other, through which it is conceived.

107   God is the absolutely infinite being. The infinite is the | affirmation of itself.[153] The infinite of thought is distinct from the infinite of imagination. The latter is the bad infinite, namely, the infinitude

---

150. [*Ed.*] See *Ethics* I, def. 2 (*Collected Works* 1:408; *Opera*, ed. Paulus, 2:35; *Opera,* ed. Gebhardt, 2:45).

151. [*Ed.*] See *Ethics* I, def. 3, where Spinoza actually says "what is in itself and is conceived through itself," not, as Hegel has it, "what is conceived within itself and through itself." In Hegel's subsequent text, "the second moment" cites def. 4 and "the third moment" cites def. 5. See *Collected Works* 1:408–409; *Opera,* ed. Paulus, 2:35; *Opera,* ed. Gebhardt, 2:45.

152. *Thus Gr; Lw reads:* how the determinations ensue, whence the understanding comes,

153. [*Ed.*] See *Ethics* I, prop. 8, schol. 1 (*Collected Works* 1:412; *Opera*, ed. Paulus, 2:39; *Opera,* ed. Gebhardt, 2:49).

of space or time, or the infinite series of mathematics, of numbers.[154] Yet this is the infinity we usually have in view when we speak of infinity. Philosophical infinity is the affirmation of itself. Here too Spinoza employs geometrical examples to illustrate his concept of the infinite. He takes two circles that are not concentric but do not touch, although one of them lies wholly within the other. The space between the two circles is a present, complete space. It is *actu*, actual, not an [infinite] "beyond," yet the determination of this space cannot be given precisely in numerical terms. The determining does not exhaust the space, and yet the space is actual.[155] [Similarly] it can be said of any line that is limited [that is, a line segment] that it consists of infinitely many points and yet the line is extant, is present, is determinate. The infinite should be represented as actu-

154. [*Ed.*] In his Letter 29 (12 in Gebhardt), to Ludwig Meyer, Spinoza sets forth the different senses of infinity (*Chief Works* 2:317–321; *Opera*, ed. Paulus, 1:526–530; *Opera*, ed. Gebhardt, 4:53–58). He distinguishes: (1) what is infinite by its nature or definition, from what is infinite owing to its cause; (2) what is infinite because unlimited, from what is finite in magnitude although its parts cannot be expressed by number; (3) what is understandable but not imaginable, from what is imaginable as well. The key to this issue lies in the distinction between the existence of indivisible substance and the existence of the modes, which are divisible. Quantity, duration, and number apply only to the modes, not to substance itself. Each of these three can in turn be either viewed superficially, by the imagination, as finite and divisible, or understood as infinite and indivisible. See *Ethics* I, prop. 15, schol. (*Collected Works* 1:420–424; *Opera*, ed. Paulus, 2:47–51; *Opera*, ed. Gebhardt, 2:57–60). Spinoza's example (cf. Hegel's bad infinite), similar to the "Achilles and the Tortoise" paradox of Zeno, is that of an hour of time viewed as infinitely divisible and therefore unable to be traversed. A similar procedure would generate the infinite series: 1, ½, ¼, ⅛, 1/16, and so on, yielding an infinite that is not actual (*actu*). Unlike Spinoza, however, Hegel accepts that numerical relations express a genuine—quantitative—infinite, for instance, the fraction 1/1–a as distinct from the series $1 + a + a^2 + a^3 \ldots$, or the fraction 2/7 as distinct from the decimal expression 0.285714. . . . See *GW* 11:159 and 21:242–244 (cf. *Science of Logic*, pp. 250–252), as well as *W* 15:382.

155. [*Ed.*] It is not clear whether Spinoza's example of the circles in Letter 29 is in terms of plane geometry or solid geometry. The reference to the space between the two circles, and matter in motion within this space, suggests solid geometry. But reference to infinitely many different straight-line distances between the two circles suggests a two-dimensional figure such as Spinoza introduces elsewhere concerning the study of fluids. Hegel's mention of the line segment example in the next sentence probably refers to an earlier passage in the same letter. See *Chief Works* 2:319, 321; *Opera*, ed. Paulus, 1:528, 530–531; *Opera*, ed. Gebhardt, 4:56, 59–60.

ally present. The genuine infinite consists in the cause producing itself (*causa sui*).[156] As soon as the cause has over against it an other, the effect, then finitude is present. In the case of the genuine infinite, however, this other that sought to limit it is at once sublated, and the infinite is itself again. God, therefore, is the absolutely infinite being or the substance that consists of infinite attributes, each of which ˉexpresses itsˉ[157] eternal and infinite essence. ˉThese determinations, however, are universal and thus completely formal.ˉ[158]

The main thing is that Spinoza says that substance consists of infinite attributes. This seems to mean that there should be infinitely many attributes. But Spinoza only speaks of two | attributes, so that "infinite" must refer to their character. He does not indicate how these two[159] proceed from the one substance, however, nor say why he speaks only of two. As with Descartes, the two of them are thought and extension,[160] each by itself being the entire totality in such a way that both have the same content, except that it is posited in one case in the form of thinking and in the other case in the form of extension. The understanding grasps these attributes, it grasps them as totalities. They express the same being, God, but in a form that the understanding, so to speak, brings with it, a form that pertains to the understanding. Both are the same totality, or, as he puts it, the order or system of extended things is the same as the order of thinking things,[161] it is one and the same system. Recently

108

---

156. [*Ed.*] See *Ethics* I, prop. 7, and prop. 8, schol. 1 (*Collected Works* 1:412; *Opera*, ed. Paulus, 1:38–39; *Opera*, ed. Gebhardt, 2:49).

157. *Thus Pn, Lw; Gr reads:* constitutes its *An reads:* constitutes an

[*Ed.*] See *Ethics* I, def. 6 and expl. (*Collected Works* 1:409; *Opera*, ed. Paulus, 2:35–36; *Opera*, ed. Gebhardt, 2:45–46).

158. *Thus Gr; Pn reads:* Now this is very formal, with the eternal, infinite essence expressed by each attribute.

159. *Thus Gr, Pn, An; Lw adds:* nor why only they

160. [*Ed.*] See *Ethics* II, props. 1 and 2 (*Collected Works* 1:448–449; *Opera*, ed. Paulus, 2:78–79; *Opera*, ed. Gebhardt, 2:86). Although Hegel rejects the view that by "infinite attributes" Spinoza means "infinitely many attributes," the passage cited in the following note suggests that Spinoza thought there are more than two attributes, since it speaks of extension and "the other attributes." For Descartes's view that there are only two kinds of things, thinking things and extended things, see n. 116, p. 000 above.

161. [*Ed.*] See *Ethics* II, prop. 7 and schol. (*Collected Works* 1:451–452; *Opera*, ed. Paulus, 1:82–83; *Opera*, ed. Gebhardt, 2:89–90).

this idea has been served up to us again in the following terms, namely, that the thinking world is implicitly the same as the extended world, and [the two just are] in distinct forms.[162] But the question here is: ˉWhence comes it that the understanding appliesˉ[163] these two forms to the absolute substance, and whence come these two forms? Here the unity of being (extension) and thinking is therefore posited in such a way that ˉthinking is in itself the totality, and likewise what is extendedˉ[164] is the same totality. So we have two totalities. In themselves they are the same, and the distinctions are only attributes or determinations of the understanding, which is an added factor. This is the general view, that the attributes ˉare just nothing in themselves, they are no distinctions in themselves.ˉ[165]

The third [moment] consists of the modes or *affectiones*.[166] In extension these are rest and motion, in thinking they are *intellectus* and | *voluntas*, cognition and will; they are mere modifications. Whatever relates to this distinction and is in particular posited by it is nothing in itself. These, then, are Spinoza's general forms.

Several other forms that are more determinate remain to be men-

109

162. [*Ed.*] Hegel's criticism is directed against Schelling's Identity-philosophy (see below, pp. 000–000).

163. *Thus An, Lw; Gr, Pn read:* How does the understanding come (*Pn:* now come) to apply

164. *Thus Pn; Sv reads:* thinking is in itself totality, *Gr reads:* the thinking universe is in itself the whole absolute, divine totality, and the corporeal universe

165. *Thus Gr; Pn reads:* are just not the [being] in itself of what is differentiated. *An reads:* are just not in themselves.

166. [*Ed.*] See the definition of mode as given on p. 000 above. Hegel's justification for designating mode as "the third moment" is that from his standpoint he identifies substance, attribute, and mode with universal, particular, and singular respectively. The analogy between singular and mode becomes particularly clear in W 15:391: "The singular as such pertains to these modes [namely, rest and motion, or understanding and will]; it is through them that what is called singular distinguishes itself." As evidence in favor of Hegel's interpretation we may cite, for instance, *Ethics* I, prop. 25, corol.: "Particular things are nothing but affections of God's attributes, *or* modes by which God's attributes are expressed in a certain and determinate way" (*Collected Works* 1:431; *Opera*, ed. Paulus, 2:59; *Opera*, ed. Gebhardt, 2:68). Hegel's subsequent statement about cognition and will is based on *Ethics* I, prop. 32, dem. and corol. 2 (*Collected Works* 1:435; *Opera*, ed. Paulus, 2:63; *Opera*, ed. Gebhardt, 2:72–73). Spinoza's text implies that motion and rest are to be considered as modes too.

tioned. Spinoza has this to say about evil:[167] "It is alleged that God is even the author of evil because God is the author of everything; it is alleged that what is evil is God himself. I affirm that God is the absolute author of everything that is positive reality or essence (Letter 36). Now if you can prove to me that error, depravity, or evil, is something that expresses an essence, I will freely grant you that God is the author of evil. But I have abundantly demonstrated that the form of evil is not in something that [expresses] an essence, ˉthat it is nothing in itself genuinely real,ˉ[168] and therefore it cannot be said that God is the author of evil. Nero's matricide, for instance, so far as it has a positive, volitional content, is another matter. His vice was just disobedience, ruthlessness, and ingratitude. But that is no essence, so God is not the cause of the evil in his action. Inasmuch as God does not consider the case abstractly ˉand no more reality pertains to things thanˉ[169] God imparts to them, it follows that such privation holds only with regard to our understanding and not with regard to God. Evil and the like is only privation; God is what is utterly real."[170]

It is all very well to say this, but it does not satisfy us. Our view of the freedom of the subject protests vehemently against the

---

167. [Ed.] Although it is shown as a single quoted passage, the remainder of this paragraph, except for the last sentence, is in fact a conflation of points from Spinoza's Letters: 31, from Willem van Blyenbergh; 32 and 36, Spinoza's replies (*Chief Works* 2:329, 333, 347; *Opera,* ed. Paulus, 1:538–539, 543, 581–582; *Opera,* ed. Gebhardt, 4:82–84, 91–92, 147 = Letters 18, 19, 23). Cf. W 15:406–407 (Ms?). In replying, Spinoza compares the matricide of Nero and that of Orestes. The two acts are alike in essence, that is, in intention and deed, in which respect both were caused by God. Nero is blameworthy in a way that Orestes is not, however, because Nero's attitude was vicious; it did not express essence and so was not caused by God.

168. *Thus Gr; Sv reads:* and so it [evil] also could not be taken as something positive,

169. *Gr reads:* and things do not have true reality other than what

170. [Ed.] For Spinoza's concept of privation, see his Letter 34, to van Blyenbergh (*Chief Works* 2:339; *Opera,* ed Paulus, 1:566–567; *Opera,* ed. Gebhardt, 4:128–129 = Letter 21). Spinoza says that privation, as the attribution of a deficiency (for instance, to a blind person who cannot see) is merely a product of our reason or imagination, not the result of God's causing something to be taken away (from that person). When certain qualities do not fall within the scope of something's nature, as determined by God's will and understanding, then that circumstance is properly called negation, not privation.

Spinozistic substance, since the fact that I exist as subject, as individual spirituality and the like, is, according to Spinoza, nothing but a modification or transient form. This is what is shocking in the inner content of Spinoza's system and what gives rise to the animosity toward it. For we have the self-consciousness of freedom and [are aware] | that spirit is in and for itself essentially the negative of the corporeal, and that it is only in positing an antithesis to the corporeal that one is what one truly is. Both in theology and in sound common sense people have held fast to this negative element. This form of the antithesis is first of all that what is free is actual, that evil exists. It is no explanation if I call it all mere modification; the moment of the negative is what is lacking and deficient in this one, rigid, motionless substantiality. The pattern of the antithesis is that, in distinguishing itself explicitly from the corporeal, spirit is substantial and actual, that *spirit is,* and is no mere privation or negation. In the same way *freedom is,* and is no mere privation. This actuality is set against the Spinozistic system, which is correct in formal thought. The actuality rests, for one thing, upon feeling. But beyond that there is the fact that in and for itself the idea contains within itself the principle of movement or of vitality, the principle of freedom and hence the principle of spirituality. Spinoza did not grasp that. On the one hand the defect of the Spinozistic system is that it does not correspond to actuality. On the other hand, however, the defect has to be grasped in a higher way—to be precise, in such a way that the Spinozistic substance is [seen to be] the idea only as wholly abstract and not in its vitality.

There are many other particular propositions from Spinoza to which I could refer, but they are very formal in character and constantly repeat one and the same thing. In this vein he says that the actual being of the *mens humana* [human mind] is the idea of a singular, existing thing.[171] It certainly does include this characteristic, but that is only ⁻one mode, one affection.⁻[172] What is lacking

171. [*Ed.*] See *Ethics* II, prop. 11 (*Collected Works* 1:456; *Opera,* ed. Paulus, 2:86; *Opera,* ed. Gebhardt, 2:94); cf. W 15:395 (Ms?).

172. *Thus Lw; Gr reads:* one *modus affectionis. Pn reads:* one mode. *Sv reads:* one modification.

[*Ed.*] See *Ethics* II, prop. 9, and prop. 10, corol. (*Collected Works* 1:453–454; *Opera,* ed. Paulus, 2:84–85; *Opera,* ed. Gebhardt, 2:91–93).

is the infinite form, which we can call knowing, freedom, spiritual-
111 ity. [173]To set up a system of form and | to grasp how the One
is organized within itself as Bruno did—that is a task Spinoza
renounced.

Spinozism is said to be atheism.[174] This is correct in one respect
at any rate, since Spinoza does not distinguish God from the world
or from nature. He says that God is all actuality, but all actuality
insofar as the idea of God explicates itself in particular fashion, for
instance, in the existence of the human spirit. So it can be said that
this is atheism, and that is said insofar as Spinoza does not distinguish God from the finite, from the world, from nature. We have
already noted ˉthat in any case the Spinozistic substance does not
fulfill the concept of God,ˉ[175] since God has to be grasped as spirit.
But if one wants to call Spinozism atheism for the sole reason that
it does not distinguish God from the world, this is a misuse of the
term; it could better be called acosmism, because all natural things
are only modifications. Spinoza himself maintains that there is no
such thing as what is called a world, that it is only a ˉform of God
and is nothing in and for itself, that the world has no genuine actu-
ality.ˉ[176] [But today] what continually intrudes is the mistaken view

173. *Thus An; precedes in Gr:* I have already indicated that Lull and Bruno
attempted
[*Ed.*] On Bruno, see p. 000 with n. 169 above. In *W* 15:408 Hegel also refers
in this connection to Raymon Lull; see also p. 000 above.

174. [*Ed.*] This assertion is found, for instance, in Christian Wolff's *Theologia
naturalis,* pars posterior, § 716. Hegel knew the assertion principally through
Jacobi, who in both his *Spinoza-Briefe,* p. 223 (*Werke* 4, pt. 1:216 and note) and
his preface to the *Werke* (pp. xxxvi–xxxvii) stated categorically that Spinozism is
atheism. In the explanation that follows directly in our text, Hegel is probably not
referring to a specific passage but reproducing the sense of arguments advanced at
various places in the *Ethics.* See in particular I, prop. 14 with corol. 1, and II, prop.
11, corol. (*Collected Works* 1:420, 456; *Opera,* ed. Paulus, 2:46, 87; *Opera,* ed.
Gebhardt, 2:56, 94–95).

175. *Thus Gr; Pn reads:* that surely the Spinozistic substance does not involve
cognitive knowledge of the concept of God,

176. *Thus Gr; An reads:* transient phenomenon.
[*Ed.*] Use of the term "acosmism" for Spinoza's philosophy and in opposition
to the charge of atheism may be traced back to Salomon Maimon's autobiography,
Lebensgeschichte, ed. K. P. Moritz, 2 vols. (Berlin, 1792). The philosopher Salomon
Maimon (d. 1800) affirms that Spinozism and atheism are diametrically opposed,
the latter denying the existence of God while the former denies the existence of the

that singular things are genuine actualities just as they are in their finitude. The reproach that Spinoza does not distinguish God from the finite is therefore of no account, since Spinoza casts all this [finite being] into the abyss of the One Identity. According to him, finite actuality (the cosmos) has no truth; what is, is God and God alone. Thus Spinozism is far removed from being atheism in the ordinary sense, although his system could well be termed atheism in the sense that God is not grasped as spirit. ⌐But there are many others, even theologians, who say God is the unknown, and speak of God only as the almighty | and highest being, and the like.⌐[177]   112 They are worse atheists than Spinoza, for they accord the status of what is true to the finite as such.

We still have to speak about Spinoza's system of morals. His principal work is the *Ethics*. Its main principle is simply that the finite spirit has its truth in the moral sphere, and is therefore moral, when it directs its knowing and willing toward God—to the extent that it has true ideas. This alone is the knowledge of God. So we can say that there is no more sublime morality than this, since it

---

world, and that therefore Spinozism should be called the "acosmic" system (1:154). Alternatively, Hegel may have encountered this interpretation of Spinozism in Christoph Theophil de Murr's *Adnotationes* on the *Theologico-political Treatise* (The Hague, 1802), which Hegel studied during his collaboration, in summer 1802, on the Paulus edition of Spinoza's *Opera* (cf. the editorial report to *GW 5*). In adopting the concept of acosmism here—as well as in W 15:404, 408, in the *Philosophy of Religion* (1:377), and in the 1827 and 1830 editions of the *Encyclopedia* (§§ 50 and 573, notes)—Hegel is at odds with Jacobi, who contended (in 1818–1819) that the distinction between atheism and acosmism is "basically only a play on words" (Jacobi, *Werke* 4, pt. 1:xxxiv–xxxv). The assertion that the world is only a form of God and has no genuine actuality is not found in Spinoza. Hegel is rather educing what seems to him to follow from Spinoza's basic viewpoint, in light of the commentators' discussion of acosmism.

177. *Thus Gr with An; Pn reads:* But then matters are no different [with] many philosophies and modes of theology, where God is not grasped as spirit.

[*Ed.*] Hegel's general criticism is directed against (1) Enlightenment—and especially eighteenth-century French—philosophy (see W 15:521 on Robinet's talk of "an unknown God"); (2) deism and "natural theology" (such as that of Herbert of Cherbury), which affirms the knowability of God but conceives God only as "necessary being" or "most perfect being"; (3) the critique of the knowability of God, by Kant, Jacobi, and their philosophical and theological disciples. Designation of God as "highest being" (*Wesen*) is also found, inter alia, in Schleiermacher's *Glaubenslehre* (Berlin, 1821), §§ 9–10.

requires only the having of a clear idea of God. The works of the righteous, that is, of those who have a clear idea of God, are, he says, that they direct all their thoughts and actions to the God whom they know. The wicked are those who do not have this idea and are directed solely to earthly things, who act according to singular and personal interests and opinions. Everything that is proceeds necessarily from God's eternal laws and counsels, and the truth, which is genuine cognitive knowledge, consists in considering everything *sub specie aeterni* [in its eternal aspect].[178] The necessity of things is the eternal will of God. The affections are what constitute human slavery, because in them human beings only have something determinate as end. Spirit has the ability to refer all corporeal affects and all representations of corporeal things back to God, for whatever is, is in God, and nothing is apart from God. In this way human beings gain power over their affects.[179] This is the return of spirit to God, and that is genuine human freedom.[180]

178. [*Ed.*] Most of the content of the three preceding sentences is not in fact taken from the *Ethics* but from Spinoza's Letter 36, to van Blyenbergh (*Chief Works* 2:347–348; *Opera*, ed. Paulus, 1:582; *Opera*, ed. Gebhardt, 4:148–149 = Letter 23). The reference to *sub specie aeterni*, however, comes from *Ethics* II, prop. 44, corol. 2; see also IV, prop. 62, and V, prop. 29 (*Collected Works* 1:481, 581, 609–610; *Opera*, ed. Paulus, 2:118, 250, 288–289; *Opera*, ed. Gebhardt, 2:126, 257, 298–299). For the following remark, on the necessity of things, see *Ethics* I, prop. 33, schol. 2 (*Collected Works* 1:436–437; *Opera*, ed. Paulus, 2:65–66; *Opera*, ed. Gebhardt, 2:74–75).

179. [*Ed.*] Spinoza's *Ethics* IV deals with human bondage to the affects, with the inability to moderate and restrain them. (Our text uses both "affects" [*Affekte*] and "affections" [*Affektionen*].) On the connection of the affects with the desiring of individual finite things, see *Ethics* III, prop. 56, dem. (*Collected Works* 1:527; *Opera*, ed. Paulus, 2:178; *Opera*, ed. Gebhardt, 2:185), as well as the preceding note. On referring corporeal affections back to God, see *Ethics* V, prop. 14 (*Collected Works* 1:603; *Opera*, ed. Paulus, 2:280; *Opera*, ed. Gebhardt, 2:290); cf. W 15:404 (Ms?). On the being in God of whatever is, see *Ethics* I, prop. 15 (*Collected Works* 1:420; *Opera*, ed. Paulus, 2:46; *Opera*, ed. Gebhardt, 2:56). On power over one's affects, see *Ethics* V, prop. 6 (*Collected Works* 1:599; *Opera*, ed. Paulus, 2:275; *Opera*, ed. Gebhardt, 2:284); cf. W 15:404 (Ms?).

180. [*Ed.*] In this connection Spinoza does not refer explicitly to a "return to God." However, see *Ethics* IV, prop. 66, schol., which calls those who are guided solely by affect "slaves" and those who are guided by reason "free" (*Collected Works* 1:584; *Opera*, ed. Paulus, 2:254; *Opera*, ed. Gebhardt, 2:260).

These ideas are true insofar as they are related to God.[181] From this cognition, from knowledge of the One, of what is true, springs the intellectual love of God—a joyfulness that at the same time includes the representation of its cause, and this cause is God. God loves himself with an infinite intellectual love, for God can have only himself as end and cause, | and the vocation of the subjective spirit is to direct itself to God.[182] This then is the highest and greatest morality; but [it] remains still [caught up] in this [abstract] universality.

113

4. Nicolas Malebranche

We have to mention another form that can be set alongside Spinozism. It too is a development of Cartesian philosophy—the form in which Malebranche presented this philosophy. Because [unlike Spinoza] he presented it in theological form, Malebranche was not reproached with atheism.

Malebranche was born in Paris in 1638.[183] He was sickly and deformed in body, ¯and was therefore brought up with very delicate care. He was¯[184] shy and loved solitude. In his twenty-second year he was accepted into the Congrégation de l'Oratoire, a kind of spiritual order, and devoted himself to the sciences. He happened to see in a bookseller's shop a work by Descartes that so interested him that his heart beat faster and he was seized by a compelling

181. *Gr adds:* This then is not philosophical cognition.
[*Ed.*] See *Ethics* II, prop. 32 (*Collected Works* 1:472; *Opera,* ed. Paulus, 2:107; *Opera,* ed. Gebhardt, 2:116); cf. W 15:404 (Ms?).
182. [*Ed.*] On the intellectual love of God, see *Ethics* V, prop. 32, corol. (*Collected Works* 1:611; *Opera,* ed. Paulus, 2:291; *Opera,* ed. Gebhardt, 2:300); cf. W 15:405 (Ms?). On God's self-love, see *Ethics* V, prop. 35 (*Collected Works* 1:612; *Opera,* ed. Paulus, 2:292; *Opera,* ed. Gebhardt, 2:302), although Spinoza does not say here that God can have only himself as end. On the subjective spirit's vocation, see *Ethics* V, prop. 36, schol., and IV, prop. 28 (*Collected Works* 1:612, 559; *Opera,* ed. Paulus, 2:293, 221; *Opera,* ed. Gebhardt, 2:303, 228), as well as n. 178 just above.
183. [*Ed.*] Hegel's account of Malebranche's life in this paragraph is taken from Buhle (*Geschichte* 3, pt. 2:430–431), although it omits the derogatory undertones ("a well-nigh exaggerated piety") found there. The work by Descartes that so affected Malebranche was the *Treatise on Man.*
184. *Thus W; An reads:* delicate,

inclination toward philosophy. He was ¯a pious, gentle man of excellent character.¯[185] He died in Paris in 1715, at the age of seventy-six.

His principal work bears the title *De la recherche de la vérité*. One part is entirely metaphysical, but the greater part of it proceeds in an empirical, logical way; for instance, it deals with errors in sight, hearing, and the imaginative power.[186] What is most important is the way Malebranche represents the nature and origin of our knowledge. Like Descartes, he locates the essence of the soul in thinking and that of matter in extension.[187] His main thought is that the soul cannot obtain its representations or ¯concepts¯[188] from | external things. How do thinking and what is extended come together? This is always an important point: How does the extended, the manifold, come into what is simple, into spirit, ¯since [extension] is mutual externality, the contrary of the simple, and of what relates [itself] to itself?¯[189] ¯Furthermore: "The soul also

114

185. *Thus Pn with An; Gr reads:* a man of most noble character and of the purest, most unwavering piety. *Lw reads:* noble, gentle, of pure piety. *Sv reads:* pious.

186. [Ed.] *The Search after Truth*, Malebranche's first and most extensive work, appeared in six editions between 1674 and 1712. Hegel used the 4th ed., 2 vols. (Amsterdam, 1688). He is probably referring here to its headings: bk. 1, "Errors of the Senses"; bk. 2, pts. 1 and 2, "The Imagination," and pt. 3, "The Contagious Communication of Strong Imaginations"; bk. 3, pt. 1, "The Understanding or Pure Mind [Spirit]," and pt. 2, "The Nature of Ideas." Hegel is probably speaking of this last part as "entirely metaphysical." See the English translation (of the 6th ed.), by Thomas M. Lennon and Paul J. Olscamp (Columbus, 1980), which is bound together with the English translation, by Lennon, of Malebranche's *Elucidations of the Search after Truth.*

187. [Ed.] See Malebranche, *The Search after Truth*, bk. 3, pt. 1, chap. 1 (Lennon, p. 198; *Œuvres* 1:381). For Malebranche we do not cite page references in the 4th ed., used by Hegel, but instead in the *Œuvres complètes*, ed. André Robinet, 20 vols. (Paris, 1958–1965).

188. *Gr reads:* concept
[Ed.] That external objects themselves transmit to the soul the species that depict or represent them is the first of five different ways of defining the relationship between the soul and external objects; Malebranche considers and rejects it. See *The Search after Truth*, bk. 1, pt. 2, chap. 1 (Lennon, pp. 219–221; *Œuvres* 1:417).

189. *Thus Gr; Pn reads:* [since] spirit is, after all, the very contrary of what is manifold? *An reads:* [since] extension is in fact the contrary of the simple?

cannot beget the ideas from itself."⁻[190] "Say not that ye yourselves only are your own light."[191] The upshot is then that it is in God that we are cognizant of all external things, it is in God that we see all things. God is omnipresent and united with spirit in the most intimate way; God is the locus of spirits (namely, thought, the universal, God), just as space is the locus of bodies. What we know we know in God, insofar as God represents[192] created beings. In God things are intellectual or spiritual, and we too are intellectual, and hence we behold things in God, in the intellectual way they are in God.

Malebranche then speaks of the universal, of thinking in general, of the infinite. He says that the universal is not a confused representation, it is no confusion of single ideas nor yet a union of single things; on the contrary, the particular, and particular representa-

190. *Thus W; Lw reads, similar in Gr:* Also, it [the extended] cannot beget itself, or be born, from itself.
[*Ed.*] Malebranche here (in the reading of the main text, but not the variant) refers to the second way of viewing the relationship, another empiricist view that he also rejects. According to it, the impressions that objects make on the body, though not themselves images of those objects, nevertheless move the soul to produce our ideas of those objects. See *The Search after Truth*, bk. 3, pt. 2, chap. 3 (Lennon, p. 222; *Œuvres* 1:422).

191. [*Ed.*] This quotation occurs in Malebranche in another context. After rejecting the third possible way of defining the relationship of soul to its objects—the hypothesis of innate ideas (not mentioned here by Hegel, but cf. W 15:412)—Malebranche proceeds to discuss and refute the fourth viewpoint, one touched on by Descartes in the Third Meditation (Descartes: *Writings* 2:28; *Œuvres* 8, pt. 1:41) and subsequently advanced by Louis de La Forge, a physician and a Cartesian, namely, the view that the soul can discover all external objects by considering itself and its own perfections. To support his refutation, Malebranche cites Augustine's injunction (*Dic quia tu tibi lumen non es*) from his Eighth Sermon, rendered by Malebranche as: "Say not that you are your light to yourself." It is Malebranche's version that Hegel renders in German. See *The Search after Truth*, bk., 3, pt. 2, chap. 5 (Lennon, pp. 228–229; *Œuvres* 1:433–434). The following sentence of Hegel's text gives the fifth way of viewing the relationship, the only one Malebranche accepts. See *The Search after Truth*, bk. 3, pt. 2, chap. 6 (Lennon, p. 230; *Œuvres* 1:437).

192. [*Ed.*] Hegel here renders Malebranche's *représenter* as *darstellen*. This sentence and the next are based on *The Search after Truth*, bk. 3, pt. 2, chap. 6 (Lennon, p. 230; *Œuvres* 1:437). Cf. also the partial translation of this Malebranche passage in W 15:412–413 (Ms?).

tions, are only participations in the universal idea of the infinite. ⁻The universal does not receive its determinate being from the particular things.⁻ ¹⁹³ The idea of the universal is the first idea in human beings, it must take precedence; if we wish to think something particular, we must first think the universal.¹⁹⁴ The universal is the foundation of the particular in the same way that all bodies have their foundation in space as an all-embracing mutual externality. The universal is in and for itself, it does not arise through the particular. When we see a triangle within the universal, we cannot say that | we see something particular.¹⁹⁵ No account can be given of how spirit is cognizant of abstract and universal truths except it be through the presence of ⁻him who can illumine the spirit,⁻ ¹⁹⁶ the one who is the universal in and for itself. Only through the presence of God does the soul have the consciousness of the universal, of God. We can only have clear cognitive knowledge through union with God, and this is not a created knowledge or idea but is in and for itself. Everything else is only a special case of this basic principle.

115

It is the same as with Spinoza;¹⁹⁷ the One Universal is God. We have knowledge of the universal and, insofar as it is determinate,

193. *Thus Pn, An; Gr reads, similar in Lw:* As God does not have his determinate being from what is created, so the infinite does not have its determinate being from finite things.

[*Ed.*] This and the preceding sentence are based on *The Search after Truth*, bk. 3, pt. 2, chap. 6 (Lennon, p. 232; *Œuvres* 1:441–442). Cf. the translation in *W* 15:414–415 (Ms?).

194. [*Ed.*] See *The Search after Truth*, bk. 3, pt. 2, chap. 6 (Lennon, p. 232; *Œuvres* 1:441). Free and abridged translations of this passage and that cited in the preceding note are reproduced in *W* 15:412–415, probably as derived from Hegel's own manuscripts. The versions of them in our text, as taken from the transcripts, are a further abridgment of Malebranche's text.

195. [*Ed.*] See *The Search after Truth*, bk. 3, pt. 2, chap. 6 (Lennon, p. 232; *Œuvres* 1:441). Cf. the translation of the unabridged quotation in *W* 15:414 (Ms?).

196. *Thus W and Malebranche; Lw reads:* what maintains the spirit,

[*Ed.*] The conclusion of this paragraph, on how God's presence enables our consciousness of the universal, is based on *The Search after Truth*, bk. 3, pt. 2, chap. 6 (Lennon, p. 232; *Œuvres* 1:441). Cf. Hegel's somewhat free and selective translation of this passage, in *W* 15:414 (Ms?). The main text here (except for the final sentence), taken from the transcripts, is presumably derived from this translation. See n. 194 just above.

197. [*Ed.*] Hegel is referring to the proposition that all determinacy is negation of the universal; see above, p. 000 with n. 143.

it is the particular; we see this particular only in the universal, as we see bodies in space. Augustine says that we see God *dès cette vie*, already in or from this life, that is, through the cognition we have of eternal truths. ‾This truth is‾[198] infinite, immeasurable, in and for itself, ‾uncreated;‾[199] it is true through itself, ‾not by any finite thing.‾[200] This [truth] is what makes the creature more perfect, and of their own volition spirits seek to know [it]. This perfection is only in God, and God is therefore the truth; when we have knowledge of infinite truth, we intuit God. Malebranche says, just as did Spinoza in using his ethical standard,[201] that it is impossible for God to have an end other than himself. Therefore it is not only necessary that our natural love strives after God, but it is likewise impossible that the light and the knowledge that God gives to our spirit should permit the knowing of anything other than what is in God. All natural love has God as its end, and still more so the knowledge or the willing of what is true, for all movements of the will toward [*für*] the creature are only motions toward the creator, who is his own | cause.[202] Thus we see in Malebranche's noble soul   116
the very same content as in Spinoza, only in a more pious form.

These are the principal ideas of Malebranche. The rest of his work is partly formal logic, partly empirical psychology—the form of how we arrive at truth.[203]

198. *An reads:* These truths are
199. *Thus W and Malebranche; An reads:* not innate;
200. *Thus Gr; An reads:* wholly encompassing the perfections.
[Ed.] In this and the next two sentences Hegel reproduces a passage in Malebranche, *The Search after Truth*, bk. 3, pt. 2, chap. 6 (Lennon, pp. 233–234; Œuvres 1:444), that follows a lengthy quotation from Augustine, *On the Trinity*, bk. 14, chap. 15. Cf. Hegel's abridged translation of Malebranche in W 15:415–416 (Ms?).
201. [Ed.] Hegel is probably referring to Spinoza's notion of the intellectual love of God (see above, p. 000 with n. 182). The paraphrase that follows in the text is from *The Search after Truth*, bk. 3, pt. 2, chap. 6 (Lennon, p. 233; Œuvres 1:442–443). Cf. the translation in W 15:415 (Ms?), the basis for Hegel's text here as transmitted by the transcripts, both of which speak of "movements of the will for (*für*) the creature . . . for the creator"; Malebranche has *pour* for each preposition, so we (following Lennon and Olscamp) use "toward."
202. [Ed.] Again Hegel is probably being influenced by Spinoza in his portrayal of Malebranche's thought, here by Spinoza's concept of *causa sui* (see above, p. 000 with n. 149).
203. [Ed.] Hegel's presentation takes into account only the metaphysical parts

C. CRITIQUE AND SECOND PERIOD OF METAPHYSICS: LOCKE, LEIBNIZ, AND OTHERS

Locke and Leibniz stand each by himself and in opposition to the other. The general feature that they have in common is that, in contrast with Spinoza and Malebranche, what they make into their principle is the particular, finite determinateness and the singular. Locke especially is concerned with knowledge of the universal, with "general ideas," [which are really] "representations," and with their origin. The reverse was the case for Spinoza and Malebranche, where substance or God, the One, is the universal or what is true, what is in and for itself, without origin and eternal—and the particulars are only modifications of it. On the contrary, what come first for Locke are the finite, and finite knowledge or consciousness, and the universal has to be derived from that. Leibniz likewise takes as his principle the monad, the singular or the individual, which in Spinoza only perishes and is transitory. ˜To this extent the two coincide in their reasoning.˜[204]

1. John Locke

John Locke was born in 1632 at Wrington. He studied the Cartesian philosophy at Oxford and there devoted himself to the science of medicine, though he did not in fact practice it owing to his frail health. In 1664 he came for a time to Berlin in the company of an English ambassador. After his return [to England] 117 he became associated with | the current earl of Shaftesbury, as his

---

of *The Search after Truth,* in bk. 3, pt. 2. The preceding and following books lie outside his concern, though in the *Science of Logic* (p. 161; cf. *GW* 21:148) he does in addition refer to Malebranche's *Elucidations of the Search after Truth* (Amsterdam, 1677–1678; revised editions through 1712), no. 10, "On the Nature of Ideas."

204. *Thus Pn; Gr reads:* It is in this regard that I place these two together.

[*Ed.*] The other philosophers treated in this section (Grotius, Hobbes, Hume and various other Scottish philosophers, Wolff) are exponents either of empiricism or of rationalism and, as such, have affinities either with Locke or with Leibniz. In discussing Locke, we translate Hegel's *allgemeine Vorstellungen* as "general ideas," which approximates to Locke's own terminology. Hegel indicates (p. 000 below) that Locke's "ideas" are really "representations" acquired from sense experience, and so they differ from what Hegel himself means by "idea" in other contexts.

˜physician.˜²⁰⁵ When Lord Shaftesbury subsequently became lord chancellor of England, he appointed Locke to an office; but Locke became caught up in the current change of ministry and lost his post when his patron fell from power. In 1675 he betook himself to Montpellier for the sake of his health. He was restored to his post, but soon thereafter he was dismissed again ˜when his patron was again deposed,˜²⁰⁶ and he even had to flee. He went to Holland, which was opposed to all oppression, whether political or religious, and was a refuge for exiles where the most famous and liberal-minded men of the day were to be found. He returned to England with William of Orange in 1688. Locke published his famous work *An Essay concerning Human Understanding* in 1694. He died on 28 October 1704.²⁰⁷

His philosophy itself is very well known. It is on the whole still the philosophy of the English and the French; in a certain sense it has also been the philosophy of the Germans and even today still is so in part. In brief, Locke's philosophical thought is that our general ideas rest upon experience, that what is true or what we know rests upon experience. ˜Experience is observation and the analysis of it according to general characteristics extracted from it.˜²⁰⁸ This is a metaphysical sort of empiricism, and it is the procedure in the ordinary sciences. In his method Locke adopted the procedure op-

205. *Thus An; Gr reads:* tutor.
[*Ed.*] Actually Locke was tutor to the earl's son.
206. *An reads:* when his new patron was deposed, *Lw reads:* upon a new change in ministry,
207. [*Ed.*] The biographical data of this paragraph are based on Buhle (*Geschichte* 4, pt. 1:238–241) and incorporate Buhle's errors; there is no evidence that Hegel consulted any other source. The mission of Sir William Vane, to whom Locke was secretary, was to the court of the Brandenburg Elector, Frederick William, in the Duchy of Cleves. Locke's flight to Holland in 1683 took place some months after Shaftesbury's death. He returned to England not with William of Orange but in February 1689, with Princess Mary at her invitation. The first edition of Locke's *Essay* appeared in London at the end of 1689 and bore the date 1690. When giving page numbers and quotations, we refer here to the critical edition by Peter H. Nidditch (Oxford, 1975).
208. *Thus An with Pn; Gr reads, similar in Lw:* Prescribed as the course or procedure of knowing are, on the one hand, experience and observation, and on the other the analysis (*Lw adds:* of it), the extraction, of general characteristics. *Sv reads:* We must on the one hand observe experience, and then work up its materials.

posed to that of Spinoza. Spinoza begins from definitions, ˘which he sets up first.˘²⁰⁹ Locke, on the contrary, shows that these general ideas—substance, cause and effect—stem from experience. In the

118 method of Spinoza and Descartes one can fail to notice | that they do not give the origin of the ideas but just take them up as they come—ideas such as substance, the infinite, and so on. There is a need, however, to show where these ideas or thoughts come from and by what means these representations are grounded and validated. Locke satisfies the need arising from this deficiency by providing the grounding for our general ideas.

But this ˘origin,˘²¹⁰ as Locke designates it, concerns only the empirical origin, namely, what course it takes within our consciousness. Everyone knows that he or she begins from experiences, from sensations, from wholly concrete states, and that general ideas come later in time. They have some connection with the concrete [object] of sensation; the general ideas are contained in it. When I see this sheet of paper, I see something spatially extended, for the universal [aspect], space, is also contained in it. This universal, space, only comes to my consciousness later than what is in space, the species comes later than ˘the individual, the concrete˘²¹¹ in which the universal is contained; hence one must *arrive* at the distinction of the universal from this particular. To draw out the universal is the operation of my consciousness. So the course Locke adopted is quite correct.

But it is another question whether these universal determinations are true in and for themselves, and where they come from, not only in my consciousness or in my understanding but in the things themselves. ˘Space, cause, effect, and the like are categories;˘²¹² how do

209. *Thus Lw; Sv reads:* and general ideas.
210. *Thus Pn, An; Gr reads:* grounding,
[*Ed.*] Locke says (*Essay,* bk. 1, chap. 1, § 3; Nidditch, p. 44): "*First,* I shall inquire into the *Original* of those *Ideas,* Notions, or whatever else you please to call them, which a Man observes, and is conscious to himself he has in his Mind; and the ways whereby the Understanding comes to be furnished with them."
211. *Thus An; Gr reads:* the singular *Pn reads:* this [one] animal *Lw reads:* the concrete
212. *Thus Gr; Lw reads:* What connection have these categories such that they are necessary, and

these categories come together in the particularity, in the concrete? How does universal space attain ˉthis particularity and [these] concrete properties?ˉ²¹³ But the question [*Standpunkt*] whether these determinations of the infinite, of substance, and so forth, are true in and | for themselves gets completely lost from sight. ˉFor Plato the infinite as identical with the finite is what is true.ˉ²¹⁴ [For Plato] it matters not whence the truth of this content derives, but in Locke the truth of the content gets completely lost from sight.

As to Locke's more specific thoughts, they are very simple. For Descartes the ideas are innate. Locke contests the so-called innate ideas and appeals to the fact that they are not found in children and in many adults; for instance, many people are unfamiliar with the proposition, "What is, is," and the like.²¹⁵ This is a very weak objection, for it presupposes that we understand innate ideas to be the sort of thing we would have in consciousness forthwith, as fully formed, just as we are born with the hands we have from infancy on. But reason's development within consciousness is something other than its implicit potential [*das Ansich*], so that the expression "innate idea" is in any event quite misleading.

The next point, then, is that Locke goes on to say that all people are conscious that they think, and that what the mind [*Geist*] occupies itself with is ideas. People have different "ideas" [*Ideen*]. These are really "representations" [*Vorstellungen*], for by "idea" *we* understand something different. In Locke's case "ideas" are

---

213. *Thus Pn; Gr reads:* the point of determining itself?

214. *Thus Pn; Gr reads:* Plato investigated the infinite and the finite and determined that neither is by itself what is true; they are what is true only when both are positing one another identically. *Lw reads:* Only the infinite to the extent that it posits itself identically with the finite and vice versa is what is true.

[*Ed.*] Hegel is referring to his own interpretation of Plato's *Philebus*.

215. [*Ed.*] On innate ideas for Descartes, see p. 000 and n. 111 above. Chapters 2–4 of the first book of Locke's *Essay* combat the hypothesis of innate ideas (although his particular target here is more likely the Cambridge Platonists than it is Descartes). See especially chap. 2, §§ 1, 4, and 5 (Nidditch, pp. 48–51), where Locke argues that it is contradictory to say truths can be "imprinted on the soul" and not be perceived by it. Hence the absence of "universal assent" to alleged innate truths sufficiently disproves their existence. "Whatsoever is, is," and "'Tis impossible for the same thing to be, and not to be," are Locke's examples of allegedly innate speculative principles. Cf. the translations from §§ 4 and 5 in W 15:426 (Ms?).

such things as the ideas of elephant, white, hardness, softness, rest, motion, and so forth. The question then is how we come by these representations. If we presuppose the mind to be a blank paper with no writing on it, then how is it furnished with them? The answer, in a word, is: by experience. All our knowing is founded on experience; by experience we acquire images—determinate sensation transforms itself into representation. Everything is experience, not merely the sensible but also ˉwhat determines or moves my spirit;ˉ[216] in other words, | I must myself be it and have it. The consciousness of what I have and am *is* experience, and it is absurd [to suppose] that we would know, and so forth, something that is not in experience. Take, for example, humanity. We are all human. I do not need to have seen everyone, however, for I am human myself, I have activity, will, and consciousness of what I am and what others are, and so all this is experience in any case. Locke's starting point therefore is that everything is experience, and from our experience we fashion for ourselves general ideas.[217]

120

Locke next distinguishes between objects and their qualities. In this context he draws a distinction between primary and secondary qualities. For Descartes the primary qualities are extension, rest, and motion; these are the qualities of what is corporeal, ˉjust as thinking is the quality of what is spiritual.ˉ[218] The prime qualities [for Locke] are extension and solidity, whereas qualities that pertain to the nature of sensation and to feeling are secondary, for instance, colors, sounds, and smells.[219]

216. *Thus Gr; An reads:* what moves my spirit; *Lw reads:* what puts my spirit into activity; *Pn reads:* the kinds of activities that are active in my spirit;

217. [*Ed.*] For the most part this paragraph faithfully reflects Locke's position in the *Essay*, bk. 2, chap. 1, §§ 1–3 (Nidditch, pp. 104–105), with the following exceptions. First, the remark about Locke's ideas really being *Vorstellungen* is Hegel's own. Second, "determinate sensation" stands for Locke's "sensible qualities." Third, where our text says that "determinate sensation transforms itself into representation" (transmitted by *Pn* only), Locke says "the senses convey into the mind . . . what produces there those *Perceptions.*"

218. *Thus Gr; Lw reads:* [as] thinking [is] in the case of spirit.

219. [*Ed.*] For Descartes's view of qualities, see p. 000 with n. 120 above. In the *Essay*, bk. 2, chap. 8, § 7 (Nidditch, p. 134), Locke distinguishes between ideas or perceptions, bodies (objects), and qualities ("modifications of matter in the Bodies that cause such Perceptions in us"). The remainder of this chapter (Nidditch, pp.

After the foregoing is presupposed, the next point is that it is the understanding, the intellect,[220] that now finds and invents the universal. General ideas [*allgemeine Ideen*] enter into the mind neither through sensation nor through ˉreflection or inner sensibility.ˉ[221] On the contrary, they are the creatures, the creations ˉor inventions,ˉ[222] of the understanding. The understanding makes them through representations that it has obtained from ˉsensation and reflection.ˉ[223] Thus the understanding is active too, but it is only a combining activity, which consists in the compounding of such general ideas. Locke says that with regard to its simple forms or modes the understanding is wholly passive. These simple determinations include force, number, infinity, and so forth. The understanding is wholly passive with regard to them, for it receives them from the existence and operation of things in the way that sensation and reflection offer them to it, | without its making any sort of [simple] idea at all. Hence the understanding is no more than the apprehension [*Auffassung*] of the abstract determinations that are contained in the object. But then Locke draws a distinction between simple and mixed forms; for example, causality is a mixed mode, from cause and effect.[224]

121

134–143), which discusses other aspects of these simple ideas and their correlates in experience, includes Locke's views of: primary qualities ("Solidity, Extension, Figure, Motion, or Rest, and Number"; § 9, pp. 134–135); secondary qualities ("Colours, Sounds, Tastes, etc."; § 10, p. 135), which are powers to produce sensations in us and are not elements in the objects themselves; a third type not mentioned by Hegel, namely, a power in bodies to produce qualities in other bodies (§ 10, p. 135); the relationship of primary and secondary qualities to ideas (§ 15, p. 137). Unlike Descartes, Locke does not here speak of qualities of the spiritual domain.

220. [*Ed.*] Hegel used English, Latin, and German terms here. The German reads: "das understanding, intellectus, der Verstand . . . "

221. *Thus An; Pn, Lw read:* reflection, *Gr reads:* affection [namely, affects],

222. *Lw reads:* of the sensations,

[*Ed.*] Locke himself says "inventions"; see the following note. *Lw*'s unsuitable term (in the context of this sentence) may be due to mistaking *Erfindungen* as *Empfindungen*.

223. *Thus Lw; Gr reads:* affection and sensation.

[*Ed.*] In the *Essay*, bk. 2, chap. 2, § 2, and in a footnote thereto that first appears in the fifth edition (1706), Locke states that we construct general or complex ideas out of combinations of the simple ideas that we derive from sensation and reflection (pp. 119–120 in Nidditch, which, however, omits the footnote).

224. [*Ed.*] The *Essay*, bk. 2, chap. 22, § 2, states that the mind is passive in

175

Locke now explains in detail the way in which the understanding acquires general ideas [*allgemeine Vorstellungen*] from concrete representations, but his explanation is extremely trivial and tedious. It takes up the greater part of his work [the *Essay*]. Space, for instance, is a general idea. We construct it through sight and feeling, from the perception of our distance from bodies and of their distance from one another.[225] The distance of bodies from one another, however, is nothing else but space; space is only another word for it. Attention fixes upon this one characteristic of spatiality among bodies. There is no deduction here, but only a leaving aside of the other characteristics. We arrive at the concept of time through the uninterrupted succession of representations in the waking state, for they continually follow upon one another, and in this way we obtain general ideas of time. If we pay attention to this and leave aside what is particular, then we have succession as such, which is itself time.[226] Similarly we obtain the idea of cause and effect through our sensory information about the perpetual alteration of things. In this perceiving we see that different particulars (substance and quality) begin to exist, and we notice that their existence stems from the appropriate application and operation of some other thing. Something begins to exist because another thing is duly applied. This gives us the idea of cause and effect. For example, we see that wax melts in front of the fire. The wax becomes soft and alters its shape, so we regard the fire as what operates on

---

receiving the simple ideas from sensation and reflection, but active in combining them to form complex ideas (Nidditch, pp. 288–289). Cf. Hegel's abridged translation of this passage, and comment, in W 15:432 (Ms?). Earlier in the same book, chap. 12, §§ 4 and 5, Locke discusses the "modes," which are complex ideas that are dependent on substances (another class of complex ideas); a simple mode combines simple ideas of the same sort (such as "dozen" from "units"), whereas a complex or mixed mode such as "beauty" combines different simple ideas of figure and color (Nidditch, p. 165). The intervening chapters (13–21) treat the simple modes exhaustively, including those mentioned by Hegel, except that Locke speaks of "power" instead of "force." On causality, see below, n. 227.

225. [*Ed.*] On space, see *Essay*, bk. 2, chap. 13, § 2 (Nidditch, p. 167).

226. [*Ed.*] Hegel here disregards Locke's distinction that time is derived from the idea of duration (the distance between any parts of succession), and so is not duration itself but the measure of duration (*Essay*, bk. 2, chap. 14, §§ 3 and 17; Nidditch, pp. 181–182, 187).

it. This is the idea of cause and effect. But in this ongoing change we also see subsistence, and this is substance.[227] We can say that nothing can be more superficial, | nothing can be more trivial, than this so-called derivation of the idea [*Idee*], in which attention is drawn to one determination that is contained in a concrete relationship. ¯The action of the understanding is only the fixation of one determination and the leaving aside of the others.¯[228] Thus Locke's philosophy commends itself by its clarity and lucidity, and there can be nothing clearer than the derivation that we have just exhibited.

122

This, then, is how we obtain general ideas or generic concepts, although they are mere nominal essences that serve to provide species or kinds for us to recognize. But we do not know what the real essence of nature is.[229] As an example to prove that species are nothing in and for themselves, Locke points to the births of deformed creatures; if the species were something in and for itself, then there would be no deformed births.[230] This is a very weak argument, one overlooking the fact that existence also belongs to the species. The existential aspect of the species is just what is essentially dependent on other determining circumstances. The universal steps forth and makes itself finite in such a way that ¯there is a casting out of the individual aspects of the concrete idea into

227. [*Ed.*] The discussion of cause and effect, including the example of the wax, follows closely *Essay*, bk. 2, chap. 26, §§ 1–2 (Nidditch, pp. 324–325); cf. the partial translation in *W* 15:433–434 (Ms?). In bk. 2, chap. 23, § 1, Locke speaks of the substratum we suppose as that in which simple ideas subsist, which substratum we call "substance" (Nidditch, p. 295).

228. *Thus Pn, similar in Lw; Gr reads:* So the understanding only abstracts and on the other side fixates. *An reads:* since the understanding only abstracts.

[*Ed.*] On abstraction, see *Essay*, bk. 3, chap. 3, § 6 (Nidditch, pp. 410–411), as well as the following note.

229. [*Ed.*] The *Essay*, bk. 3, chap. 3, § 13, states that essences of species are but abstract ideas in the mind that the understanding has constructed from the similitudes observed in things (Nidditch, pp. 415–416). In § 15 Locke goes on to distinguish nominal essence and real essence (Nidditch, p. 417). Hegel's remark that we do not know the real essence of nature may also refer to Locke's comment, in discussing deformed births (see the following note), about the erroneous "supposition of essences that cannot be known."

230. [*Ed.*] See *Essay*, bk. 3, chap. 3, § 17 (Nidditch, pp. 417–418).

mutual externality.¯²³¹ In this way the existence of the species can become outwardly distorted. One interest of philosophy is to know what is true, and in Locke this is to be achieved in empirical fashion. Calling attention to the general characteristics [of things] is useful, but the perspective that this [knowing] should have truth in and for itself is left out of account.

123 Locke's philosophy is, if you like, a metaphysics. In all its formality it deals with general characteristics or universal thoughts, and this universal aspect is to be derived from experience and observation. Another feature is his | practical procedure, which operates in the same fashion, namely, that thought applies itself to objects, or that thoughts—the indwelling, essential universal—are abstracted from the objects. This metaphysical empiricism has on the whole become the foremost mode of treating issues or of cognitive knowing in England and in Europe; and what we in general call the sciences, and in particular the empirical sciences, have this procedure to thank for their origin. This scientific method is the observation of objects and the investigation or drawing out of their inner law. (The converse method is on the one hand that of Scholasticism, and on the other that of metaphysical [rationalism], namely, proceeding from basic principles or definitions.) The philosophical method that is practical in this way, the philosophizing of argumentative [räsonnierenden] thinking, is what has now become universal, and through it the entire revolution in our mental attitude has come about.

2. Hugo Grotius

The same method is evident in the work of Hugo Grotius, where it has been applied on the one hand to physical objects and on the other to political and legal objects. ¯Hugo Grotius wrote¯²³² *De*

231. *Thus An with Pn; Gr reads, similar in Lw:* there is the sphere where singular, particular things act upon one another;

232. *Thus An, similar in Pn, Lw; Gr reads:* Hugo van Groot, born in Delft in 1583, was a jurist, attorney general, and syndic [corporate legal representative]. As implicated in the prosecution of Barneveldt, however, he had to flee in 1619, and he remained for a long time in France until he in 1634 entered the service of Queen Christina of Sweden. In 1635 he became Swedish ambassador in Paris. He died at

jure belli et pacis (1625), which no one reads any longer, although it was extremely influential. He derived many of his points historically, even from the Old Testament; he compiled the different stances that peoples have adopted toward one another historically in diverse circumstances of war and peace.[233] Through his wholly empirical compilation of the behavior of peoples toward one another, coupled with empirical | argumentation, he had the   124 effect of making people conscious of general principles, principles of the understanding and of reason, so that they became recognized as valid—such as the principle that prisoners of war may not be killed, since the purpose is to disarm the enemy and make them incapable of waging war, and once this is accomplished one is not to do them further harm.[234] ⌐General principles of this kind have had their basis in their [historical] object.⌐[235] Such proofs or de-

---

Rostock in 1645, while journeying from Stockholm to Holland. His principal work is

[*Ed.*] The actual title is: *De jure belli ac pacis libri tres* (Paris, 1625); English translation by Francis W. Kelsey et al. (from the 1646 ed.), *The Law of War and Peace* (Indianapolis and New York, 1925).

233. [*Ed.*] This sentence does not make clear the methodological function such examples have for Grotius. In his view the ultimate ground of right or law lies in rational concern for the social community, as the end toward which the social instinct tends. The specifications of the law of nations (*ius gentium*), as distinguished from natural law (*ius naturale*), he bases on consensus of the nations (*consensus gentium*) extracted from his diverse historical sources, including the Old Testament with its own distinction between divine and human law (*ius Dei et ius hominum*). See *The Law of War and Peace,* prolegomena 6, 11, 17, 40, 46–48 (Kelsey, pp. 11, 13, 15, 23–24, 26–27); the prolegomena of the 1646 Latin edition do not have numbered paragraphs.

234. [*Ed.*] In book 3 of *The Law of War and Peace* Grotius concludes, contrary to Hegel's account, that the laws of warfare do permit the killing of prisoners; see especially chap. 4, §§ 10–12 (Kelsey, pp. 649–650). Refraining might be due to preferring what is morally right over what is merely permissible (chap. 4, § 2; Kelsey, pp. 641–643), or due to expediency (chap. 7, § 5.3; Kelsey, p. 692). Hegel's formulation may be based on Grotius's quotation (in bk. 3, chap. 11, § 13.1; Kelsey, pp. 737–738) of a passage from Augustine's First Letter to Boniface, which states that because the enemy is killed in battle out of necessity and not by an act of will, pity ought to be shown to captives.

235. *Thus An; Gr reads:* This is the establishing of universal principles that have their ultimate basis in the objects themselves. *Lw reads:* These principles had their universal basis more or less in the nature of the object. *Pn reads:* These principles are inherent in the nature of the object.

ductions do not satisfy us, but we must not fail to appreciate what they accomplished in their time.

3. Thomas Hobbes

ˉIt was in England that reflection on topics of constitutional law in particular flourished.ˉ[236] Hobbes is noteworthy and celebrated on account of the originality of his views. He was born in Malmesbury in 1588 and he died in 1679. A prolific author, he also wrote the *Elements of Philosophy*, dealing with philosophy in general. The first part of it, the *De corpore*, appeared in London in 1655. In this first part he deals initially with logic, secondly with *philosophia prima* or ontology, thirdly *de rationibus motuum et magnitudinum* [the proportions of motion and magnitude], then fourthly with the physics or nature of phenomena, sound, smell, and the like. The second part was to be *De homine* and the third *De cive*.[237]

125   In the preface to the *Elements of Philosophy* he says | that Copernicus paved the way in astronomy and Galileo in physics, for before them there had been nothing certain in these sciences. He also says there that Harvey [elaborated] the science of the human body, and that Kepler, Gassendi, and others further developed general physics and astronomy.[238] All this counts as philosophy according to the viewpoint we mentioned previously. ˉHobbes himself proceeds according to immediate perception and reflective understanding.ˉ[239] He further says that, as for political philosophy or

236. *Thus An, similar in Lw; Pn reads:* In England in particular there was a revolution in political views. *Gr reads:* England in particular developed the conditions of domestic constitutional law, for their distinctive form of government led the English to reflection on this issue.

237. [*Ed.*] *Elements of Philosophy* is not the name of a single work but the overall title for Hobbes's philosophical system. He actually published the third part, *De cive* (*The Citizen*), first, in 1642. The first part, *De corpore* (*The Body*), appeared in 1655, and the second, *De homine* (*Human Nature*), in 1657.

238. [*Ed.*] These statements are in the Epistle Dedicatory to the 1655 edition of *De corpore*; see *The English Works of Thomas Hobbes,* ed. Sir William Molesworth, 11 vols. (London, 1839–1845), 1:viii–ix; cf. Hegel's excerpt from it in *Berliner Schriften,* p. 689. Hegel's next statement in the text, that all this counts as philosophy, refers back to his characterization of Locke's position, p. 000 above.

239. *Thus Pn; Gr reads:* In it the reflective understanding seeks knowledge of the universal.

philosophia civilis, it is no older than his own book *De cive.*[240] His book *Leviathan,* a quite notorious work, has the same content. He sought to deduce the principles of state authority, monarchical authority, and the like from universal determinations, and his theses are too original for us to omit mention of them.

He says at the beginning that civil society derives its origin from mutual fear, and that every society is organized for individual advantage or from ambition or self-interest. All human beings are by nature equal, but he proves this equality on grounds characteristic for him, namely, that each person is capable of killing the other, that each is the ultimate power over the other. Therefore it is likewise the case that each is weak and susceptible to being killed by the other. Equality is therefore based upon universal weakness, not as in more recent times upon absolute freedom or autonomy. He says further that in the natural state we all have the will to harm one another.[241] He is right about that. He apprehends the natural state in its authentic sense: there is no idle talk of a naturally good condition, for the natural state is rather the bestial state, the state of desire, of the unsubdued self-will. All have the will to injure one another, and equally the will to secure themselves against the pretensions of others and | to acquire greater rights and advantages   126 for themselves. So there is mistrust of all toward all. Hobbes characterizes this natural state more precisely as a *bellum omnium contra omnes,* a war of all against all.[242] That is [the] quite correct view of the natural state.

The expression "nature" has a double sense, an ambiguity. We understand "nature" to mean that our human nature is our spirituality, rationality, and freedom; and that, of course, is not what is meant by "natural state." The other condition, the natural state,

240. [*Ed.*] Also in the Epistle Dedicatory, p. ix; see n. 238 above.
241. [*Ed.*] This account of the origin of civil society in mutual fear and the like is from *De cive,* chap. 1, especially §§ 2–4; cf. §§ 5–6; see the critical edition of *De cive,* ed. Howard Warrender (Oxford, 1983), pp. 90–93. In § 3 Hobbes states that civil law is responsible for introducing the present inequality among persons. In § 4 he says the will to harm one another arises from various causes, and in some cases (such as defense of one's possessions and freedom) is less blameworthy than in others (such as ambition and presumptuousness).
242. [*Ed.*] See *De cive,* chap. 1, § 12; Warrender, p. 96.

is when human beings behave according to their natural being, when they act according to their desires, inclinations, and the like, and not yet according to what is right. Rationality is achieved only when the universal gains mastery over what is immediately natural. According to the "right" of what is immediately natural, this "right" grants us an irresistible power of lordship over those who cannot resist, and it is absurd to let those we have under our control become free and strong again. From this Hobbes draws the conclusion that human beings must go forth from the natural state, *exeundum esse e statu naturae.* This is correct, for the condition of [authentic] right is in no way the natural state. The particular will must be subordinated to the universal will, to the law of reason, which [for Hobbes] is the will of the sovereign who is not accountable [to anyone else]. Since the universal will is made to reside in the will of one person, the monarch, the state of complete despotism thus follows from a viewpoint that is [initially] quite correct.[243] But a lawful condition is something other than one in which the caprice of one [sovereign will] is simply said to be the law.

There is this much, at least, in Hobbes's thesis: that right and the general organization of the state ought to be established on the foundation of human nature, of human characteristics and inclinations. The English have been greatly concerned with the principle of passive obedience, according to which kings are said to have their authority from God. In one respect this is quite correct. In another, however, it has been understood to mean not only that kings have no accountability but that it is their blind caprice or their sheerly subjective will that must be obeyed.[244] |

127

243. [Ed.] On the natural right to dominate others, see *De cive,* chap. 1, § 14; Warrender, p. 97. Hobbes's conclusion that human beings must go forth from the natural state actually follows from the "war of all against all," for one needs allies so as not to have to fight alone (§ 13; Warrender, pp. 96–97). He treats the need for all wills to be subordinated to a single will, in chap. 5, § 6 (Warrender, p. 133), and the sovereign as not accountable to anyone else, in chap. 6, § 12 (Warrender, p. 141). "Despotism" is Hegel's own term here, for Hobbes speaks of the ruler's absolute right, and the citizens' duty of simple obedience so that the state may function (chap. 6, § 13; Warrender, pp. 141–144).

244. [Ed.] In this sweeping remark about "the English" Hegel probably has in mind both *De cive* and also Hobbes's *Leviathan* (1651). There is no evidence that

Reflective thought assumed a prominent and essential role in the struggle to make the relationships of right explicitly secure in the state, ˜to ground the organization of public affairs.˜[245] As did Hugo Grotius, so have the English and PUFENDORF in similar fashion made the human instincts (artistic, social, and so on—all that is immanently human) into principles.[246]

The other aspect [of the empiricist revolution] is that thought has likewise been applied to nature, and in this field Newton is famous by virtue of his mathematical discoveries as well as his physics.[247]

Hegel was familiar with any other seventeenth-century English political philosophy of a formal sort; that is unlikely in any case, for his sources on the history of philosophy mention none. The most extensive presentation of the issue is in Buhle (*Geschichte* 3, pt. 1:263 ff. and 308 ff.), who discusses Hobbes only. Nevertheless, from his study of history, including Hume's *History of Great Britain* (cf. n. 342 below), Hegel was surely familiar with Tudor and Stuart theories of the divine right of kings.

245. *An reads:* to organize civic rights. *Gr reads:* to ground a legal constitution. *Lw reads:* to ground the organization of public affairs in struggle. *Pn reads:* and strove to impart organization [to it].

246. *Gr adds:* He [Samuel Pufendorf] was born in 1621 in Saxony. He studied constitutional law, philosophy, and mathematics in Leipzig and Jena. In 1658 he entered the service of Sweden, and in 1686 he switched to the service of Branden-burg. He died in 1694 in Berlin, while holding the office of privy councillor. He wrote several works on constitutional law, of which his *ius naturae et gentium* is particularly noteworthy.

[*Ed.*] Pufendorf's actual year of birth is 1632. *Lw* alone transmits "so have the English," and it is uncertain to whom the reference is made. Hegel could have been thinking of Locke's *Two Treatises of Civil Government* (1690), but it is uncertain whether he was familiar with them. There is no evidence that Hegel had read Pufen-dorf's *De jure naturae et gentium libri octo* (Lund, 1672; the English translation of the 1688 edition, *On the Law of Nature and Nations*, is by C. H. Oldfather and W. A. Oldfather, Oxford and London, 1934). But he did possess a copy of the 1739 edition of Pufendorf's *De officio hominis et civis juxta legem naturalem libri duo* (Lund, 1673; the English translation of the 1682 edition, *The Two Books on the Duty of Man and Citizen according to the Natural Law*, is by Frank Gardner Moore, New York and London, 1927). Unlike Grotius, Pufendorf linked the social instinct with the thought of the person. He also furthered the dissociation of secular natural-law doctrine from theological doctrine, stressed the independent significance of the social order, and introduced sociological, historical, and cultural elements into an expanded framework of natural law (so that he "made the human instincts . . . into principles," as Hegel states). His execution of this program furnished ample instances of the coupling of empirical materials and rational reflection.

247. *Gr adds:* He was born in 1642 at Walstrope [*Ed.*: Woolsthorpe] in Lin-colnshire. He studied mathematics in particular, and in 1669 he became professor

His maxim was: "Physics, beware of metaphysics," that is to say, beware of thinking. But ⁻physics⁻²⁴⁸ can do nothing without thinking; attraction and the like are metaphysical categories established by Newton on the basis of thinking. The issue is just the way in which the categories are to be applied.

In England since Newton's day the experimental sciences have had the name "philosophy"; the English call mathematics and physics "Newtonian philosophy." This expression is still in use today. The economy of the state and the achievement of material welfare have [also] been examined; [Adam] Smith's political economy has become famous in England.²⁴⁹ General principles, such as 128 the current emphasis on free trade, | the English call philosophical principles, they call them philosophy. Six months ago at a gathering where people were drinking to his health, Canning delivered a speech in which he said England is to be congratulated for having a ministry that applies philosophical principles in its administration.²⁵⁰ Thus in England the expression "philosophy" has been

of mathematics at Cambridge and subsequently president of the Royal Society in London. He died in 1727.

[Ed.] In discussing the work of Sir Isaac Newton (1642–1727), several contemporary writers such as Buhle (Geschichte 4, pt. 1:115) quote the maxim that follows in our text, the source of which is Newton's Opticks (London, 1706), p. 314. The ensuing comment about attraction points to a fundamental difference in judging the relation of Newton's work to metaphysics. Newton says he is far removed from hypotheses, including metaphysical hypotheses, since he explains phenomena on the basis of gravitational force but does not inquire into their causes; see his Principia mathematica (1687), next to last paragraph of the General Scholium to book 3, "The System of the World" (English translation by Andrew Motte, revised by Florian Cajori, Sir Isaac Newton's Mathematical Principles, Berkeley, 1946, pp. 546–547). But in Hegel's view the adoption of gravitational force to explain phenomena, in particular Newton's contention that gravitational force is actually present, is the unacknowledged use of a metaphysical category.

248. Thus Gr; Pn reads: mathematicians

249. [Ed.] Hegel possessed a copy of Adam Smith's Wealth of Nations (edition published at Basel, 1791) and also, in German translation from the English, a copy of John Steuart, Untersuchung der Grundsätze der Staats-Wirthschaft; oder, Versuch über die Wissenschaft der innerlichen Politik in freyen Staaten . . . (Hamburg, 1769–1770).

250. [Ed.] The report on the anniversary dinner of the Ship Owners' Society, which quoted Canning's remark that government ministers have it "in their power to apply to the state of the country the just maxims of profound philosophy," ap-

extolled in one mode of usage, whereas in Germany philosophy has become more a term of jest. The English everywhere call "philosophy" those general principles that pertain to physics, chemistry, and rational political science—principles that rest upon ˉreflective experience,ˉ[251] the knowledge of what in this sphere shows itself to be necessary and useful. From this empirical mode of philosophy, for which Locke furnishes the metaphysics, we now pass over to Leibniz.

4. Gottfried Wilhelm Leibniz[252]

Gottfried Wilhelm, Baron von Leibniz, was born in Leipzig in 1646, where his father was professor of philosophy.[253] He studied jurisprudence at Leipzig and occupied himself also with philosophy. As required by the current curriculum, he studied philosophy first, and applied himself especially to it. At Leipzig he also defended philosophical theses, a few of which are still contained in his works; they concern in particular the principle of individuation, which constitutes the abstract principle of his philosophy generally.[254] He acquired a great deal of historical information in order to gain the degree of doctor of laws, but the faculty of law denied him graduation on the pretext of his youthfulness, and it may be that this happened because they did not look kindly on | the fact   129
that he was much occupied with philosophy. He then left Leipzig and went first to Jena and from there to Altdorf, where he gradu-

---

peared in *The Morning Chronicle* of 14 February 1825. Hegel made extracts from it; see *Berliner Schriften*, p. 701; the full text of the article is reproduced by M. J. Petry, "Hegel and the Morning Chronicle," *Hegel-Studien* 11 (1976):31–32. George Canning was governor-general of India (1822–1827) and then prime minister for a brief period before his death in 1827.

251. *Thus Gr: denkende Erfahrung; An reads:* experience plus additional consideration,

252. *Thus An, Gr, Lw, Sv; Pn adds:* the German Philosopher

253. [*Ed.*] A main source cannot be established for the following statement of Leibniz's biography. In addition to Brucker, Buhle, Tennemann, and Tiedemann, Hegel was also acquainted with *La vie de M. Leibniz* in the introduction to the *Essais de théodicée* . . . (Amsterdam, 1734). See also the following notes.

254. [*Ed.*] See Leibniz, *Opera omnia* . . . , ed. Louis Dutens (Geneva, 1768), 2, pt. 1:400, for a list of philosophical propositions he set forth publicly in Leipzig on 30 May 1663.

ated with honors. In Nuremberg he entered into the employment of a society of alchemists, to make abstracts of alchemical treatises. ˉThen he becameˉ[255] tutor to a son of von Boineburg, chancellor to the elector of Mainz.[256] In his extant correspondence there are very many letters to this Herr Boineburg.[257] He traveled to Paris with this young man, received a pension from the elector of Mainz when the young man's education had finished, and remained in Paris by himself for four years. After the elector's death his pension was withdrawn.[258] After that he toured Holland, where he made the acquaintance of the mathematician Huygens, and England, where he got to know Newton.[259] Later [at the end of 1676] he entered the service of [the Duchy of] Braunschweig-Lüneburg, becoming councillor and librarian in Hanover. In 1677 he discovered the differential and integral calculus. He fell into a controversy about this

255. *Thus An, similar in Lw, Sv; Pn reads:* He entered employment as

256. [*Ed.*] His stay in Jena in summer 1663 followed immediately upon his Leipzig disputation. Thereafter Leibniz went directly to Altdorf, where he received his degree in November 1666. His stay in Nuremberg lasted from spring to autumn of 1667, whereupon he went to Frankfurt am Main and to Mainz. Hegel passes over Leibniz's diverse activities in the circle of the elector, Johann Philipp von Schönborn, and of Baron Johann Christian von Boineburg; there is no proof that he was a tutor at this time.

257. [*Ed.*] For this correspondence, see *Commercii epistolici Leibnitiani . . .*, ed. Johann Daniel Gruber (Hanover, 1745), as well as a work of similar title, ed. Johann Georg Heinrich Feder (Hanover, 1805); cf. Leibniz, *Sämtliche Schriften und Briefe,* edited by the Prussian Academy of Sciences, first series, vol. 1 (Darmstadt, 1923).

258. [*Ed.*] Leibniz went to Paris in March 1672. His principal task was to settle some private business in which von Boineburg was involved, and also to further the Consilium Aegypticum, the effort to divert the political interests of the French king, Louis XIV, away from Germany and the Low Countries and toward Egypt. Boineburg's son, Philipp Wilhelm, came to Paris subsequently, in November 1672; supervising his studies was only a sideline of the stay in Paris. The elector, von Schönborn, died just three months later in February 1673. At this time Leibniz was not receiving payment for being a tutor but rather a stipend for his service to Mainz, as well as a stipend, up until September 1673, for services rendered to the Boineburg family. He remained in Paris until 1676, in the service of the electors, Lothar Friedrich von Metternich and Damian Hartard von der Leyen. Therefore Hegel's remark in the text applies only to the cessation of service to the Boineburg family.

259. [*Ed.*] Leibniz made the acquaintance of Christian Huygens (1629–1695) in autumn 1672 in Paris, not in Holland. His first trip to London, January–February 1673, was in the service of his German employers. A second and shorter stay in London took place in 1676 while he was traveling from Paris to Hanover via England and Holland. It is very unlikely that he met Sir Isaac Newton.

with Newton and the Royal Society of London, in which Newton and the London Society treated him dishonorably.[260] He made many journeys from Hanover in the service of his prince, particularly to Italy in order to gather documents related to the house of Este, which had ties with that of Braunschweig-Lüneburg; and he edited writings concerning the history of the house of Braunschweig-Lüneburg.[261] Then he became imperial councillor in Vienna. His circle of acquaintances included the elector of Hanover and also Princess Sophie Charlotte, consort of Frederick I of Prussia, through whom he brought about the founding of the Berlin Academy of Sciences. In Vienna he also became acquainted with Prince Eugene.[262] He died in Hanover in 1716.

Leibniz put his hand to the most diverse sciences and disciplines and accomplished much, in particular in | mathematics, ˉand he is the creator of the method of integral and differential calculus.ˉ[263] We do not have an elaborated system of his philosophy, but only

130

260. [Ed.] Leibniz discovered the differential calculus in his final year in Paris, 1676. Hegel's remark here should not be taken as claiming the credit for Leibniz alone; the *Science of Logic* discusses Newton's calculus (pp. 255 ff.; GW 11:165 ff. and 21:253–263). He is simply being critical of attempts to detract from Leibniz's contribution to this discovery; see, for example, his criticism (in W 15:451) of the omission of any praise of Leibniz in the later editions of Newton's *Principia mathematica*.

261. [Ed.] His first journey to Italy for this purpose took place in 1689–1690. Hegel could not have known of this research from the final form in which Leibniz cast it in the manuscript (still unpublished at the time of his death) *Annales rerum Brunsvicensium*. But it is also unlikely that he knew it from Leibniz's published versions, *Lettres sur la connexion ancienne des maison de Brunsvic et d'Este* (1695) and *Scriptores rerum Brunsvicensium illustrationi inservientes* (1707–1711). Reports about this aspect of Leibniz's work are in the histories of philosophy that Hegel utilized. See *Leibniz: Gesammelte Werke,* ed. Georg Heinrich Pertz, first series (Hanover, 1843–1846; reprint, Hildesheim, 1966), vols. 1–3, *Annales Imperii occidentis Brunsvicensis.*

262. [Ed.] Hegel does not distinguish the two initial stays in Vienna of 1688 and 1690 on trips to and from Italy, from the third in 1700, the fourth in 1708, and the fifth in 1712–1714, during which time Leibniz was designated imperial councillor. He may already have become acquainted with Prince Eugene in Hanover in 1708. The Academy of Sciences was founded in 1700. On Leibniz's relation to Princess Sophie Charlotte, electress of Brandenburg and queen of Prussia, see Leibniz, *Werke,* series 1, *Historisch-politische und staatswissenschaftliche Schriften,* ed. Onno Klopp, vol. 10 (Hanover, 1877), which contains their correspondence.

263. *Thus Gr; Lw reads:* of which he can be called a creator, as discoverer of the differential method.

˜individual˜[264] essays he wrote on this subject. For example, he wrote a *Treatise concerning the Principles of Grace,* addressed to Prince Eugene of Savoy, [as well as] a refutation of Locke's essay on human understanding.[265] His most famous work, his *Theodicy,* is a popular writing done for the benefit of Queen Sophie Charlotte and directed against Bayle. Bayle was a keen dialectician who followed in general the line mentioned in our discussion of Vanini. When Bayle attacks the dogmas of religion, he says that they cannot be proved by reason; they are not to be known by reason, but faith submits [to them].[266] Leibniz's *Theodicy* is a very famous work but one no longer to our taste; it is a justification of God with respect to the evil in the world. The view defended in it is optimism, that the world is the best. Leibniz demonstrates that God has chosen the most perfect from many possible worlds, insofar as it can be perfect in view of the finitude that it is supposed to embrace within

264. *Thus An, Pn; Gr, Lw, Sv read:* brief

265. [*Ed.*] That this statement about *The Principles of Nature and Grace, Based on Reason* (1714) is correct is probably due to a double error. J. J. Koethen, in his Latin translation of the *Monadology* (Geneva, 1737), erroneously labeled that work as dedicated to Prince Eugene (*Theses metaphysicae in gratiam serenissimi principis Eugenii*). The same error passed into the Dutens edition of the *Opera,* which Hegel used, and was only first corrected by C. J. Gerhardt in his edition, *Die philosophischen Schriften,* 7 vols. (Berlin, 1875–1890), 6:483 ff., 598, 607. So in describing *The Principles* as addressed to Prince Eugene, Hegel is perhaps inadvertently correcting the error in Dutens. Or perhaps Hegel was aware of the correct account given in Jacobi's *Spinoza-Briefe,* pp. 387–388; cf. Jacobi's *Werke* 4, pt. 2:118. Leibniz first wrote a short piece on Locke's *Essay* in 1696, which he later augmented with a very large work, *New Essays concerning Human Understanding,* which was only published posthumously by Rudolf Eric Raspe, in *Leibniz: Œuvres philosophiques latines et françoises* (Amsterdam and Leipzig, 1765). It is in French and occupies the whole of volume 5 in Gerhardt; see the English translation by Peter Remnant and Jonathan Bennett (Cambridge, 1981).

266. [*Ed.*] Leibniz published his *Theodicy: Essays on the Goodness of God, the Freedom of Man, and the Origin of Evil,* in 1710; see the abridged translation by E. M. Huggard, ed. Diogenes Allen (Indianapolis, 1966). The *Theodicy* originated in conversations in Berlin during 1701–1702 with Queen Sophie Charlotte about the *Historical and Critical Dictionary* (Rotterdam, 1695–1697) of Pierre Bayle (1647–1706). It also bears upon Bayle's *Réponse aux questions d'un Provincial* (Rotterdam, 1704), which the queen had read; cf. Bayle, *Œuvres diverses* (The Hague, 1727), vol. 3. For Bayle's position as Hegel describes it here, see his account of Bredenbourg's defense against the charge of being a Spinozist, in the article on Spinoza in the *Dictionary* (*Œuvres diverses* 3:2637). On Vanini, see p. 000 above.

itself.[267] That can perhaps be asserted in a general sense, but this perfection is no definite thought, and the nature of evil or of the negative is not explained by it.

In his philosophizing Leibniz proceeded in the way that we still do, for example, in physics, by formation of hypotheses. We have at hand some data that are to be explained. We are supposed to form a hypothesis or a general viewpoint from which the particular can be deduced. This general ˉviewpointˉ[268] must be framed in this way or in that, in light of the existing data. Leibniz's system is still wholly metaphysics, and it stands in essential and glaring contradiction to Spinozism, to the principle of substantial unity where everything determinate is only something transitory.[269] | Over   131
against this principle of absolute unity Leibniz made the absolute multiplicity ˉof individual substancesˉ[270] his principle—although this multiplicity is unified in God, the monad of monads.[271]

He then calls these substances what is individual [*das Individuelle*], or monads, which he distinguishes from atoms. Monads are what is utterly singular, indivisible, simply one. The proof that these monads are what is true in everything is very simple and is based on superficial reflection. There are in fact composite things the principle of which must therefore be something simple; "composite being" means a unity of what is internally a multiplicity.[272]

267. [*Ed.*] The term "optimism" does not appear in the *Theodicy*; its first application to that work seems to be in a review of it by the Jesuits of Trévoux, in *Mémoires pour l'histoire des sciences et des beaux-arts*, February 1737. For the argument that God must choose the best of all possible worlds, see *Theodicy*, pt. 1, § 8 (Allen, p. 35; *Schriften*, ed. Gerhardt, 6:107).

268. *Thus Gr; Lw reads:* hypothesis

269. [*Ed.*] See pp. 000–000 above.

270. *Thus Pn; Sv reads:* of substances, *Gr reads:* [of] the individual substance, *An reads:* of universal substance

271. [*Ed.*] On this term, see p. 000 below.

272. [*Ed.*] On the simplicity of monads, see *Principles of Nature and Grace*, § 1, in *Gottfried Wilhelm Leibniz: Philosophical Papers and Letters*, ed. Leroy E. Loemker, 2d ed. (Dordrecht and Boston, 1969), p. 636; *Schriften*, ed. Gerhardt, 6:598. Cf. the translation of this passage in *W* 15:455 (Ms?). The following statement in the text, to the effect that composites are aggregates of simples, refers to § 2 of the *Monadology*, and the subsequent distinction of monads from Epicurean atoms may refer to § 3 (Loemker, p. 643; *Schriften*, ed. Gerhardt, 6:607), where Leibniz calls monads the "true atoms."

Thus there is the quite trivial category of the composite, from which the simple can be easily derived. The monads, therefore, are what is primary. But they are not the Epicurean atoms—for the atoms are what is internally devoid of determination, where the determination comes only from their aggregation. The monads are instead substantial forms—a fine expression borrowed from the Scholastics; they are entelechies, nonmaterial and nonextended, and they do not originate and perish in a natural manner but are originated through a creative act of God.[273] The expression "creation" is familiar from religion, but it must be defined much more precisely in order for it to be a thought or to have philosophical significance.

Monads therefore are [in the second place] what is simple. Each is a substance on its own account, each is independent vis-à-vis the others. They are without effect upon one another, so that one is not cause in relation to another nor does it posit itself in the other, else it would be no entelechy. The relationship of influence, says Leibniz, is a relationship of crude philosophy [*Vulgärphilosophie*], for we cannot conceive how material particles of one kind or material qualities of one substance can pass over into the other substance; therefore we must abandon the image of influence. If we accept independent substances, as Descartes | did, then no causal nexus can be thought, for that presupposes an influence, a connection of one to the other, and so the other is no substance.[274]

132

273. [*Ed.*] On Epicurean atoms, cf. W 14:487. On monads as substantial forms and as entelechies, see Leibniz, *On Nature Itself; or, On the Inherent Force and Actions of Created Things,* § 11 (Loemker, pp. 503–504; *Opera,* ed. Dutens, 2, pt. 2:55; *Schriften,* ed. Gerhardt, 4:511); *Monadology,* §§ 18, 74 (Loemker, pp. 644, 650; *Schriften,* ed. Gerhardt, 6:609–610, 619). "Entelechy" is an Aristotelian term, in this context designating something that contains within itself the principle and goal of its own development. On the origin and perishing of monads, see *Monadology,* §§ 3–6 (Loemker, p. 643; *Schriften,* ed. Gerhardt, 6:607); cf. *Principles of Nature and Grace,* § 2 (Loemker, p. 636; *Schriften,* ed. Gerhardt, 6:598). In his treatment of the Scholastics Hegel does not take up the topic of substantial forms. Unlike Aquinas, Leibniz includes in the domain of substantial forms the individual itself, with the effect of converting Aquinas's *haecceitas* ("thisness," or specific individuality) into an intelligible essence. W 15:456 refers to substantial forms as "Alexandrian metaphysical points"; cf. Plotinus, *Enneads* 5.7, "On Whether There Are Ideas of Particulars."

274. [*Ed.*] On the mutual independence of monads, see *Monadology,* § 7, which characterizes them as "windowless" (Loemker, p. 643; *Schriften,* ed. Gerhardt,

In the third place the monads must be distinguished from one another, they must be intrinsically distinct. Here then the Leibnizian principle of indiscernibles enters the discussion; popularly stated, no two things are identical with each other. This thesis of difference, taken superficially, is uninteresting. This very matter was the topic of philosophizing at the court. ˉA courtier did not want to believe it, so the electress challenged him to seekˉ²⁷⁵ two identical leaves, but he found none. Two drops of milk examined under a microscope are distinct.²⁷⁶ It matters not to us whether or not there are two things [that look] identical, for this is the superficial sense that does not concern us here. The more precise sense [of identity] is that each is in itself something determinate, each is in itself something distinct from every other thing. ˉWhether two things are identical or not identicalˉ²⁷⁷ is only a comparison that we make, one that has its locus in us. The more precise point, however, is the determinate distinction in the things themselves. If two things are distinct merely through the fact that they are two, then each is one; but the twoness still constitutes no diversity, for they

---

6:607–608). Criticism of the idea of physical influence, according to which material parts or qualities of one substance pass over into another substance, occurs in *Troisième éclaircissement du système de la communication des substances,* published in the *Journal des sçavans,* 19 November 1696 (*Opera,* ed. Dutens, 2, pt. 1:73; *Schriften,* ed. Gerhardt, 4:501). Cf. *W* 15:457 (Ms?). Cf. also *Monadology,* § 51 (Loemker, p. 648; *Schriften,* ed. Gerhardt, 6:615), which states that monads have only an *ideal* influence upon one another, and this only through divine intervention. At the conclusion of this *Third Clarification,* Leibniz opposes the Occasionalism of Malebranche, which Hegel finds already present in Descartes (see above, pp. 000–000 with n. 133); then the only possible remaining view is that of a preestablished harmony. The Cartesian view of an influence of soul upon body Leibniz criticizes in *Monadology,* §§ 80–81 (Loemker, p. 651; *Schriften,* ed. Gerhardt, 6:620–621).

275. *Thus Lw; An reads:* [Leibniz cites the] story of his friend and the electress, who sought

276. [*Ed.*] On the qualities of monads whereby they are different from one another, and on the necessity of this difference, see *Monadology,* §§ 8–9 (Loemker, p. 641; *Schriften,* ed. Gerhardt, 6:608). On the incident involving the leaves and the drops of milk, see Leibniz's *Fourth Letter to Clarke* (1716), § 4 (Loemker, p. 687; *Opera,* ed. Dutens, 2, pt. 1:128–129; *Schriften,* ed. Gerhardt, 7:372); cf. *W* 15:457 (Ms?). Cf. also *New Essays on Human Understanding,* trans. Remnant and Bennett, p. 231; *Œuvres,* ed. Raspe, p. 190; *Schriften,* ed. Gerhardt, 5:214.

277. *Thus Gr; Pn reads:* Identity or nonidentity

are identical. The main thing is rather the determinate distinction in itself.

The Leibnizian monad is therefore a determinate unity [*Monas*].[278] Its determinacy is expressed more precisely by saying that it is [actively] representational [*ist vorstellend*], and from that standpoint the Leibnizian system is the system of an intelligible world; everything material is an [active] representing, something percipient. More specifically, this idealism involves the fact that what is simple is something differentiated in itself and, regardless of its implicit differentiation, | regardless of its manifold content, it still is and remains only one. Take, for example, I, my spirit; I have many representations, there is an abundance of thoughts within me and yet, regardless of this internal manifoldness, I am only one. ¯This is ideality,¯[279] that what is [inwardly] differentiated is at the same time sublated, is determined as one. This is the most interesting point of Leibniz's system.

Thus the monad is an [active] representing, something percipient. The expression that the monad "has representations" is just what is inapt, because we ascribe the having of representations only to consciousness and to consciousness as such. Leibniz, however, also accepts representations without consciousness, in sleep or in a swoon, in which states there are representations without consciousness.[280] What we call matter is then for Leibniz what is suffering

278. [*Ed.*] Here Hegel implicitly opposes the Leibnizian monad—as determinate—to the Pythagorean unity (ἑνάς, μονάς), which he characterizes as essentially indeterminate Monas insofar as it is only the abstract One and is regarded by the Pythagoreans themselves sometimes as what is determined by the Dyad and sometimes as determining the Dyad; cf. W 13:245–247. On the representational and percipient character of monads, see *Monadology*, §§ 11–14 (Loemker, pp. 67–68; *Schriften*, ed. Gerhardt, 6:608–609); a monad is "actively representational" because changes in it, that is, in its representations, derive from an internal principle rather than from external causes (§ 11). Cf. also *Principles of Nature and Grace*, § 2 (Loemker, p. 636; *Schriften*, ed. Gerhardt, 6:598). On the reduction of the material domain to what is percipient, see *Monadology*, § 17 (Loemker, p. 644; *Schriften*, ed. Gerhardt, 6:609). On the soul as a simple substance that nevertheless has a multitude of contents in its perception, see *Monadology*, § 16 (Loemker, p. 644; *Schriften*, ed. Gerhardt, 6:609).

279. *Thus Gr; Sv reads:* Idealism is this,

280. [*Ed.*] Whereas in this section Hegel uses "representation" and its derivatives more often than "perception," the latter is the term consistently used by Leibniz

or passive, [or] is an aggregate of monads. The passivity of matter consists in the obscurity of its representations, in a kind of stupor that does not come to ¯self-consciousness.¯[281] Bodies are such aggregates of monads—agglomerations that can no more be called "substance" than can a flock of sheep. So their continuity is their arrangement or extension.[282] Organic bodies are the sort in which one monad, an entelechy, rules over the rest, although in this context "ruling" is an inappropriate expression. The conscious monad distinguishes itself from what Leibniz calls the bare monad through the clarity of its representing,[283] although this is only a formal distinction.

---

himself. On the states having perceptions without consciousness, see *Monadology*, § 20 (Loemker, p. 645; *Schriften*, ed. Gerhardt, 6:610) and *Principles of Nature and Grace*, § 4 (Loemker, p. 637; *Schriften*, ed. Gerhardt, 6:600).

281. *Thus An; Gr reads:* activity.

[*Ed.*] The preceding sentence, probably abbreviated in transmission, which couples passivity and aggregation, relates to the distinction between "first matter" (without soul or life) and "second matter" (body as consisting of multiple substances, as in a school of fish or a flock of sheep) that is drawn in Leibniz's letter of 4 November 1715 to Nicholas Remond (*Opera*, ed. Dutens, 2, pt. 1:214–215; *Schriften*, ed. Gerhardt, 3:657). Linkage of passivity and incomplete perceptions occurs in *Monadology*, § 49 (Loemker, p. 647; *Schriften*, ed. Gerhardt, 6:615); §§ 23–24 refer to this state as a kind of stupor (Loemker, p. 645; *Schriften*, ed. Gerhardt, 6:610–611). Cf. *W* 15:461, which presents the obscurity as a consequence of passivity and in a footnote cites Leibniz's *On the Soul of Beasts* (1710), §§ 2–4. The textual variant "activity" reflects this correlation of distinct perception with activity; perhaps Hegel used both formulations.

282. [*Ed.*] On the inability of extension or geometric nature itself to give rise to action or motion, see Leibniz's *On the Inherent Force and Actions of Created Things* (1698), § 11 (Loemker, p. 503; *Opera*, ed. Dutens, 2, pt. 2:55; *Schriften*, ed. Gerhardt, 4:510–511). *Monadology*, § 2 designates a compound as an aggregate of simple substances (Loemker, p. 643; *Schriften*, ed. Gerhardt, 6:607). Extension is not itself a kind of substance, according to the *Clarification of the Difficulties Which Mr. Bayle Has Found in the New System of the Union of Soul and Body* (1698) (Loemker, p. 496; *Opera*, ed. Dutens, 2, pt. 1:79; *Schriften*, ed. Gerhardt, 4:523); it is instead a nonsubstantial continuity, according to the letters to Bartholomew des Bosses of 21 July 1707 and 15 February 1712 (Loemker, pp. 600–601; *Opera*, ed. Dutens, 2, pt. 1:280, 295; *Schriften*, ed. Gerhardt, 2:339, 435–436); cf. also the extract from the letter published in the *Journal des sçavans* of 18 June 1691 (*Opera*, ed. Dutens, 2, pt. 1:237; *Schriften*, ed. Gerhardt, 4:464–467).

283. [*Ed.*] On the ruling monad that is the soul of an animal, see *Principles of Nature and Grace*, § 4 (Loemker, p. 637; *Schriften*, ed. Gerhardt, 6:599). On what Hegel calls the "bare" (*nackt*) monad, see *Monadology*, § 24 (Loemker, p. 645;

Leibniz then posits the distinction of the human being or the conscious monad more precisely in the fact that it is capable of recognizing eternal and necessary truths, that it represents to itself what is universal, something universal that rests upon two fundamental principles. One is the principle of [the identity of] indiscernibles, and the other is the principle of | sufficient reason.[284] The latter principle seems to be a superfluous addition, but Leibniz understands it to refer to reasons as determination of purpose. What enters the discussion here is the distinction between efficient and final causes. The stones and beams of a house are merely natural causes, whereas the final cause is a destination, the [completed] house—the sufficient reason that these beams and stones and such things have been placed in this way. These therefore are the principal moments. But a further consequence is the fact that what follows from these eternal truths is the existence of God.[285] What

134

Schriften, ed. Gerhardt, 6:611); the Latin text has "bare" or "naked" (*nudus*), as do the French (*nu*) and Loemker, whereas the standard German translation of this passage has "simple" (*einfach*)!

284. [*Ed.*] On the capacity of human beings (but not animals) to know eternal and necessary truths, see *Monadology,* § 29 (Loemker, p. 645; *Schriften,* ed. Gerhardt, 6:611), and *Principles of Nature and Grace,* § 5 (Loemker, p. 638; *Schriften,* ed. Gerhardt, 6:600–601). On the two great principles, that of contradiction and that of sufficient reason, see *Monadology,* §§ 31–32 (Loemker, p. 646; *Schriften,* ed. Gerhardt, 6:612). In contrast with *W* 15:463, where *Monadology,* §§ 31–32 is given in abbreviated form, in our text Hegel mistakenly substitutes the identity of indiscernibles for the principle of contradiction. The substitution is probably due to the fact that Hegel derives the principle of contradiction from the principle of identity, and in turn sets the latter in connection with the identity of indiscernibles, which *W* 15:563 formulates as: whatever is not distinguished in thought is not distinct.

285. [*Ed.*] Hegel's reduction of sufficient reason to final causality strips the Leibnizian principle of its theological dimension, which comes into prominence particularly in inquiries about the sufficient reason not only of rational truths but also of factual truths. For factual truths infinitely many efficient and final causes can be given without arriving at sufficient reasons. See *Monadology,* §§ 37–39 (Loemker, p. 646; *Schriften,* ed. Gerhardt, 6:613), which concludes by positing as the final reason of things a necessary substance, God, who is one and sufficient. Cf. *Principles of Nature and Grace,* §§ 8, 11, where Leibniz states (in § 11) that laws of motion cannot be explained by efficient causality alone; one must turn to final causality, to the principle of fitness, and thus to God (Loemker, pp. 639–640; *Schriften,* ed. Gerhardt, 6:603). Cf. *Monadology,* §§ 43–45 (Loemker, p. 647; *Schriften,* ed. Gerhardt, 6:614).

follows is the eternal truth or consciousness of what is in and for itself universal and absolute, ⁻and this universal, this absolute in and for itself, is God. As a monad it is one with itself.⁻²⁸⁶ God is the monad of monads, the absolute monad. But if the μονάς μοναδῶν, or God, is the absolute substance, then of course the substantiality of the other monads comes to naught.²⁸⁷ This is a contradiction that is internally unresolved, that between the one substantial monad and the many individual monads that are supposed to be independent, the basis of whose independence is that they do not stand in relation to one another. So there is an unresolved contradiction. The monads are said to be created by God, that is, posited by God's will, but only the monads under the aspect of substance.

The more precise specification of the relationship of the monad of monads and of its activity is that it is the preestablishing element [das Prästabilisierende] in the changes in the monads. Each monad is in itself totality, each is in itself the universe; the bare monad is as such implicitly the universe, and its differentiation is the unfolding of this totality within it. Leibniz says that the whole universe in its entire development can be conceived from a grain of sand.²⁸⁸

286. *Thus Gr, similar in Lw; An reads:* God. *Sv reads:* of God.

287. [*Ed.*] The expression μονάς μοναδῶν or "monad of monads" is not found in Leibniz. Hegel may have adopted it from the literature on Leibniz, for instance, Wendt's edition of Tennemann's *Grundriss der Geschichte der Philosophie für den akademischen Unterricht* (Leipzig, 1825), § 357. It is well suited for grasping God's relation to the other monads, since for the Pythagoreans it is a relationship of μίμησις (imitation) or μέθεξις (participation)—cf. W 13:260–262—and, despite the paradigm of created being, Hegel discovered this relationship again in the *Monadology,* §§ 47–48 (Loemker, p. 647; *Schriften,* ed. Gerhardt, 6:614–615). Giordano Bruno also uses the expression; see *Opera latine conscripta,* ed. F. Fiorentino et al., 3 vols. in 8 (Naples, 1879–1891; reprint, Stuttgart, 1962), 1, pt. 3:146. Nor is the other expression, "absolute monad" or "absolute substance," found in Leibniz. Hegel introduces it to designate the difference that Leibniz himself expresses (in *Monadology,* § 47) through the distinction between the "original" substance and "created" monads; cf. his letter of 12 August 1711 to Friedrich Wilhelm Bierling (*Opera,* ed. Dutens, 5:375; *Schriften,* ed. Gerhardt, 7:502).

288. [*Ed.*] On the foundation in God of preestablished harmony, see *Principles of Nature and Grace,* § 15 (Loemker, p. 640; *Schriften,* ed. Gerhardt, 6:605), which speaks of a community of which all (monads) are members, and of a perfect harmony between God as architect and God as monarch, between a nature that leads to grace and a grace that perfects nature; cf. *Monadology,* § 78 (Loemker, p. 651;

135   This looks like a splendid thought. But the world is more than a grain of sand. | Much that is missing must still be added, so that the representation adds more than exists in this grain of sand. Each monad is therefore ⁻implicitly the universe, and the important thing is for the universe to come⁻[289] into existence [in it].[290] The monad is active, it represents, it perceives, and this perception unfolds within it according to the laws of desire, of activity. ⁻Just as the movements of its outer world unfold according to the laws of bodies, so the unfolding from itself of the representing within itself, of the spiritual, follows the laws of desire.⁻[291] For Leibniz this has the following more precise relation to the representation of freedom. He says that the nature of the compass needle is to point north, and that a magnet with consciousness would represent to it-

---

Schriften, ed. Gerhardt, 6:620). On each monad as totality, as in itself the universe, see *Principles of Nature and Grace,* § 13 (Loemker, p. 640; *Schriften,* ed. Gerhardt, 6:604); none but God, however, is a fully conscious totality. Leibniz does not speak of a grain of sand as totality, but of a bit of matter (*Monadology,* § 65: Loemker, p. 649; *Schriften,* ed. Gerhardt, 6:618); cf. also § 62, as well as *Theodicy,* pt. 1, § 9 (Loemker, p. 649; *Schriften,* ed. Gerhardt, 6:617, 107–108; Allen, pp. 35–36), and the sixth letter to Louis Bourget, 2 July 1716 (*Opera,* ed. Dutens, 2, pt. 1:337; *Schriften,* ed. Gerhardt, 3:595).

289. *An reads:* implicitly the universe, and the important thing is for it [the monad] to come *Lw reads:* implicitly the infinite, but the important thing is for it [the infinite] to come *Gr reads:* in itself [and] so for the universe and its unfolding to be conceived it must in any event come

290. *Lw adds:* which is for Leibniz consciousness, or clarity of representation.

[*Ed.*] Hegel could be thinking of *Monadology,* § 61 (Loemker, p. 649; *Schriften,* ed. Gerhardt, 6:617), which says that each body responds to every happening in the universe, although a soul can "read" within itself only those events that it represents clearly.

291. *Thus W; Gr reads, similar in Lw:* In the movement of the outer world are the determinations of the monads, which unfold within them according to the laws of bodies and within the spiritual according to the laws of desire.

[*Ed.*] On the connection of activity with perceiving, see p. 000 above, and *Monadology,* § 49 (cited in n. 281 above). The statement linking perception with the laws of desire is probably inadequately transmitted by our sources. The assumption is that Hegel wished to contrast the distinctive modes of operation of souls and bodies; see *Monadology,* § 79 (Loemker, p. 651; *Schriften,* ed. Gerhardt, 6:620), which states that souls act through appetition, according to the laws of final causes, whereas bodies act according to the laws of efficient causes, or motion; cf. *Principles of Nature and Grace,* § 3 (Loemker, p. 637; *Schriften,* ed. Gerhardt, 6:598–599).

self that ˜the alignment toward the north˜²⁹² is its own determination, but this would only be representation.²⁹³

Because the monads are closed off [that is, "windowless"] and each develops within itself, there must then also be a harmony of their development, ˜an organic whole. We represent this or that to ourselves, we will this or that; our activity is applied in this way and brings about changes, our inward determination becomes in this way bodily determination and then outward changes, we appear as causes having effects on other monads. But this is only an illusion. The fact that there is nevertheless agreement between the determination of our willing and the change that we intend to bring about by it is something due to an other, it comes²⁹⁴ from without,˜²⁹⁵ and this other is God, who preestablishes this harmony. This is the well-known preestablished | harmony, which therefore   136
comes from without. It is approximately the same as what we saw in the case of Descartes with his "assistance."²⁹⁶ Whatever we do is thus the action in concert of an infinite number of monads within us. The soul does not act upon the bodily monad. But since changes take place in one monad, corresponding changes take place in the other monad, and this correspondence is a harmony that is posited by God.²⁹⁷

292. *Gr reads:* it *Lw reads:* this *Pn reads:* therein
293. [*Ed.*] For Leibniz's criticism of Descartes on the freedom of the soul to affect the body, see *Monadology,* § 80 (Loemker, p. 651; *Schriften,* ed. Gerhardt, 6:620–621). See also *Theodicy,* pt. 3, § 291 (Allen, pp. 137–138; *Schriften,* ed. Gerhardt, 6:289–290). *Theodicy,* pt. 1, § 50, contains the example of the compass needle (Allen, p. 51; *Schriften,* ed. Gerhardt, 6:130).
294. *Gr adds:* not
295. *Thus Gr (but see preceding note), similar in Lw; Sv reads:* This harmony comes from without, from God,
296. [*Ed.*] On the "windowless" character of monads, see *Monadology,* § 7 (cf. n. 274 above). On the preestablished harmony, see above, pp. 000–000 with n. 288. Hegel's comparison of Leibniz with Descartes overlooks the fact that Leibniz sets his system of preestablished harmony apart from the position of Descartes in particular, and it also overlooks the fact that Leibniz views the relationship of "assistance" (on which, see pp. 000–000 above) as not at all Cartesian.
297. [*Ed.*] *Monadology,* § 81 (Loemker, p. 651; *Schriften,* ed. Gerhardt, 6:621), states that souls and bodies each act as if the other did not exist, and also act as if each influenced the other. That is, each is "windowless" and so independent, but each is also a perception of the universe as a whole of interrelated members.

These are the principal moments of the Leibnizian philosophy. We see therefore that the Leibnizian system is a metaphysics that proceeds from the limited determinations of the understanding concerning absolute multiplicity, such that coherence can only be grasped as continuity, and as a result absolute unity is annulled from the outset. Absolute being-for-self is abstractly presupposed, and God must then mediate among the individuals and determine the harmony in the changes of the individual monads. It is an artificial system that is grounded on the categories of the understanding concerning the absolute being of multiplicity or abstract singularity. The most important point in regard to Leibniz ˉresides in the fundamental theses, the principle of individualityˉ²⁹⁸ and the proposition concerning indiscernibles.²⁹⁹

5. Christian Wolff

The Wolffian system is affiliated with ˉLeibniz's system.ˉ³⁰⁰ Wolff's philosophy is a systematizing of Leibniz and one even speaks of Leibnizian-Wolffian philosophy. Wolff has earned great and undying credit for raising Germany to a culture of the understanding.³⁰¹ |

137

Wolff was the son of a baker³⁰² in Breslau, where he was born in 1679. At first he studied theology, then philosophy, and in 1707

298. *Thus Gr; Pn reads:* is the fundamental thesis of intelligibility *Lw reads:* consists in the representation of intellectuality

299. [*Ed.*] See p. 000 above.

300. *Pn reads:* the systematization of the Leibnizian system.

301. [*Ed.*] The following account of Wolff's life largely agrees with that in W 15:474–475; Heinrich Wuttke states that the account in W is full of misinformation; see *Christian Wolffs eigene Lebensbeschreibung,* edited by Wuttke together with an essay on Wolff (Leipzig, 1841). Wuttke's edition and essay (208 pp.) are reprinted in *Christian Wolff: Gesammelte Werke,* division 1, vol. 10, Biography, ed. Hans Werner Arndt (Hildesheim and New York, 1980). Also reprinted in that volume are these biographies: *Vita, fata et scripta Christiani Wolfii philosophi* (Leipzig and Bratislava, 1739), by Friedrich Christian Baumeister (but published anonymously), 126 pp.; *Historische Lobschrift des weiland hoch- und wohlgebornen Herrn Christians, des Heiligen Römischen Reiches Freyherrn von Wolf . . .* (Halle, 1755), by Johann Christoph Gottsched, 152 pp. with supplements and appendix (108 pp.). Hegel took his misinformation about Wolff from Buhle. The notes that follow correct the errors.

302. [*Ed.*] Buhle reports that Wolff was a baker's son (*Geschichte* 4:571); actually his father was a tanner, as reported by Baumeister (p. 12) and Wuttke (p. 110).

he became professor of mathematics and philosophy at Halle.[303] [He] had opponents: the Pietist theologians in Halle treated him in the basest manner; when he brought their writings into disrepute, they resorted to intrigues. They brought charges to King Frederick William I, a military enthusiast, saying that Wolff taught determinism, that according to him human beings have no free will and hence that soldiers do not desert of their own will [but rather] under ⁻divine direction.⁻[304] They pointed, of course, to the danger this doctrine could pose if it were to spread among the soldiers. Frederick William I became very angry about this, and ⁻in 1723⁻[305] Wolff had to leave Halle and the Prussian States within forty-eight hours, under threat of hanging. The theologians compounded the scandal by preaching against him, and the pious Francke, founder of the orphanage, thanked God on his knees in church for Wolff's removal, that the state was freed of the atheist.[306] Wolff went to Kassel, and then became the first professor of philosophy at the University of Marburg. The academies of sciences in London, Paris, and Stockholm named him a member—an honor that was then still an honor. Peter the Great made him vice-president of the Academy of St. Petersburg.[307] In Berlin a commission was convened in order

303. [Ed.] Wolff was called to Halle as professor of mathematics—according to Wuttke, mathematics and physics. From 1709 on he also lectured on metaphysics, logic, and morals.

304. Thus Pn; Lw reads: a particular influence of God. W reads: a particular arrangement (preestablished harmony) of God.

305. Thus An, Pn, Sv; Gr reads: on 23 November 1723

306. [Ed.] This is taken almost word for word from Buhle (Geschichte 4:579). But according to the account of Gottsched (p. 67), who relies on Wuttke (pp. 196–197), the usually mild Pietist professor August Hermann Francke (1663–1727), on the Sunday after Wolff's departure (which, according to Gr, was in late November), preached with zeal on the Gospel text of Matt. 24:19–20 (cf. Mark 13:17–18): "And alas for those who are with child and for those who give suck in those days! Pray that your flight may not be in winter or on a sabbath." Francke's zeal was clearly directed at Wolff's wife, who was in the last stages of pregnancy and had remained behind in the city.

307. [Ed.] Regarding Wolff's admission to the scientific academies, Hegel follows Buhle (Geschichte 4:581). He was admitted to the Berlin Academy in February 1711, and to the London Academy shortly before that (cf. Wuttke, n. 1 to p. 148). Buhle's erroneous report about admission to the Stockholm Academy was probably prompted by the fact that the king of Sweden had also been the count of Hesse

to render an expert opinion on his philosophy, and ˉit was ab-
138 solved of all harmfulness.ˉ³⁰⁸ The theologians opposed to it | were
silenced and forbidden to ˉspeakˉ³⁰⁹ about it. Within the lifetime
of Frederick William I, Wolff was recalled to Halle. He did not accept right away the offer to occupy anew his professorship at Halle,
but only did so after Frederick II ascended the throne in 1740 and
reaffirmed the offer. Wolff became vice-chancellor of the university,
and in 1745 he was elevated to the rank of baron by the elector of
Bavaria.³¹⁰ He then remained in Halle right to the end, to his death
in 1754.

(where Marburg is located) since 1730. The report may also have rested upon a
confusion of names, since Wolff was named a member of the Bologna Academy in
1752 (Gottsched, p. 130). Only the admission to the French Academy occurred during Wolff's Marburg period, in 1733 (see Gottsched, supplements and appendix,
p. 46, and Wuttke, p. 158). Hegel's sarcastic remark that such admission "was then
still an honor" refers obliquely to the recent efforts of Schleiermacher to exclude
him from the Royal Prussian Academy of Sciences—even at the cost of dissolving
the philosophical section of the Academy; cf. Hegel, *Briefe* 2:449–450; 3:440–442.
The transcripts abridge the report about St. Petersburg, whereas W 15:474–475
contains a more satisfactory, though not wholly correct, account. In the spring of
1723 Peter the Great offered the vice-presidency of his planned academy of sciences to Wolff, and he renewed the invitation after Wolff's expulsion from Halle;
see Gottsched, supplements d and p, appendix, pp. 31–32 and 41–42. Wolff de-
clined the offer, but in 1725, after the Academy had been founded by the empress
Catherine I, he was made an honorary member; see Gottsched, supplement s, appendix, pp. 44–45.

308. *Thus An, similar in Gr, Lw; Pn reads:* it declared him to be not harmful.
[*Ed.*] The commission was established in 1736. Three years before this, Wolff
had been summoned to return to Prussia; see Gottsched, p. 89 with supplement y.

309. *Thus Lw; W reads:* contend
[*Ed.*] Hegel's statements here go beyond his sources (Buhle and Tiedemann) and
resemble a remark made by Wolff in 1723 and reproduced in Gottsched (appendix,
p. 38 with n.) that refers to the Pietists being silenced "unless they wish to beat the
air in vain."

310. [*Ed.*] The first summons to return to Halle was in 1733, prior to his actual
rehabilitation. In 1739 Wolff was again called to Prussia, first to Frankfurt-on-
the-Oder, but then also to Halle; see Gottsched, pp. 100–101. He was initially
vice-chancellor at Halle, but was named chancellor after the death of Chancellor
Ludewig in 1743. After Karl VII died, Maximilian Joseph, the elector of Bavaria,
became regent of the empire. Hegel could not have gotten the correct date of Wolff's
elevation to baronial rank either from Tiedemann (*Geist* 6:517) or from Buhle
(*Geschichte* 4:581); but see Gottsched, pp. 123–124 with supplement g.

Wolff gained great fame in mathematics[311] and likewise through his philosophy, which was dominant in Germany for a long time. We can call it in general a philosophy of the understanding as extended to all objects that fall within the realm of knowledge. We might say that Wolff first made philosophy properly indigenous to Germany. It is especially important that most of his treatises were written in the German language; Leibniz wrote in Latin, and for the most part in French. The usual titles [of Wolff's essays] are "Rational Thoughts" concerning God, the world, the human soul, nature, and so forth. His writings comprise ˜twenty-four˜[312] quarto volumes. So Wolff wrote in German, and Tschirnhausen and Thomasius share with him the merit of propagating the German language in philosophy.[313] A science can only be truly said to belong to a people when it is written in their own tongue, and this is especially necessary in the case of philosophy.

On the whole it is then the Leibnizian philosophy that Wolff systematized; but this statement refers only to the main views of Leibniz's *Monadology* and his *Theodicy,* to which Wolff re-

311. [*Ed.*] See in particular his chief mathematical work, *Elementa matheseos universae,* 5 vols. (Halle, 1713–1741), especially the fifth (= *Gesammelte Werke,* division 2, vol. 33).

312. *Thus An; Gr, Lw read:* twenty *Sv reads:* twenty-five
[*Ed.*] Wolff lectured in German from the outset of his professorship in Halle. He wrote: "I have found that our language serves much better for the sciences than does Latin, and that one can convey in the pure German language what sounds quite barbaric in Latin," in his *Ausführliche Nachricht von seinen eigenen Schrifften, die er in deutscher Sprache von den verschiedenen Theilen der Welt-Weisheit heraus gegeben auf Verlangen ans Licht gestellet* (Frankfurt am Main, 1733), chap. 2, § 16, p. 27 (in *Gesammelte Werke,* division 1, vol. 1). Hegel's specimen titles may call to mind Wolff's *Vernünfftige Gedancken von Gott, der Welt und der Seele des Menschen, auch allen Dingen überhaupt* (Halle, twelve editions, 1720–1752); see *Gesammelte Werke,* division 1, vols. 2–3. The actual number of his quarto volumes is twenty-six; cf. Wuttke's essay on Wolff, p. 100.

313. [*Ed.*] Hegel is probably referring to the mathematician and scientist Ehrenfried Walther von Tschirnhaus (1651–1708), author of *Zwölf nützliche Lebensregeln . . .* ; see Buhle (*Geschichte* 4:528). On the rationalist theologian Christian Thomasius (1655–1728), Buhle remarks (*Geschichte* 4:541) that he also lectured first in German rather than Latin and scarcely suspected what vast consequences his action would have for German literature after him. There is no evidence that Hegel himself undertook a study of Tschirnhaus or of Thomasius.

mained faithful.[314] In addition, he gave philosophy the division into branches that has held good right up to the most recent times.[315] First, there is theoretical | philosophy, which consists of: (a) logic, purified of the endless Scholastic elaboration, for which purification we are indebted to Petrus Ramus and others—it is the logic of the understanding that Wolff has systematized; (b) ontology, the doctrine of the abstract and universal categories of philosophizing, namely, being, one, substance, phenomenon—this, therefore, is an abstract, universal metaphysics; (c) pneumatology, or the philosophy of the soul; (d) cosmology, or the general doctrine of bodies; (e) natural theology. Second, practical philosophy contains: (a) natural right [or law]; (b) morals and ethics; (c) civics [*Völkerrecht*] or politics; (d) economics. The whole is laid out in strict geometrical form—axioms, theorems, scholia, corollaries, and so forth. Wolff tended on the one hand toward a vast and wholly universal scope, and on the other toward a strictness of method with regard to propositions and their proofs. The content is partly extracted from the Leibnizian philosophy, with regard to the general views, and partly taken empirically from our inclination and sensibility.

The strictness of the method has certainly become in part very pedantic; the syllogism is the principal form, and it has often degenerated into an outlandish pedantry of unbearable verbosity. The customary examples from individual sciences are treated in the manner of geometrical exercises and solutions. For instance, the

314. [*Ed.*] With this judgment Hegel follows a widespread understanding that culminates in the statement by Wolff's student, Georg Bernhard Bilfinger (1673–1750), about the "Leibnizian-Wolffian philosophy." Wolff himself resisted that view; see his *Eigene Lebensbeschreibung* (pp. 141–142 in Wuttke)—published only after Hegel's death—as well as Wuttke's essay (p. 102). In this autobiography (pp. 82–83) Wolff expresses his serious reservations about Leibniz's theory of monads and his *Theodicy.*

315. [*Ed.*] In what follows Hegel draws upon the divisions of Wolff's *Vernünfftige Gedancken* . . . (cf. n. 312 above). See also the list of divisions in *W* 15:478. The French humanist Pierre de la Ramée (Petrus Ramus, 1515–1572) discarded "artificial" Scholastic logic, replacing it with a "natural" logic keyed (under the influence of Cicero) to spontaneous human thought as expressed in speech. Hegel's inversion of the order of pneumatology and cosmology may be motivated by the sequence in Kant's *Critique of Pure Reason* (see the full citation in n. 353), in the section on paralogisms of pure reason (B 399–432), in which psychology is treated before cosmology.

fourth theorem in his military science reads: "The approach to the fortress must be made ever more difficult for the enemy, the closer he comes." The proof is: "For the closer the enemy approaches to the fortress, the closer comes the danger for the besieged; the closer the danger for the besieged becomes, the greater it is, and all the more must they ward it off through the obstacles with which they oppose or repel the enemy. On this account, the closer the enemy comes to the fortress, the more difficult the approach must be made for him. Q.E.D."[316] Wolff proceeds in this quite trivial manner with every possible content. |

6. Metaphysical and Popular Philosophy

The stages of philosophy that we have considered so far have the character of being metaphysics, of proceeding from general determinations of the understanding, although linking with them experience and observation ‾of how natural objects present themselves to spirit.‾[317] One aspect of this metaphysics is that the antitheses of thought have been brought to consciousness and interest has been directed to the resolution of contradiction: thought and being, God and the world, good and evil, divine prescience and human freedom—these contradictions, the antitheses of soul and spirit, of representations and material things and their reciprocal relation, are what have occupied attention. Second, the resolution of these antitheses and contradictions has been given, and this resolution has been posited in God. God is therefore that in which all these contradictions are resolved. This is the common feature of all these philosophies according to their principal aspect.

What is noteworthy in this connection is that these antitheses are not resolved in themselves, that the nullity of the antitheses and their presuppositions has not been exhibited in the domain of the antitheses themselves. Hence no truly concrete resolution has come to pass, and although God is thought of as resolving all contradic-

---

316. [Ed.] See *Christian Wolff: Der Anfangs-Gründe aller mathematischen Wissenschaften anderer Theil* (Halle, 1757), which includes "Anfangs-Gründe der Fortification oder Kriegs-Bau-Kunst . . . ," in *Gesammelte Werke*, division 1, vol. 13, pp. 592–740; the quotation in our text is based on p. 604.

317. *Thus Lw; Gr reads:* —in general the empirical mode.

tions, God and the resolution of those contradictions have been more talked about than grasped and conceived. When God is grasped according to his attributes of prescience, omnipresence, omniscience, and so on, when the divine attributes of power, wisdom, goodness, and justice are treated as attributes of God himself, then these antitheses also lead to contradictions, such as of prescience with the creation of free beings. Leibniz sought to soften and annul these contradictions by saying that these attributes moderate one another;[318] they are conjoined in such a way that their contradiction is eliminated. But that gives us no grasp of the resolution of such contradictions. From this perspective this metaphysics contrasts with | the ancient philosophies to which we can ever again return and find satisfaction in ˉthemˉ[319] at their level, for they do not occupy this standpoint as the modern ones do. In this modern metaphysics the antitheses are developed to the absolute contradiction, and therefore developed more profoundly than in ancient philosophy and so to something higher than we find in the ancients. Their resolution is also given, to be sure—[namely,] God; but God remains the beyond, and all the contradictions remain on this side, unresolved according to their content. God is only named as the mediator but is not grasped as such—as the one in whom the contradictions eternally resolve themselves; God is not grasped as spirit, as the triune one. It is only in God as spirit, as triune spirit,

141

318. [*Ed.*] In the second edition of the *Logic* ("Book One: The Doctrine of Being") Hegel repeats the contention that *temperieren* ("to moderate") is "a Leibnizian expression of mediation"; see *Science of Logic* (p. 112; *GW* 21:100). The representation of mediation that Hegel reproaches as inadequate is, to be sure, found a number of times in Leibniz. See *Principles of Nature and Grace,* § 9 (Loemker, p. 639; *Schriften,* ed. Gerhardt, 6:602), which describes justice as "nothing but goodness conforming with wisdom"; also, the preface to the *Theodicy* (Allen, p. 4; *Schriften,* ed. Gerhardt, 6:36), which describes God as absolute power but with a wisdom that permits no capricious or despotic application of that power. But in fact it is not Leibniz but Wolff who uses the expression *temperieren*; cf. his *Theologia naturalis methodo scientifica pertractata,* pars prior, §§ 1067 and 1070 (in *Gesammelte Werke,* division 1, vol. 7, pt. 1), which uses both verbal (*attempero*) and nominative (*temperamentum*) Latin forms in speaking of the relation of divine goodness and wisdom. Jacob Boehme frequently used the German verb *temperieren* as an expression for mediating, though not in connection with the issues cited here from Wolff's discussion.

319. *Pn reads:* it [this metaphysics]

that this antithesis to himself is contained within himself, and with it the resolution too. This determinate concept of God is not yet taken up into that philosophy. The resolution of the contradictions is only an otherworldly resolution.

Over against this metaphysics there has now arisen what can be called popular philosophy, reflective philosophy, or reflective empiricism—an empiricism that is more or less metaphysical just as, conversely, the metaphysical philosophy becomes empirical in its particular application. Firm and fundamental theses or principles have been sought over against those contradictions—unshakable, secure theses that are immanent in the human spirit and breast. Instead of the resolution taking place only in God and in the beyond, these fixed principles are this-worldly, something secure and independent. These fundamental theses have generally been directed against the otherworldly metaphysics, against the artificiality of metaphysical constructions, against "assistance," preestablished harmony and optimism—the best [of all possible] worlds.[320] An understandable and this-worldly position has emerged and this-worldly principles have been created from what is called sound reason, sound human understanding, natural feeling; they are principles derived from the content found in the breast of the cultivated person. |

These principles can be good if our human inclination, feeling, and heart are cultivated in the same measure as our understanding. If our heart is ethically formed and our spirit is cultivated for thinking and reflecting, then beautiful feelings can prevail within us and the content that these fundamental theses express can be a content that ought generally to be acknowledged in any case. But when ˉthe sound human understanding or the natural heart in generalˉ[321] is made into the fundamental thesis, then what we find ˉis a natural sensibilityˉ[322] [and] knowing, as when the Hindus pray to the cow

142

320. [Ed.] On artificiality, see p. 000 above. Hegel regards the "system of assistance" as something already present in Descartes, and more explicitly in Malebranche; see above, p. 000, n. 133. Mention of "preestablished harmony" and "optimism" refers again to Leibniz; see above, nn. 267, 274, 288.
321. *Thus An with Pn; Gr reads:* what we call sound understanding or reason, or what is implanted in the human heart,
322. *Pn reads:* are natural sensibilities

and the ape, the Egyptians to [a particular] bird or to the bull, Apis. The uncivilized Turks have natural sensibilities and sound human understanding too, in company with the greatest cruelties. But when we speak of sound human understanding or of natural feeling, we always have in mind a cultivated spirit. We forget that ˉthe ethical or the rightˉ [323] that is found in the human breast is the product of cultivation and education, that they made these fundamental theses into natural feelings in the first place and gave them the stamp of habit; [only] then do that religion and ethical life become immediate knowledge for us. Here [in popular philosophy] natural feelings and sound human understanding are therefore made into the principle, and much that ought to be acknowledged falls under this head. This is the shape of philosophy in the eighteenth century. French, Scottish, and German philosophy all belong to it, and the German form we designate by the expression *Aufklärung* [Enlightenment].

A few characteristics have to be provided here in more detail. Natural understanding or sound reason, the content of which is taken from the human breast, directed itself on the one hand against the religious aspect [of culture]. Its attack came in distinct moments—first of all against the positive, Catholic religion, and then on the other | side, or as the German Enlightenment, against the ˉProtestantˉ [324] religion too, insofar as it has a content that it has received from revelation and from ecclesiastical definition.

143

The first attack therefore was directed against the form of authority in general, the other one against the content. This form of thinking can fairly easily dispose of the content, since such thinking is not what we properly understand reason to be but is rather what must be called understanding. It is easy for this understanding to discover contradictions in a religious content whose ultimate foundation can only be grasped by speculative reason. Since the principle of the understanding is abstract identity, the understanding applied this measuring stick to the religious content, exhibited contradictions in it, and declared it to be invalid. The

323. *Thus Gr; An reads;* religiosity or ethical life
324. *Thus Gr, Pn, An, Lw; Sv reads:* positive aspect of the Protestant

understanding proceeds in the same fashion against a speculative philosophy. The German Enlightenment did this and so did French philosophy—the one in the attack on the Lutheran religion, the other in the attack on the Catholic religion. There is no occasion for us to go into the distinction between the two religions any further here, since we have already elaborated upon it for the medieval period.[325] The argumentation of sound human understanding is turned against both the authority of positive religion and its content. All that then remains is what is called Deism, that is, a general belief in a God. This is now the content, something left over in a very general form in many theologies, and it is this same content that is also found in Islam, which worships one God. The Qur'ān acknowledges Christ as a great teacher and prophet, and in some ways it places him higher than he has been placed often in recent [Christian] theology.[326] This is the reconciliation of the Islamic religion with the Christian religion.

But this orientation of the argumentative understanding in opposition to religion was not the end of the matter, for the argumentative understanding also moved on to [espouse] materialism, atheism, and naturalism. | We ought not, however, to attach the label of "atheism" to anyone lightly. It is easy to accuse a philosophy or an individual of atheism because of views concerning God that deviate from those that others hold. But, all the same, many of the argumentative philosophers did move on to atheism in the most definite way. The universal, what is grasped as the ultimate ground of everything, as what is substantial, efficacious, and active, these philosophers called "nature" or "matter." We can say that on the whole this is Spinozism, that what is represented

325. [*Ed.*] See pp. 000–000 above.
326. [*Ed.*] The Qur'ān acknowledges Jesus, the son of Mary, as one of those sent by Allah (2:81, 130, 254; 3:78; 4:156, 161, 169; 5:79; 33:7; 42:11; 57:27; 61:6), as illumined by the Holy Spirit (2:81, 254; 5:50, 109–115), as a servant of Allah (4:170; 43:57–64; 61:14), as one of those near to Allah (3:40; 4:156). It even concedes—in contrast with the radical wing of Enlightenment criticism of religion—the supernatural creation of Jesus (3:40–55; 19:16–35; 21:91; similar to Adam's creation—3:52), but it contests that Jesus is God's son (5:19, 76; 9:30–35) and rejects the doctrine of the Trinity as tritheism (4:169; 5:77, 116). It is unlikely that Hegel knew the Qur'ān at first hand.

as this ultimate ground is the Spinozistic substance—the One of substance.[327]

This movement took place among the French philosophers especially, although a few of them such as ROUSSEAU are not to be reckoned in the same group. In Rousseau's *Emile* there is a "profession of faith by a Savoyard vicar" that is pure Deism. The residue [of religion] in the German Enlightenment is just what is found in the Qur'ān, in Rousseau, and in Voltaire.[328] Others have moved on expressly to naturalism. Here we must mention in particular the *System of Nature* of HOLBACH (a German baron who lived in Paris). It consists of very superficial thoughts. "Le grand tout de la nature," the great whole of nature, is the ultimate thing here. Things originate and perish through laws, attributes, and connections. The aggregate of qualities and their changes is "le grand

327. [*Ed.*] Hegel is probably referring to Paul Henri Thiry, Baron d'Holbach (1723–1789), whose *Système de la nature*, 2 vols. (Amsterdam and London, 1771), published under the name of Mirabaud, embodies a thoroughgoing materialism, yet one that rejects the Cartesian doctrine of the homogeneous and inert character of matter and instead treats it as consisting of diverse kinds of atoms that are essentially endowed with motion and energy. See: *Système* 1:28, 39; *The System of Nature*, trans. Samuel Wilkinson, 3 vols. (London, 1820–1821; reprint, New York and London, 1984), 1:31–32, 42.

328. [*Ed.*] Jean-Jacques Rousseau (1712–1778) published *Emile*, a book on the education and moral development of the person, in 1762. The profession of faith of the Savoyard priest presents three articles of the Deist's creed (the existence of divine will and divine intelligence, and the immortality of the human soul) and an explicit critique of all revelation. Hegel's estimation does not take into account the expression at the end of the profession of faith (and admittedly marginal to it) that goes beyond the priest's spontaneous skepticism in saying: "Yes, if the life and death of Socrates are those of a philosopher, the life and death of Christ are those of a God." See: Rousseau, *Œuvres complètes*, ed. Bernard Gagnebin and Marcel Raymond, 4 vols. (Paris, 1959–1969), 4:380; *Emile*, trans. Barbara Foxley (London, 1911; reprint, 1974), p. 270. The works by Voltaire (François-Marie Arouet, 1694–1778) in Hegel's library were limited to historical titles. There are few indications as to which of his writings criticizing religion Hegel was familiar with. We may assume his acquaintance with *Candide* (1759) and the *Philosophical Dictionary* (1764), as well as with lesser-known essays on Lord Bolingbroke (1784) and on the Bible (1776); on the latter two, see *Philosophy of Religion* 1:339 with n. 155. Hegel's sweeping reference to the German Enlightenment is likewise difficult to pin down. He could be alluding to the rationalistic writings of Hermann Samuel Reimarus (1694–1768) and of the "neologist" theologians Johann Joachim Spalding (1714–1804) and Johann Wilhelm Friedrich Jerusalem (1709–1789).

tout."[329] Because of its great superficiality such a presentation is lamentable.

The second aspect of this argumentative understanding is morals, a topic highly developed by German, French, and, in particular, Scottish philosophers. We can say no more about English philosophy, for although CUDWORTH, CLARKE, WOLLASTON, and others lived in the eighteenth century, they operated within the forms of very commonplace metaphysics of the understanding.[330] The Scottish philosophers in particular devoted themselves to the cultivation of morals and politics. As cultured men they studied the moral nature of humanity, considering how it presents itself to cultured reflection, and they sought to bring moral obligations under one principle—under sociability and the like. Garve has | translated   145

329. [*Ed.*] Baron d'Holbach's first chapter speaks in this fashion of "the great whole that results from the assemblage of diverse substances, their diverse combinations, and the diverse motions that we observe in the universe" (*Système* 1:10; *Système* 1:12–13); cf. *W* 15:519–520 (Ms?); see also n. 327 above. Although Hegel owned d'Holbach's book, he is excerpting from a reference in Buhle (*Lehrbuch* 8:62–63).

330. [*Ed.*] *Pn* is the only one of our sources that transmits Cudworth's name, but it probably does so authentically. Ralph Cudworth (1617–1688) actually lived in the seventeenth century, not the eighteenth. For that reason Tennemann, Buhle, and Rixner treat him separately from Clarke and Wollaston. *W* 15:445 mentions Cudworth's main work, *The True Intellectual System of the Universe* (London, 1678), but characterizes it very negatively as "an insipid metaphysics of the understanding." It cannot be established whether Hegel based his view on his sources for the history of philosophy (which treat Cudworth in a positive tone), on Cudworth's book itself, or on its widely known Latin translation by Johann Lorenz Mosheim (Jena, 1733; 2d ed., Leiden, 1773). Hegel could have been informed about William Wollaston (1659–1724) and Samuel Clarke (1675–1729) from Buhle (*Geschichte* 5, pt. 1:321–328) and Rixner (*Handbuch* 3:140–142). Buhle focuses only on Clarke's *Discourse concerning the Unchangeable Obligations of Natural Religion* (1704–1705). Tennemann (*Geschichte* 9:370–388) does not take up Wollaston but does refer to others of Clarke's writings, including his *Letter to Mr. Dodwell* (1706) on the immortality of the soul, and *A Demonstration of the Being and Attributes of God* (1705); Hegel's remark in the text about a "very commonplace metaphysics of the understanding" may refer to these treatises; see *The Works of Samuel Clarke*, 4 vols. (London, 1738; reprint, New York and London, 1978). Buhle (pp. 322–323) mentions Wollaston's *The Religion of Nature Delineated* (London, 1724), saying that Wollaston based morals solely on reason as a cognitive faculty. On Wollaston's doctrine of the connection of morals with knowledge of truth ("conformity to truth"), see Rixner (*Handbuch* 3:141–142).

many of their writings into German, in particular those of Ferguson (and others). These are popular [writings] with good ethical principles, presented in the style of Cicero.[331] We find among these Scottish philosophers in particular a third tendency, namely, that they have also sought to provide a more definite account of the principles of knowing. But on the whole they proceed on the same basis that has been established as the principle in Germany too.

Thus THOMAS REID was born in 1704 and died in 1796, as professor at Glasgow.[332] He investigated the principle of cognitive knowing. His view is that there are unproven and indemonstrable fundamental truths, which common sense accepts as immediately decisive and decided. They are fundamental principles within spirit, an immediate knowing in which an inner, independent source is posited. These indemonstrable truths do not require the support of science, nor do they submit to its criticism, for they are the root of knowing and of philosophy—truths that of themselves bring immediate insight. There are comparable determinations for ethical life—such as philanthropy, social inclination, perfection of the

331. [Ed.] Adam Ferguson (1724–1814) wrote the *Institutes of Moral Philosophy* (London, 1769). Hegel could have been familiar with Christian Garve's German translation of this work (Leipzig, 1772). There is no evidence that Hegel knew Ferguson's more comprehensive *Principles of Moral and Political Science*, 2 vols. (Edinburgh, 1792). Garve translated works of other Scottish philosophers, including James Porter, Henry Home, Alexander Gerard, and Adam Smith, as well as works of the Englishman Edmund Burke; cf. the bibliography in Garve's *Popularphilosophische Schriften über literarische, ästhetische und gesellschaftliche Gegenstände,* a collection of photographically reprinted writings, ed. Kurt Wölfel (Stuttgart, 1974). Hegel certainly knew Adam Smith's *Wealth of Nations* (London, 1776), for a later edition of it was in his library, but there is no clue that he also knew Smith's *Theory of Moral Sentiments* (London, 1759). In *W* 15:504–505 Hegel refers to philosophers who have written about morals (and judges them less positively than he does in our text), mentioning Adam Smith among them; but this reference could be derived from the treatment of Smith in Buhle (*Geschichte 5*, pt. 1:328–331) or Rixner (*Handbuch* 3:265–266). Hegel's mention of Cicero in this connection may be due to the fact that together with his work on the Scottish philosophers Christian Garve translated and commented on Cicero's *De officiis*; he also translated Aristotle's *Ethics* and *Politics.*

332. [Ed.] Reid was actually born in 1710; Wendt (*Grundriss,* p. 442) has 1704. Since only *Gr* among the transcripts has a birthdate for Reid, Griesheim probably added it later, after referring to Wendt.

whole—by which individuals must gauge their actions. This is Reid's view.[333]

JAMES BEATTIE, born in 1735, was professor of morals at Edinburgh and at Aberdeen, and he died in 1803. ˉBeattie posited plain human understandingˉ[334] as the source of all knowledge, all religion and ethics. Truth is that which we must grant as valid according to the natural disposition of spirit or of the soul. ˉCertain truths are the foundation for everything else.ˉ[335] The existence of the divine being is a fact within our consciousness that is exalted above all doubt, all argumentation.[336] This is the same thesis that had also been posited as the principle in Germany at that time: an inner revelation, one that does not come into us in an outward

333. [*Ed.*] This presentation of Reid is a slightly abridged version of that in *W* 15:503 (Ms?), which is almost literally excerpted from Rixner (*Handbuch* 3:259). Rixner bases his account on Reid's *An Inquiry into the Human Mind on the Principles of Common Sense* (London, 1769). The expression "philanthropy, social inclination" has not been found in any of Hegel's sources.

334. *Thus Pn with Lw; Gr reads:* Common sense is posited by him

[*Ed.*] Beattie's year of birth appears only in *Gr*, whereas all five transcripts give his year of death. Hegel's sources agree on these dates: Tennemann, *Geschichte* 9:480; Wendt, *Grundriss*, p. 404; Rixner, *Handbuch* 3:261. This brief account of Beattie's philosophy is based—as is also clear from *W* 15:504 (Ms?)—on Rixner (3:261–262), who in turn relies on a German translation by Andreas Christoph Rüdinger (Copenhagen and Leipzig, 1772) of Beattie's *An Essay on the Nature and Immutability of Truth; in Opposition to Sophistry and Scepticism* (Edinburgh, 1770). What Rixner provides, however, is not, as he implies, a citation from Beattie but a sketchy and misleading summary of Beattie's first chapter: "Of the Perception of Truth in General." Hegel's account has reference to Rixner's phrase, "common sense of plain human understanding"; but the German translation distinguishes terminologically between "understanding" as that power of the soul whereby we know the truth of a proof, and "common sense" (*gesunde Vernunft*) as the faculty for knowing a truth that is self-evident.

335. *Thus Lw; An reads:* It [the nature of spirit] is the foundation whenever there is doubt. *Gr reads:* Convictions as wholly certain are the foundation for actions.

336. [*Ed.*] This statement comes not from Beattie but from James Oswald (c. 1704–1793). It abbreviates a reference to Oswald in Rixner (*Handbuch* 3:262); cf. *W* 15:504 (Ms?), where it is correctly ascribed to Oswald. It comes from Oswald's *An Appeal to Common Sense on Behalf of Religion* (Edinburgh, 1766); German translation by Friedrich Ernst Wilmsen, 2 vols. (Leipzig, 1774).

146 way, | a knowing, by the conscience, of principles or content—a knowing in fact of God and God's being.[337]

DUGALD STEWART is the most recent of the Scots, for he is still alive.[338] On the whole England stands on the same ground; there is the same sphere of reflection.

Here we can bring in what the French call "ideology." It is nothing else but logic, ontology, and abstract metaphysics, namely, the enumeration and analysis of the simplest thought-determinations. They are not handled dialectically and are not investigated according to their sources. Instead the stuff is taken from our reflection, from our thought and representation, and it is analyzed minutely and its further determinations exhibited.[339] It is Humean skepticism, however, that makes the direct transition to Kantian philosophy.[340]

---

337. [*Ed.*] See p. 243 below. Rixner (*Handbuch* 3:260) points in this connection to Jacobi's philosophical novel, *Woldemar: Ein Seltenheit aus der Naturgeschichte* (Flensburg and Leipzig, 1779).

338. [*Ed.*] Dugald Stewart (1753–1828) was a disciple of Thomas Reid. In the sources on the history of philosophy Hegel used, Stewart is mentioned only as author of a biography of Reid (see Rixner, *Handbuch* 3:261), for most of his publications were more recent titles, such as his *Elements of the Philosophy of the Human Mind* (London, 1792) and *Philosophical Essays* (Edinburgh, 1810). Since in W 15:505 as well Hegel does not deal any more concretely with Stewart, and remarks there that he seems to be the last and least noteworthy of the Scottish philosophers, it is unlikely that Hegel had read him in detail, though he certainly knew the review bearing on Stewart in *The Quarterly Review*; see n. 24, p. 116 above.

339. [*Ed.*] Only Rixner (*Handbuch* 3:466–467) among Hegel's sources on the history of philosophy introduces "ideology," and his presentation is scarcely correct. Nevertheless, Hegel's characterization of ideology can serve as a very abbreviated description of the procedure adopted by Antoine Louis Claude Destutt de Tracy, the most notable of the ideologues, in the first and most important part of his *Elémens d'idéologie*, namely, *Idéologie proprement dite* (Paris, 1817). Destutt de Tracy refers freely to the "sensualism" of Etienne Bonnot de Condillac (1715–1780), though without the latter's genetic perspective (p. 25), and he reduces thinking to four faculties of sensibility: sensation, memory, judgment, and will (p. 27). The analysis of these faculties, and therefore of the whole realm of our ideas, makes up "ideology" proper (p. 213). Hegel's evaluation of ideology as "abstract metaphysics" may have in view the circumstance that Destutt de Tracy sets out from empirical, subjective thinking, leaving aside the existence of external objects, which are only demonstrated subsequently, in chapter 7, "On Existence" (pp. 107–142).

340. [*Ed.*] At this point in the 1825–26 lectures Hegel puts aside concerns for exact chronology in order to be able to pass over directly from Hume to Kant.

7. David Hume

David Hume counts as a skeptic. He was born in 1711 in Edinburgh, and he died in 1776 in London. He spent a long time in diplomatic circles.[341] His *Essays* have made him most well-known on the philosophical side. In them he treated philosophical objects, although not systematically (but more as a cultured and thoughtful man of the world), not in a logical system, and also not with the scope that his thoughts properly might have attained or could have grasped. The main thing is that he presupposes the philosophical standpoint of Locke and Bacon (the philosophy of experience). It has to confine itself to a matter that is given through outer intuition or through sensibility of what is inner, including right, ethics, the religious; all this, then, is the content.[342] |

147

Hume's philosophy belongs chronologically before the French philosophy and Scottish philosophy just discussed, for Reid et al. constitute a reply to Hume. The structure of these lectures resembles that of the first Berlin lectures of 1819, as well as of the second (1821-22) and the last (1829-30). In the lectures of 1823-24, and similarly in those of 1827-28, Hegel follows Christian Wolff with—in this order—Hume, Scottish and French philosophy, and then Jacobi as the transition to Kant.

341. [Ed.] This short biographical notice is partly erroneous and partly misleading. Tennemann and Tiedemann do not expressly name Hume's place of death, but their presentation suggests Edinburgh, which is correct. Of the transcripts, only *Gr* gives London, probably based on Rixner (*Handbuch* 3:248). Hume was actually in the diplomatic service only for comparatively short trips to Vienna and Turin (with General St. Clair, 1747-1748) and to Paris (with Count Hertford, 1763-1766), as well as for two years (1767-1769) spent as under secretary of state.

342. [Ed.] In referring to Hume's *Essays,* Hegel probably has in mind especially those that deal with philosophical and moral issues, for instance, *An Enquiry concerning Human Understanding* (London, 1748) and *An Enquiry concerning the Principles of Morals* (London, 1751), each being a revision of a part of his *A Treatise of Human Nature* (London, 1739-1740). Buhle (*Geschichte* 5, pt. 1:195) and Tennemann (*Geschichte* 11:419) agree in reporting that these essays met with a favorable reception. Hume was also renowned for his six-volume *History of Great Britain* (London, 1754-1762), being in some circles better known for that than for his philosophical works; Hegel refers directly to it in other lecture series on the history of philosophy (cf. *W* 15:493). Hegel's characterization of Hume's method as unsystematic does not derive from his sources but rather calls to mind Hegel's own presentation of Bacon; see pp. 000 above. For the standpoint of Bacon and Locke that Hegel says Hume presupposed, see pp. 000 and 000 above. Tennemann (*Geschichte* 11:426–427) in particular underscores the significance of Locke for Hume. Hegel may have in mind Hume's *An Enquiry concerning Human Understanding,* which attributes the mind's creative power to the compounding, transposing, and

When Hume examines more closely what is subsumed under experience, he finds further determinations, and in particular the determination of the universal and of universal necessity. Hume consistently drew attention to the fact that when we keep to this [empirical] standpoint, then experience, outer and inner, is indeed the foundation of what we know, but the characteristics of universality and necessity are not contained or given within experience. Necessity in particular is comprised in the relation of cause and effect,[343] but what we perceive is only the fact that now something occurs and then something else follows upon it. Immediate perception relates simply and solely to a content [in] the nexus of time, in the succession of time. So the content and the succession fall within perception, but the connection of cause and effect does not. It is the same with respect to the universal. What we perceive are single phenomena, single sensations or perceptions, the fact that now this is so and then that. It can even be the case that we perceive

so forth, of the materials furnished to it by the senses and experience: "all the materials of thinking are derived either from our outward or inward sentiment"; "all our ideas or more feeble perceptions are copies of our impressions or more lively ones"; see *An Inquiry concerning Human Understanding*, edited with an introduction by Charles W. Hendel (Indianapolis, 1955), pp. 27–28, 30. There are many examples of such compound ideas; Hegel's "right, ethics, the religious" may be suggested by the examples mentioned by Hume in this context, for instance, the idea of God and the ideas of revenge, friendship, generosity, and the like, which arise from our temperament and experience.

343. [*Ed.*] It is clear here and in the following paragraphs that Hegel is not presenting Hume's position in its own terms, but from the perspective of Kant's critique of it. This is especially clear from the frequent mention of universality and necessity—concepts not found in this form in Hume. Also, Hegel does not mention the principles enunciated by Hume for the connection of representations: resemblance, contiguity in space and time, causality (*Inquiry,* ed. Hendel, sec. 3, p. 32); nor does he mention Hume's division of the objects of human reason into relations of ideas and matters of fact (*Inquiry,* ed. Hendel, sec. 4, p. 40). Actually Hegel's summary refers only to Hume's "matters of fact" and not to his "relations of ideas." Hegel's statement that "universality and necessity are not contained or given within experience" may be based on Hume's contention (*Inquiry,* ed. Hendel, sec. 4, p. 40) that the contrary of every matter of fact (such as the sun rising tomorrow) "is still possible, because it can never imply a contradiction and is conceived by the mind with the same facility and distinctness as if ever so conformable to reality." On the following page Hume discusses cause and effect as the foundation of reasoning about matters of fact; later he notes (sec. 4, p. 46) that experience is the foundation of all reasoning about cause and effect.

the same characteristic many times over, but that is still far re-moved from universality, for universality is the sort of determi-nation that is not given to us through experience.[344] We can call this a completely correct remark if we understand "experience" to mean outer experience. ˉExperience senses that something exists, but the universal is still not in that experience.ˉ[345]

From this vantage point Hume then considered legal, ethical, and religious determinations, and disputed their absolute validity. In fact, when it is presupposed that our knowledge derives from experience and that only what we have through experience is true, then it is indeed according to experience that something counts as right. For example, it is true that we find in our feeling the sense ˉthat murder, for instance, is something wrong;ˉ[346] [we find this] in our sensibility and in the | sensibility of others, and thus it be-comes generally valid. But it can also be shown readily that other peoples have entirely different views of what is right. There are those who do not have the sense that theft is wrong, for instance, the Lacedaemonians or the so-called innocent peoples of the South Sea islands. What one people regards as ˉreligious,ˉ[347] or as un-ethical or shameful, is not regarded that way by another.[348] Such

148

344. [Ed.] According to Hume, what is perceived in single instances is not the necessary connection of events but sheer succession (Inquiry, ed. Hendel, sec. 7, pp. 74–75). He subsequently argues (p. 86) that the constant conjunction observed in a number of instances does not itself yield necessary connection, which comes rather from a habit of the observing mind that expects the second event to accompany the first in future occurrences as it has done repeatedly in the past. Hegel here speaks of "universality" and construes it in a strict Kantian sense, thus giving too little con-sideration to the significance Hume assigns to observable uniformity in natural events, and to "custom," in the representation of a necessary causation. For Hume we must have "the constant *conjunction* of similar objects and the consequent *infer-ence* from one to the other" if we are to form the idea of a necessary connection between events (Inquiry, ed. Hendel, sec. 8, p. 92).

345. *Thus Gr; Pn reads:* It cannot be said that something exists in universal fashion.

346. *Thus An; Gr reads, similar in Lw:* that the murderer or the thief must be punished;

347. *Thus Lw; Gr reads:* irreligious

348. [Ed.] Here Hegel probably has in mind Hume's distinction between popu-lar and philosophical objections to moral arguments (Inquiry, ed. Hendel, sec. 12, pp. 166–169). Hegel's presentation creates the false impression that skepticism in matters of morality and right is Hume's final result. In this lecture series Hegel leaves

matters rest upon experience, and the individual subject has its own subjective experience. The subject finds religious feelings within itself, but one subject finds one shape or specification for God in its religious feeling, while another finds within itself God in another shape, in another determination. Hence if truth rests upon experience, then the determinations of universality, of validity in-and-for-itself and the like, come from elsewhere; they are not justified by the uniquely valid source, namely, experience.[349]

Hume therefore explained this kind of universality, as well as necessity, not as something that exists objectively but rather as something subjective only. Custom is a subjective universality of this kind. We have the custom of counting a certain thing as what is right or ethical, and others do not. Something has universality for us, but something subjectively universal is limited to us, since others have other customs. This is a correct and perceptive distinc-

out of account Hume's arguments against excessive (Pyrrhonian) skepticism, in particular the thought of overcoming skepticism through the strong power of the natural instinct to act and reason even when certainty is unattainable (*Inquiry*, ed. Hendel, sec. 12, pt. 2, pp. 168–169); but cf. W 15:499–500. Hume also invokes this power of instinct or sentiment as proof of the universality of "moral evidence," in *An Enquiry concerning the Principles of Morals*, appendix 1, "Concerning Moral Sentiment"; see *Hume's Ethical Writings*, ed. Alasdair MacIntyre (New York, 1965), pp. 124–132. See also n. 350 below. The examples that Hegel introduces would be accounted popular and not philosophical objections, for the latter rely on the uncertainty of the causal relation; see Hume's comment that experience, not a priori thought, is the foundation of moral reasoning (*Inquiry*, ed. Hendel, sec. 12, pt. 3, p. 172). Hegel's examples do not correspond precisely with any given in either of Hume's *Enquiries* we have been discussing, or in his *Natural History of Religion* (London, 1757). Hegel may have drawn them from discussions in his own day; see his critical remarks on the view that primitive peoples embody an original spiritual perfection (*Philosophy of Religion* 3:97 with n. 99).

349. [*Ed.*] Hegel's remarks about the subjective character of religious feelings could have in view the presentation of differing religious practices and doctrines that Hume provides in his *Natural History of Religion*, but without consideration of Hume's conclusion in section 15 of that work, "General Corollary from the Whole." There Hume speaks on the one hand of the weakness of human reason that is shown in religious principles that have been dominant in the world, but also of its natural propensity to believe in a single creator god envisioned in the manner proposed by the physicotheological, or teleological, proof; see *The Natural History of Religion ...*, ed. A. Wayne Colver (Oxford, 1976), pp. 92–95. It is thus more likely that Hegel is here only reiterating his polemic directed against appeal to immediate knowledge of God.

tion in relation to experience taken as the source of knowledge. The Kantian reflection sets out from this beginning, and we now pass over to it.[350]

D. RECENT PHILOSOPHY:
KANT, FICHTE, JACOBI, SCHELLING

We shall also discuss Jacobi here, in conjunction with Kant.[351] | 149

1. Immanuel Kant: Transcendental Aesthetic and Analytic

[352]The general sense of the Kantian philosophy is that, as Hume has shown, categorial determinations [*Bestimmungen*] such as universality and necessity are not to be found in perception, and there-

350. [*Ed.*] Hume stresses custom in *An Enquiry concerning Human Understanding*. Custom is the propensity to renew or repeat an act or operation without being driven to do so by reason or understanding. He calls it "the great guide of human life" that makes experience useful to us and gives us the expectation that future sequences of events will be like those experienced in the past (*Inquiry*, ed. Hendel, sec. 5, pp. 56–59). But Hume does not furnish this account in the context of his moral philosophy. Hegel does not discuss the elaboration of the specific principles of moral evidence in Hume's *An Enquiry concerning the Principles of Morals*, nor the opposition Hume draws (in the appendix) between reason and moral sentiment. Hume states that reason discerns the utility of various actions but assigns no moral blame or approbation to them. It is sentiment (a feeling for the happiness of persons) that leads us to prefer one means or action over another (see *Hume's Ethical Writings*, pp. 124–132); the social significance of this natural sentiment of benevolence is discussed in sec. 5, pt. 2 (pp. 65–77). On the difference between Kant and Hume with respect to custom and universality, see Kant's *Critique of Pure Reason*, B 5. Perhaps Hegel is referring here to Kant's remark, in the foreword to his *Prolegomena to Any Future Metaphysics*, that Hume awakened him from his dogmatic slumber; see the English translation by Paul Carus (La Salle, 1902), p. 7.

351. [*Ed.*] In the 1825–26 lectures only, Hegel intersperses parts of his treatment of Kant with his remarks on Fichte and Jacobi. After Fichte's *Wissenschaftslehre* he returns to Kant's Transcendental Dialectic, and after general remarks on Jacobi he returns to Kant's practical philosophy with reference to Fichte. Then he couples further aspects of Kant with Jacobi's view of faith. For details, see the Editorial Introduction, p. 00 above.

352. *Precedes in Gr:* Kant was born in 1724 in Königsberg. At first he studied theology there, in 1755 he emerged as an academic instructor, and in 1770 he became professor of logic. He died in Königsberg on 12 February 1804. The Kantian philosophy has an immediate connection with what we have just discussed concerning Hume's thought.

fore they have a source other than perceiving. This other source is the subject or the I, the subject in its self-consciousness.[353] This is the principal thesis of the Kantian philosophy, which is also called critical philosophy because its first aim is to be a critique of knowing. Knowing is represented as the instrument or the means by which we want to take possession of the truth. So in advance, before we can get to the truth itself, we must first investigate the nature or type of the instrument in order to see whether it is capable of accomplishing what is required of it.[354] Kant's subjection of knowing to examination in this way was a great and important step. This critique of knowing applies equally to the empiricism or knowledge that allegedly grounds itself only upon experience, and to that more metaphysical type of philosophizing associated with Wolff and German philosophy in general. Even before Kant, German philosophy had already taken the turn toward that empirical style which we have sketched. What prevailed in the practical domain prior to Kant was the so-called "theory of happiness," the concept and vocation of humanity and how this concept should be realized. This vocation is grasped as happiness.[355] There was also

353. [Ed.] Hegel is referring to Kant's expressions directed to the connection between his program in his *Critique of Pure Reason* (Königsberg, 1781; Riga, 1787) and Hume's critique of knowing; see n. 350 above, and B 127 of the *Critique* (English translation by Norman Kemp Smith; London, 1929, 1933), which states that Hume tried to derive such a priori concepts from a subjective necessity arising in connection with repeated experiences, since he did not see that the understanding itself, through the use of these concepts, is the very author of that experience. Cf. B 793, which says Hume regarded such a priori principles as fictitious, as habits arising from experience. The "Transcendental Deduction of the Pure Concepts of Understanding" (B 129–169) exhibits the grounding of these categories in the pure subject. On Hume's significance for Kant's development of transcendental idealism, see also Kant's *Critique of Practical Reason* (1788), trans. Lewis White Beck (Indianapolis, 1956), pp. 53–59; original in *Gesammelte Schriften,* edited by the Royal Prussian Academy of Sciences, 22 vols. (Berlin, 1902 ff.), 5:52–57.

354. [Ed.] Mention of knowing as an instrument is an allusion to the *Critique of Pure Reason,* B 24–25, which speaks of an organon of pure reason whereby a priori knowledge could be acquired; similar language about knowing as an instrument occurs in § 73 of Hegel's *Phenomenology* (p. 46). Kant, however, does not speak in this passage of a critique that leads to an actual system of pure reason, but of one that is a propaedeutic to it (cf. B xliii).

355. [Ed.] On this popular philosophy, see pp. 000–000 above, where, however, Hegel cites no names from German philosophy apart from Garve's translations; nor,

still in vogue a rational metaphysics of the Wolffian kind, as illustrated, for instance, by Mendelssohn. This rational metaphysics maintained itself in distinction from the merely empirical procedure, but its main activity consisted in taking as basic the categories [*Gedankenbestimmungen*] of the understanding, such as possibility, | actuality, and so on, and with them devising rational arguments about God and the like.[356] Kant's philosophy is directed first of all against both of these approaches. Its principal thesis is the quite simple one that we have already indicated, and it is just made difficult by the range and prolixity ˜with which it is presented. The same point is repeated often, which is frequently beneficial for the beginner.˜[357] It is also made difficult by its own characteristic kind of terminology.

150

The principal moments of Kant's philosophy are as follows. The first and most universal is his outright acknowledgment that the determinations of necessity and universality are not to be found in perception. ˜The question then becomes: Where are they to be found? The answer is that˜[358] they are only to be found in self-

---

in W 15:485 ff. and 530 ff., does he cite any names from a pre-Kantian empiricism in German popular philosophy. It cannot be determined with certainty what authors and works Hegel is alluding to when he mentions the "theory of happiness" of the practical domain; his sources on the history of philosophy are of little help on this point. Buhle does mention (*Geschichte* 6, pt. 1:350) the work of the philosophically inclined scientist Pierre Louis Moreau de Maupertuis (1698–1759). It is more probable, however, that Hegel has in mind the works of a number of nearly forgotten authors, such as Gotthilf Samuel Steinbart's *System der reinen Philosophie oder Glückseligkeitslehre des Christenthums . . .* (Züllichau, 1778, 1780), §§ 81–82, or Johann Georg Heinrich Feder's *Untersuchungen über den menschlichen Willen, dessen Naturtriebe, Veränderlichkeit, Verhältniss zur Tugend und Glückseligkeit . . .*, 3 vols. (Linz, 1785–1787), especially vol. 3, bk. 4.

356. [*Ed.*] This remark is directed especially at Moses Mendelssohn's *Morgenstunden; oder, Vorlesungen über das Daseyn Gottes*, pt. 1 (Berlin, 1786), in particular pp. 284–305.

357. *Thus An; Gr, similar in Lw, reads:* in which it [the philosophy] is represented. At the same time the range also has one advantage, for the same point is repeated often, so that one can remember the principal theses and not at once lose sight of them.

[*Ed.*] In the German edition the text lemma encompasses only "It is also made difficult" (in the following sentence). We have relocated it to eliminate redundancy.

358. *Thus Gr with Lw; Pn reads:* But *An reads:* Instead

consciousness; they belong to it, to subjective thinking.[359] More precisely, these determinations of thinking are of the type that are determinations of universality or of unity generally, that is to say, the conjunction of diverse determinations, and in that respect Kant calls thinking a synthesizing, a joining into unity.[360] But thinking already contains these conjunctions within itself, in its own determinations, for thinking is a union, a uniting of distinctions. The distinctions are the stuff that is given through experience, and in order to conjoin this stuff the ability to do so must already be in the subjective determinations. Cause and effect or causality, and the others, are categories of thought.[361] They are intrinsically conjunction.

Kant poses the philosophical question therefore in this way: How are synthetic judgments a priori possible?[362] Judgments are conjunctions of categories of thought such as subject and predicate; "synthetic" means "conjoining." There are a priori judgments, that

359. [Ed.] The remark about his outright acknowledgment that universality and necessity "are not to be found in perception"—or more generally in experience— indicates that Hegel is thinking of B 3–4, a passage in the introduction to the Critique of Pure Reason, which states that whereas experience only yields comparative universality, through induction, necessity and strict universality are indicative of a priori knowledge. See also B 123–124, as well as n. 353 above. Kant's criticism of Hume (in B 127) states that Hume never realized that the understanding itself is the author of experience, since it finds in experience concepts that, although lacking connection in the understanding alone, are given in experience as connected of necessity in the object. Cf. B 131 ff., and also n. 375 below.

360. [Ed.] On Kant's concept of synthesis, see B 102–103 of the Critique of Pure Reason. Synthesis is the spontaneous activity of thought in putting representations together in a certain way so that the manifold of them may be conceived in a single cognitive act. See also the "Transcendental Deduction of the Pure Concepts of Understanding" (B 129–169, especially 129–131); B 143 ff. treats the synthesizing function of the categories.

361. [Ed.] The Critique of Pure Reason (B 104–105) explains that the same function that unites representations in a judgment also unites the synthesis of representations in an intuition, and that we call this unity the pure concept of the understanding. Thus the a priori concepts, which Kant calls "categories" (after Aristotle), function both in logic and in the structure of experience. In Kant's table of categories (B 106), causality and dependence, or cause and effect, occupy the second position in the categories of relation.

362. [Ed.] See the Critique of Pure Reason, B 19.

is, conjunctions of thought that are not given through experience.[363] Cause and effect are categories of thought. Hume already showed that they are not | in experience. Sense perception has only space 151 and time as its binding element, not cause and effect.[364] Hence these conjunctions are a priori, that is, they are in self-consciousness.[365] Kant calls this philosophy "transcendental philosophy."[366] "Transcendent" and "transcendental" must be distinguished. In "transcendent mathematics" the determination of the infinite is especially employed. In this sphere of mathematics we say, for example, that the circle consists of an infinite number of straight lines; the circumference is represented as straight, and since the curvature is represented as straight the procedure *passes beyond* [*übergeht*] the geometric determination and is in that way transcendent, it lies beyond the understanding. Kant defines "transcendental philosophy" as a philosophy that does *not* go beyond the sphere of the finite in its use of categories but that exhibits the source of what can perhaps become transcendent. "Transcendentalism" therefore only refers to the source of the determinations that can become transcendent, and this source is consciousness. Consciousness is what is universal.

363. [*Ed.*] The *Critique of Pure Reason* states (B 12–13) that experience itself cannot be the conjoining factor, because in the judgment the connection is made not just with a higher degree of universality but with necessity, a priori, on the basis of the sheer concepts; cf. B 2.

364. [*Ed.*] On this sentence and the preceding one, see p. 000 with nn. 343 and 344.

365. [*Ed.*] The *Critique of Pure Reason* states that reason is the faculty that furnishes the principles of a priori knowledge (B 24), and it calls the unity of pure or original apperception the "transcendental unity of self-consciousness" (B 132).

366. [*Ed.*] On Kant's concept of transcendental philosophy, see the *Critique of Pure Reason*, B 27–30, 829. Hegel disregards the fact that for Kant this critique is not itself called transcendental philosophy (B 27); it embodies the complete idea of transcendental philosophy, but is not itself equivalent to that science (B 28). The ensuing distinction of "transcendent" from "transcendental" is given in B 352. There is no indubitable source for Hegel's particular explanation of the idea of transcendental philosophy that follows in our text. He could be referring to the *Critique of Pure Reason*, B 90–91, where Kant defines the analytic of concepts as a "dissection of the faculty of the understanding itself," which locates a priori concepts in the understanding alone and by doing so explains their possibility. Cf. also B 24–25.

Kant proceeds only psychologically, that is, historically. Sensibility, understanding, and reason are present in human [experience]. Kant tells the story in this way by taking it up quite empirically, without developing it from the concept.[367] First, there is sensible nature in general. Within that he first of all distinguishes sensation generally, as outer sensation (for instance, red, bitter, hard) or inner sensation (of the right, the ethical, anger, agreeable things, religious matters, and so forth).[368] These inner sensations are subjective only. But there is also a universal sensible element within this sensible domain. This universal element is space and time. ([In Kant's view of] sensation and intuition, "intuition" means setting sensation outside us, sundering it from us, seeing it either within time as succession or in space as coexistence.[369] Nowadays people have no such concept of intuition. They understand it to mean immediacy of consciousness, | and they speak of an intuition of God,[370] although God belongs only to thought.) Space and time therefore are

152

367. [Ed.] This statement may be directed in particular to the formulation at the end of the introduction to the *Critique of Pure Reason* (B 29), which, in anticipation of what is to follow, simply declares that sensibility and understanding are the two stems of human knowledge. Just before, however, Kant had said that concepts that contain any empirical element must not be admitted (B 28) and that transcendental philosophy involves pure, speculative reason and only that (B 29). But Kant makes these remarks in connection with the delimiting of speculative reason as distinct from practical reason.

368. [Ed.] This is probably a reference to the extended footnote at the end of the preface to the second edition of the *Critique of Pure Reason* (B xl-xli); cf. B 66, 275–279, 400–401, 405, 519, 700. But the examples adduced in our text are not found in this passage or other passages in Kant. Kant does mention briefly the perception of red, in connection with his account of degrees of magnitude in sensations (B 211); but that example has a character and a context different from those of Hegel's distinction between outer and inner sensation. Here Hegel is bringing together the "inner sensation" of the transcendental aesthetic with the sensation (understood as feeling) discussed in the practical philosophy.

369. [Ed.] On space and time as the two pure forms of sensible intuition, see *Critique of Pure Reason,* B 36. On the relation of sensation and intuition, see B 35, which states that when we remove from the representation of a body all the elements supplied by the understanding and by sensation respectively, the remainder (extension and figure) is what belongs to pure intuition. Hegel's explanation of this relationship is not true to its actual wording in Kant. He could also have in view another passage (B 38), which says that the representation of space must be the basis for my referring any sensation to something outside of me. See also B 38–39, 48–49, on inner and outer intuition.

something universal, the universal of the sensible itself, or what Kant calls the a priori forms of sensible nature.[371] For that reason space and time do not even belong to sensation as such, insofar as it is determined outwardly or inwardly. ⁻I have this or that sensation,⁻[372] it is something particular and singular, [whereas] space and time, the universal in sensation, belong to sensible nature a priori, to the subjective.[373] Kant calls this way of judging "aesthetic," the "transcendental aesthetic"; nowadays we take "aesthetic" to mean "acquaintance with the beautiful."[374] In Kant the aesthetic is the doctrine of intuition with respect to what is universal in intuition, that is, to what lies within the subject as such or belongs to it, namely, space and time. I sense something hard, and the hardness is my sensation. My intuition is that I locate something hard outside me in space; but now I also locate my sensation itself outwardly in space. With this division between subjectivity and objectivity, the contents in space are mutually external and are outside me. That this is so is the doing of the a priori sensible nature. Space is this projection of the determinate being, of this content, outside me and separate from me. In time I project it in such a way that another [instant] takes the place [of the present one].

370. [Ed.] See below, p. 000 with n. 459.
371. [Ed.] See the Critique of Pure Reason, B 34 ff., in particular B 36. Kant himself speaks of the unity, not the universality (so Hegel), of space and time, since they are intuitions rather than concepts; cf. B 39, 47.
372. Thus Gr; Lw reads: I have this or that content before me,
373. [Ed.] The Critique of Pure Reason emphasizes that space is "the subjective condition of sensible nature, under which alone outer intuition is possible for us" (B 42); elsewhere (B 49, 51) Kant says that time is "a subjective condition under which all intuitions can occur in us." Hegel does not go fully into Kant's doctrine of the empirical reality and transcendental ideality of space and time.
374. [Ed.] The Critique of Pure Reason (B 35) introduces the term "transcendental aesthetic" for the a priori science of all the principles of our sensible nature. The change in terminology noted by Hegel is not simply post-Kantian. In a footnote to the same passage Kant notes that in Germany since the time of Alexander Gottlieb Baumgarten (1714–1762) "aesthetic" has designated what is elsewhere called the "critique of taste." Kant objects to Baumgarten's usage and seeks to return "aesthetic" to its place in the classical juxtaposition of αἰσθητά (sensation) and νοητά (thought). Of course Kant's own talk in his subsequent Critique of Judgment (1790) of a power of "aesthetic judgment" contributed further to the very shift in meaning to which he is objecting.

The second [faculty] is understanding. Kant calls the spontaneity of thinking "understanding." This expression stems from the Leibnizian philosophy. Understanding is active thinking, I myself, this activity, the pure apperception of self-consciousness. This quite empty, abstractly empty ⁻I⁻[375] is *what I am*. Apperceiving is determining in general, whereas perceiving [*Perzipieren*]—another Leibnizian expression—has more the meaning of sensing or representing. Apperceiving is rather the activity through which something | is posited in my consciousness.[376] I am what is simple, hence what is completely universal, wholly devoid of determination, abstract. Insofar as I now posit or apperceive some sort of empirical content or manifold in the I, it must be within this simple [element]. In order for it to enter within this one or this simple [element], it must itself be simplified, and thus the content is, so to speak, infected by the unity. Within consciousness a content itself becomes one, it becomes my content. I am I, this one, and in that the content becomes mine it becomes posited in the unity and thus it becomes one. This unity of the manifold is posited by my spontaneity; thinking is in general this synthesizing of the manifold.[377] This is an important awareness, a momentous knowledge. But the fact that I am *one*—as thinking, active, positing unity—Kant does

153

---

375. *Thus Gr, Sv; An reads:* One *Lw reads:* pure element
[*Ed.*] The *Critique of Pure Reason* calls the understanding the mind's power of producing representations from itself, the spontaneity of knowing, in contrast with sensibility, which is the mind's receptivity (B 75). Leibniz says there is in us a wonderful spontaneity that makes the resolves of the soul independent of physical influences from other creatures (*Theodicy*, pt. 1, § 59: Allen, p. 53; *Schriften*, ed. Gerhardt, 6:135); see also n. 293 above. Kant calls this act of spontaneity "pure or original apperception." It is the self-conscious "I think," but without accompanying representation; it is the transcendental unity of self-consciousness or of apperception (B 132). Kant's emphasis here and elsewhere is that it is a thinking and not an intuiting (B 157), that it is an *act* of the understanding (B 130).
376. [*Ed.*] In the *Critique of Pure Reason* (B 376–377) Kant distinguishes the perception that is sensation (modification of the state of a subject) from objective perception or knowledge (which is either intuition or concept). For Leibniz's use of "perception" and "apperception," see n. 278 above.
377. [*Ed.*] The synthesis of the manifold is due not to the senses but to the spontaneous act of the power of representation (*Critique of Pure Reason*, B 129–130); cf. B 132, and n. 360 above.

not explain so precisely. What thinking produces is thus the unity, and so it produces only itself, for it is what is one.

With regard to the manifold, the unity can be called "connection" [*Beziehung*]. There are then varieties of this unity, for the connections determine themselves more precisely, and these modes of connection are the categories or universal thought-determinations. The problem with these universal thought-determinations is that Kant takes them from that part of the ordinary logic where the types of judgment are classified. He sets up different kinds of judgment as kinds of connection: positive, negative, infinite, singular, and the other judgments are at the same time particular modes of connecting.[378] Insofar as these particular modes of connection are picked out, they are categories. Kant adopts them empirically, just in the way they have been ordered in logic. He does not think about proceeding from unity to the kinds or determinations of unity— about developing the distinctions out of unity.[379] He has twelve fundamental categories, which fall into four kinds, and composite

378. [*Ed.*] In the first four sentences of this paragraph, Hegel's exposition is closely based on selected passages in the *Critique of Pure Reason*. The concept of an object unites the manifold of a given intuition (B 137). The categories are the conditions under which this sensible manifold comes together in a unitary consciousness, and "categories" is another term for functions of judgment when applied to intuition (B 143). Kant's table of categories shows that there are the same number and kinds of pure categories, applicable a priori to objects of intuition, as there are logical functions of possible judgments (B 105–106; cf. B 95). In naming the kinds of relation, however, Hegel is using the terminology of his own logic of judgment; see *Science of Logic*, pp. 630 ff.; *Wissenschaft der Logik*, vol. 2 (*GW* 12:60–73). Kant's table of judgments (B 95) lists "affirming" [*bejahend*] rather than "positive," "denying" [*verneinend*] rather than "negative," and "individual" [*einzeln*] rather than "singular" [*singulär*]; the English translation by Kemp Smith does not reflect all of these distinctions.

379. [*Ed.*] Kant criticizes Aristotle for having no principle for a derivation of the categories, for just collecting the first ten hastily and then later thinking he had discovered five more (*Critique of Pure Reason*, B 107). Hegel rejects Kant's claim to have derived the categories systematically from a common principle, the faculty of judgment (B 106), because this *Critique* itself states (B 95) that, if we look at the sheer form of understanding involved, we find that thought in judgment comes under *four* heads, each of which has in turn three moments. As examples of a development of distinctions from unity, Hegel could cite the thought of Proclus and perhaps also that of Pythagoras; cf. W 15:75 ff. and 13:243 ff.

categories. First are the categories of quantity: (a) one, (b) many, and (c) all (or: unity, plurality, totality). It is remarkable, and a great merit on Kant's part, that each class in turn constitutes a
154   triad.[380] Triplicity, this ancient form of the | Pythagoreans, the Neoplatonists, and the Christian religion,[381] emerges here again, albeit quite externally. Unity is followed by difference or plurality, and the third is the positing of the first two in one; plurality, once it is closed, is totality. The second kind are the categories of quality: (a) positive, (b) negative, and (c) limitation or the boundary (this last counts as positive and negative). The third kind are the categories of relation, or of relation*ship*: (a) substance and accidents, (b) causal relationship or relationship of cause and effect, and (c) reciprocity.[382] The fourth kind are the categories of modality, that is, the connection of objects with our thinking: (a) possibility, (b) actuality, and (c) necessity.

The reflective understanding therefore is the source of the categories or wholly universal thought-determinations.[383] These categories pertain to thinking [and as such] are empty or unfulfilled; in order for them to be fulfilled and gain significance there is required the stuff of perception or intuition, of feeling, and so forth. They

380. [*Ed.*] Instead of categories that are "fundamental" and those that are "composite," Kant speaks of "original and primitive concepts" in relation to "derivative and subsidiary ones," of *Prädicamenten* in relation to *Prädicabilien* (*Critique of Pure Reason*, B 106–108). It is "remarkable" not only that there are three categories in each class of original concepts but also that the third in each class arises from the combination of the first two in it.

381. [*Ed.*] See *Philosophy of Religion* 3:80 ff., 192 ff., 279 ff.

382. [*Ed.*] Kant uses the Latinate *Relation* in his table of categories. Hegel prefers the Teutonic *Verhältnis*. In this section on Kant we render these terms as "relation" and "relationship" respectively. *Beziehung*, which we sometimes render elsewhere as "relation," is here "connection."

383. [*Ed.*] Kant's table of categories (*Critique of Pure Reason*, B 106) gives the second, third, and fourth classes respectively as follows. Quality: reality, negation, limitation. Relation: inherence and subsistence (substance and accidents), causality and dependence (cause and effect), community (reciprocity between agent and patient). Modality: possibility-impossibility, existence-nonexistence, necessity-contingency. The understanding contains in itself, a priori, all these pure concepts of synthesis (B 106).

are the connection, the positing in unity, of the manifold stuff of feeling, the stuff of intuition; they have significance only through their bonding with this stuff of intuition.

This bonding of the categories with the stuff of perception is what Kant understands by "experience."[384] And that is quite correct. There is perceiving in experience, there is stuff in it that belongs to feeling, to intuition. But this stuff is not apprehended merely according to its singularity or immediacy. To the contrary, it is posited in the very bonding ˘with those˘[385] categories (such as cause and effect) or, in short, ˘with what we call˘[386] natural laws, universal determinations or genera. The latter are not immediate perceptions. What we immediately perceive are not the laws of the heavens but only the changes in position of the stars, namely, that when one is in view another is too, that one star is a certain distance from another and comes back into view in this same position. | But what is perceived in this way is fixed or brought under   155
the categories, it is experience. In this way universal categories of thought are present within experience. Whatever is experience has to be universal, valid for all times.

According to Kant there are then two enduring components in experience. On the one side is the empirical component of ˘perception.˘[387] On the other is the second moment, the categories, cause and effect, substance and accident, the genus or universal.[388] When [the] cause is specified, then the effect must necessarily be present too. This analysis is quite correct. In experience we meet with both of these determinations. Kant joined to this the thesis that experience contains only phenomena and that we do not, through this knowledge that we have by experience, know things as they are in

384. [Ed.] "Experience is possible only through the representation of a necessary conjunction of perceptions" (Critique of Pure Reason, B 218); cf. B 219.

385. Thus An; Lw reads: with the Gr reads: through the Sv reads: through

386. Thus An, similar in Lw; Gr, Sv read; through

387. Thus Gr, Pn; An reads: feeling, intuition. Lw reads: perception of individual phenomena. We often call this "experience" too.

388. [Ed.] The two components of knowledge, namely, the concept (or categories) and intuition, are cited in the Critique of Pure Reason, B 146; cf. B 161, 195, 218.

themselves.[389] ~The perception in the experience Kant calls~[390] the subjective, the sphere of the contingent; in contrast, the objective component in experience is the categories, through which this stuff is posited as connected, the unity introduced by thought. The "objective" means here the law or the universal, what pertains to thinking. The stuff ~of experience~[391] on the other hand is something generally subjective, which means that it only *is* in the way it is in my sensation. That I see, hear, or otherwise sense something, is the receptivity of my organ. I only know about the sensation, not about the thing—my receptive knowing is altogether subjective. The objective component, or what Kant calls the category, is of course the antithesis to the subjective component, but it too is something subjective—not, of course, in the sense that it belongs to my feeling but because it belongs ~to the pure I of my self-consciousness, to the | realm of reflective understanding.~[392] ~On the one hand I have a feeling-content while on the other I am active over against it, I do not leave it in its contingent determination, I make it universal, but this activity is subjective too.~[393] So we do not in this way know the thing in itself; instead we have on the one hand only determinations of feeling that are connected with our organs, and on the other hand categories of thought, that is, determinate modes of

156

389. [*Ed.*] We can know objects only as appearances, in sensible intuition, but not as things in themselves (*Critique of Pure Reason,* B xxv–xxvi).

390. *Thus Gr; Sv reads:* The experience or intuition Kant calls *Lw reads:* In experience we have feelings, intuition. This is, Kant continues,

391. *Thus Pn, Lw; Gr reads:* of the realm of intuition *An reads:* of intuition *Sv reads:* and the feeling

[*Ed.*] On the distinction between the subjective and objective elements in experience, see the *Critique of Pure Reason,* B 233–234, and 218–219.

392. *Thus Gr, similar in Lw; Sv reads:* to the self-consciousness, to the reflective understanding. *Pn reads:* to my thinking. *An reads:* in the pure circle of the reflective consciousness.

[*Ed.*] The synthetic unity of consciousness is an objective condition for any intuition becoming an object for me (*Critique of Pure Reason,* B 138). It is a subjective condition of thought that has objective validity, as conditioning the possibility of all knowledge of objects (B 122).

393. *Thus Gr, similar in Lw; Sv reads:* The objective component in experience is also *my* activity.

the activity that I am. Thus what we know and define are only phenomena.[394] This is Kant's principal thesis.

2. Johann Gottlieb Fichte: *Wissenschaftslehre*

[395]The relationship of Fichte's philosophy to this Kantian position is that it should be regarded as a more consistent presentation and development of Kant's philosophy. Fichte's earliest writings are entirely Kantian. ¯Fichte begins¯[396] with the point we have just gone over, with the I, with the transcendental unity of self-consciousness ¯in which I am one. This I or this unity is the same for Fichte and is what is first.¯[397] Kant further declares the I to be the source of the categories. This I is what is certain, it is the *cogito* of Descartes,[398] the | certainty of myself; this certainty is my connection with myself; what I know is posited in me, and this pure, abstract knowing is I myself. Thus the beginning [for Fichte] is just as it was for Kant. [But] Kant adopted the ¯thought-determinations,¯[399] the categories, empirically, just as they have been worked out in [traditional] logic, that is, just as the universal forms are found in the [table of] judgments.[400] This procedure is empirical and philosophically unjustified. Fichte went beyond this, and that is his great merit. He called for, and sought to complete, the derivation or con-

157

394. [*Ed.*] See above, n. 389.

395. *Precedes in Gr:* Fichte was born at Rammenau, near Bischofswerda, in 1762. He studied in Jena, Leipzig, and Wittenberg, and in 1793 he became professor of philosophy at Jena, a position he resigned in 1800 owing to the unpleasantness he incurred on account of his essay, *Concerning the Ground of Our Belief in a Divine Government of the World* (1798). He lived from independent means for a few years in Berlin. He became a professor in Erlangen in 1805, and in Berlin in 1809, where he died on 29 January 1814.

396. *Thus Pn, An, Sv; Gr, similar in Lw, reads:* Where Fichte attained the greatest determinateness in his presentation, he begins

397. *Thus Gr; Sv reads:* or with the I.
[*Ed.*] Kant's discussion of this point is presented on pp. 000, 000 above.

398. [*Ed.*] On Descartes, see above, p. 000 with n. 98.

399. *Thus Sv; Gr reads:* determinations of the pure I, *An reads:* determinations, *Lw reads:* thought-determinations of the I,

400. [*Ed.*] See above, n. 379.

struction of the categories of thought from the I, and he did in part carry out this project.[401]

The I is active, it is determining, it produces its determinations.[402] What are the determinations that it produces, and what is their necessity? The I is consciousness, but the necessity of this activity, of the fact that I produce determinations such as cause and effect, lies beyond my consciousness. *I* do it, but I instinctively produce the category, [for instance,] the conjunction of cause and effect, without knowing that I do it.[403] Fichte then defines philosophy as ˜artificial˜[404] consciousness or the consciousness of consciousness, and so I may have consciousness of what my consciousness does. It has been said, on the contrary, that we cannot get behind consciousness to discover how consciousness has arrived at its result. "I have consciousness" then means that I discover *that* my con-

---

401. [*Ed.*] Hegel is referring to Fichte's *Grundlage der gesammten Wissenschaftslehre als Handschrift für seine Zuhörer* (1794), commonly called simply the *Wissenschaftslehre*; English translation by Peter Heath and John Lachs under the title *Science of Knowledge* (New York, 1970). Here Fichte derives the first category, that of reality, from his first principle, A = A, construed as the self's pure activity of positing itself. See J. G. Fichte, *Gesamtausgabe der Bayerischen Akademie der Wissenschaften*, ed. Reinhard Lauth and Hans Jacob, division 1 (Stuttgart–Bad Cannstatt, 1964 ff.), 2:261; cf. *Science of Knowledge*, p. 100. In like fashion Fichte derives the category of negation from his second principle, not-A is not equal to A (*Gesamtausgabe* 2:267; *Science of Knowledge*, p. 105), and the category of determination (limitation, for Kant) from his third principle, A in part equals not-A and vice versa (*Gesamtausgabe* 2:282; *Science of Knowledge*, p. 119). He does something similar with the grounding of reciprocity (*Gesamtausgabe* 2:290; *Science of Knowledge*, p. 151) and other categories.

402. [*Ed.*] Fichte understands the "I am" not only as the expression of a fact of consciousness but also as the expression of the self's own pure activity (*Gesamtausgabe* 2:259; *Science of Knowledge*, p. 97).

403. [*Ed.*] Here Hegel is very likely touching on the theme of unconscious production to which he already devoted extensive space in his early essay, *The Difference between Fichte's and Schelling's System of Philosophy* (1801), trans. H. S. Harris and Walter Cerf (Albany, 1977), pp. 120–122, 130 (*GW* 4:43–44, 51). He may be pointing to passages in Fichte's *Wissenschaftslehre* that stress the fact that the self cannot be consciously aware of its activity in producing the objects it intuits, that they first enter one's understanding through the medium of imagination (*Gesamtausgabe* 2:371, 374–375; *Science of Knowledge*, pp. 205, 208).

404. *Thus Gr, Lw; Sv reads:* having artificial

[*Ed.*] The text has *künstlich*, the variant *kunstmässig*. Fichte clearly states that these "facts of consciousness" are brought forth philosophically by an "artificial" reflection (*Gesamtausgabe* 2:363, 365; *Science of Knowledge*, pp. 196–197, 199).

sciousness has done this; but *how* consciousness has conducted its operations, how I am supposed to arrive at this knowledge, that is what is said to involve difficulties.[405] When I philosophize, however, or when I know what my "I" does, then this too is a consciousness; I go *behind* my ordinary consciousness—but *not above | and beyond* it. When I sleep I am above and beyond consciousness, but in sleep I am stupefied. When I philosophize I am in a state of consciousness and, as consciousness, I am object, for I can make my ordinary consciousness into an object for me, something ordinary consciousness itself does not do. Instead ordinary consciousness occupies itself only with other objects, interests, and the like, and does not make its own consciousness into its object. When we philosophize about being, cause, effect, and so forth, then we make being, cause, and effect into our consciousness. When I say, "the paper is white," ¯I maintain thereby that the paper is white. But when I maintain that it *is*, then I make being—a pure category—into [an object for] my consciousness, and so I make my consciousness into [an object for] consciousness and in this way I stand behind my ordinary consciousness.¯[406] I am always in the state of knowing, and in this instance I make that knowing into my object. To that extent we know our knowing and there is no difficulty about it. ¯It was Fichte who first brought the knowing of knowing to consciousness. What is more, by doing that, Fichte also posited philosophical consciousness or the aim of philosophy as the knowing of knowing.¯[407] For that reason he called his philosophy the

158

405. [*Ed.*] Hegel is very likely referring to Wilhelm Traugott Krug (1770–1842), author of *Entwurf eines neuen Organon's der Philosophie; oder, Versuch über die Prinzipien der philosophischen Erkenntniss* (Meissen and Lübben, 1801). Krug maintains (pp. 60–61) that such investigation can at most reach simple or primordial facts of consciousness, but consciousness itself as the original synthesis can never be explained or conceived philosophically, because I can never rise above my own individual consciousness to examine the origin of consciousness itself. The natural consciousness is not transparent to itself; I can only say that the being and knowing of my being are in an original unity in me, but I cannot say how and why that is the case (p. 74).

406. *Thus Gr with Lw; Sv reads:* ordinary consciousness grasps the relation "white" and "paper," but does not grasp the "it is."

407. *Thus Gr, similar in Lw; Sv reads:* Philosophical consciousness has as its object the knowing of knowing.

"science of knowledge" [*Wissenschaftslehre*] or the knowing of our knowing. And here "knowing" means our activity or our knowing ˜within the categories.˜[408]

Fichte *constructed* the categories as follows. The I is what is first. I equals I, I is simple, it is none other than a relating of the I to I—I know myself.[409] Insofar as I am consciousness, I know an object. When I say that I intuit something, I have a representation of it, that is, this content is also mine; I am also in this object. I = I is the identity stated generally or in abstract form. I is a relation of itself to itself. Relation [*Beziehung*] requires two sides, | but here they are the same. That is the first thesis or the first definition in Fichte's philosophy.

The second thesis is that I set a not-I, an object, in opposition to myself; I posit myself ˜as˜[410] not posited. This not-I is the object as such, the negative of myself. "Not-I" is a good expression, although at first glance it may look somewhat bizarre. A great deal of ridicule has been directed at the I and not-I, for "not-I" is a new word and hence it strikes us Germans as quite curious even though the expression is correct. ˜The French say *moi et non moi* in a similar sense.˜[411] They find nothing to laugh at. Not-I is the other to me; the object, what is over against me or what is not I, is the not-I. So this second thesis says that the I posits itself as limited, as not-I.

159

[Ed.] Apart from the title of the *Wissenschaftslehre* itself, Fichte stated explicitly, in *Ueber den Begriff der Wissenschaftslehre oder der sogenannten Philosophie . . .* (Weimar, 1794) p. 18, that his philosophy could be called simply "knowledge" or "the science of knowledge"; cf. *Gesamtausgabe* 2:118.

408. *Gr reads:* of the categories. *Lw reads:* within the category. *Sv reads:* from the categories.

409. [Ed.] See the further specification of the first principle in the *Wissenschaftslehre*: "the absolutely posited X can be expressed as I = I, I am I" (*Gesamtausgabe* 2:257; *Science of Knowledge*, p. 96).

410. *Thus Gr, Pn, An; Sv reads:* as limited, as

[Ed.] Fichte's second principle expresses this limitation, in the certainty that a not-I is utterly opposed to the I (*Gesamtausgabe* 2:266–267; *Science of Knowledge*, p. 104).

411. *Thus Pn with Gr, similar in Sv; Lw reads:* In this matter the French are far more rational than the Germans. They speak quite unreservedly of *moi et non moi*, and find that phrase expresses what ought to be expressed. It is poor manners on our part to find something bad just because it is expressed in a suitable though unusual way.

Fichte says this second thesis is just as absolute as the first even though from one side it is conditioned by the first, namely, in that the not-I is taken up in the I, that I posit it in opposition to me, that it is an other to me. Despite this, the negative in it is still something absolute.[412]

The third thesis is the determination of these two theses by one another, that I posit the not-I as ‟limiting me,‟[413] or again that I posit myself as limiting or bounding the not-I so that it is only object. I am constantly posited in my relation to the not-I. ‟When I am limited by the not-I, then I am posited as passive.‟[414] One of these theses is the thesis of the theoretical domain, of intelligence, the other the thesis of the practical domain, of the will.[415] In fact, insofar as I am conscious of myself as determining the object, | I am then making myself active in relation to an object, the not-I, and I know this. [But] the theoretical proposition is that I am object to myself, so that I come to be limited by the not-I. In intuition we say that I have an object before me, that the object governs me; between the two there is a relationship, they limit one another; at one time I prevail, and at another I am something passive, I am

160

412. [Ed.] See n. 410 above, as well as the way in which the *Wissenschaftslehre* employs the second principle in the deduction of the third, in which the not-I gets taken up into the I (*Gesamtausgabe* 2:268–269; *Science of Knowledge*, pp. 106–107). This second principle is absolutely unconditioned in form, as is the first, although it is conditioned as to its matter (*Gesamtausgabe* 2:266–267; *Science of Knowledge*, p. 104).

413. *Thus An, Lw; Pn reads:* limited, *Gr reads:* limiting me, the synthetic activity,

[Ed.] Fichte states the third principle as: "In the I, I oppose a separable not-I to the separable I" (*Gesamtausgabe* 2:272; *Science of Knowledge*, p. 110). Hegel's formulation anticipates the (subsequent) theoretical part of the *Wissenschaftslehre*, specifically, two principles stated in § 4: (1) "The I posits the not-I as bounded by the I"; (2) "The I posits itself as bounded by the not-I" (*Gesamtausgabe* 2:285; *Science of Knowledge*, pp. 122–123). Hegel presents the two in reverse order from their sequence in the *Wissenschaftslehre*.

414. *Thus An with Gr; Lw, similar in Gr, reads:* Either I am limited, or I posit myself as the I that is limiting or bounding; thus [in the latter case] I am activity [*Aktivität, Tätigkeit*], and the not-I is bounded by me.

415. [Ed.] See the two principles in n. 413 above. The *Wissenschaftslehre* assigns the first one (in Fichte's sequence, not Hegel's) to the practical domain, and the second to the theoretical domain (*Gesamtausgabe* 2:286; *Science of Knowledge*, pp. 122–123).

limited by the not-I. This latter aspect is the theoretical aspect, the fact that whenever I intuit I receive this not-I for the content, that it determines me. The representation arises from the content, and I have this content within me, the very content that is outside me. This is on the whole just like the Kantian experience, I and a stuff or a content; so there is here a not-I through which the I is determined. The I functions equally as determining (active, thinking) and determined. In theoretical consciousness I know that I am determined by the not-I, by the object. In ordinary consciousness, however, I do not know that in theoretical consciousness I also function as active, as determining; only the philosophical consciousness knows this.

This activity is the category, and Fichte now seeks more precisely to derive from it the particular categories in their necessity. That is what is important in Fichte's philosophy. No one else since Aristotle has thought about how to exhibit the determinations of thinking in their necessity, their derivation, their construction; Fichte tried to do this.[416] We can see, however, that his presentation is from the outset burdened with an antithesis—in Kant it was the I and the representation, and then the thing-in-itself; in Fichte it is the I and the not-I.

The I is supposed to be the ideal principle and the not-I the real principle. Herr Krug has talked a great deal of nonsense about this, for in Germany at that time there were many philosophers such as Krug, Fries, Bouterwek, Schulze, and the like, who did nothing but snap up their random thoughts from these two, from Kant and Fichte, or from Schelling, and yet they made polemics against them although they have taken their thoughts from them, if indeed they have any thoughts.[417] | With *these* philosophers, therefore, we do

416. [*Ed.*] On Fichte's systematic derivation of the categories, see above, p. 000 with n. 401.

417. [*Ed.*] The *Wissenschaftslehre* states that the not-I is qualitatively opposed to the I and thus is the real ground of determination in it, whereas the I is only quantitatively opposed to itself and thus is merely the ideal ground of its own determination (*Gesamtausgabe* 2:325; *Science of Knowledge*, p. 161). Krug (see above, n. 405) held that the I is the real principle, not the ideal principle, and he refused to identify either the ideal principle or the real principle simply with the not-I. His 1801 *Entwurf*, directed against Schelling's 1795 essay, *Of the I as Principle of Phi-

not concern ourselves. They only introduce modifications or adjustments, and for the most part their changes mean no more than that the great principles have been made paltry and barren, that precisely the living point of unity has been destroyed; or they mean that subordinate forms have been employed, by means of which a different principle is then supposed to be erected—but upon closer examination we find left over the principles of one of *those* philosophies [Kant's, Fichte's, or Schelling's]. So we can take solace in the fact that we are unable to say anything further about all these philosophies, for we would only have to tell a tale of thievery. Their modifications of [philosophical] forms are either just the semblance of an alteration, or more probably a degradation, of the principles of those other philosophies.

Fichte's ideal principle is that I am what determines, what posits.[418] But something negative is also involved in this, namely, that I find myself to be determined. The I is just equal to itself, that is, it is infinite; and infinity in thinking just means thinking's being at home with itself, its not relating itself to an other or to a limit. "The bounds of human reason" is an empty expression. It is a natural fact that the subject's reason is bounded and dependent, a fact determined by human nature itself. [But] thinking is independent. The place where we are infinite is precisely in thinking. It is self-

losophy, declares (pp. 10–20) that the real principle of *philosophical* (that is, abstract and reflective) knowledge, its *principium essendi*, its inner ground or source, is the unitary, philosophically knowing subject, the I. The ideal principle, the *principium cognoscendi*, is what serves the derivation of determinate philosophical knowledge; it is plural, and consists of material principles of knowing in general and formal principles of scientific knowing. Cf. Hegel's criticism of Krug in *GW* 4:112, 174–187; English translation, "How the Ordinary Human Understanding Takes Philosophy (as displayed in the works of Mr. Krug)," pp. 292–310 in *Between Kant and Hegel: Texts in the Development of Post-Kantian Idealism*, translated and annotated by George di Giovanni and H. S. Harris (Albany, 1985). For his criticism of the *System der Logik* of Jakob Friedrich Fries (1773–1843), see *GW* 12:311–312. For his criticism of Friedrich Bouterwek (1766–1828), see *GW* 4:95–104 and *W* 15:645–646. For his criticism of Gottlob Ernst Schulze (1761–1823), whose anonymous defense of skepticism, *Aenesidemus* (n.p., 1792), was reviewed by Fichte, see *GW* 4:197–238; English translation of the defense and the review, in di Giovanni and Harris, pp. 104–157.

418. [*Ed.*] See the preceding note.

evident that, apart from thinking, human beings are also dependent and finite, but we must not seek to carry this dependence over into reason, into thinking. [If we do,] then infinitude too can be very abstract, and in this way it too is finite in its turn, although despite that it remains infinitude within itself.

For Fichte the I is infinite, it is thinking. But this I finds that it is together with a not-I. It is an absolute contradiction⁴¹⁹ that the I, which is supposed to be utterly alone with itself [*bei sich selbst*]— this I that is defined as being utterly free—is now said to be together with another. In Fichte's thought the resolution of the contradiction is a resolution only called for [and not one achieved]. It remains a kind of resolution in which the I | can constantly surpass [*aufhe-ben*] the boundary but in which there always remains a limit, beyond which it can go forth once more, and so on *ad infinitum,* namely, into the bad infinite—although according to this resolution I always again find a new limit, a not-I. With the surpassing of one limit a new one always shows up, so that there is a continuous alternation of negation and affirmation, an identity with self that collapses into negation once more and is ever again reestablished out of the negation. This is the standpoint of Fichte's philosophy in its theoretical aspect.

162

3. Kant: Transcendental Dialectic

Kant's presentation places reason as the third element in the progression. The second was understanding, or reflective determination, but reason is thinking insofar as it makes the infinite or the unconditioned its object. Kant calls this infinite or unconditioned the idea.⁴²⁰ Only since Kant's time has the distinction between reason and understanding become normal in philosophical usage.

419. [*Ed.*] The *Wissenschaftslehre* states that the I equal to itself is posited as indivisible, whereas the I to which the not-I is opposed is posited as divisible; the latter I is thus in opposition to the absolute I (*Gesamtausgabe* 2:271; *Science of Knowledge,* p. 109).

420. [*Ed.*] See the *Critique of Pure Reason,* B 368 ff.; in B 378 Kant speaks of particular a priori concepts "that we can call pure concepts of reason, or transcendental ideas." See also B 379, where the transcendental concept is said to be "the totality of conditions for any given conditioned," or "a ground of the synthesis of the conditioned."

This distinction is necessary. Among the earlier philosophers, on the contrary, the distinction was not drawn in this way. So in discussing them we too have used these expressions interchangeably. But if we are to speak in a definite way, then this distinction must be observed. Understanding is thinking within finite relationships, whereas reason—according to Kant—is thinking that has the unconditioned or the infinite as its object, and this unconditioned he calls "idea," an expression he borrows from Plato.[421] The idea is of course the unconditioned. But the unconditioned must be grasped in its concreteness, and this is where the main difficulty arises. Reason needs to know the infinite or the unconditioned cognitively, that is, to define it, to discover and derive its determinations. Hence the unconditioned should become known. We talk a lot about thinking, knowing, and cognition, and yet we never say what this knowing, thinking, and cognition is. In philosophy, however, the very point is that what is presupposed as known [bekannt] is to be known cognitively [erkannt]. What is at issue here therefore is | cognitive knowledge of the unconditioned. This is the object of reason. Reason has the infinite for its object, and it has the drive toward cognitive knowledge of the infinite. But it cannot accomplish this, and the ground Kant adduces is in the first place that the infinite is not given in experience, that there is no intuition corresponding to the infinite, that it is not given in outer or inner experience.[422] We must assuredly concede that the infinite is not given in the world, in sense perception. If we presuppose that our knowing is experience, a synthesizing of thoughts with the materials of feeling, then we cannot have cognition of the infinite at all in the sense of having a sensible perception of it. No one will want to require a sense perception as the confirmation of the infinite too, however, since the infinite is present only for spirit, because it is essentially spiritual.

The second point is that for the infinite to become known it

163

---

421. [Ed.] The *Critique of Pure Reason*, B 370, says that Plato used the term "idea" for what surpasses not only objects of the senses but also concepts of the understanding, and with which nothing in our experience is congruent.

422. [Ed.] See the preceding note, as well as the *Critique of Pure Reason*, B 383–384.

must become determinate. We have nothing to serve that purpose but the forms of thinking, which we call categories. These furnish what Kant calls objective determinations, but do so in such a way that in themselves the categories are nonetheless only something subjective once more. So if we want to use these categories to determine the infinite, we become entangled in false conclusions and contradictions (antinomies).[423] This is an important aspect of the Kantian philosophy, the specification that, so far as it is determined by categories, the infinite loses itself in contradictions. Kant says that these contradictions are necessary and that in them reason becomes transcendent.[424] If, for instance, the [infinite] object were the world, then we should know cognitively whether or not the world has a beginning and an end, whether it is limited in space and time.[425] But the world is the universe or the whole, and thus it is something universal, an idea, and this idea could be determined as limited or as unlimited. If we now apply these categories to the problem, we fall into contradictions. We can maintain both sides [of the antinomy], for the one thesis is necessary and so is the other. Thus reason falls into contradiction. The | necessity of the contradiction is the interesting aspect of which Kant made us aware. In accord with ordinary metaphysics people imagined that one thesis must be valid and the other must be contradicted, although the necessary occurrence of contradictions of this kind is precisely what is interesting in the Kantian treatment.

164

423. [Ed.] Here the term "false conclusions" (or, as Kant says, "pseudorational conclusions") refers not to all three kinds of dialectical syllogisms but especially to the first kind, the transcendental paralogisms, which proceed from the transcendental unity of the subject to its absolute unity, of which we cannot truly have any concepts; see the *Critique of Pure Reason*, B 397–398. The second kind of inference, the antinomy, draws opposed conclusions from the transcendental concept of the totality of conditions for any appearance; see B 398.

424. [Ed.] Hegel is referring to Kant's doctrine of transcendental illusion; see the *Critique of Pure Reason*, B 349 ff., especially B 354–355, which stresses that it is natural and inevitable (albeit unjustifiable) that human reason will make these misleading transcendent judgments and so get entangled in the dialectic of pure reason. See also the concluding remark (B 593) to the section on the antinomy of pure reason.

425. [Ed.] This remark refers to the first pair of opposed theses in the antinomy of pure reason; see the *Critique of Pure Reason*, B 454–455.

Kant then also comes to the idea of God. He says that God is the most real being [*Wesen*], which is the Wolffian definition. Then the point is to prove that God is not merely a thought but that God *is,* that God has existence, actuality, being [*Sein*].⁴²⁶ Kant calls the latter case the "ideal" to distinguish it from the idea; the ideal is the idea as having being.⁴²⁷ Thus, in art we call "ideal" the idea that is realized in a sensible mode, whereas in the case of God [we mean by "ideal"] that this universal idea *is.* The [logical] determination to which Kant holds firmly is that being cannot be plucked out of the concept.⁴²⁸ From this it follows that although reason has thoughts of the infinite or the indeterminate, this idea [of God] is altogether separate from determination and in particular from the determination that is called being.

The ideas do not show themselves in experience, and so the ideas of reason are not confirmed through experience. If the ideas are determined merely through categories, then contradictions arise. If the idea is on the whole to be exhibited only as it [truly] is [*als seiend*], then it is only subjective, only a concept, and the being of what is existing, namely, the objective, is forever distinct from it. Therefore what remains of reason is nothing but the form of its unity, or the identity of the idea; and all that this suffices for is the systematizing of the manifold laws and conditions of the under-

426. [*Ed.*] Hegel is referring to the third of the dialectical inferences, that of the ideal of pure reason; see the *Critique of Pure Reason*, B 595 ff. Wolff does not actually speak of an *ens realissimum* (most real being) but of an *ens perfectissimum* (most perfect being); see his *Theologia naturalis methodo scientifica pertractata*, pars posterior (Frankfurt am Main and Leipzig, 1741), § 6. Baumgarten uses both terms for God, in his *Metaphysica*, 7th ed. (Halle, 1779), § 806. Baumgarten counts existence among the "realities" and so concludes that a most perfect being has existence; see § 810. Hegel is referring only to the ontological proof, because Kant regards the demonstrations of the cosmological and physicotheological proofs as depending on the demonstration of the ontological proof.

427. [*Ed.*] On Kant's understanding of "ideal," see the *Critique of Pure Reason,* B 595 ff. The ideal is the idea *in individuo,* as an individual thing (B 596). The concept of an *ens realissimum* is the only proper or true ideal of which human reason is capable; it is the concept of the supreme condition of the possibility of all that exists, as a thing wholly determined in and through itself and represented as an individual (B 604).

428. [*Ed.*] The *Critique of Pure Reason* uses the apt term "pluck out" in the criticism of proofs for the existence of God (B 631).

standing. Reason orders the classes, species, and kinds, as well as the laws of spirit, of nature, and so forth, seeking to bring them into unity.[429] That is what theoretical reason is for Kant. It is in this respect that Jacobi's philosophy attaches itself immediately to 165 Kant. |

4. Friedrich Heinrich Jacobi: General Orientation

[430]Friedrich Heinrich Jacobi was a gifted and very noble man of deep scientific cultivation who served long in the affairs of the state and was very conversant with French philosophy. By chance he became involved in controversy with Mendelssohn over a biography of Lessing that Mendelssohn wanted to produce. Jacobi maintained that Lessing had been a Spinozist. Hence those who regarded themselves as specialists, that is, specialists in philosophy, and who thought they had a monopoly on Lessing's friendship, such men as Mendelssohn, Nicolai, and others, began a dispute with Jacobi. ¨In his correspondence Jacobi displayed a deep acquaintance with Spinozism, and he even showed that Mendelssohn was wholly ignorant about this system.¨[431] This episode led to explanations that

429. [Ed.] In the preceding sentence Hegel may not have in mind the transcendental doctrine of method (p. 000 above) so much as the appendix to the Transcendental Dialectic, entitled "The Regulative Employment of the Ideas of Pure Reason" (Critique of Pure Reason, B 670–696). Reason seeks to make knowledge systematic, to show how its parts are connected according to a single principle, by proceeding from the assumption that knowledge is a whole (B 673). On the necessity of ordering of species and kinds in a hierarchical and systematic unity, see B 679–680. On the laws of spirit and of nature, see B 677–678.

430. Precedes in Gr: Jacobi was born in 1743 in Düsseldorf. He held civil-service positions in the Grand Duchy of Berg and afterward in Bavaria. In 1804 he became president of the Academy of Sciences in Munich, a post he resigned, however, in 1812. He died in Munich on 16 March 1819.

[Ed.] See n. 433 below.

431. Thus An with Pn, similar in Sv; Gr reads: They showed not only shallowness of philosophical insight but even ignorance.

[Ed.] Gotthold Ephraim Lessing (1729–1781), the eminent dramatist and man of letters, also wrote essays on philosophical and religious subjects. His friend Moses Mendelssohn (1729–1786) was a thinker of decidedly rationalistic bent and a purveyor of popular philosophy, as was Friedrich Nicolai (1733–1811). Jacobi reported an alleged confession by Lessing: "The orthodox conceptions of the deity are no longer for me; I cannot take pleasure in them. Ἐν χαι Πᾶν ["One and All"]! I know no other" (Jacobi, Spinoza-Briefe, pp. 22 ff., 62; in Jacobi's Werke 4, pt. 1:54 ff.,

gave Jacobi the occasion to develop and present his philosophical views more precisely, especially his views about knowledge.

The biographical details for Kant and Fichte were omitted, and we will make up for that briefly here. Kant was born in Königsberg in 1724, and he died [there] on 12 February 1804. Fichte was born on 19 May 1762, in Rammenau, and he died on 19 March 1814, in Berlin.[432] Jacobi was born in Düsseldorf in 1743. He held administrative positions in the civil service, and ultimately he was president of the Academy in Munich. After resigning that position he retired to private life, and he died on 16 March 1819.[433]

Jacobi has the following to say about cognitive knowledge. We conceive a thing when we can deduce it from its proximate cause, not from a remote cause. The most remote cause is always God, whom we cannot bring into play for this purpose, for that would be superficial. We must have the proximate, wholly determinate cause in order to deduce the thing from it. | We know the thing when we have insight into its immediate conditions in their succession. [For instance,] we conceive the circle when we have insight into ˉthe conditionsˉ[434] of its generation. This insight must be clear. This, then, is in general what cognition is, namely, knowing the conditions of something determinate and, in doing so, having insight into it as something conditioned, as something brought about by another, something produced by a cause.

Jacobi's view about the enterprise of wanting to know the unconditioned is consistent with this. In the human mind there are

166

---

89). See also *Spinoza-Briefe,* pp. 1–4 (*Werke* 4, pt. 1:37–39), especially 4, where Jacobi indicates that he had written to Elise Reimarus: "Lessing was a Spinozist." A useful resource for this controversy is *Die Hauptschriften zum Pantheismusstreit zwischen Jacobi und Mendelssohn,* ed. with historical-critical introduction by Heinrich Scholz (Berlin, 1916).

432. [*Ed.*] The correct date of Fichte's death is 29 January 1814. The date in our text is transmitted by *Pn* alone; *Lw* gives the year of his death as 1809. Perhaps Hegel gave the wrong date, as also for Jacobi (see the following note).

433. [*Ed.*] The correct date of Jacobi's death is 10 March 1819. On this point, see Friedrich Köppen, in Jacobi's *Werke* 4, pt. 1:iii. The date in our text is transmitted by *Pn, Lw,* and *Gr.*

434. *Thus Gr, An, Lw; Pn reads:* the precise mechanism

[*Ed.*] Jacobi himself uses the term "mechanism" when stating the example of the circle. See his *Spinoza-Briefe,* supplement VII, p. 419 n.; cf. *Werke* 4, pt. 2:149n.

representations of the conditioned and the unconditioned, and the two are bound together inseparably, [are] identical; but the bond is such that the representation of the conditioned presupposes that of the unconditioned, and the representation of the former can only be given through that of the latter. Our conditioned existence and knowledge then rests upon an infinite number of mediations, our researches have before them an infinite field ˜[in which we] must ascend from one condition to the next.˜⁴³⁵ But knowing the unconditioned would mean wanting to discover unconditioned conditions or to give conditions to the unconditioned, wanting to treat the inconceivable as having an existence conceivable to us, namely, a merely natural way of being—for everything that is conceivable for us must arise in a conditioned manner. As long as we are conceiving, we have a chain of conditioned conditions; when this chain ceases, then our conceiving ceases and with it the nexus that we call nature, and then we are no longer able to know. ˜We would have to have the concept of the unconditioned apart from this [conceiving].˜⁴³⁶ For if the unconditioned is said to be conceived, then it must cease being unconditioned, for it would have to acquire conditions.⁴³⁷ |

167

So this, then, is Jacobi's thought. But everything that lies outside this sphere—the nexus of the conditioned—is outside our clear cognition, so that knowledge of it through the concept cannot be de-

---

435. *Gr reads:* of conditions [leading] to [other] conditions. *Sv reads:* of conditions through which we must ascend.

436. *Thus Pn; Lw reads:* The possibility of the existence of nature itself would be the concept of the unconditioned itself, insofar as this concept is not the natural presupposition or the unconditioned condition of nature.

437. [*Ed.*] The topic of this whole paragraph, wanting to know the unconditioned, is covered in Jacobi's *Spinoza-Briefe,* supplement VII, pp. 423–426 (cf. *Werke* 4, pt. 2:152–155). There Jacobi states that we have within us both representations (the conditioned and the unconditioned) as inseparable. The representation of the unconditioned is presupposed by that of the conditioned; we need not seek the unconditioned, for "we have an even greater certainty of its existence than we have of our own conditioned existence." Conditioned existence rests on endless mediation. When we discover the mechanism of such mediation for a thing, then we construct the thing in a representation, we conceive it; what we cannot construct in this way we cannot conceive. Therefore: "To discover conditions for the unconditioned, to find out a possibility for the absolute necessity, to seek to construct it in order to be able to conceive it, seems evidently to be an absurd undertaking." The remainder of the passage in Jacobi continues in the same vein as our text.

manded. The supernatural, therefore, cannot be apprehended by us in any except an immediate way; it can only be apprehended as an actual fact [*Tatsache*]; it *is,* it is this immediate reality, and what is, or this infinite essence, all tongues call "God."[438] Conceiving means knowing the conditions of the conditioned. The supernatural is precisely what has no conditions, what cannot be conceived; for *us* it *is* only as a fact, only in an immediate, nonmediated way.

The distinction between the view of Kant and that of Jacobi is that for Kant the categories are of no help here; [they are applicable only to] finite, limited circumstances. For Kant knowledge is only a knowledge of phenomena, not of what is in-itself, and this is because the categories are only subjective. It is not because of their content or because they are limited and finite, for the main point is always rather that they are subjective even though they constitute the objective element in experience. For Jacobi, on the contrary, the main point is not just that the categories are subjective but that they are only conditions, and conditioned conditions at that, and conceiving therefore means positing the nexus through the categories, that is, through conditioned conditions. This is an essential distinction, but the two positions are in mutual agreement as to the result. Jacobi has also called immediate knowing "faith,"[439] and we will have more to say about that later.

438. [*Ed.*] See Jacobi, *Spinoza-Briefe,* supplement VII, pp. 426–427; cf. *Werke* 4, pt. 2:155–156. Hegel introduces the word "immediate" in this passage. Jacobi simply says of the supernatural, which lies outside the nexus of what is naturally mediated, that "the supernatural cannot be apprehended by us in any other way than as it is given to us, namely, as fact—it is!"

439. [*Ed.*] Hegel is referring to the heading "VI. The element of all human knowledge and efficacy is faith," in Jacobi's *Spinoza-Briefe,* pp. 228–229 (*Werke* 4, pt. 1:223). In another passage Jacobi declares to Mendelssohn that we are born and situated in faith just as we are born and situated in human society, and that the striving for certainty presupposes a certainty already known. "This leads to the concept of an immediate certainty, which not only requires no grounds but absolutely excludes all grounds. . . . Conviction arising from grounds is a conviction at second hand. . . . If then every instance of holding something to be true that does not derive from rational grounds is faith, then conviction arising from rational grounds must itself come from faith, and receive its strength from faith alone. Through faith we know that we have a body, and that outside us there are present other bodies and other thinking beings. . . . without [the] you, the I is impossible"

5. Kant and Fichte: Practical Philosophy

The first moment in the Kantian philosophy was intelligence, the theoretical aspect; the second is the practical aspect, the will, what the principle of willing is. Kant divides willing into the lower and the higher faculties of desire, and this is ˉa badˉ[440] way of putting it. The lower | faculty of desire consists of the appetites, inclinations, and the like. The higher is the will as such, which does not have external or singular goals but universal ends; hence it is a higher faculty of the soul.[441] So the question is: What is the principle of willing, what is supposed to determine human beings in their actions? The principle people have generally adopted is benevolence, sociability, general happiness. But Kant says that determinations of this kind, which are taken from our inclinations, are principles that are heterogeneous in relation to our will, or that when it makes things of this sort into its end and its determination the will is heteronomous, it takes its law from something other than itself. The nature of the will, however, is to be free and self-determining, for it is independent, it is absolute spontaneity, it is autonomous. Its own freedom is the only end or goal the will can have.[442] This is a very important and defining characteristic of the Kantian philosophy. As we seek after this or that goal for ourselves and our activity, as we seek for standards by which to judge the world and its history, what should we adopt as the *final* end for the will? Well, there is no other end for the will than the one

---

(see *Spinoza-Briefe*, pp. 215–217, in *Werke* 4, pt. 1:210–211). See also Jacobi's dialogue, *David Hume über den Glauben; oder, Idealismus und Realismus* (Breslau, 1787), pp. 44, 47 (*Werke* 2:161, 163). Hegel resumes the discussion of faith on pp. 000–000 below.

440. *Thus Lw; Gr reads:* not an unsuitable

441. [*Ed.*] In his *Critique of Practical Reason*, Kant says that reason is the higher faculty of desire only insofar as it determines the will rationally rather than in service to the inclinations (the pathologically determinable lower faculty); in this passage he does not speak of faculties "of the soul." See *Schriften* 5:24–25; Beck, pp. 23–24.

442. [*Ed.*] The *Critique of Practical Reason* states (*Schriften* 5:33) that the autonomy of the will is the sole principle of all moral laws and duties, that heteronomy of choice [or caprice] is contrary to the principle of duty and the will's ethical life, and (5:48) that the idea of freedom is a faculty of absolute spontaneity (Beck, pp. 33, 49).

created out of the will itself, the goal of its own freedom.[443] The establishment of this principle was a great advance; human freedom is the ultimate pivot upon which humanity turns, the ultimate and absolutely firm pinnacle that is not open to influence, such that we grant validity to nothing, to no authority of whatever form, if it goes against human freedom. This grand principle has won widespread diffusion and sympathy for the Kantian philosophy, in the aspect that humanity finds within itself something utterly firm and unwavering. There is a firm center point, the principle of freedom; everything else that does not rest firmly upon this point is precarious, with the result that nothing is obligatory in which this freedom is not respected. This is the principle.

The next point is that initially this freedom is empty or formal, that it is the negative of everything other to it; no bond, nothing other, obligates me.[444] In the fact that the will is alone with itself [*bei sich selbst*] it is undefined, there is [just] the will's identity with itself, its freedom. But | in this inward solitude there is no content or determination; the sole form that this principle has is that of identity with self. ˉWhat is duty? What binds the free will? All Kant had for duty was the form of identity, of noncontradiction—which is the law of the abstract understanding.ˉ[445] But with identity we

169

443. [*Ed.*] See the *Critique of Practical Reason* (*Schriften* 5:29; Beck, p. 28).

444. [*Ed.*] According to the *Critique of Practical Reason*, the law of the pure will does not stem from the empirical domain, and its (non-natural) necessity "can consist only in the formal conditions of the possibility of a law in general" (*Schriften* 5:34; Beck, p. 34). For instance, the requirement to promote the happiness of others arises strictly from the formal requirement to extend the maxim of self-love to others as well if it is to be objectively valid, that is, conformable to pure practical reason (*Schriften* 5:34–35; Beck, p. 35). Only such a formal law can determine practical reason a priori (*Schriften* 5:64; Beck, p. 66).

445. *Thus Pn (but excluding: which is the law of the abstract understanding); An reads:* The next thing is the content or the determination that the free will gives to itself. That is duty, which is the form of non-self-contradiction, of identity with self. *Gr reads, similar in Lw:* For the specification of duty—for the abstract question is: "What is duty for the free will?"—Kant has thus had nothing but the form of identity, of non-self-contradiction, which is the law of the abstract understanding.

[*Ed.*] The *Critique of Practical Reason* states: "The concept of duty thus requires of action that it objectively agree with the law, while of the maxim of the action it demands subjective respect for the law as the sole mode of determining the will through itself" (*Schriften* 5:81; Beck, p. 84).

advance not one step further. God is God, plant is plant, and no further determination follows. Some sort of content must be given. Each content that is put into this form [of identity] avoids self-contradiction, but that amounts to the same thing as if it is not put into this form at all. Take, as an example, property. In my actions I must respect property, but property can be entirely removed from the picture; it is in no way contradictory if I do not acknowledge property and say that there is no such thing as "property," that everything is mere "possession." The defect of the Kantian principle of freedom is that it is indeterminate, merely formal. It is the same with Fichte, where the practical sphere is defined in such a way that the I is determinative of the not-I, that in that sphere I am alone with myself. In order to have a determination, however, there must also be a not-I, for it is through the not-I that a content first enters the picture. Kant initiated the grounding of right upon freedom, and Fichte authored a book on *Natural Right* in which he made freedom into the principle.[446] This was an important beginning, but they must make or adopt presuppositions in order to arrive at something particular.

6. Kant and Jacobi: Teleology, Faith, and
    Knowledge of God

The third moment in Kant is the emergence of the demand for the concrete. This has in the main two shapes, for we shall leave to one

---

446. [*Ed.*] For Kant's grounding of right upon freedom, see his *Metaphysische Anfangsgründe der Rechtslehre* (Königsberg, 1797), p. xxxiii, § C (*Schriften* 6:230). On Fichte's not-I, see above, n. 413. The introduction to Fichte's *Grundlage des Naturrechts nach Principien der Wissenschaftslehre* (Jena and Leipzig, 1796) explains how, in ascribing freedom to others as well as to oneself, I limit myself by leaving room for their freedom. "Accordingly, the concept of right is the concept of the necessary relations of free beings with one another" (*Gesamtausgabe* 3:319). In the body of that work he states that the task of the science of right is to explain how it is that persons are free, yet exist in reciprocal influence upon one another and so not as solely independent, that is, to explain how a community of free beings is possible (*Gesamtausgabe* 3:383). Hegel's remarks in the text neglect the distinctions drawn in practical philosophy by Kant and Fichte, in particular the significance given to the problem of recognition by Fichte, namely, the connection between the positing of myself as a free person and the positing of other free persons.

side the third, the aesthetic aspect.[447] One form of the demand is the way in which we consider living things. Kant's presentation of the living thing in his critique of reflective judgment is that | when 170 we consider it, we have before us something sensible, whether plant or animal. On the one hand we treat this sensible being according to the categories of the understanding, according to cause and effect. In our consideration of the living organism, however, we do not stay with these categories of the understanding but instead treat what is alive as also being the cause of itself, as self-producing; this is the living thing's self-maintenance.[448] What is lifeless just endures, whereas what is alive (albeit transitory) is, insofar as it lives, self-producing and self-maintaining.[449] Its members are means, but at the same time it is purpose within itself, it is its own end [*Selbstzweck*], it is an organic product of its own nature; all of its members are both means and ends at the same time. [There is] no external teleology here, for the end is not external to the matter as it is

---

447. [*Ed.*] This enumeration of three forms in which the requirement of the concrete appears does not appropriately reproduce Kant's systematic presentation. By the third shape or form Hegel means Kant's aesthetic judgment, which constitutes part 1 of the *Critique of Judgment* (Berlin, 1790); by the first shape he means the topic of teleological judgment, which constitutes part 2 of that *Critique*. What he calls the second is the doctrine of postulates (see p. 000 below), which he interprets from the perspective of the moral proof for God in the appendix to the *Critique of Judgment* rather than from the perspective of the *Critique of Practical Reason*. Therefore the purported three shapes of the concrete correspond respectively to: (1) the analytic and dialectic of teleological judgment (§§ 61–78 of the *Critique of Judgment*); (2) the appendix to part 2, namely, the methodology of teleological judgment (§§ 79–91); (3) the analytic and dialectic of aesthetic judgment (§§ 1–60).

448. [*Ed.*] The *Critique of Judgment*, § 61, states that interpreting nature's forms and combinations according to purposes affords an additional principle for bringing natural phenomena under rules, when the laws of mechanical causality do not suffice to do that (*Schriften* 5:360); see the English translation by J. H. Bernard (New York, 1951), p. 206. In § 64 Kant states that "a thing exists as a natural purpose [*Naturzweck*] if it is cause and effect of itself," and he also distinguishes three types of such self-maintenance. In the first a tree reproduces itself generically, by generating another tree; in the second the tree produces itself as an individual organism, by growing; in the third each interdependent part of the tree acts reciprocally as both cause and effect of the other parts (*Schriften* 5:370–371; Bernard, pp. 219–220). See also p. 000 and n. 156 above, on the concept of *causa sui* for Spinoza.

449. *Gr adds:* Indeed it has conditions necessary for that purpose, but it does produce itself. In addition, it is a means.

in the case of a house. The purpose of a house is to be dwelt in, and the means for that are external, the wood or the stones that are used to build it. But inner purposiveness signifies that something is in itself both end and means. This is the Aristotelian concept.[450] In the organic products of nature, therefore, we have the intuition of the immediate unity of concept and reality; vitality (or soul) and existence are identical, the universal (or vitality) and the particularization are identical; we intuit them in a unity in the case of the organic products of nature, but not in inorganic nature. It is at this point that Kant has need of the concrete, the fact that the concept or the universal is determinative of the particular.[451]

Kant's second point [about living things as purposive] is that this is a mode of our reflective power of judgment; we do not know that the living thing is this way but we are compelled to consider it so, and this is the maxim of our reflection about what is natural. It is this way in art too, where the idea is sensibly presented, for in the work of art reality and ideality (particular and universal) are immediately one.[452] |

171

The other way in which the need for the concrete emerges in the Kantian philosophy—the second form—is immediately tied to the practical domain.[453] Practical reason has an end, this end in its full

450. [Ed.] Kant distinguishes outer and inner purposiveness, in §§ 63, 66, and 82 of the Critique of Judgment (Schriften 5:366 ff., 376 ff., 425; Bernard, pp. 212–216, 222–224, 274–279). Aristotle's account of how living things carry out their life processes both "by nature" and "for an end" occurs in the Physics 2.8. 199a17–32. Aristotle's point is that it is the form in the living thing that gives rise to its purposive action ("for the sake of"); this is the famous entelechy, the immanent form that accounts for the goal-directed changes in and by living things.

451. [Ed.] Hegel may be thinking of the formulation in § 64 of the Critique of Judgment to the effect that if we are to see a thing as possible only as far as it is purposive, we must see that even our empirical knowledge of it, of its causes and effects, presupposes the employment of rational concepts (Schriften 5:369–370; Bernard, p. 216). The formulation in our text is not wholly intelligible, however, since Kant's teleological perspective on nature involves only the reflective judgment, not the function of judgment that is determinative of the very structure of experience. See also the following note.

452. [Ed.] These remarks do not actually bear upon Kant's critique of aesthetic judgment but rather upon Hegel's own Lectures on the Philosophy of Art; see W 10, vols. 1–3.

453. [Ed.] The discussion that follows, up to the introduction of God, concerns on the one hand the doctrine of postulates from the Critique of Practical Reason

universality is the good, and this good is an idea, it is my thought. Present at the same time, however, is the absolute demand that the good also should be realized in the world. Natural necessity should correspond to the law of freedom or to the good, it should not only be the necessity of an external nature but [it should be realized] everywhere in and by the world, through what is right and ethical, through human life and the life of the state, so that the world in general would be good. The good is the absolutely final end; it determines reality in human life and in the external world.[454] This harmony of the good and reality is the absolute demand inherent in reason.

For the single individual this harmony is happiness, although subjective reason is not able to achieve its realization. In every good action the human agent brings about something good, but only a limited good. The universal good or the universal and final end of the world can only be realized through a third factor, and this power over nature and over the world, which has for its final end good in the world, is God. Hence God is a postulate of practical reason, a postulate that must be believed.[455] The content here is

---

(Schriften 5:121–134; Beck, pp. 126–139) and on the other hand the doctrine of method from the Critique of Judgment, §§ 83 ff. (Schriften 5:429 ff.; Bernard, pp. 279 ff.). Here Hegel does not distinguish between the two. By stressing the concept of purpose, however, his presentation shows that he primarily has in view the form in the Critique of Judgment.

454. [Ed.] For Kant a final end is one that requires no other as a condition of its possibility; see Critique of Judgment, § 84 (Schriften 5:434; Bernard, p. 284). What Kant regards as the final end of the creation is not simply the good, as Hegel indicates in our text, but rather the human being under the moral laws; similarly, he defines the highest purpose of the human being, noumenally considered, as "the highest good in the world," or "the highest good in the world possible through freedom" (Critique of Judgment, §§ 84–85: Schriften 5:434–435, 445, 448, 450; Bernard, pp. 284–285, 296, 299–301).

455. [Ed.] The succinct argument in § 87 of the Critique of Judgment states that happiness is the highest physical good possible in the world and is therefore the final purpose we have to further in the world, with the stipulation that we be worthy of happiness according to the law of morality. That happiness, which is the due of moral freedom, we cannot represent as something brought about automatically by natural causality. Therefore we must assume a moral author of the world who brings about happiness in proportion to morality (Schriften 5:450; Bernard, p. 301). The formulation that "Hence God is a postulate of practical reason, a postulate that

therefore on the one hand the worldly and on the other hand the good. The good itself embodies the specification that it is to be realized. Initially the good is an idea within us, within thinking, but as human subjects we cannot fully bring about the good. Nature has its own proper laws, and these independent and singular relations are without reference to the good. It is characteristic of thinking or of reason, however, to demand the unity of the good within the world, to have within itself and to will this unity as what is essential and substantial. The antithesis—a contradiction between the good and the world—is | contrary to this identity; reason must therefore demand the supersession of this contradiction, it must demand that there be a power that is good on its own account and is power over nature, and only God is that. So this is the place of God in the Kantian philosophy. It is not demonstrable that God is—this remains a demand. God is thus a postulate of practical reason. We have these two factors, the world and the good. Goodness—virtue or morality—is good only insofar as it is in struggle; virtue requires opposition to itself. On the one hand it is posited that the contradiction cannot be resolved, while on the other hand the unity or harmony of the two is necessary. The deficiency is that ⁻this unity⁻[456] is not demonstrated and cannot be demonstrated. This deficiency arises because, by the standard of Kant's dualism, it cannot be shown that the good as an abstract idea, as merely subjective in itself, consists in sublating its subjectivity; nor can it be shown that nature, or the world in itself, consists in sublating its externality and difference from the good, and in exhibiting as its truth something that appears as a third factor (with regard to nature and the good) but is at the same time defined as what is first. In Kant's view God can only be believed in, God is only a postulate of practical reason. Jacobi's "faith" connects with this and is the point where Jacobi coincides with Kant—so we need to insert it here.

172

---

must be believed" echoes the *Critique of Practical Reason* (*Schriften* 5:124, 126; Beck, pp. 128–130). On the concept of practical belief in relation to what theoretical reason cannot substantiate, see also the *Critique of Judgment*, § 91 (*Schriften* 5:467–472; Bernard, pp. 318–325).

456. *Thus Pn; Gr, Lw read:* God

We have already mentioned what Jacobi calls faith, namely, that God—being in-and-for-itself, the absolute as such, the unconditioned, and so forth—cannot be demonstrated, because demonstrating or conceiving means discovering the conditions for something, deriving it from conditions. A derived absolute or a derived God for that very reason would not be an absolute or something unconditioned, would not be a God but a creature.[457] We do have a consciousness of God, and this consciousness is so constituted that there is immediately conjoined with this representation of God the knowledge that God *is*. Neither for Jacobi nor for Kant can this be a demonstrated knowledge. It is therefore | not something mediated within our knowing, but an immediate knowledge. We can appeal to this immediate knowing in the human mind, for in representation and thinking we go beyond what is natural and finite, we move on to something supernatural and supersensible. It is as certain for us that this supernatural something *is,* as it is that we ourselves exist; the certainty that it *is,* is identical with our own self-consciousness; it is as certain that God *is* as it is that I am. This immediate knowing of God is the point that is firmly posited in Jacobi's philosophy, and Jacobi even calls it "faith" too. But Kant's faith and Jacobi's faith are different. For Kant faith is a postulate of practical reason, the demand for the resolution of the contradiction between the world and the good. For Jacobi, however, faith is an immediate knowing on its very own account, and it is represented as such.[458] Since Jacobi's time everything said and even written by philosophers such as Fries, and by theologians, amounts to the contention that what we know of God we know immediately through intuition—primordial intuition, intellectual intuition, or immediate knowledge of the spiritual. This immediate knowledge is even called revelation, but in a different sense from revelation in

173

457. [*Ed.*] On Jacobi's view of faith, see above, nn. 438 and 439. See also *Jacobi an Fichte* (Hamburg, 1799), preface, p. ix: "A God who could be *known* would be no God at all" (in *Werke* 3:7).
458. [*Ed.*] See the preceding note, as well as Jacobi's preface to vol. 4, pt. 1 of his *Werke*: "Certainly we must set out from feeling and intuition, for there is no merely speculative route to awareness of God . . ." (p. xxxix). On Kant's view of faith, see above, p. 000 with n. 455.

the theological sense or the usage of the church.[459] Revelation as immediate knowing is within us ourselves, whereas the church apprehends revelation as something imparted from without; faith in the theological sense is faith in something that is given outwardly through teaching, not an immediate knowing from within us. Hence it is a deception, so to speak, when the expressions "revelation" and "faith" are employed here ˉin a philosophical sense, and in a theological sense as well.ˉ[460] This is Jacobi's standpoint, and whatever has been said about it by philosophers and theologians

174 since his time has been very eagerly taken over and | disseminated, so that we find everywhere nothing but the repetition of this thought of Jacobi's.

This immediate knowing is set in opposition to philosophical, cognitive knowing on the part of reason and is judged to be superior to philosophy. In this context people speak of cognition and

459. [Ed.] See, for example, the first (anonymous) edition of On Religion: Speeches to Its Cultured Despisers (Berlin, 1799), by the theologian Friedrich Schleiermacher (1768–1834), p. 50: "The essence of religion is neither thinking nor acting, but rather is intuition and feeling." In his book Wissen, Glaube und Ahndung (Jena, 1805), the philosopher Jakob Friedrich Fries (1773–1843) defined "the feeling or recognition of the eternal in the finite, which we call presentiment" as a special organ that stands over against knowing and faith (p. 176; cf. pp. 64, 178, 218, 233 ff., 326). The theologian Wilhelm Martin Leberecht de Wette (1780–1849) adopted Fries's concept, in his Lehrbuch der christlichen Dogmatik (Berlin, 1813) and in his Ueber Religion und Theologie (Berlin, 1815). See also Jacobi's disciple, the philosopher Friedrich Köppen (1775–1858), who in his Ueber Offenbarung, in Beziehung auf Kantische und Fichtische Philosophie, 2d ed. (Lübeck and Leipzig, 1802), affirms "our most joyful conviction" that truth rests not upon demonstration or a clear conception but upon inner feeling—that we can be immediately certain of it (p. 139). He also says that the Kantian moral argument for God does not satisfy our human impulse because it clarifies only how we can wish for the existence of such a God but not how we can affirm it with full conviction (pp. 52–53). Jacobi's treatise Von den göttlichen Dingen und ihrer Offenbarung (Leipzig, 1811) even claims the proper meaning of revelation for this inner awareness alone: "A revelation through outer phenomena . . . can at best only relate to the inner, original revelation, as speech relates to reason. . . . The true God can no more appear outside the human soul than a false god can exist outside it on its own account" (Werke 3:277).

460. Thus Pn; Gr, with Lw, reads: and represented as though one were speaking of faith and revelation in the theological sense, although what ought to be the philosophical sense is entirely different here, and yet one pursues this "faith" with an air of Christian piety. Sv reads: This [is found] in all theological writings of the time.

faith in the way that the blind speak of colors. In their sense of philosophy all believe themselves to be philosophers and to be capable of judging philosophy, because all have within them the same measuring stick. They concede, to be sure, that someone who is not a shoemaker cannot make shoes even though having on himself the measure of the shoe, that is, a foot, as well as having hands to do the work. But, in contrast, immediate knowing holds of philosophy the opinion that all are philosophers just as they stand, that everyone is an authority in philosophy and all can make pronouncements as they choose. Reason comprises on the one hand mediated cognition or revelation of God within us, and on the other hand precisely intellectual intuition itself; reason is knowledge of what has being-in-and-for-itself, it is the revealing of God, whereas understanding is the revealing of the finite. But faith, or knowing as immediate, comprises every other content—I believe that I have a body, that paper lies here, and so forth—everything that I know immediately is faith. The expression "faith," which had been reserved for religious content, Jacobi uses in the sense of immediate knowing for a content of every other sort as well.[461]

461. [Ed.] On revelation within the person, see the preceding note, as well as Jacobi's preface to vol. 3 of his *Werke* (p. xx), where he declares his agreement with Friedrich Schlegel on the thesis that "the original revelation of God to human beings is no revelation in image and word, but an emergence in inner feeling." See also his preface to vol. 4, pt. 1 of his *Werke*, which speaks of a sense for the supersensible that he calls "reason" (p. xxi), and which identifies the root of philosophy as human knowledge proceeding from revelation (pp. xxii–xxiii); cf. p. xxxvi. Jacobi first distinguished between understanding and reason in his later writings. In *Ueber das Unternehmen des Kriticismus die Vernunft zu Verstande zu bringen* . . . (Hamburg, 1802), Jacobi criticized Kant's placement of reason above understanding (in Jacobi's *Werke* 3:59–195). In his treatise *Von den göttlichen Dingen und ihrer Offenbarung* (Leipzig, 1811), however, Jacobi himself ranked understanding below reason; see pp. 175 ff. Schelling directed his satirical piece *Denkmal der Schrift von den göttlichen Dingen etc. des Herrn Friedrich Heinrich Jacobi* . . . (Tübingen, 1812) against Jacobi. There he calls this ranking Jacobi's greatest error, and declares: "In all human language and speech, understanding was set above reason. Prior to the Kantian terminological confusion it occurred to no one to doubt this"; in Schelling's *Sämmtliche Werke*, ed. K. F. A. Schelling, 14 vols. in 2 divisions (Stuttgart and Augsburg, 1856–1861), 8:616, 618. Jacobi, however, maintained the view that understanding was subordinate to reason, in the introduction to the edition of his *Werke* and in a supplemental footnote to his (1787) dialogue, *David Hume*; in *Werke* 2:61 ff., 98 ff., 221–222 (note). On faith as immediate knowing, see above, n. 439.

This is the most widespread standpoint of ˉour time.ˉ⁴⁶² Its characteristic is immediate knowing, whether we call it faith, knowledge, or what have you. This is the first step. When we ask for this knowing's content, then ˉit is [simply said] that *God is.*ˉ⁴⁶³ This immediate knowledge is individual knowledge, it belongs to each individual, [to the] individual as such. The I is, and it knows immediately that God, the universal, is. Here God is | generally defined and interpreted as a spiritual being with the attributes of power, wisdom, and the like. We [in contrast] call wholly universal knowing "thinking," we call singular, external knowing "intuition" or "representation," and we call the introduction of categories of thought "understanding." It is absurd when thinking is spoken about without knowing what it is. ˉEvery universal activity is thinking. Religious feeling exists only insofar as it is the feeling of a thinking being, only insofar as its determinations proceed from thinking.ˉ⁴⁶⁴ An animal has no religious feeling.

This One or God is the universal, taken abstractly, and God is wholly abstract, even in his personality—the absolutely universal personality. One forgets in this context that what is revealed in immediate knowing is the universal. Immediate knowing proper, however, is natural, sensible knowing. And when humankind has come so far as to know God as solely object of spirit, then this result is mediated via teaching, through a lengthy and progressive cultivation. The ˉHindusˉ⁴⁶⁵ and the Egyptians have known just as immediately that an ox is God, that God is an ox or a cat, and the Hindus still know other things of this sort today. It is thus a deficiency of simple reflection not to know that the universal or God, as

462. *Thus Gr, An, Lw; Pn reads:* philosophy.
463. *Thus Pn; Gr reads:* [it is that] God is known and that *God is.*
464. *Thus Pn; Gr reads:* The universal element in the human mind is thinking. An example is religious feeling. Animals do not have it, it is a human feeling, and insofar as it is religious it is such as the feeling of a thinking being; and the determination of the feeling is not a determination of a natural impulse and the like, but a determination of thinking.
465. *Thus Pn, Lw; An reads:* Phoenicians
[*Ed.*] This sentence refers to Apis the bull, of the ancient Egyptians, as well as to their reverence for cats. See *Philosophy of Religion* 2:746 with n. 83, and n. 339 (2:633–636).

what is spiritual, is within itself by no means something immediate; not to know instead that this immediacy is only the consequence of a revelation from the side of religion, that it is the consequence of the education of the human race[466] and therefore is mediated. When we grant validity to immediate knowing, then all can suit themselves and everything is justified, for each person can subjectively and immediately know something different; one person can know this and another one that, and everything is permitted—idolatry, | irreligiousness, and so on. The affirmation that the human being knows God immediately is therefore quite false. The immediate is what is natural, and knowing God as something spiritual is therefore essentially only the result of mediation and teaching. 176

The second step is that immediate knowing is set in opposition to mediated knowing. The distinctions between immediacy and mediation are very poor and abstract determinations, and it would be a very limiting and very impoverished enterprise if we wanted to build religion and philosophy upon such views. These determinations are only the sort of forms that have no subsistence or truth on their own account. The ultimate form here, the fact that immediacy is grasped as what is most absolute, shows the lack of all critical thought, all logic. Kantian philosophy is the critical philosophy, but the very point in it that has been forgotten is that the infinite cannot be constituted from finite categories. Such categories belong to the finite and limited understanding, and, as Kant himself says, they are incapable of grasping what is true.[467]

A more precise account of what the opposition involves is that all knowing can be immediate and equally not be immediate. All

466. [Ed.] This may be a deliberate allusion to Lessing's rationalistic theological essay *The Education of the Human Race* (1780), in Lessing's *Sämtliche Schriften*, vol. 13; trans. F. W. Robertson, in *Lessing's Theological Writings*, ed. Henry Chadwick (London, 1956), pp. 82–98.

467. [Ed.] Here Hegel turns one result of the *Critique of Pure Reason* against the post-Kantian effort to grasp the absolute from the forms of immediacy. He does not mention, however, that Kant's critical philosophy would also contest the possibility of Hegel's own program of a rational knowledge of God. The Kantian categories are finite because their cognitive function is restricted to the domain of experience, and in particular to the knowledge of phenomena, and does not extend to things in themselves; see above, n. 389.

immediate knowledge is also internally mediated; we know this in our own consciousness, we can observe it in the most commonplace phenomena, and it is absurd to forget it. Here in Berlin I know immediately about America, and yet this knowledge is highly mediated. If I am to see American soil immediately before my eyes, then this would first involve as a mediation my having made the journey there; first Columbus must discover America, ships must be built, and so forth, for all these discoveries and inventions play a part in my seeing. ˜That it is immediate˜[468] is the result of an endless number of mediations. I know immediately that in a right triangle the sum of the squares on the legs is equal to the square on the hypotenuse. I know this immediately, | and yet I have learned it and become convinced of it only through the mediation of the proof. Immediate knowledge is thus everywhere mediated. The distinction between mediated and immediate is therefore only psychological.

177

It is equally easy to see that the reputedly immediate knowledge of God is just as much a mediated knowledge too. Immediate humanity is natural humanity with its natural behavior and its desires, with no knowledge of the universal and no thoughts— ˜children or savages, uncultivated and ignorant,˜[469] who know nothing of God. Natural human beings are as they ought not to be, for mediation is part of being human. We have true knowledge only through elevation above the natural, only by arriving at consciousness of the universal, of what is higher. Then we do indeed know immediately what is higher, but that point is reached only via mediation. All thinking is immediate. But this very thinking is a process within itself, it is movement and vitality, and all vitality is internal movement or internal process, it is mediated. This is even more the case with spiritual vitality, for the movement is the passing-over from the one to the other, from the merely natural or sensible to the spiritual, and that is mediation. The antithesis between immediate and mediated knowledge is thus wholly vacuous, and it is one of the most utterly superficial or empty bubbles to

468. *Thus Pn; Gr reads:* What we now know immediately *Lw reads:* That I know it immediately *Sv reads:* But however this immediacy arises, it
469. *Thus Pn; Gr, similar in Lw, reads:* namely, children, Eskimos, and the like,

which thinking can give birth if we take the antithesis of mediate and immediate knowledge to be authentic. Only the most barren and impoverished understanding supposes that in an antithesis such as immediacy and mediation it has hold of something firm and ultimate. Philosophy does nothing but bring this mediation to consciousness; ˉphilosophy exhibits the mediation implicit according to the subject matter, as in religion, for instance, or some other topic. |

But since every standpoint has an aspect in which it is justified, there liesˉ[470] in this standpoint [of immediate knowing] the great [truth] that to accept that the human spirit knows God immediately is to acknowledge human freedom, the human spirit. The source of the knowledge of God is in this acceptance. In this principle all externality or authority is therefore superseded, for this is the principle, but also no more than the principle, of the freedom of spirit. It is the greatness of our time that this form, however little its self-understanding, still bears within it this [truth] that freedom—the peculiar possession of spirit—is acknowledged, that spirit is inwardly at home with itself [in sich bei sich ist] and has this consciousness within it. But this principle is only abstract. The next point is that this principle of the freedom of spirit, which is abstract, should come back to pure objectivity, that not everything that enters my head or rises up within me or is revealed to me is for that very reason what is true, except it be purified and attain its authentic objectivity. This it does only through thought, which strips away what is particular and contingent—[attaining] an objectivity that is independent of mere subjectivity and that is in and for itself, but in such a way that the principle of freedom is still respected in it. It is basic to the Christian religion that God is a Spirit,[471] and that one's own spirit must bear witness to this. But that to which spirit witnesses must be spirit. The content must be the authentic content, but this is not established [simply] by the fact that it is revealed or certified to me. Such is the standpoint [of

470. *Thus Gr; Sv reads:* this is the current state of affairs. There lies *Lw reads:* The third point is to notice that
471. [*Ed.*] See above, n. 209, p. 000.

immediate knowledge], and we have now seen both its deficiency and the greatness of the principle that lies within it.

If God is believed in according to this Kantian-Jacobian standpoint (and we for the moment concede it), then it by all means involves a return ˉto the absolute.ˉ[472] But then the question is: What is God? "The supersensible" is an anemic expression, and so are "the universal," "the abstract," "what subsists in-and-for-itself"; | all the epithets that I bestow on God still say nothing. What then is the concrete determination of God? If we want to pass over to [genuine] determinations, then the consequence harmful to this standpoint is that we are passing over to a cognitive knowing, which means knowing an object that is inwardly concrete, is determinate. According to this immediate knowing we only get to the point that God (in some general sense) *is,* that we have God with the characteristic of the unlimited, the universal, the indeterminate. For that reason, so it is said, God could not be known cognitively, for in order to be known cognitively God would have to be concrete and would therefore contain at least two determinations; and the two are mediated in their connection, because a knowledge of the concrete is at once mediated knowledge or cognition. But since this standpoint repudiates mediation, it remains with the indeterminate. When Paul—in the Acts of the Apostles—addresses the Athenians, he appeals to the altar that they had dedicated to the unknown god. The standpoint that we are dealing with leads us back again to the unknown god. Immediate knowledge remains at the standpoint of the Athenians.[473] Paul taught them what God is, that God is not something unknown.[474]

179

474. *As a transition to the next chapter there follows in Gr:* All vitality, whether of nature or of spirit, is mediation within self, and Schelling's philosophy has now passed over to that point. *In Lw:* We have noted that what is spiritual is essentially concrete, and Schelling's philosophy has passed over to that point.

472. *Thus Gr; Pn reads:* to the truth.

473. [*Ed.*] See Acts 17:23. In the 1823–24 lectures Hegel made this same comparison between the standpoint of the late Enlightenment and of Romanticism, that God cannot be known cognitively, and the standpoint of the Athenians who dedicated an altar to the unknown god. He borrowed it from Jean-Baptiste Robinet's *De la nature,* 3d ed. (Amsterdam, 1766). See W 15:521 (Ms?), which cites Robinet (chap. 3, p. 16): "We could once again place on the gate of our temples the inscription to be read on the temple erected on the Areopagus: *Deo ignoto.*"

7. Friedrich Wilhelm Joseph Schelling: Identity Philosophy

[475]Schelling's philosophy has, to begin with, passed over to cognitive knowledge of God, having taken Fichte as its starting point. Schelling's first essays are still wholly Fichtean, and only gradually did | he disengage himself from this Fichtean form. Fichte's form 180 of the I involves ambiguity between "I" as absolute I, or God, and "I" in my particularity; this gave [Schelling] his impulse.[476] On the one hand Schelling began from the Fichtean philosophy, and on the other he adopts as his principle the intellectual intuition that the

475. *Precedes in Gr:* Schelling was born at Schorndorf in Württemberg in 1775. He studied in Leipzig and Jena, where he became more closely associated with Fichte. For many years he has been secretary of the Academy of Fine Arts in Munich.

[*Ed.*] Schelling was actually born in Leonberg, near Stuttgart (and not far from Schorndorf), on 27 January 1775. He studied at Tübingen (1790–1795), subsequently was a tutor for a private family in Leipzig, and went to Jena as a professor in 1798. It is surprising to encounter so many errors in *Gr* about the early career of a person who had then been such a close associate of Hegel. In 1806 Schelling became the first director of the new Academy of the Arts, a division of the Bavarian Academy of Sciences. He long outlived Hegel, and died on 20 August 1854 at the spa of Bad Ragaz, Switzerland.

476. [*Ed.*] The early writings Hegel has in mind are *On the Possibility of a Form of All Philosophy* (1794) and *Of the I as Principle of Philosophy; or, On the Unconditional in Human Knowledge* (1795); see Schelling's *Sämmtliche Werke* 1:85–112 and 1:149–244 respectively; see also the new historical-critical edition, *Friedrich Wilhelm Joseph Schelling: Werke*, ed. Hans Michael Baumgartner, Wilhelm G. Jacobs, Hermann Krings, and Hermann Zeltner (Stuttgart–Bad Cannstatt, 1976 ff.), 1:247–300 and 2:1–175 respectively; see the English translation of these two essays by Fritz Marti, in his *F. W. J. Schelling: The Unconditional in Human Knowledge: Four Early Essays (1794–1796)* (Lewisburg, 1980), pp. 33–58 and 59–149. Hegel's contention that these essays are still wholly Fichtean overlooks the differences between Fichte and Schelling that already exist here—such as in the formulation of the initial or basic principles. Hegel uses the Fichtean technical term *Anstoss* ("impulse") in suggesting that it was the very ambiguity in Fichte's view that drove Schelling beyond that formulation. On Fichte's concept of the absolute I, see above, p. 000 and n. 419. On God as absolute I, see also Schelling's letter to Hegel of 4 February 1795; in Hegel's *Briefe* 1:22; also in *F. W. J. Schelling: Briefe und Dokumente,* ed. Horst Fuhrmans (Bonn, 1962 ff.), 2:65. In it Schelling says: "*God* is nothing but the absolute I, the I insofar as it has negated everything theoretical, and therefore God is equal to zero in the *theoretical* philosophy. Personality arises by means of the unity of consciousness. Consciousness, however, is not possible without any object; but for God, that is, for the absolute I, there is no object at all, for through the object it would cease to be absolute—accordingly there is no personal God." On Hegel's evaluation of the double significance of a beginning from the I, see the *Science of Logic*, pp. 75 ff. (*GW* 11:38–39).

human mind, and the philosopher in particular, must have. The content of this intuition, or what in it becomes the object, is the absolute or God, what has being in-and-for-itself; but this content is expressed as concrete and internally self-mediating, as the absolute unity of the subjective and the objective—in other words, as the absolute indifference of the subjective and the objective.[477]

Thus Schelling's philosophy makes its beginning from immediate knowing, from intellectual intuition. The second point, however, is that its content is no longer the indeterminate, the essence of essences, but the absolute as concrete. We have already said what the form of intellectual intuition involves.[478] Nothing could be more convenient than to posit cognition on the basis of immediate knowing, of what pops into one's head. But immediate knowledge of God as a spiritual being exists only for Christian peoples and not for others, it is not in the consciousness of other peoples. This immediate knowledge appears to be even more contingent [when presented] as intellectual intuition of the concrete or, more precisely, of subjectivity and objectivity. Since the presupposition of philosophy is that the subject has an immediate intuition of this identity of the subjective and the objective, philosophy thus appears as an artistic talent or genius in individuals that comes only to

477. [Ed.] On the concept of intellectual intuition, see Schelling's *System of Transcendental Idealism* (1800); *Sämmtliche Werke* 3:369–370; translation by Peter Heath (Charlottesville, 1978), pp. 27–28. In this passage an intellectual intuition is defined as an absolutely free knowing (in contrast with sensible intuition), as a producing of its own object. The I itself involves such an intuition, since its free act of knowing itself is productive of itself as object; hence the I is a permanent intellectual intuition. This intellectual intuition (the I as self-producing) is the organ and sole object of all transcendental philosophy. On the concept of the unity of subjective and objective in this same treatise, see *Sämmtliche Werke* 3:600–601 (Heath, pp. 208–209). This absolute identity, or the ground of the identity of subject and object, is here said to be neither subject nor object itself, nor both at the same time. As what is absolutely simple, what is without objectification or predicates (albeit as eternal mediator, behind the scenes, between free action and natural law), this absolute identity can never be an object of knowledge. To this account Schelling adds, in the *Darstellung meines Systems der Philosophie* (1801), that by *reason* he means absolute reason, or reason thought of as total *indifference* of the subjective and the objective (*Sämmtliche Werke* 4:114).

478. [Ed.] See above, p. 000.

"Sunday's children" [namely, to the favored few].[479] By its very nature, however, philosophy can become universal, for its soil is thinking, the universal, and that is the very thing that makes us all human. The principle therefore is one that is utterly universal; but if a determinate intuition or consciousness is required | such as 181 consciousness or intuition of the identity of subject and object, then what is being required is a determinate or particular thinking.

In this form of the knowledge of the absolute as concrete (and more precisely, in the form of the unity of subject and object), philosophy has now once again separated itself from representation, from the ordinary and representational mode of consciousness and of its reflection. The beginning of this separation from the ordinary mode of consciousness had already been made by Kant. The outcome—that the true cannot be known cognitively and that philosophy is therefore superfluous—has been generally established and accepted as useful. With the Fichtean philosophy ordinary consciousness has divorced itself from philosophy even more. Fichte's I is supposed not merely to have consciousness of the empirical but also to be cognizant of, or know, some determinations that do not fall within ordinary consciousness. It is most notably Schelling's philosophy, however, that has severed itself from the ordinary representations of the reflective consciousness. Fichte still had the tendency toward popularization. His later essays in particular are written for this purpose, in an attempt to force the reader

479. [Ed.] This criticism may be directed at formulations that appear at various spots in Schelling's writings. See, for example, the *System of Transcendental Idealism,* which states that failure to comprehend transcendental philosophy is due to lack of the organ for that purpose, namely, intellectual intuition, and also suggests that lack of this special sense is no more surprising than the lack of some other sense in certain individuals (*Sämmtliche Werke* 3:369–370; Heath, pp. 27–28). In his 1803 lectures *On University Studies,* Schelling says: "Those who do not have intellectual intuition cannot understand what is said of it, and for this reason it cannot at all be given. A negative condition of its possession is the clear and sincere insight of the nothingness of all merely finite cognition. One can develop it within oneself; in the philosopher it must become, so to speak, one's character—a constant organ, a skill for seeing everything only as it presents itself in the idea"; see *Sämmtliche Werke* 5:256; the English translation by E. S. Morgan, ed. Norbert Guterman (Athens, Ohio, 1966), renders this passage too loosely (pp. 49–50).

to an understanding, but he never managed to achieve a popular appeal[480] and Schelling did so even less. For Schelling the concrete is by its very nature at once speculative. The concrete content— God, life, or whatever particular form it has—is indeed a content of ordinary consciousness; and in its religious determination, when we relate ourselves to God, it is a consciousness of something concrete. But the difficulty is that we *think* what is contained in the concrete, the thoughts become concrete, we think the different determinations. The standpoint of the understanding is to distinguish the thoughts, to define them in contrast with one another, while the requirement of philosophy is to bring these different thoughts back together. Of course natural consciousness has the concrete as its object, but understanding is what causes the cleavage, understanding is the reflection that holds fast to finite categories of thought, and the difficulty is to grasp the unity and hold on to it firmly. Finite and infinite, cause and effect, positive and negative— each of these pairs the understanding regards as utterly opposed.

182   Thinking *begins* at this point, which is the realm of | reflective ˉconsciousness where the old metaphysical consciousness was able to play its part.ˉ[481] But the speculative involves having these antitheses before oneself and yet resolving them, knowing them as identical.

Here with Schelling, speculation proper has therefore come to the fore again, and philosophy has thus regained its own special character; the principle of philosophy—thinking in itself or rational thinking—has received the *form of thinking*. Accordingly, in Schelling's philosophy the content or the truth has once more become

480. [*Ed.*] Hegel's choice of words alludes to the subtitle of Fichte's *Sun-clear Report to the General Public about the Actual Essence of the Most Recent Philosophy: An Attempt to Force the Reader to Understand* (1801); see *Gesamtausgabe*, division 1, 7:165–268. In the *Werke* (*W* 15:613, 640) there are references to two of Fichte's series of popular lectures, *On the Nature of the Scholar and Its Manifestations* (1805) and *The Way towards the Blessed Life; or, The Doctrine of Religion* (1806), both published in Berlin in 1806; see *Fichte: Ausgewählte Werke in sechs Bänden*, ed. Fritz Medicus (Leipzig, 1910), 5:1–102 and 103–307; English translations by William Smith, in *Fichte's Popular Works* (London, 1873), pp. 133–231, 381–564. Fichte's works after 1806 remained unpublished in his lifetime.

481. *Thus Gr; Pn reads:* understanding, the old metaphysics.

the main thing, whereas in the Kantian and the other subsequent philosophies the concern most particularly expressed was that knowledge, cognition, or subjective cognition should be investigated. It appeared plausible that we should first investigate cognitive knowing, the instrument, although there is an old story told of the σχολαστικός who would not enter the water until he had learned to swim.[482] ⁻To investigate cognitive knowing means to know it cognitively; but how one is to know without knowing is not stated.⁻[483] This, then, is the general standpoint of Schelling's philosophy.

A defect of Schelling's philosophy is that the point of indifference of the subjective and the objective is presupposed, not proved.[484] This proof could only be carried out by investigating the subjective and the objective each on its own account in its logical determinations, namely, in its essential determinations. From this investigation it then must follow that the subjective is self-transforming, that it does not remain subjective but makes itself objective, and that the objective is what does not remain objective but makes itself subjective. The result would thus be that each makes itself into its opposite, and only the identity of the two is the truth. The understanding is astonished at this transformation and calls [it] sophistry, hocus-pocus, legerdemain, and the like.

Schelling did indeed hold this view in a general way, | but he · 183 did not follow it through in a determinate, logical fashion. In one of his first essays, his *System of Transcendental Idealism,* he indicated the relationship in the following way. There are two poles, the one being nature and the objective, the other the subjective or knowing. These two poles mutually presuppose and require one

482. [*Ed.*] This anecdote is contained in a collection of witticisms written in Greek, known as Φιλογέλως ("Friend of Laughter"), collected in late antiquity by Hierocles of Alexandria and Philagrios the Grammarian. See *Philogelos der Lachfreund: Von Hierokles und Philagrios,* ed. A. Thierfelder (Munich, 1968), p. 28: § 2. "A Scholastic who wanted to swim was nearly drowned. He swore never again to go into the water until he had learned to swim." Hegel also uses this anecdote in the *Philosophy of Religion* 1:139 with n. 60, and 169 with n. 51.

483. *Thus Gr; Pn reads:* One wants to know it cognitively before one engages in it.

484. [*Ed.*] See above, n. 477.

another. There must therefore be two fundamental sciences: the embodiment [*Inbegriff*] of everything objective is called nature, and that of everything subjective is the I, or intelligence. Either the one or the other can be made the starting point, and this must happen to each [in turn]—the I must be made the first principle, and nature as well.

When the objective is made first we begin with the natural sciences, and their striving is to attain to what is intelligent; the highest goal is the spiritualization of natural laws into laws of thinking. The phenomenal, the material, and the like must vanish and laws alone remain. The ˉcompleted theory of natureˉ[485] would be one on the strength of which the whole of nature resolves itself into intelligence. The lifeless products of nature are to be regarded only as abortive attempts at self-reflection on the part of nature; lifeless nature is to be grasped as immature intelligence, as torpid, petrified intelligence. Only through its highest reflection does nature reach the highest goal, that of becoming object to itself; this occurs in the human being, which, through itself or through reason, returns into itself, and what is revealed through this return is ˉthat nature is identical with what is consciousness and intelligence in us.ˉ[486]

When on the contrary the subjective is made first, the task is to

---

485. *Thus Gr, Lw; Sv reads:* highest perfection of natural science

486. *Thus Pn, similar in Gr; Sv reads:* that matter has ceased, and the whole world is grasped no longer objectively, but subjectively, in thought.

[Ed.] See the opening statements of the Introduction to the *System of Transcendental Idealism,* where the concept of transcendental philosophy is outlined (*Sämmtliche Werke* 3:339–341; Heath, pp. 5–6). In this paragraph Hegel gives a fair account of the points he chooses to mention. In Schelling's version the identity of subjective and objective in knowing calls for explanation, and the explanatory endeavor requires undoing the identity; that is what gives rise to the alternative procedures in which each in turn is given priority. Starting with nature (the objective) leads to intelligence (the subjective) in two stages; there is not only the drive of natural science to formulate general laws of natural phenomena but also the higher, philosophical task of "the complete spiritualizing of all natural laws into laws of intuition and thought," for "the more lawfulness emerges in nature itself the more the husk disappears, the phenomena themselves become more mental and at length vanish entirely." It is at nature's apex, human reason, that nature becomes fully object to itself and identical with conscious intelligence.

show how an object ˉenters in that coincides with the subject.ˉ487 This would then be the authentic transcendental philosophy, starting out from the subject and letting the objective | arise from it. 184 The foundation of this philosophy is the I, as in Fichte's case. Presupposed here is the fact of knowing, I = I, I as pure act; and from this standpoint the objective has to be exhibited by showing how the I advances to the objective. Here the highest mode of objectivity, the identity of the objective and the subjective, is the I that attains objectivity and abides in it.

This highest stage is [what] Schelling calls the power of imagination [*Einbildungskraft*]. The objectivity of intellectual intuition is art, poetic art and the like. So art ˉis grasped as what is highestˉ488

487. *Thus An; Gr reads:* comes to the subject, how it coincides with it, becomes one with it.

[*Ed.*] This sentence and the next draw upon directly subsequent statements (see the preceding note) in the *System of Transcendental Idealism* (*Sämmtliche Werke* 3:341–342; Heath, pp. 6–7).

488. *Thus Gr, similar in Lw; Sv reads:* presents the subjective objectively

[*Ed.*] Schelling presents the concept of imagination more clearly in the Introduction to the *System of Transcendental Idealism* than he does in the body of that work. In this Introduction (*Sämmtliche Werke* 3:349–351; Heath, pp. 12–14) he states that the identity of the unconscious activity of nature with the conscious activity of the subject occurs in the consciousness that is both conscious and unconscious activity at once, that is, in aesthetic activity with its artistic products. "The ideal world of art and the real world of objects are therefore products of one and the same activity." The world of objects, or nature, is "the original, as yet unconscious, poetry of the spirit." Art brings this poetry to consciousness, and the philosophy of art, "the universal organon of philosophy," is where the identity is fully grasped. To understand philosophy two conditions are requisite: a person must be engaged in producing these original acts of intelligence and must also be constantly reflecting upon the production. The proof that this reflection is possible only through an aesthetic act of the imagination gets deferred to the end of the treatise, part 6, entitled "Deduction of a Universal Organ of Philosophy; or, Essentials of the Philosophy of Art according to the Principles of Transcendental Idealism" (*Sämmtliche Werke* 3:612–634; Heath, pp. 219–236). Here Schelling explains further the concept of imagination and states that art itself, or aesthetic intuition, *is* intellectual intuition become objective (*Sämmtliche Werke* 3:625–626; Heath, pp. 229–230). Here also he discusses "the obscure concept of genius" and ascribes to it the power to unite, or to express the original identity of, the poetry that is inborn and unconscious with the art that is learned and conscious; genius "is for the aesthetic what the self is for philosophy, namely, the supreme absolute reality, which never itself becomes objective but is the cause of everything that is so" (*Sämmtliche Werke* 3:616, 619; Heath, pp. 222, 224).

and philosophizing is represented as being this genius-character [*Genialität*] of art. But *we* soon recognize that the power of imagination, or art, is not what is highest, for the idea of spirit cannot be expressed in the authentically highest way in art; ˉart brings forth the idea in the mode of the sensible, of intuition,ˉ[489] and because of its form of existence the work of art cannot be adequate to spirit. Since the ultimate point is designated as imaginative power, as art, this standpoint itself is only a subordinate and subjective standpoint, and so this [ultimate] point itself is not the absolute identity of subjective and objective; art is not yet the totality itself.

The two sides are, on the whole, expressed very definitely here. One side involves the thorough leading [*Durchführung*] of nature to the subject, and [the other that] of the I to the object. The [project's] authentic execution [*Durchführung*], however, can only take place in a logical mode, for logic embodies pure thought. Pure thought and its development or process is the soul of nature as well as of the subject. But the consideration of the logical is what Schelling never gets to in his presentation. The genuine proof that this identity is what is true would in any event have to be carried out in the way indicated. | And then the identity would be proved as what is true, as a result—or, in Jacobi's terms, it would be posited as conditioned, as derivative. Because it is the result, however, the true sense is precisely the sublating of this one-sidedness—the sublating of its form as the result, its being only something mediated— and hence also the sublating of this mediating itself, for it is as much immediate as it is mediated: it is a process that as such is self-contained mediation [*das Vermitteln in sich*].

Because his presentation needed to begin with the idea of the absolute as the identity of subjective and objective, Schelling repeatedly sought to demonstrate this idea in his later presentations; he tried especially hard to do so in the *Neue Zeitschrift für speku-*

185

---

489. *Pn reads:* art brings forth something in the mode of the sensible, of intuition, *An reads:* art brings the idea, *Gr reads:* this is always the mode of intuition, *Lw reads:* for this is the sensible mode, intuition, *Sv reads:* art brings the idea to intuition in a sensible mode,

lative Physik.[490] But these proofs are carried out in the most for-
malistic [*formell*] way, so that in fact they always presuppose what
is supposed to be proved. The identity in question is declared to be
the absolute indifference of the objective and the subjective, so that
both have their true determination in it.[491] But the expression "indifference" [*Indifferenz*] is not apt, since the indifference is what
is neutral [*das Gleichgültige*] with regard to both. By this criterion
it can seem as if ˉthe absoluteˉ[492] is neutral toward both aspects,
or that it would be remote from them. Schelling speaks also of the
identity of essence and form, of finite and infinite, of positive and
negative.[493] These antitheses can be employed, but they are only
abstract and relate only to different stages of development of the
logical itself.

In the later presentations, therefore, Schelling begins from this
absolute identity. A detailed presentation of his philosophy is contained in the *Zeitschrift für spekulative Physik,* vol. 2, part 2. Like
Spinoza, Schelling here employs a geometrical method, proceeding
from definitions, axioms, then propositions that guide the proof,

490. [*Ed.*] The references to "presentations" and "later presentations" would
seem to mean those essays subsequent to the 1800 *System of Transcendental
Idealism* that bear the word *Darstellung* ("Presentation") in their titles. The *Neue
Zeitschrift für speculative Physik* was a journal edited by Schelling. Schelling's
Darstellung meines Systems der Philosophie (1801) appeared in the *Zeitschrift für
spekulative Physik* (Jena and Leipzig), a predecessor to the *Neue Zeitschrift* . . . that
he also edited; see *Sämmtliche Werke* 4:105–212. At this point in the lectures Hegel
may have mentioned this essay as well as another by Schelling in the first issue of
the *Neue Zeitschrift* (Tübingen, 1802), entitled *Fernere Darstellungen aus dem System der Philosophie* (in *Sämmtliche Werke* 4:333–510), and his auditors failed to
hear or understand him correctly owing to unfamiliarity with the names of the essays. In the *Fernere Darstellungen* Schelling states that whoever stands outside the
unity of thinking and being, of subjective and objective, has lost the demonstrative
principle of identity (p. 364).

491. [*Ed.*] On the concept of absolute indifference, see the end of n. 477 above,
and also the *Fernere Darstellungen,* which speaks of the absolute as the indifference
of essence and form in which even all contrast of quantitative and qualitative unity
disappears (*Sämmtliche Werke* 4:379–380).

492. *Thus Pn; Gr reads:* the fulfilling of indifference, whereby it is concrete, *An
reads:* it [*viz., the indifference*]

493. [*Ed.*] For a whole range of polarities that the absolute identity unites see,
for example, the *Fernere Darstellungen* (*Sämmtliche Werke* 4:367–368).

and then derivative propositions; but this method has no authentic application to philosophy. In this procedure he presupposed certain forms of distinction that he calls "potencies," [an expression] that he took over from Eschenmayer.[494] People have often sought | to make philosophy mathematical. That was not Schelling's plan, to be sure, but he made use of the form of potencies [that is, the mathematical "powers" of square and cube] as ready-made distinctions. In developing the philosophy of nature in this presentation, he proceeded only as far as organism. What the aspect of spirit involves he had, however, given in greater detail in his earlier treatise, the *System of Transcendental Idealism*. With regard to the practical domain he has not proceeded much further than Kant did in his essay *Vom ewigen Frieden*; there is no full-blown [practical] philosophy of spirit. One particular work, a *Treatise concerning Freedom,* is of a deeper and more speculative sort, but it deals only with this one point.[495]

So Schelling has been preeminently the author of the modern philosophy of nature. On the whole, "philosophy of nature" means nothing else than treating and conceiving nature in a thinking fashion. Ordinary physics has its metaphysics too, for its definitions of forces, laws, and the like are thoughts. But when philosophy goes beyond the form of the understanding and has grasped the speculative concept, then it must become conversant with the categories

494. [*Ed.*] On this essay in the *Zeitschrift,* see n. 490 above. Near its beginning (p. 113), Schelling declares that he has taken Spinoza as his model not just because of the content of Spinoza's philosophy but also because its geometrical form is most conducive to economical presentation and to evaluation of the evidence for the proofs; on the same page he also credits some of his formulations to Eschenmayer. Adam Karl August Eschenmayer (1768–1852) was his friend and sometime disciple. Later Schelling wrote a cordial reply to Eschenmayer's critique of his essay *Of Human Freedom* (1809); both critique and reply appear in *Sämmtliche Werke* 8:137–189. Eschenmayer's "potencies" express mathematical powers.

495. [*Ed.*] Kant published *Vom ewigen Frieden* in Königsberg in 1795; see *Schriften* 8:341–381; English translation by Lewis White Beck under the title *Perpetual Peace,* in *Kant: On History,* ed. Beck (Indianapolis, 1957, 1963), pp. 85–135. The full title of Schelling's treatise mentioned here is *Philosophical Investigations concerning the Essence of Human Freedom and the Issues Connected with It* (Landshut, 1809); see *Sämmtliche Werke* 7:331–416; English translation by James Gutmann under the title *Schelling: Of Human Freedom* (Chicago, 1936).

The University of California Press takes full responsibility for the errata below. None of the errors should be attributed to the editor, Robert F. Brown.

Lectures on the
History of Philosophy
edited by Robert F. Brown
ERRATA

Page 20 n. 8, line 11, *read* pp. 125–130
Page 37 n. 50, line 10, *read* p. 60
Page 39 n. 58, line 1, *read* pp. 153–154
Page 43 n. 66, line 2, *read* pp. 17–24
Page 49 n. 78, line 1, *read* pp. 27–35
Page 55 n. 94, line 5, *read* pp. 142–143;
  n. 95, line 3, *read* p. 239
Page 56 n. 102, line 1, *read* pp. 139–141;
  n. 103, line 3, *read* n. 195, p. 91
Page 60 n. 112, line 1, *read* p. 36
Page 68 n. 135, line 4, *for* Ramon *read*
  Raymon
Page 70 n. 140, line 1, *read* p. 72 with
  n. 143; line 2, *read* p. 92; line 2, *read*
  p. 188
Page 71 n. 141, line 4, *read* p. 60
Page 72 n. 143, line 20, *read* p. 70; line 20,
  read p. 92; line 20, *read* p. 188
Page 73 n. 146, line 6, *read* p. 77
Page 77 n. 157, line 1, *read* p. 73
Page 78 n. 161, line 4, *read* pp. 82–87
Page 79 n. 152, line 9, *read* pp. 162–163;
  line 10, *read* p. 162; n. 164, line 6, *read*
  pp. 247–248
Page 80 n. 164, line 6, *read* pp. 155–156
Page 82 n. 170, line 5, *read* p. 79
Page 87 n. 181, line 3, *read* p. 88
Page 94 n. 203, line 1, *read* pp. 46–47
Page 102 n. 223, line 2, *read* p. 108
Page 109 n. 8, line 8, *read* p. 134
Page 110 n. 10, line 2, *read* pp. 52–94
Page 117 n. 29, line 1, *read* pp. 247–248
Page 118 n. 31, line 6, *read* p. 119; line 22,
  read p. 119
Page 119 n. 37, line 3, *read* p. 123
Page 123 n. 47, line 4, *read* p. 126
Page 126 n. 57, line 1, *read* pp. 203–205
Page 132 n. 79, line 5, *read* p. 17
Page 139 n. 95, line 1, *read* pp. 251–258;
  n. 96, line 2, *read* pp. 229–232
Page 140 n. 99, line 1, *read* p. 239 with
Page 142 n. 105, line 2, *read* n. 94, p. 55
Page 143 n. 106, line 6, *read* pp. 243, 251–
  258
Page 144 n. 109, line 1, *read* pp. 167–169
Page 145 n. 114, line 6, *read* pp. 153–156
Page 146 n. 118, line 2, *read* pp. 155–159
Page 147 n. 119, line 5, *read* p. 156; n. 120,
  line 2, *read* p. 174
Page 150 n. 127, line 1, *read* p. 153; line 3,

  read p. 160; n. 130, line 2, *read* p. 190;
  line 2, *read* p. 197
Page 151 n. 133, line 5, *read* p. 165
Page 155 n. 147, line 1, *read* pp. 185, 189–
  190
Page 158 n. 160, line 7, *read* p. 146
Page 159 n. 162, line 2, *read* pp. 263–271;
  n. 166, line 1, *read* p. 156
Page 162 n. 173, line 2, *read* pp. 81–82; line
  2, *read* pp. 82–84
Page 168 n. 197, line 2, *read* p. 154
Page 169 n. 201, line 2, *read* p. 165; n. 202,
  line 2, *read* p. 155
Page 170 n. 204, line 6, *read* p. 173
Page 173 n. 215, line 1, *read* p. 144
Page 174 n. 219, line 1, *read* p. 147
Page 180 n. 238, line 5, *read* p. 178
Page 188 n. 266, line 10, *read* pp. 92–93
Page 189 n. 269, line 1, *read* pp. 153–155;
  n. 271, line 1, *read* p. 195
Page 191 n. 274, line 10, *read* pp. 150–151
Page 196 n. 291, line 4, *read* p. 192
Page 197 n. 296, line 2, *read* pp. 195–196;
  line 6, *read* pp. 150–151
Page 198 n. 299, line 1, *read* p. 194
Page 205 n. 320, line 1, *read* p. 198; line 3,
  read p. 151
Page 207 n. 325, line 1, *read* pp. 94–103
Page 212 n. 337, line 1, *read* p. 243; n. 338,
  line 9, *read* p. 116
Page 213 n. 342, line 12, *read* p. 111; line
  13, *read* pp. 109, 111–117, 171–178
Page 217 n. 351, line 6, *read* p. 10
Page 218 n. 355, line 1, *read* pp. 205–206
Page 221 n. 364, line 1, *read* pp. 214–215
Page 223 n. 370, line 1, *read* pp. 251–252
Page 229 n. 397, line 2, *read* pp. 220, 228;
  n. 398, line 1, *read* p. 139
Page 234 n. 416, line 1, *read* pp. 229–230
Page 240 n. 429, line 2, *read* (B 733 ff.)
Page 244 n. 439, line 4, *read* pp. 250–254
Page 247 n. 447, line 6, *read* p. 249; n. 448,
  line 11, *read* p. 158
Page 251 n. 458, line 4, *read* p. 249
Page 257 n. 471, line 1, *read* p. 97
Page 259 n. 476, line 15, *read* p. 236
Page 260 n. 478, line 1, *read* p. 251
Page 266 line 32, *for* für *read* über
Page 268 n. 495, line 1, *for* Vom *read* Zum

and thought-determinations of nature on its own account. Kant had already taken the first steps in [speculative] thinking about nature.[496] But it was Schelling who sought to set the concept of nature in place of the ordinary metaphysics of the understanding [*Verstandesmetaphysik*] of nature. Schelling called nature a benumbed intelligence,[497] that is, the outward mode of existence of the system of thought-forms, just as spirit is the existence of the same system but in the form of consciousness. It is Schelling's great merit to have introduced the concept and the form of the concept into the consideration of nature, to have put the concept in place of the ordinary metaphysics of the understanding.

The main form at the basis [of his theory] is that of triplicity, the form of the first, second, and third potency. He begins with "matter" and says that A = A, the absolute indifference in its initial immediacy, is matter.[498] From there he passes over to further deter-

496. [*Ed.*] The reference is to Kant's *Metaphysical Foundations of Natural Science* (1786); in *Schriften* 4:465–566; English translation by James Ellington (Indianapolis, 1970).

497. [*Ed.*] This is probably a reference to the *System of Transcendental Idealism* (*Sämmtliche Werke* 3:341; Heath, p. 6).

498. [*Ed.*] Schelling instead says in the *Darstellung* that the first relative totality (that is, the first potency) is matter (*Sämmtliche Werke* 4:38). The potency theory recurs in various forms and contexts throughout the many decades of Schelling's long career as writer and lecturer. One place to see its full expression is in the *Darstellung*, §§ 23, 30, 40, 42–44 (*Sämmtliche Werke* 4:124, 128, 133–136). The threefold form, however, is not so dominant here as one might think from Hegel's words. He may actually have in mind a section of the *Fernere Darstellungen* entitled "On the Opposition of the Real [*reel*] and Ideal [*ideel*] Series, and the Potencies of Philosophy" (*Sämmtliche Werke* 4:412–423), which stresses that "the form of philosophy as a whole, and each individual construction, reverts to the three potencies (finite, infinite, and eternal), positing them with absolute equality."

499. [*Ed.*] Schelling thought the three potencies are replicated at ever-higher levels of complexity in nature, which is why he compared the third potency (chemical process) of the inorganic domain with the third (reproduction) of the organic domain and so on. At each level the third potency is a totality inclusive of the other two; for example, (inorganic) chemical process is inclusive of magnetism and electricity. On the three inorganic potencies see, for instance, the *Darstellung* §§ 113–114, and on the organic potencies see §§ 141 ff. (*Sämmtliche Werke* 4:184–187, 202 ff.). Schelling's substitution of sensible forms for mathematical ones, a procedure Hegel criticizes, is done quite openly, as when Schelling designates the plant as the carbon pole and the animal as the nitrogen pole, or when he says (§ 152, p. 207) that the female gender is to the male as the plant is to the animal. This sort

187 minations. But the progression of forms | appears more as an out-
wardly imposed schema [than as an inward necessity]. The logical
aspect of the progression is not justified on its own account. For
that reason the philosophy of nature has fallen into particular disrepute, because it is carried on in a wholly external fashion, because
it takes a ready-made schema for its basis and imposes it on natural phenomena. For Schelling these [ready-made] forms were the
potencies.

Instead of these mathematical forms or the typology of thoughts
[*Typus von Gedanken*], however, one can try to use some schema
of sensible forms as the theoretical basis. In this vein the magnetism, electricity, and chemical process in nature have been defined as the three potencies, so that in the case of the organism, for
instance, reproduction has been called the chemical process, ir-
ritability the electricity, and sensibility the magnetism.[499] This mis-
chief of applying to one sphere of nature forms adopted from
another sphere—a play of analogies—has been carried very far
when, for example, one calls the wood fibers of plants "nerves,"
as Oken does.[500] For we are dealing with thought, and nerves are
not thoughts any more than are the expressions "pole of contrac-
tion and expansion," "masculine and feminine," and the like. This
formalism of foisting an external schema upon a sphere of nature
one wants to examine is a completely external way of doing the
philosophy of nature. One can fantasize in this way, but it all takes
place as a way of avoiding thought—and thought is still the one
and only determination that is relevant.

This is the final form [of philosophy] that we have to consider.
The main thing in Schelling's philosophy is that it deals with a con-

---

of sensible imagery for the potencies is omnipresent in the numerous essays that set
forth Schelling's philosophy of nature. The specific correlation that Hegel gives here
is found in the *Erster Entwurf eines Systems der Naturphilosophie* of 1799 (in
Sämmtliche Werke 3:1–268)—that is, before Schelling had arrived at the "typology
of thoughts"; see especially 3:203–218.

500. [*Ed.*] Lorenz Oken (1779–1851) was an avid disciple of Schelling's philosophy of nature and the author of *Lehrbuch der Naturphilosophie*, 3 vols. (Jena,
1809–1811), from which this reference comes (division 3, first and second part,
p. 112).

tent, with something concrete and true. His [entire] philosophy has been called philosophy of nature, but the philosophy of nature is only one part of the whole. Schelling grasped the relationship of nature within this concrete totality in the following way. The absolute or God makes itself into the ground, as something presupposed,[501] and God as sheer ground is nature. God makes himself into the ground, but [as such God is] only ground and not cause, and nature must be known in that aspect [namely, as ground]. The absolute, | however, is what sublates this ground and makes itself into intelligence.[502]

188

8. Conclusion

This then is the latest interesting and authentic shape of philosophy. What it lacks is the form of development, which is the logical aspect, the necessity of the progression. This concrete idea is the result of the labor of spirit over two and a half millennia. The stages are: the idea, and in Neoplatonism the concrete idea; but the work of the modern era has been to grasp this idea as spirit, as the self-knowing idea. The progression from the idea to the self-knowing idea involves the antithesis [of abstract and concrete] making itself absolute, the idea having come to knowledge, to consciousness of

501. [Ed.] One passage in which Schelling sets forth compactly this view of God as ground occurs in his 1812 attack on Jacobi (see n. 461 above). He says there that God is *ground of himself,* that God makes a nonintelligent aspect of himself the ground for his own self-development. Contrary to Jacobi, who thought that what stands first must be superior, Schelling holds that God subordinates this initial and nonintelligent aspect of himself to his higher (and subsequent) nature in its rational and ethical transcendent life, "just as the human being first truly transfigures himself into intelligence and an ethical nature, by subordinating the irrational part of his nature to the higher part" (*Sämmtliche Werke* 8:71–72).

502. [Ed.] This terse summary scarcely does justice to Schelling. See *Of Human Freedom,* where the doctrine of a ground in God is initially presented in its fullness. There Schelling states: "This ground of his existence, which God has within himself, is not God absolutely considered, i.e., so far as he exists; for it is indeed only the ground of his existence, it is *nature*—in God; an essence inseparable, yet still distinct, from God" (*Sämmtliche Werke* 7:358; Gutmann, p. 32). The later *Ages of the World* (1811–1815, though unpublished in Schelling's lifetime) makes it clear that the ground or nature in the bipolar deity is not itself the created nature of the world but only the basis for that finite, physical nature; see *Sämmtliche Werke* 8:195–344; English translation by Frederick de Wolfe Bolman, Jr. (New York, 1942).

its absolute cleavage; this has been the work of the modern era. With Descartes pure thinking rose above this cleavage that had to become self-conscious, and progressed to the antithesis of the subjective and the objective. The true reconciliation or resolution of the antithesis is the insight that this antithesis, pushed to its absolute extreme, resolves itself, that, as Schelling says, in themselves the opposites indeed are identical,[503] although it is not only that they are identical in themselves but also that eternal life is just this eternal producing of the antitheses and the eternal positing of them in identity.

This then is the standpoint of the current age, and with it I now conclude the series of spiritual configurations.[504] I have tried to exhibit their necessary procession out of one another, ˉso that each philosophy necessarily presupposes the one preceding it.ˉ[505] Our standpoint is the cognition of spirit, the knowledge of the idea as spirit, as absolute spirit, which as absolute opposes itself to another spirit, to the finite spirit. To recognize that absolute spirit can be *for it* is this finite spirit's principle and vocation.

503. [Ed.] This is probably a reference to § 12 of Schelling's *Darstellung*: "The absolute identity is the only thing that is absolutely or *in itself*, and therefore everything is in itself only insofar as it is the absolute identity itself, and insofar as it is not the absolute identity itself, it is not in itself" (*Sämmtliche Werke* 4:119).

504. [Ed.] This closing reference to "the series of spiritual configurations [*die Reihe der geistigen Gestaltungen*]" echoes the words of the *Phenomenology* (p. 265 et passim), in the introduction to division BB. Spirit, where Hegel says that spirit must "by passing through a series of shapes [*Gestalten*] attain to a knowledge of itself."

505. *Thus Gr; Pn reads:* [for] the later [standpoint] is mediated, is the result of the preceding standpoint.

APPENDIXES

GLOSSARY

The glossary contains a selection of frequently used and/or technical terms, especially those posing problems in translation. General principles of translation are discussed in the Editorial Introduction. The glossary has served only as a guide, to which the translators have not felt obliged to adhere when context or English idiom have required different renderings. When more than one English word is given, the generally preferred terms are listed first, while terms following a semicolon may be suitable in less technical contexts. "Cf." indicates related but distinguished German terms, which generally are translated by different English equivalents. Adjectives are listed without endings. This glossary is indexed only on German terms; the indexes to each volume serve partially as English-German glossaries.

German	English
German	*English*
absolut	absolute
Absolute	the absolute
abzuleiten	deduce (cf. "herleiten")
allgemein	universal, general
Allgemeine	the universal
Andacht	devotion, worship
Anderssein	other-being, otherness
anerkennen	recognize, acknowledge (cf. "erkennen")
Anerkenntnis	recognition (cf. "Erkenntnis")

angemessen	suitable, appropriate, commensurate, fitting
anschauen	intuit, envisage
Anschauung	intuition, envisagement (cf. "Wahrnehmung")
an sich	in itself, implicit (cf. "in sich")
Ansich	in-itself, implicit being
Ansichsein	being-in-self
Anundfürsichsein	being-in-and-for-self
Arbeit	labor (cf. "Werk")
auffassen	comprehend, grasp (cf. "begreifen," "fassen")
Auffassung	comprehension
aufheben	sublate; transcend, supersede, annul
Aufhebung	sublation; transcendence, supersession, annulment
auflösen	resolve, dissolve
Auflösung	resolution, dissolution
Bedeutung	meaning, significance (cf. "Sinn")
Begierde	desire, appetite
beglaubigen	verify, attest, confirm
Beglaubigung	verification, attestation
begreifen	conceive
Begreifen	conception, conceiving
Begriff	concept
bei sich	with self, present to self, at home
Beisichsein	presence with (to) self, self-communion, at home with self
beobachten	observe
Beobachtung	observation (cf. "Betrachtung")
Beschäftigung	occupation, concern
besonder	particular
Besonderheit	particularity
bestehen	subsist, endure, consist
Bestehen	subsistence

bestimmen	determine, define, characterize, specify
bestimmt	determinate, definite
Bestimmtheit	determinateness, determinacy
Bestimmung	determination, definition; character(istic, -ization), destination, vocation, specification, attribute
betrachten	consider, treat, deal with
Betrachtung	consideration, treatment, examination, discussion (cf. "Beobachtung")
Bewusstsein	consciousness
beziehen	relate, connect, refer to
Beziehung	relation, connection, reference (cf. "Verhältnis," "Zusammenhang")
Bild	image
bildlich	imaginative, figurative
Bildung	culture, formation, cultivation
bloss	mere, simple, sheer
Boden	soil, ground, territory
darstellen	present, portray, set forth
Darstellung	presentation, portrayal, exposition (cf. "Vorstellung")
Dasein	determinate being, existence (cf. "Existenz," "Sein")
Denkbestimmung	category, thought-determination
denken	think
Denken	thinking, thought (cf. "Gedanke")
denkend	thinking, thoughtful, reflective
eigentümlich	characteristic (adj.), proper
Einbildung	imagination (cf. "Phantasie")
Eine (der, das)	the One, the one
einfach	simple
Einzelheit	singularity, single (or singular) individual (cf. "Individuum")
einzeln	single, singular
Einzelne	single individual (cf. "Individuum")

Element	element (cf. "Moment")
empfinden	(to) sense
Empfindung	sensibility, sensation, sentiment, sense (cf. "Gefühl")
entäussern	divest, externalize
Entäusserung	divestment, externalization
Entfremdung	estrangement
entgegensetzen	oppose
Entgegensetzung	opposition
Entzweiung	cleavage, rupture, severance; cleaving, split
erfassen	apprehend, grasp (cf. "auffassen," "fassen")
erheben	elevate, raise up
Erhebung	elevation, rising above
Erinnerung	recollection (cf. "Gedächtnis")
erkennen	know, cognize, recognize, learn, discern, know cognitively (cf. "anerkennen," "kennen," "wissen")
Erkenntnis	cognition; knowledge, cognitive knowledge (cf. "Anerkenntnis," "Kenntnis," "Wissen")
erscheinen	appear (cf. "scheinen")
Erscheinung	appearance, phenomenon (cf. "Manifestation")
Erziehung	education
Existenz	existence (cf. "Dasein"—when the distinction is important, the German is given in square brackets)
existieren	exist (cf. "sein")
fassen	grasp (cf. "auffassen," "begreifen," "erfassen")
Form	form (cf. "Gestalt")
für sich	for (by, of) itself, on its own account, explicit
Fürsich	for-itself

Fürsichsein	being-for-self, explicit being
Gebiet	field, realm
Gedächtnis	memory (cf. "Erinnerung")
Gedanke	thought, thoughts (cf. "Denken")
Gedankenbestimmung	category of thought
Gedankenbildung	ratiocination
Gefühl	feeling (cf. "Empfindung")
Gegensatz	antithesis, contrast; antipathy, opposition (cf. "Entgegensetzung")
Gegenstand	object, issue, topic
gegenständlich	objective
Gegenwart	presence, present
Geist	spirit (capitalized when clearly referring to God)
gelten	count, be valid
Gemeinde	community
Gemüt	mind, soul, heart (cf. "Gesinnung")
Genuss	enjoyment, pleasure, communion
geoffenbart	revealed (cf. "offenbar")
Geschichte	history; story (cf. "Historie")
geschichtlich	historical (often synonymous with "historisch")
Gesinnung	conviction, disposition
Gestalt	figure, shape
Gestaltung	configuration
Gewissen	conscience
Glaube	faith, belief
glauben	believe
Gleichgültigkeit	indifference, unconcern
Gleichheit	equivalence
Glück	fortune
Glückseligkeit	bliss, happiness
Grund	ground, reasons, basis
gründen	(to) base
Grundlage	foundation

herabsetzen	degrade, reduce
herleiten	derive (cf. "abzuleiten")
hinausgehen	overpass, go beyond
Historie	history (cf. "Geschichte")
historisch	historical (often synonymous with "geschichtlich")
ideal, ideell	ideal
Idee	idea
Individuum	individual (cf. "Einzelne")
in sich	within itself, into self, inward, internal, self-contained (cf. "an sich")
jenseitig	otherworldly
Jenseits	the beyond, the other world
kennen	know (cf. "wissen")
Kenntnis	information, acquaintance (cf. "Erkenntnis," "Wissen")
Kraft	force, strength, energy; power (in compounds) (cf. "Macht")
Kultus	cultus
Lehre	teaching, doctrine
lehren	teach
Leidenschaft	passion
Macht	power (cf. "Kraft")
Manifestation	manifestation (cf. "Erscheinung")
Mannigfaltigkeit	manifold(ness)
Mensch	human being (to avoid sexist connotations, frequently: one, we, they, people)
Menschheit	humanity
mit sich	with self; integral
Moment	moment (cf. "Element")
Moral	morals
Moralität	morality (cf. "Sittlichkeit")
nachdenken	(to) deliberate, meditate, ponder
Nachdenken	deliberation, meditation, meditative thought

Natur	nature
natürlich	natural
Natürliche	the natural
Natürlichkeit	natural life, natural state, naturalness; simplicity, unaffectedness
offenbar	revelatory, manifest (cf. "geoffenbart")
Offenbaren	revealing
Offenbarung	revelation
partikulär	private (cf. "besonder")
Perzeption	perception
perzipierend	percipient
Phantasie	phantasy; fanciful imagination (cf. "Einbildung")
Positive	the positive, positivity
Räsonnement	argumentation, reasoning
realisieren	realize (cf. "verwirklichen")
Realität	reality (cf. "Wirklichkeit")
Recht	right
reflektiv	reflective
Reflexion	reflection
rein	pure
Sache	matter, subject matter; thing, fact, case
Schein	semblance, show
scheinbar	seeming
scheinen	seem
schlechthinning	utter, simple (cf. "absolut")
schliessen	conclude, infer
Schluss	syllogism, conclusion
Schmerz	anguish, sorrow; pain
seiend (part. and adj.)	having being, subsisting
Seiende(s)	(God and cognates:) actual being (finite objects:) being, entity, subsisting being
sein (verb)	be: is (God and cognates); is, exists, occurs, etc. (finite objects)
Sein (noun)	being

setzen	posit
Setzen	positing
Sinn	sense, meaning (cf. "Bedeutung")
sinnlich	sensible, sentient, sensuous, sense (adj.)
Sinnlichkeit	sensuousness, sensible nature
sittlich	ethical
Sittlichkeit	ethics, ethical life, ethical realm (cf. "Moralität")
spekulativ	speculative
Spekulative	the speculative, speculation
Subjekt	subject
Subjektivität	subjectivity
substantiell	substantive, substantial
teilen	(to) divide
Teilung	division, separation (cf. "Urteil")
trennen	(to) separate, part (from)
Trennung	separation
Trieb	drive, impulse, instinct
Übergang	transition, passing over
übergehen	pass over
übergreifen	overreach
überhaupt	generally, on the whole; altogether, after all, in fact, as such, etc.
Überzeugung	conviction
umfassen	embrace, contain
unangemessen	incongruous, unsuitable, inadequate, incommensurate
Unglück	misery, unhappiness
unmittelbar	immediate (cf. "unvermittelt")
Unmittelbarkeit	immediacy
unterscheiden (verb)	distinguish, differentiate
Unterscheidung	differentiation, distinction (cf. "Unterschied")
Unterschied	distinction (cf. "Unterscheidung")

unterschieden (past part. and adj.)	distinguished, differentiated (part.); distinct, different (adj., cf. "verschieden")
unvermittelt	unmediated (cf. "unmittelbar")
Urteil	judgment, primal division (cf. "Teilung")
urteilen	(to) judge, divide
Vereinzelung	singularization
Verhalten	attitude, comportment, behavior
sich verhalten	comport oneself, relate oneself, function
Verhältnis	relationship, condition (cf. "Beziehung," "Zusammenhang")
Verhältnisse (pl.)	conditions, circumstances, state of affairs
vermitteln	mediate
Vermittlung	mediation
Vernunft	reason
vernünftig	rational
verschieden (adj.)	different, distinct, diverse (cf. "unterschieden")
Verschiedenheit	difference, diversity
versöhnen	reconcile
Versöhnung	reconciliation
Verstand	understanding
verwirklichen	actualize (cf. "realisieren")
Verwirklichung	actualization (cf. "Wirklichkeit")
vollendet	consummate; perfect, complete, final
Vollendung	consummation
vorhanden	present, at hand, extant
vorhanden sein	be present, be at hand, exist (cf. "sein")
vorstellen	represent; imagine
vorstellend	representational, representative
Vorstellung	representation; image, imagination, view
wahr	true
Wahre	the true
wahrhaft(ig)	true, genuine, authentic, truthful
Wahrheit	truth

Wahrnehmung	(sense) perception (cf. "Anschauung")
Werk	work (cf. "Arbeit")
Wesen	essence; being
Widerspruch	contradiction
Willkür	caprice, arbitrariness; free choice, free will
wirklich	actual
Wirklichkeit	actuality (cf. "Realität")
wissen	know (cf. "kennen," "erkennen")
Wissen	knowledge, knowing (cf. "Erkenntnis," "Kenntnis")
Wissenschaft	science, scientific knowledge
Zeugnis	witness, testimony
Zufall	chance
Zufälligkeit	contingency
Zusammenhang	connection, connectedness, nexus, coherence, correlation (cf. "Beziehung," "Verhältnis")
Zweck	purpose; end, goal, aim
zweckmässig	purposeful, expedient
Zweckmässigkeit	purposiveness, expediency

BIBLIOGRAPHY OF HEGEL'S SOURCES
FOR MEDIEVAL AND MODERN PHILOSOPHY

This bibliography includes all of the sources to which Hegel explicitly makes reference in this volume of the *Lectures on the History of Philosophy* or which can be inferred with reasonable certainty from his formulations. Works cited in the footnotes as evidence for ideas contained in the lectures, but which cannot be established as sources upon which Hegel himself drew, are not included in the bibliography.

In the footnotes, works are frequently cited in abbreviated form, without full bibliographical information. In those few cases where a short title may not be immediately recognizable from this bibliography, it is so designated in parentheses at the end of the entry. Frequently cited works by Hegel are listed at the beginning of this volume.

The bibliography does not list specific works of many of the authors—e.g., individual dialogues of Plato—but rather editions or collections with which Hegel is likely to have been familiar. In the footnotes, classical works are cited in the abbreviated form customary today (as in *The Oxford Classical Dictionary*), followed by book, chapter, and section references, but without indicating the editions that Hegel himself used or modern editions. Works with both Greek and Latin titles are cited only with the Latin title.

The sources given in this bibliography fall into four groups:

— Works listed in the Auction Catalogue of Hegel's library are designated by an asterisk (*).
— Works to which Hegel refers in these lectures or elsewhere, and of which he almost certainly made use, are designated by a dagger (†).

- Works probably used by Hegel, but for which there are no explicit references, are listed without a sign.
- Modern editions or English translations to which reference is made in the footnotes are indented following the original entries. Otherwise modern editions are not included.

Anselm of Canterbury. *Opera*. 2d ed. Paris, 1721.
* Aristotle. *Opera quaecunque hactenus extiterunt omnia*. Edited by Desiderius Erasmus. 2 vols. in 1. Basel, 1550. (Hegel owned the edition of 1531.)
* ———. *Physik*. Translated and edited by C. H. Weisse. Leipzig, 1829.
* Bacon, Francis. *Opera omnia, quae extant: Philosophica, moralia, politica, historica* . . . With a biography of the author. Frankfurt am Main, 1665.
———. *The Works of Francis Bacon*. Edited by James Spedding, Robert Leslie Ellis, and Douglas Denon Heath. 7 vols. London, 1857–1874.
* Baumgarten, Alexander Gottlieb. *Metaphysik*. 2d ed. Halle, 1783.
———. *Metaphysica*. 7th ed. Halle, 1779.
Bayle, Pierre. *Dictionaire historique et critique*. 3d ed. Revised, corrected, and enlarged by the author. 4 vols. Rotterdam, 1720.
———. *Œuvres diverses*. 4 vols. The Hague, 1725–1727.
Beattie, James. *An Essay on the Nature and Immutability of Truth; in Opposition to Sophistry and Scepticism*. Edinburgh, 1770.
———. *Versuch über die Natur und Unveränderlichkeit der Wahrheit; im Gegensätze der Klügeley und der Zweifelsucht*. Translated by Andreas Christoph Rüdinger. Copenhagen and Leipzig, 1772.
* Boehme, Jacob. *Theosophia revelata; Das ist, Alle göttliche Schriften des gottseligen und hocherleuchteten deutschen Theosophi*. Edited by Johann Otto Glüsing. [Hamburg,] 1715.

————. *Sämtliche Schriften*. Edited by Will-Erich Peuckert. 11 vols. Stuttgart, 1955–1961. (Facsimile reprint of *Theosophia revelata,* edited by Johann Wilhelm Ueberfeld, 10 vols., Amsterdam, 1730, which is an improved version of the 1715 edition, which Hegel owned.)

* Brucker, Jacob. *Historia critica philosophiae.* 4 vols. Leipzig, 1742–1744. (Hegel owned the 1756 edition.)

† Buhle, Johann Gottlieb. *Geschichte der neuern Philosophie seit der Epoche der Wiederherstellung der Wissenschaften.* 6 vols. Göttingen, 1800–1804. (*Geschichte*)

† ————. *Lehrbuch der Geschichte der Philosophie und einer kritischen Literatur derselben.* 8 vols. Göttingen, 1796–1804. (*Lehrbuch*)

Cardano, Girolamo. *Opera.* 10 vols. Lyons, 1663. (Vol. 4 contains: Arithmetic, Geometry, Music. Vol. 5 contains: Astronomy, Astrology, Oneirocritics.)

————. *The Book of My Life.* Translated by Jean Stoner. London, 1930.

Cicero. *Opera.* 5 vols. Leipzig, 1737.

————. *Opera omnia.* From the edition of Jacob Gronovius, with the addition of various selections from Pearce, Graeve, and Davis, together with the arguments of individual works and with a historical index of events and a philological-critical index of terms. Edited by J. Augustus Ernesti. Leipzig, 1737.

Descartes, René. *Œuvres de Descartes.* 11 vols. Edited by Victor Cousin. Paris, 1824–1826.

————. *Œuvres de Descartes.* Rev. ed. Edited by Charles Adam and Paul Tannery. 13 vols. Paris, 1964–1972. (*Œuvres*)

————. *The Philosophical Writings of Descartes.* Translated by John Cottingham, Robert Stoothoff, and Dugald Murdoch. 2 vols. Cambridge, 1985. (*Writings*)

————. *Meditationes de prima philosophia, in quibus Dei existentia, et animae humanae a corpore distinctio, demonstrantur: His adjunctae sunt variae objectiones doctorum virorum in istas de Deo et anima demonstrationes; cum responsionibus auctoris.* Latest ed., including additions and emendations. Amsterdam, 1663.

* ———. *Principia philosophiae.* New ed., carefully reviewed and corrected. Amsterdam, 1656.

Destutt de Tracy, Antoine Louis Claude. *Elémens d'idéologie. Première partie: Idéologie proprement dite.* Paris, 1817.

Ferguson, Adam. *Grundsätze der Moralphilosophie.* Translated from the English by Christian Garve. Leipzig, 1772.

Fichte, Johann Gottlieb. *Die Anweisung zum seligen Leben, oder auch die Religionslehre: In Vorlesungen gehalten zu Berlin, im Jahre 1806.* Berlin, 1806.

* ———. *Grundlage der gesammten Wissenschaftslehre als Handschrift für seine Zuhörer.* Leipzig, 1794. (*Wissenschaftslehre*)

———. *Science of Knowledge.* Translated by Peter Heath and John Lachs. New York, 1970.

* ———. *Grundlage des Naturrechts nach Principien der Wissenschaftslehre.* Jena and Leipzig, 1796.

———. *Ueber das Wesen des Gelehrten und seine Erscheinungen im Gebiete der Freiheit: In öffentlichen Vorlesungen, gehalten zu Erlangen, im Sommerhalbjahre 1805.* Berlin, 1806.

———. *Ueber den Begriff der Wissenschaftslehre oder der sogenannten Philosophie, als Einladungsschrift zu seinen Vorlesungen über diese Wissenschaft.* Weimar, 1794.

———. *Ausgewählte Werke in sechs Bänden.* Edited by Fritz Medicus. Leipzig, 1910.

———. *Fichte's Popular Works.* Translated by William Smith. London, 1873.

———. *Gesamtausgabe der Bayerischen Akademie der Wissenschaften.* Edited by Reinhard Lauth and Hans Jacob. Division 1. Stuttgart–Bad Cannstatt, 1964 ff.

† Fries, Jakob Friedrich. *System der Logik: Ein Handbuch für Lehrer und zum Selbstgebrauch.* Heidelberg, 1811.

* Gassendi, Pierre. *De vita et moribus Epicuri libri octo.* Revised edition, expanded and corrected. The Hague, 1656. (Hegel owned the 1654 edition.)

———. *Miscellanea*. Vol. 5. Lyons, 1658.

Gottsched, Johann Christoph. *Historische Lobschrift des weiland hoch- und wohlgebohrnen Herrn Christians, des Heiligen Römischen Reiches Freyherrn von Wolf*... Halle, 1755.

* Grotius, Hugo. *De jure belli ac pacis libri tres, in quibus jus naturae et gentium, item juris publici praecipua explicantur*. With the author's annotations and his Dissertation on the Freedom of the Seas. And with J. F. Gronovius's examination of the whole work on The Law of War and Peace. From the second edition of Johann Barbeyracius. 2 vols. Leipzig, 1758.

———. *The Law of War and Peace*. Translated by Francis W. Kelsey et al. Indianapolis and New York, 1925.

† Hjort, Peder. *Johann Scotus Erigena; oder, Von dem Ursprung einer christlichen Philosophie und ihrem heiligen Beruf*. Copenhagen, 1823.

* Hobbes, Thomas. *Elementorum philosophiae sectio prima: De corpore*. London, 1655.

* ———. *Elementorum philosophiae sectio tertia: De cive*. Amsterdam, 1696.

———. *De cive*. Edited by Howard Warrender. Oxford, 1983.

———. *The English Works of Thomas Hobbes*. Edited by Sir William Molesworth. 11 vols. London, 1839–1845.

* d'Holbach, Paul Henri Thiry [Mirabaud, pseud.]. *Système de la nature ou des loix du monde physique et du monde moral*. New edition, to which have been added several pieces by the best writers on the same topics. 2d ed. 2 vols. London, 1771.

———. *The System of Nature*. Translated by Samuel Wilkinson. 3 vols. London, 1820–1821.

Hume, David. *Essays and Treatises on Several Subjects*. 4 vols. Edinburgh and London, 1753.

————. *An Inquiry concerning Human Understanding.* Edited, with an introduction, by Charles W. Hendel. Indianapolis, 1955.

————. *Hume's Ethical Writings.* Edited by Alasdair MacIntyre. New York, 1965.

————. *The Natural History of Religion.* Edited by A. Wayne Colver. Oxford, 1976. (Bound with: *Dialogues concerning Natural Religion.* Edited by J. V. Price.)

† Jacobi, Friedrich Heinrich. *David Hume über den Glauben; oder, Idealismus und Realismus: Ein Gespräch.* Breslau, 1787.

* ————. *Jacobi an Fichte.* Hamburg, 1799.

† ————. *Ueber die Lehre des Spinoza in Briefen an den Herrn Moses Mendelssohn.* New, enlarged ed. Breslau, 1789.

————. *Die Hauptschriften zum Pantheismusstreit zwischen Jacobi und Mendelssohn.* Edited, with historical-critical introduction, by Heinrich Scholz. Berlin, 1916.

* ————. *Von den göttlichen Dingen und ihrer Offenbarung.* Leipzig, 1811.

————. *Werke.* Edited by Friedrich Roth. 6 vols. Leipzig, 1812–1825. (Vols. 1–3 were in Hegel's library.)

* Kant, Immanuel. *Critik der practischen Vernunft.* Riga, 1788.

————. *Critique of Practical Reason.* Translated by Lewis White Beck. Indianapolis, 1956.

† ————. *Critik der reinen Vernunft.* 2d ed. Riga, 1787.

————. *Critique of Pure Reason.* Translated by Norman Kemp Smith, from R. Schmidt's collation of the first (A) and second (B) editions. London, 1929, 1933.

* ————. *Critik der Urtheilskraft.* Berlin and Libau, 1790.

————. *Critique of Judgement.* Translated by J. H. Bernard. New York, 1951.

* ————. *Metaphysische Anfangsgründe der Naturwissenschaft.* Riga, 1786.

————. *Metaphysical Foundations of Natural Science.* Translated by James Ellington. Indianapolis, 1970.

* ————. *Metaphysische Anfangsgründe der Rechtslehre.* Königsberg, 1797.

* ———. *Zum ewigen Frieden: Ein philosophischer Entwurf.* Königsberg, 1795.

———. *Perpetual Peace.* Translated by Lewis White Beck. In *Kant: On History.* Indianapolis, 1957, 1963.

———. *Gesammelte Schriften.* Edited by the Royal Prussian Academy of Sciences. Berlin, 1902 ff. (*Schriften*)

———. *Prolegomena to Any Future Metaphysics.* Translated by Paul Carus. La Salle, 1902.

* Krug, Wilhelm Traugott. *Entwurf eines neuen Organon's der Philosophie; oder, Versuch über die Prinzipien der philosophischen Erkenntnis.* Meissen and Lübben, 1801.

* Leibniz, Gottfried Wilhelm. *Œuvres philosophiques latines et françoises.* From manuscripts preserved in the Royal Library of Hanover. Edited by Rudolf Eric Raspe, with a preface by Mr. Kaestner. Amsterdam and Leipzig, 1765.

† ———. *Opera omnia.* Edited by Louis Dutens. For the first time collected, classified, and furnished with prefaces and indexes. 6 vols. Geneva, 1768.

———. *Die philosophischen Schriften.* Edited by C. J. Gerhardt. 7 vols. Berlin, 1875–1890.

———. *Philosophical Papers and Letters.* Edited by Leroy E. Loemker. 2d ed. Dordrecht and Boston, 1969.

———. *Sämtliche Schriften und Briefe.* Edited by the Prussian Academy of Sciences. 40 vols. Darmstadt and Leipzig, 1923–1969.

———. *Werke.* First Series: *Historisch-politische und staatswissenschaftliche Schriften.* Edited by Onno Klopp. 11 vols. Hanover, 1864–1884.

———. *Commercii epistolici Leibnitiani, ad omne genus eruditionis, praesertim vero ad illustrandum integri propemodum seculi historiam literariam apprime facientis, per partes publicandi tomus prodromus, qui totus est Boineburgicus.* Edited by J. Daniel Gruber. Hanover, 1745.

———. *Commercii epistolici Leibnitiani typis nondum vulgati selecta speciminia.* Edited, with notes and illustrations, by Johann Georg Feder. Hanover, 1805.

* ———. *Essais de théodicée sur la bonté de Dieu, la liberté l'homme, et l'origine du mal*. New ed., augmented by a history of the life and works of the author, by L. de Neufville. Amsterdam, 1734.

———. *Theodicy*. Abridgment of the E. M. Huggard translation, edited by Diogenes Allen. Indianapolis, 1966.

———. *New Essays on Human Understanding*. Translated and edited by Peter Remnant and Jonathan Bennett. Cambridge, 1981.

Lessing, Gotthold Ephraim. *Axiomata, wenn es deren in dergleichen Dingen gibt: Wider den Herrn Pastor Goeze, in Hamburg*. Braunschweig, 1778.

———. *Eine Duplik*. Braunschweig, 1778.

———. *Die Erziehung des Menschengeschlechts*. Edited by Lessing. Berlin, 1780.

———. *The Education of the Human Race*. Translated by F. W. Robertson, revised by Henry Chadwick. In *Lessing's Theological Writings*, edited by Chadwick. London, 1956.

———. *Zur Geschichte und Litteratur: Aus den Schätzen der Herzoglichen Bibliothek zu Wolfenbüttel*. Second contribution. Braunschweig, 1773. Contains: *Des Andreas Wissowatius Einwürfe wider die Dreyeinigkeit*.

———. *Sämtliche Schriften*. Edited by K. Lachmann and F. Muncker. 3d ed. 23 vols. Leipzig, 1886–1924.

* Locke, John. *An Essay concerning Human Understanding*. In four books. 8th ed. 2 vols. London, 1721.

———. *An Essay concerning Human Understanding*. Edited, with introduction, critical apparatus, and glossary, by Peter H. Nidditch. Oxford, 1975.

———. *The Works*. A new edition, corrected. 10 vols. London, 1823.

* Maimon, Solomon. *Lebensgeschichte*. Edited by Karl Philipp Moritz. 2 vols. Berlin, 1792.

* Maimonides, Moses. *Liber* מורה נבוכים, *Doctor perplexorum*. Contains a key to the proper understanding of doubtful and more obscure Scripture passages. . . . Now, for setting forth more abundantly the understanding of the Hebrew language, and for its use and grandeur in plainly declaring Christian teaching, clearly and faithfully rendered into Latin. Translated by Johannes Buxtorf from the Hebrew version of Ibn Tibbon. 4 vols. Basel, 1629.

* Malebranche, Nicolas. *De la recherche de la vérité.* 2 vols. 4th ed. Amsterdam, 1688.

————. *The Search after Truth.* Translated (from the 6th ed.) by Thomas M. Lennon and Paul J. Olscamp. Columbus, 1980. Bound with *Elucidations of The Search after Truth,* translated by Lennon.

————. *Œuvres complètes.* Edited by André Robinet. 20 vols. Paris, 1958–1965.

* Mendelssohn, Moses. *Morgenstunden; oder, Vorlesungen über das Daseyn Gottes.* Berlin, 1786.

† *The Morning Chronicle,* 14 February 1825.

Mosheim, Johann Lorenz. *Institutionum historiae ecclesiasticae antiquae et recentioris.* Drawn from the sources themselves, emended conspicuously, enriched with many appendixes, and illustrated with various observations. 4 vols. Helmstedt, 1755.

† Neander, August. *Genetische Entwickelung der vornehmsten gnostischen Systeme.* Berlin, 1818.

* Newton, Isaac. *Philosophiae naturalis principia mathematica.* Final edition, enlarged and emended. Amsterdam, 1714.

————. *Sir Isaac Newton's Mathematical Principles.* Translation by Andrew Motte, revised by Florian Cajori. Berkeley, 1946.

* ————. *Optice; sive, De reflexionibus, refractionibus, inflexionibus, et coloribus lucis libri tres.* Latin translation by Samuel Clarke. 2d ed., enlarged. London, 1719.

Oken, Lorenz. *Lehrbuch der Naturphilosophie.* 3 vols. Jena, 1809–1811.

* Plato. *Opera quae extant omnia.* Latin translation by Joannes Serranus [Jean de Serres]. Edited by Henricus Stephanus [Henri Estienne]. 3 vols. [Geneva,] 1578.

———. *Opera omnia quae extant.* Translated and edited, with commentaries, by Marsilio Ficino. Lyons, 1590.

Plotinus. *Opera, quae extant omnia.* Translated into Latin by Marsilio Ficino from the most ancient codices. Basel, 1615. (The earlier editions of Ficino—Florence, 1492 and Perna–Basel, 1580—were not accessible to the editors.)

* Proclus. *In Platonis theologiam libri sex.* Edited by Aemilius Portus, with a short life of Proclus by Marinus Neapolitanus. Hamburg and Frankfurt am Main, 1618.

Pufendorf, Samuel. *De jure naturae et gentium libri octo.* Lund, 1672.

———. *On the Law of Nature and Nations.* Translated by C. H. Oldfather and W. A. Oldfather. Oxford and London, 1934.

* ———. *De officio hominis et civis juxta legem naturalem libri duo.* Lund, 1673. (There is no confirmation of the listing in the catalog of Hegel's library, of the 1739 Basel edition.)

———. *The Two Books on the Duty of Man and Citizen according to the Natural Law.* Translated by Frank Gardner Moore. New York and London, 1927.

† *The Quarterly Review* (London), April and July 1817.

Rixner, Thaddä Anselm. *Handbuch der Geschichte der Philosophie zum Gebrauche seiner Vorlesungen.* 3 vols. Sulzbach, 1822–1823.

Rousseau, Jean-Jacques. *Aemil; oder, Von der Erziehung.* Translated from the French, with notes. 4 parts. Berlin, Frankfurt am Main, and Leipzig, 1762.

———. *Emile.* Translated by Barbara Foxley. London, 1911.

———. *Œuvres complètes.* Edited by Bernard Gagnebin and Marcel Raymond. 4 vols. Paris, 1959–1969.

Schelling, Friedrich Wilhelm Joseph. "Darstellung meines Systems der Philosophie." *Zeitschrift für spekulative Physik* (Jena and Leipzig), edited by Schelling, vol. 2, no. 2 (1801).

* ———. *Denkmal der Schrift von den göttlichen Dingen etc. des Herrn Friedrich Heinrich Jacobi und der ihm in derselben*

gemachten Beschuldigung eines absichtlich täuschenden, Lüge redenden Atheismus. Tübingen, 1812.

———. *Erster Entwurf eines Systems der Naturphilosophie: Zum Behuf seiner Vorlesungen.* Jena and Leipzig, 1799.

* ———. "Fernere Darstellungen aus dem System der Philosophie." *Neue Zeitschrift für spekulative Physik* (Tübingen), edited by Schelling, vol. 1, no. 1 (1802).

———. *Philosophische Schriften.* Vol. 1. Landshut, 1809. Contains (pp. 397–511): "Philosophische Untersuchungen über das Wesen der menschlichen Freiheit und die damit zusammenhängenden Gegenstände."

———. *Of Human Freedom.* Translated by James Gutmann. Chicago, 1936.

* ———. *System des transscendentalen Idealismus.* Stuttgart, 1800.

———. *System of Transcendental Idealism (1800).* Translated by Peter Heath. Introduction by Michael Vater. Charlottesville, 1978.

———. *Ueber die Möglichkeit einer Form der Philosophie überhaupt.* Tübingen, 1795.

* ———. *Vom Ich als Princip der Philosophie; oder, Über das Unbedingte im menschlichen Wissen.* Tübingen, 1795.

———. *Schelling: The Unconditional in Human Knowledge: Four Early Essays (1794–1796).* Translated by Fritz Marti. Lewisburg, 1980.

———. *Vorlesungen über die Methode des academischen Studium.* Tübingen, 1803.

———. *On University Studies.* Translated by E. S. Morgan. Edited by Norbert Guterman. Athens, Ohio, 1966.

———. *Historisch-kritische Ausgabe.* First Series: *Werke.* Sponsored by the Schelling-Kommission of the Bavarian Academy of Sciences. Edited by Hans Michael Baumgartner, Wilhelm G. Jacobs, Hermann Krings, and Hermann Zeltner. Stuttgart–Bad Cannstatt, 1976 ff.

———. *Sämmtliche Werke.* Edited by K. F. A. Schelling. Division 1, 10 vols. Division 2, 4 vols. Stuttgart and Augsburg, 1856–1861. (Reissued in 6 vols., 6 supplementary vols., and 1 Nachlassband. Edited by Manfred Schröter. Munich, 1927–1959.)

———. *Briefe und Dokumente*. Edited by Horst Fuhrmans. Vols. 1–3. Bonn, 1962–1975.

† Schleiermacher, Friedrich Daniel Ernst. *Der christliche Glaube nach den Grundsätzen der evangelischen Kirche im Zusammenhange dargestellt*. 2 vols. Berlin, 1821–1822. (*Glaubenslehre*)

† ———. *Über die Religion: Reden an die Gebildeten unter ihren Verächtern*. Berlin, 1799.

* Smith, Adam. *An Inquiry into the Nature and Causes of the Wealth of Nations*. 4 vols. Basel, 1791.

* Spinoza, Benedict. *Opera quae supersunt omnia*. New ed. Edited by H. E. G. Paulus, with a life of the author and some notes on the history of the writings. 2 vols. Jena, 1802–1803.

———. *Opera*. Commissioned by the Heidelberg Academy of Sciences. Edited by Carl Gebhardt. 4 vols. Heidelberg, 1926.

———. *Chief Works*. Translated by R. H. M. Elwes. 2 vols. London, 1883.

———. *The Collected Works of Spinoza*. Translated by Edwin Curley. Vol. 1. Princeton, 1985.

* ———. *Adnotationes ad Tractatum theologico-politicum*. Edited from the author's original manuscript by Christoph Theophil de Murr, with a preface and notes on Spinoza's writings. The Hague, 1802.

* Stanley, Thomas. *Historia philosophiae, vitas opiniones, resqve gestas et dicta philosophorvm sectae cvivsis complexa . . .* From English talks translated into Latin, corrected and augmented throughout by various discussions and observations, and with a life of the author. Leipzig, 1711.

* Steuart, John. *Untersuchung der Grundsätze der Staats-Wirthschaft; oder, Versuch über die Wissenschaft der innerlichen Politik in freyen Staaten*. 2 vols. Translated from English. Hamburg, 1769–1770.

† Tennemann, Wilhelm Gottlieb. *Geschichte der Philosophie*. 11 vols. Leipzig, 1798–1819. (*Geschichte*)

———. *Grundriss der Geschichte der Philosophie für den akademischen Unterricht*. 4th ed., enlarged and improved (= 2d ed. prepared by Amadeus Wendt). Leipzig, 1825.

* Tiedemann, Dieterich. *Geist der spekulativen Philosophie*. 6 vols. Marburg, 1791–1797. (Hegel owned vols. 1–3.)

† Wagner, Johann Jakob, ed. *Journal für Wissenschaft und Kunst*. Vol. 1. Leipzig, 1805.

Wolff, Christian. *Der Anfangs-Gründe aller mathematischen Wissenschaften anderer Theil* . . . New, improved and enlarged edition. Halle, 1757.

* ———. *Elementa matheseos universae*. 5 vols. Halle, 1713–1741. (Hegel owned the edition of 1730–1738.)

* ———. *Psychologia rationalis methodo scientifica pertractata*. New, corrected edition. Frankfurt am Main and Leipzig, 1740.

———. *Theologia naturalis methodo scientifica pertractata. Pars prior, integrum systema complectens qua existentia et attributa Dei a posteriori demonstrantur*. New, corrected ed. Frankfurt am Main and Leipzig, 1739. *Pars posterior, qua existentia et attributa Dei ex notione entis perfectissimi et natura animae demonstrantur*. Second, corrected ed. Frankfurt am Main and Leipzig, 1741.

———. *Vernünfftige Gedancken von Gott, der Welt und der Seele des Menschen, auch allen Dingen überhaupt*. New, enlarged ed. Halle, 1751.

———. *Gesammelte Werke*. Newly edited by Jean Ecole, J. E. Hofmann, M. Thomann, H. W. Arndt, and Ch. A. Corr. 79 vols. Hildesheim and New York, 1962 ff.

INDEX

BIBLICAL REFERENCES

Genesis	1:27	19n
	2:9, 17	24n
	3:4–5, 22	25n
2 Kings	9:30	114n
Matthew	24:19–20	199n
Mark	13:17–18	199n
Luke	22:69	32n
John	1:14, 18	20n
	3:16, 18	20n
	4:24	97n
	14:21	99n
	15:10	99n
	16:7–14	31n
	18:36	27n
Acts	2	31n
	2:4	31n
	2:32–36	32n
	7:55	32n
	17:23	258n
Romans	8:3–4	19n
	8:7	19n
2 Corinthians	3:6	29n
	5:19	18n
1 John	4:9	20n

INDEX

NAMES AND SUBJECTS

Terms common to Hegel's philosophical and religious vocabulary occur with great frequency in the text and are indexed on a selective basis. The German for key concepts is given in parentheses.

Aaron, 86
Abelard, Peter, 53, 56–57, 62
Abimelech, 86
Absolute (*Absolute*), 132n, 258, 260, 266–267, 271
Abstract, abstraction (*Abstrakt, Abstraktion*): as empty, 81, 111, 126, 255; as formless, 80; God as, 254; as idea, 161, 177; as not true, 17; as principle, 257; as thinking, 17, 50, 101, 107; unity of spirit, 154
Academy of sciences: Bavarian (Munich), 240n, 241, 259n; Berlin (Royal Prussian), 187, 199, 200n; Bologna, 200n; French, 199–200n; London (Royal Society), 187, 199; St. Petersburg, 199; Stockholm, 199
Accident (*Akzidenz*), 37–39, 88n
Achilles, 86
Achillini, Alexander, 72n
Acosmism, 79n, 162–163
Activity (*Tätigkeit*): monad, 196–197; pure activity of self, 230–231, 234
Actuality (*Wirklichkeit*), 80–81,

143–144, 153, 154, 161–163; idea implanted in, 27
Adam, 14, 24–26, 67, 92–93, 207n
Aesthetic (*Aesthetik*), 223
Affections (*Affektionen*), 159–161; as human slavery, 164
Agrippa of Nettesheim, 85n
Ahab, 114
Alain de Lille, 30n, 58n
Albert the Great, 58n, 60–62, 65n, 71n
Alchemy, 83n, 114, 115n, 119, 186
Alexander of Alexandria, 34n
Alexander of Aphrodisias, 72n
Alexandrian philosophy, 52, 99, 107, 133n, 190n
All (*Alles*), 82, 88. *See also* Totality
Allah, 207n
Alstedt, Johann Heinrich, 85n
Amaury of Bène, 60n
Anaxagoras, 107n
Angels, 58, 67, 124n, 128
Anselm of Canterbury, 13, 53–56, 142–143
Antinomies, 238

Antithesis (*Gegensatz*), 120, 129–131, 203, 234, 250, 262, 267, 271–272; in Christianity, 33, 44, 46–47; in nature, 81–82; of mediate and immediate, 256–257; spiritual, 40–42, 51, 161; of thinking and being, 54–56, 107, 133–134; of universal and singular, 63–64. *See also* Opposition
Apollo, 88
Apperception (*Apperzeption*), 221n, 224
Aquinas, Thomas, 58, 61, 63, 65n, 71n, 72n, 190n
Arabs, 83; philosophy of, 35–39, 60n
Archimedes, 147n
Argumentation (*Rässonement*), 112, 178, 207, 209, 211
Aristotelian(ism), 37n, 52, 59, 60, 71n, 72, 73n, 77, 80, 81, 84, 115n, 133n, 190, 247. *See also* Aristotle
Aristotle, 35, 36, 37n, 58, 60, 61, 62, 70n, 71n, 72n, 81, 85, 86n, 115n, 210n, 225n, 234, 248n. *See also* Aristotelian
Arius, 34; Arians, 34–35
Art (*Kunst*), 70, 91, 239, 248, 260–261, 265–266
Astrology, 73n, 75, 114n, 129
Athanasius, 34n
Atheism, 76n, 91, 162–163, 165, 199, 207
Atomism, 37–38, 82n, 189, 190, 208n
Attributes (of substance), 156, 158–159
Augustine, 20n, 24n, 25n, 49n, 52, 57, 167n, 169, 179n
Authority, religious, 206–207, 257
Autonomy (*Selbständigkeit*), 95, 238
Averroes. *See* Ibn Rushd
Averroism, 70n, 72, 84n, 91. *See also* Double truth

Avicenna. *See* Ibn Sina

Baader, Franz von, 118n
Bacon, Francis, 9, 59n, 93n, 103n, 107n, 108, 109, 110–117, 134n, 213
Baillet, Adrien, 135n, 136n
Bamberger Zeitung, 86n
Baptism, 100
Barbarism, 41–46, 51, 69, 95, 120–121, 130
Barlaam, 71
Basilides, 34n
Basil of Caesarea, 20n
Baumeister, Freidrich Christian, 198n
Baumgarten, Alexander Gottlieb, 223n, 239n
Bayerland, Abraham Wilhelmson von, 120n
Bayle, Pierre, 70n, 72n, 188, 193
Beattie, James, 211
Being (*Sein*), 231, 239; actual, 132n, 143; composite, 189–190; determination of, 139; meaning of term, 141. *See also* Existence
Bering, Johann, 56n
Bessarion, Basilius Cardinal, 72
Bible, 28, 114; historical criticism of, 152n; inspiration of, 152; interpretation of, 29–31, 101–102; New Testament, 28, 101; Old Testament, 179
Bierling, Friedrich Wilhelm, 195n
Bilfinger, Georg Bernhard, 202n
Blyenbergh, Willem van, 160n, 164n
Bodin, Jean, 93n
Body (*Körper*), 146–148, 167, 169, 176, 193, 196. *See also* Corporeality; Matter
Boehme, Jacob, 9, 20n, 102n, 103n, 107n, 108, 117–131, 134n, 204n
Boethius, 52
Boineburg, Johann Christian von, 186

Boineburg, Philipp Wilhelm von, 186
Bolingbroke, Lord, 208n
Bosses, Bartholomew des, 193n
Bossuet, Jacques-Bénigne, 66n
Boulainvilliers, Count Henri de, 151n
Bourget, Louis, 196n
Bouterwek, Friedrich, 234, 235n
Boyle, Robert, 147n
Brown, Robert F., x, 14
Brucker, Jacob, 17n, 39n, 52n, 56n, 57n, 58n, 59n, 60n, 61n, 62n, 63n, 67n, 72n, 73n, 74n, 75n, 76n, 78n, 85n, 90n, 91n, 111n, 135n, 136n, 185n
Bruno, Giordano, 76–90, 91, 94, 162, 195n
Brutus, 86n
Buhle, Johann Gottlieb, 36n, 37n, 60n, 71n, 72n, 73n, 74n, 75n, 76n, 77n, 78, 80n, 82n, 86n, 87n, 88n, 89n, 90n, 91n, 92n, 111n, 135n, 136n, 147n, 165n, 171n, 183n, 184n, 185n, 198n, 199n, 200n, 201n, 209n, 210n, 213n, 219n
Bulaeus (C. D. du Boulaye), 52n, 53n, 60n, 63n, 66n
Burke, Edmund, 210n
Buxtorf, Johannes, 37n, 39n
Byzantine world, 41, 71, 72

Cabala, 73–74
Caecina (Tetinnus), 62
Caesalpinus, Andreas, 72n
Caesar, Julius, 86n, 91–92
Calvin, John, 77
Campanella, Tommaso, 76, 86n
Canning, George, 184
Caprice (*Willkür*), 182, 244n
Cardano, Girolamo, 74–76, 91
Carl Ludwig (elector of the Palatine), 152
Cartesian(ism), 55n, 132n, 146n, 149n, 150, 151, 165, 170, 191, 197, 208n. See also *Cogito*

ergo sum; Descartes; Malebranche
Cassiodorus, 52n
Category (*Kategorie, Bestimmung*), 146, 172–173, 184, 190, 229–232, 234, 238, 243, 255, 262; categorial determination, 81, 217–218; of thought, 84–87; of understanding, 219, 225–227
Catherine I (tzarina of Russia), 200n
Causality (*Kausalität*), 79, 155–156, 172, 175, 176–177, 190, 214–215, 220–221, 227, 230, 247–248; *causa sui*, 155–156, 158; efficient cause, 79, 116–117, 194, 196n; final cause, 79–80, 116–117, 194, 196n. See also Purpose; Teleology
Certainty (*Gewissheit*), 243n; absolute certainty, 143; inner certainty, 95–96, 98, 242n, 251; self-certainty, 139–142, 150, 229
Charles the Bald (French emperor), 52
Charron, Pierre, 93
Chenu, M. D., 30n
Cherbury, Herbert of, 163n
Christianity, 83, 84n, 133, 257–258, 260; cultus of, 18, 46–47, 96; essential principle (idea) of, 17–22, 26–28, 65, 132n, 226; historical interpretation of, 21–22. See also Bible; Church; Councils; Doctrine; Jesus Christ; Trinity
Christina (queen of Sweden), 137, 178n
Chrysoloras, Manuel, 71
Church, Christian, 40, 44–48, 65–66, 68–69; Catholic church, 91–93, 99; Protestant Reformation, 28–31, 94–103
Church fathers, 20, 27–35, 40, 57–58
Cicero, 62, 74, 85–86, 112,

202n, 210
Clarke, Samuel, 191n, 209
Clergy, 47–48, 57, 69, 96, 119, 120n, 136–137, 151–153
Cogito ergo sum, 138–143, 147n, 150, 229
Cognition (Erkenntnis), 102, 107, 134, 150, 159, 167, 237–238, 241–243, 252–253, 257, 263; reflective, 53–54, 111–112; subjective, 144, 263; sub specie aeterni, 164–165; thoughtful, 26, 27. See also Knowing
Colerus, Johannes, 151n, 153n
Columbus, Christopher, 256
Common sense, 210–211
Concept (Begriff), 112–113, 123, 156, 242, 269; conceived through itself, 156n
Concrete (Konkret), 50, 246–250, 258, 262; concrete thought, 102
Concurrence, divine (concursus dei), 145–146
Condillac, Etienne Bonnot de, 212n
Congrégation de l'Oratoire, 165
Conscience (Gewissen), 48, 96, 98, 99
Consciousness (Bewusstsein), 172–173, 192–193, 221, 230–231, 259n; "artificial," 230; as certain of itself, 142–143; of God, 251–252; ordinary, 231, 234, 261–262; as spiritual, 21, 97–98; subjective, 27; theoretical, 234. See also Self-consciousness
Contradiction (Widerspruch), 195, 203, 238, 239, 250; absolute, 236; principle of, 194n, 245–246. See also Contrarium; Opposition
Contrarium, 123, 125–131; Yes and No, 129–131
Conviction (Ueberzeugung), 43, 96, 243n

Copernicus, Nicolaus, 180
Corporeality (Körperlichkeit), 80, 161, 164; Corpus, 124n, 125, 128. See also Body; Matter
Councils, church: Ferrara, 72n; Florence, 72n, 73n; Fifth Lateran, 72n; Nicaea, 34n; Rome, 72n; Vienna, 83n
Courçon, Robert de, 60n
Cousin, Victor, 137n, 149
Cramer, Johann Andreas, 66n
Creation: creatures, 108n, 146; by God, 37–38, 138, 190
Critical philosophy, 134, 218
Crusades, 46
Cudworth, Ralph, 209
Cusanus, Nicholas, 82n
Custom (Gewohnheit), 216, 217n

Dalai Lama, 31–32
Darkness, contrasted with light, 122–123, 130
David of Dinant, 60n
Deduction (Schliessen, Deduktion), 115, 137, 139–140, 179–180. See also Induction; Logic
Deism, 163n, 207–208
Delphi, 22n
Democritus, 73n, 76n
Descartes, René, 56, 108, 109n, 131, 132, 134, 135–151, 158, 165, 166, 172, 173, 174, 175n, 190, 191n, 197, 205n, 229, 272
Desire (Begierde), 130, 181, 196, 244
Destutt de Tracy, Antoine Louis Claude, 212n
Determination (Bestimmung), 89, 141, 143, 154, 157–158, 168–169, 190, 220, 228, 230, 234, 238, 239; determinate distinction, 123–124, 191–192; simple, 175, 177; universal, 172–175
Determinism, 199

Devil, 54, 67, 92–93, 120–121, 127, 153n. *See also* Lucifer
Dialectic (*Dialektik*), 19, 65, 188; of pure reason, 238
Distinction (*Unterscheidung*), 127–128; determinate, 191–192; kinds of, 146
Docetism, 34n
Doctrine, Christian system of, 27–35, 48, 53, 56–60, 65–68, 72n, 98–102
Dominicans, 58, 59, 61, 62, 74, 77
Double truth, doctrine of, 70–71, 92–93
Doubt, 137–139
Dreams, 138, 140–141
Duns Scotus, John, 58–59
Duty (*Pflicht*), 95, 245–246
Dyad, 192n

Eadmer, 53n, 54n
Eberhard, Johann August, 24n
Education (*Erziehung, Bildung*), 254–255; Christian education, 100; conformity to good, 25–26; personal cultivation, 111
Egyptians, 69, 206, 254
Elizabeth I (queen of England), 110
Empiricism (*Empirie*), 113, 134, 166–167, 171–178, 179, 185, 202, 218, 225; metaphysical, 178; reflective, 205. *See also* Experience, philosophy of (based on)
Energy (*Kraft*), 121–122, 124–125, 128. *See also* Force; Power
Enlightenment (*Aufklärung*), 24n, 43n, 117n, 163n, 206–208
Entelechy, 190, 193, 248n
Enthusiasm (*Schwärmerei*), 117–119
Epicurean(ism), 61–62, 73, 91n, 189n, 190. *See also* Epicurus
Epicurus, 62, 150n. *See also* Epicurean

Erasmus, 67n
Erigena, John Scotus, 52–53
Error, 138, 166
Eschenmayer, Adam Karl August, 268
Essence (*Wesen*), 155, 160, 260; eternal and infinite, 158; one single in God, 121, 123
Essex (earl of), 110
Ethics (*Ethik, Sittlichkeit*), 149–150, 215; ethical, 206. *See also* Morals
Eugene (prince of Savoy), 187, 188
Eve, 67, 92–93
Evil (*Böse*), 120, 130, 150n, 160–161, 188–189; in God, 127–128; as natural state, 19; as privation, 160; as sin, 24. *See also* Sin
Existence (*Existenz, Dasein*), 80–81, 88, 155, 176–177; of God, 54–56, 142–143; of I, 139–141; of idea, 113, 239. *See also* Being
Experience (*Erfahrung*), 138, 215–216, 220–221, 227, 234; philosophy of (based on), 109, 111–117, 133, 171–178, 213–217, 218. *See also* Empiricism
Extension (*Ausdehnung*), 146–147, 150n, 158, 166, 174, 193
Externality (*Aeusserlichkeit*), 65–67, 78, 148, 166; mutual, 177–178; in religion, 47–48; removal of, 96–103, 132, 257; in thinking, 48

Fabricius, J. L., 153n
Faith (*Glaube*), 47, 53, 243, 250–258; and reason, 72n, 91–93, 96–98, 188
al-Farabī, 37n
Feder, Johann Georg Heinrich, 186n, 219n
Feeling (*Gefühl*), 228; religious, 216, 252n, 254
Ferguson, Adam, 210

Ferrara, Ricardo, ix
Ferrari, Lodovico, 76n
Fichte, Johann Gottlieb, 9, 10, 43n, 108, 135, 139, 217, 229–236, 241, 246, 259, 261, 262n, 265; Fichtean philosophy, 259, 261
Ficino, Marsilio, 72–73
Finitude (*Endlichkeit*), 145–146, 158; finite, 156, 163, 173, 237; finite spirit, 272; finite things, 146–147
Force (*Kraft*), 80–81, 122n. *See also* Energy
Forge, Louis de la, 167n
Form, 79–80, 82, 115–116, 159, 248n; substantial, 190
Franciscans, 58, 62–63
Francke, August Hermann, 199
Frankenberg, Abraham von, 118n, 120n
Frederick I (king of Prussia), 187
Frederick II (Holy Roman emperor), 60
Frederick II (king of Prussia), 200
Frederick III (Holy Roman emperor), 73
Frederick V (elector of the Palatine), 136
Frederick William (elector of Brandenburg), 171n
Frederick William I (king of Prussia), 199, 200
Freedom (*Freiheit*), 69–70, 161, 244–246, 249–250; definition of, 102; Germanic, 63; of individual subject, 18, 26, 69–70, 95–98, 150n, 153, 160–161; principle of Christian freedom, 96–98; of spirit, 18, 69–70, 95–98, 164, 257, 268; of thinking, 139. *See also* Will
French Revolution, 42
Fries, Jakob Friedrich, 234, 235n, 251, 252n

Galen, 117n
Galilei, Galileo, 147n, 180

Gans, Eduard, 114n
Garniron, Pierre, x
Garve, Christian, 209–210, 218n
Gassendi, Pierre, 62, 73, 140–141, 180
Gaunilo, 55–56
Geiler von Kaisersberg, 30n
Gellert, Christian Fürchtegott, 23n
Genus (*Gattung*), 63–64. *See also* Species
Geometrical method, 152–153, 155, 157, 202–203, 267–268
Gerard, Alexander, 210n
German(ic): language, 65, 201; peoples, 35, 40; soul, 121
Ghert, Peter Gabriel van, 118n
Gnosticism, 20n, 34
God, 66–67, 92–93, 153, 188–189, 203, 207–208; as absolute, 195, 251, 260; absolute definition of, 56; as absolute idea, 18; as absolute identity, 121; as absolutely infinite being, 158; attributes of, 124, 130, 142–144, 163, 204, 254; belief in, 216; as "beyond," 204; "birth" of, 128–129, 130; body of, 124n; as concrete, 21, 32–33; essence in nature, 118n; and evil, 160; existence of, 54–56, 91, 162, 194–195, 211, 239, 251, 254; God-world relation, 78, 122–131, 151, 162–163; as ground, 271; hidden or unknown, 123, 163, 258; human relationship to, 95–103; idea of, 239; immediate presence of, 31, 243, 251–252; monad of monads, 195; necessity of idea of, 22; otherness within, 32; as particular, 18; most perfect being, 54–56, 142–143, 163n; postulate of practical reason, 249–250; most real being, 239; as self-differentiating, 21; as spirit, 17, 97–98, 162–163,

197–198, 204–205, 257–258, 260; locus of spirits, 167–169; seven spirits of, 128; as truth, 169; union with, 168; will of, 91–92, 164; wisdom of, 126. *See also* Allah; Jesus Christ; Trinity

Godfrey de Bouillon, 46n

Good: highest, 249–250; idea of, 249; superessential goodness, 89

Göttingen University library, 78

Gottsched, Johann Christoph, 198n, 199n, 200n

Grace of God, 18, 26, 195n

Gregory IX (pope), 60

Gregory of Nazianzus, 20n

Gregory of Nyssa, 20n

Grotius, Hugo, 170n, 178–180, 183

Haecceitas, 190n

Haldane, E. S., 4

Happiness (*Glückseligkeit*), 249–250; theory of, 218, 244

Harmony: as happiness, 249; preestablished, 191n, 195n, 197, 205; universal, 88–89. See also *Temperamentum*

Harris, H. S., x, 14

Harvey, William, 180

Heart (*Gemüt*), human, 26, 30, 44, 49, 94, 96, 99, 100, 129, 205–206. *See also* Soul

Heavens, 123–125; stars and planets, 124–125, 148, 227

Heeren, Arnold Herrmann Ludwig, 60n

Hebrew language, 36, 37n, 39n, 73n, 74, 83n

Hell, 127–128, 129

Henry of Ghent, 59n

Heraclitus, 88

Hercules, 86

Herder, Johann Gottfried, 3, 152n

Herennius, C., 85–86

Hertford (count), 213n

Hesiod, 62

Hierocles of Alexandria, 263n

Hindu, Hinduism, 31n, 33n, 69, 205, 254

History, as pathway of spirit, 22

Hjort, Peder, 53

Hobbes, Thomas, 59n, 134n, 170n, 180–182, 183n

Hodgson, Peter C., ix, x, 14

Hoffmeister, Johannes, 4, 7

d'Holbach, Paul Henri Thiry, 208–209

Home, Henry, 210n

Horn, Georg, 133

Human being, humanity (*Mensch, Menschheit*): distinction from animality, 25, 194; evil of, 24–26; freedom as pinnacle of, 245; human nature, 181–182, 264; human race, 92–93; image of Trinity, 121–122; immediate, natural, 256; unity with divine nature, 17–18; universal, 64

Hume, David, 5, 134n, 170n, 183n, 212n, 213–217, 218n, 220n, 221

Huygens, Christian, 186

I (*Ich*), 127–128, 139–140, 142–143, 161, 192, 218, 224, 229–236, 246, 254, 259, 264, 265; absolute I, 259; as infinite, 236; not-I, 232–234, 236, 246. *See also* Self-consciousness

Ibn Rushd (Averroes), 37n

Ibn Sina (Avicenna), 37n

Idea (*Idee*): adventitious ideas, 144n; in Christianity, 33; compound, 214n; concrete, 112, 177–178; divine, 48; "general ideas" (Locke), 170–178; of God, 142–144, 239; innate, 144–145, 167n, 173–174; philosophical, 26–27, 44, 113, 120, 143, 236–237, 271–272; Platonic, 63; single, 167; universal, 87, 168, 239

Ideal: the "ideal," 239; "ideal" influence, 191; idealism, 63, 192; ideality, 192; principle, 234, 265n

Identity (*Identität*), 78n–79n, 126, 267; A = A, 230n; absolute, 121, 163, 260n, 267, 272; abstract, 206, 245–246; I = I, 233, 265; of indiscernibles, 191; of opposites, 272; of subjective and objective, 260–261, 263–266; of thought and being, 54–56, 140; of will with itself, 245

Ideology, 212

Image of God, 19, 108n, 121, 126

Imagination (*Einbildung, Imagination, Phantasie*), 85–86, 113, 156–157, 166, 265–266

Immediacy (*Unmittelbarkeit*), 141, 255–256; in knowing, 43, 54, 206, 210, 243, 251–258, 260; of worldly, 20–21

Impulse (*Anstoss*), 258

Imputation, 96

Incarnation, 31–35, 54, 67

Indifference (*Indifferenz*), absolute, 260, 263, 267, 269

Indiscernibles, identity of, 191, 194, 198

Individuality (*Individualität*), 198; determination of, 154, 155; individual lives of philosophers, 74, 109–110; individualism, 74; individuation, 185. *See also* Singular

Induction (*Induktion*), 115

Infinite (*Endliche*), 126, 156–158, 173, 221, 236–238; "bad" infinite, 156–157, 236; God as, 156; I as, 235–236; as spiritual, 237

Influxus physicus, 150

Inquisition, 77

Intuition (*Anschauung*), 220n, 222–223, 226–227, 232–234, 251, 254, 266; aesthetic, 265n;

of God, 222, 251–252; immediate, 139; intellectual, 251, 253, 259–261; outer, 213; productive, 230n

Inwardness (*Innerlichkeit*), 121, 123, 131–132

Irenaeus, 34n

Isaac, 62

Islam, 35, 36, 83, 207. *See also* Allah; Qu'rān

Jacobi, Friedrich Heinrich, 10, 43n, 78, 79n, 80n, 81n, 82n, 139n, 143n, 154n, 162n, 163n, 188n, 212n, 213n, 217, 240–243, 244n, 250–258, 266, 271n

Jaeschke, Walter, ix, x

Jalāl al-Dīn Rūmī, 39n

James I (king of England), 110, 114n

Jean Charlier (John Gerson), 68

Jelles, Jarig, 154n

Jerusalem, Johann Wilhelm Friedrich, 208n

Jesuits, 135, 189n

Jesus Christ, 31–35, 66, 93, 99, 120, 207, 208n; Christology, 34–35; "Firstborn Son," 20; Logos, 32–33; Son of God, 32; Sophia (wisdom), 32–33. *See also* Trinity

Jews, 36, 39, 74, 93, 114, 121, 151–153. *See also* Hebrew language

Jezebel, 114n

Joachim of Fiore, 48n

John XXII (pope), 63n

John of Salisbury, 62n

Jourdain, Amable, 37n

Judgment (*Urteil*), 225, 229; aesthetic, 223n, 246–247; synthetic a priori, 220–221; teleological, 247–248

Julian of Toledo, 65–67

Kalām, 36n, 37n

Kant, Immanuel, 9, 10, 24n, 55–

56, 79n, 108, 109n, 134n, 135, 140, 163n, 202n, 212n, 213n, 214n, 217–229, 234, 235, 236–240, 241, 243, 244–251, 253n, 255, 261, 268, 269n. *See also* Kantian

Kantian(ism), 10, 79, 212, 215, 229, 234, 238, 244–246, 250, 253n, 255, 258. *See also* Kant

Karl VII Albert (Holy Roman emperor), 200n

Kepler, Johannes, 180

al-Kindī, 36n

Kingdom of God, 27, 46

Knowing (*Wissen, Erkennen*), 139, 166–169, 218, 229–232, 237–238; immediate, 139, 251–258; knowing of knowing, 230–22; knowing things in God, 167; mediated, 255–256, 258. *See also* Cognition

Knox, T. Malcolm, 4

Koethen, J. J., 188n

Köppen, Friedrich, 241n, 252n

Krug, Wilhelm Traugott, 231n, 234

Language, human expression in, 97

Latin language, 59, 60, 152, 201

Lauer, Quentin T., 4

Law. *See* Right

Lectures, all series, 1–2, 108n; Haldane-Simson English edition, 4; *Werke* edition of (*see* Michelet)

Lectures of 1805–06, 3

Lectures of 1819, 212n

Lectures of 1820–21, 212n

Lectures of 1823–24, 3, 108n–109n, 116n, 134n, 212n, 258

Lectures of 1825–26, 4, 5, 134n, 149n, 212n–213n, 217n; editorial principles of English edition, 10–14; reconstruction of, 5–10

Lectures of 1827–28, 116n, 120n, 212n

Lectures of 1829–30, 116n

Leibniz, Gottfried Wilhelm, 35n, 108, 134, 145n, 149n, 155, 170, 185–198, 201, 204, 205n, 224n; Leibnizian philosophy, 201–202, 224

Lessing, Gotthold Ephraim, 30n, 152n, 240, 241n, 255n

Leyen, Damian Hartard von der, 186n

Life: living beings, 148; universal, 121–127. *See also* Organic life; Vitality

Light: divine, 118–119, 122, 130; of knowledge, 144, 167–169; primordial 87–89

Lightning, 128, 130

Limit (*Grenze*), 232–236, 238

Lipsius, Justus, 73n, 93n

Loans, Jacob, 73n

Locke, John, 108, 109n, 135, 145n, 147n, 149n, 170–178, 183n, 185, 188, 213

Logic, 87n, 202, 266, 269, 271; Aristotelian, 52, 115n, 225, 229; formal, 54–56, 68; logical inference, 50. *See also* Deduction; Induction; Syllogism

Louis IX (king of France), 63

Louis XIV (king of France), 186n

Louis the Pious (French emperor), 52

Love, 48, 169; divine, 123, 129; intellectual love of God, 165

Lucifer, 127–128

Ludewig, Chancellor, 200n

Ludwig of Bavaria (Holy Roman emperor), 63

Lull, Raymon (Llull, Ramon), 68n, 82–87, 162n

Lullian Art, 78, 82–87

Luther, Martin, 28, 47, 97; Lutheran faith, 95, 206–207

Machiavelli, Niccolò, 93

Magic, 61, 114

Maimon, Salomon, 162n
Maimonides, Moses, 36–39
Malebranche, Nicolas, 108, 134,
144, 145n, 149n, 151n, 165–
169, 170, 191n, 205n
Marcion, 34n
Marcurius, 119, 120, 124n
Mary (princess of England), 171n
Mary, Virgin Mother of Jesus,
61, 66, 97, 136, 207n; Im-
maculate Conception of, 77
Materialism, French, 134, 207,
208n
Mathematics, 75, 135, 136, 137,
138, 183–184, 187, 199, 201,
221, 268; calculus, 186–187
Matter (*Materie*), 79–81, 82n,
147–148, 166, 190–193, 208n,
269
Maupertuis, Pierre Louis Moreau
de, 219n
Maximilian I (Holy Roman
emperor), 74n
Maximilian III Joseph (elector of
Bavaria), 200n
Maximum and minimum, 81–82
Mechanism, 92, 147–149, 150;
"reflective mechanics," 149
Medabberim ("speakers"), 37–39
Mediation (*Vermittlung*), 97,
141, 144, 151, 242, 255–258,
266; *temperieren,* 204n
Medici, Cosimo the Elder, de, 73
Medici, Lorenzo I, de, 73
Medicine, 114n, 115n, 170
Melancthon, Phillip, 73n
Mendelssohn, Moses, 219, 240,
243n
Metaphysics (*Metaphysik*), 114n,
133–134, 141, 148–149, 150,
184, 185, 189, 198, 203–
205, 262, 268; empirical,
178; metaphysical world, 89;
"private," 108; rational, 219;
of understanding, 101, 209,
238, 269
Metternich, Lothar Friedrich von
(elector of Mainz), 186n

Meyer, Ludwig, 153, 157n
Michael Balbus (Byzantine
emperor), 52n
Michael Scotus, 60n
Michelet, Karl Ludwig, 3, 4, 5,
6, 37n, 109n
Miller, A. V., 4
Mind (*Geist*), human, 137, 153,
161–162, 173, 241–242, 254n.
See also Spirit
Mirandola, Giovanni Francisco,
73n
Mirandola, Giovanni Pico, 73, 77
Mnemonics, 85–89
Mode, 176; categories of
modality, 226; of substance,
156, 159
Monad, 170, 189–198, 202n
Montaigne, Michel de, 93
Morals, morality (*Moral,
Moralität*), 163–165, 202,
209–211, 250
Mosaic scriptures and laws, 152
Mosheim, Johann Lorenz, 35n,
209n
Motion (*Bewegung*), 147–149,
159
Murr, Christoph Theophil de,
163n
Musaeus, Johann, 153n
Mutakallimūn, 37n
Mysterium Magnum, 126
Mysticism, 67–68, 131
Mythology, 107

Naturalism, 207, 208
Natural state (*Natürliche*), 19,
181–182; negation of, 19–21,
41
Nature (*Natur*), 87–90, 92, 162,
208, 263–264, 265n, 266–270;
as body of God, 125; as evil,
19; "hidden" (inner), 118–
119; highest goal of, 264; law
of, 116; natural law, 183n;
natural sphere, 45; natural
things, production of, 79–
81; philosophy of, 268–271;

sensible, 222–223; source of, 124; unity of, 116. *See also* Natural state

Neander, August, 34n

Necessity (*Notwendigkeit*), 82, 142, 164, 214, 216, 217, 219–221, 249–250, 272

Negation (*Negation*), 141, 154, 160n, 236. *See also* Negativity

Negativity (*Negativität*), abstract, 38–39; negative, 189, 232–233, 235, 245; negative in God, 120–121, 123, 127–128, 130. *See also* Negation

Neology, 208n

Neoplatonism, 17–20, 27, 34, 52n, 60n, 87, 89, 123, 132, 133n, 226, 271. *See also* Plotinus; Porphyry; Proclus

Nero, 160

Newton, Isaac, 109n, 149n, 183–184, 186–187

Nicolai, Friedrich, 240

Nizolius, Marius, 74n

Nominalism, 62–65

Nothing (*Nichts*), 126, 127–128

Novalis (Friedrich von Hardenberg), 43n, 118n

Object (*Gegenstand*), 174, 232–233; objective, 263–265; pure objectivity, 257

Occasionalism, 151n, 191n

Ockham, William of, 62–65

Oetinger, Friedrich Christoph, 118n

Oken, Lorenz, 269

One (*Eine, Eins*), 78n, 82, 123, 126, 142, 155, 162–163, 168, 192n, 208, 254

Ontological Proof, 54–56, 142–143, 239

Opposition (*Entgegensetzung*), 232–234, 255; opposites, 151, 272; coincidence of opposites, 82n

Optimism, 188–189, 205

Orestes, 160n

Organic life, organism (*Lebendigkeit, Organische*), 79n, 193, 197, 247–248, 270. *See also* Vitality

Oriental thought, 39

Original Sin, 24–26

Orthodoxy, religious, 26, 101

Oswald, James, 211n

Other (*Ander*), 156, 232–233

Otherworldliness, 205

Pantheism, 20, 37–39, 60n, 78–79, 92n

Paris, University of (Sorbonne), 52n, 56–57, 59, 60, 92n

Participation, 168, 195n

Particular (*Besondere*), 112–113, 141, 154–155, 159n, 167–169, 170, 172–173, 248; divine particularity (*Besonderheit*), 33–35. *See also* Singular

Passions (*Leidenschaften*), 45–46, 68–69, 153

Passivity (*Passivität*), 81, 192–193, 233–234

Paul (the Apostle), 19n, 34n, 258

Paulus, H. E. G., 151n, 153n, 163n

Pelagianism, 25n

Penitence, 96, 99

Pentecost, 31n

Perception (*Wahrnehmung, Perzeption*), 174, 192–193, 196, 198n, 214, 224, 226–228, 237. *See also* Sensation

Perfection, idea of, 54–56, 142–143, 188–189

Peter Lombard (Peter of Novara), 57, 58, 59, 66

Peter the Great (tzar of Russia), 199, 200n

Petrarch, Francesco, 71

Petry, M. J., 185n

Pfefferkorn, Johann, 74n

Philagrios the Grammarian, 263n

Philip the Fair (emperor of France), 63n

Philo of Alexandria, 39, 128n

Philosophy, 129, 184–185; divisions of, 149n, 202; Greek, 35–36, 71–74, 107, 133; historical development of, 2, 113, 272; philosophical development of Christian principle, 28; political, 178–183; popular, 205; relation to theology, 58–60; Roman, 133; standpoint of, 24; thinking that thinks itself, 133n; transcendental, 221
Physics, 148–149
Pietism, 199–200
Plato, 22n, 23n, 42, 56, 62, 73n, 88n, 110, 173, 237. See also Neoplatonism; Platonism
Platonic Academy of Florence, 73
Platonism, 14, 72–73; Cambridge Platonists, 173n. See also Neoplatonism; Plato
Plethon, George Gemistos, 73n
Plotinus, 19, 34, 73n, 80n, 87n, 123n, 128n, 190n
Poetry, 113, 265
Pomp, 124n
Pomponazzi, Pietro, 72, 91n, 92n, 93n
Pores, 148
Porphyry, 52
Porter, James, 210n
Positing, (Setzen), 232–233
Possibility (Möglichkeit), 80–81
Potency (Potenz), 268–270
Power (Macht), 122n; of God the Father, 125–127
Practical domain (Praktische), 218, 233, 244–246, 248–250, 268
Presence to self, at home with self (Beisichsein), 96–99, 146, 257
Presupposition (Voraussetzung), 138–139, 142–143, 272
Proclus, 17, 19, 77n, 80n, 87n, 88n, 89, 123n, 132n, 225n
Property (Eigentum): as inner possession, 103, 107n, 108; private, 69–70, 246; spirit's

own, 102–103; worldly, 103, 107n, 108
Providence, divine, 23, 66, 92
Pseudo-Dionysius (the Areopagite), 52, 61
Pufendorf, Samuel, 183
Purpose (Zweck), 79, 247–248; human purposes, 95. See also Teleology
Pythagoras, 62, 225n
Pythagoreans, 73–74, 192n, 195n, 226; Neopythagoreans, 132, 133n. See also Pythagoras

Qualities (Qualitäten): categories of quality, 226; in God, 124–125, 128n; primary and secondary, 147, 174; of a thing, 123
Quelle (source), 123
Quellgeister (source-spirits), 124n, 125n
Quodlibetal method, 59
Qur'ān, 207, 208

Radbertus, Paschasius, 66n
Ramus, Petrus (Pierre de la Ramée), 202
Rationalism: philosophical, 134, 178; theological, 208n, 240n, 255
Raymond of Sabunde, 68
Real: medieval realism, 62–65; principle, 234, 235n, 265n
Reason (Vernunft), 81, 92–93, 113, 217n, 218n, 222n, 236–240, 244, 253, 260n; contradiction in, 238; development of, 173; law of, 182; practical, 248–250
Recognition (Anerkenntnis), 97–98, 246n
Reconciliation (Versöhnung), 18, 26–27, 42–43, 107, 272; of outer and inner, 110; religious, 98; with self, 95
Reflection (Reflexion), 175, 189

Reid, Thomas, 210–211, 212n, 213n
Reimarus, Elise, 241n
Reimarus, Hermann Samuel, 152n, 208n
Relation (*Verhältniss, Relation*), 232; categories of, 226
Religion: Catholic, 206–207; essence of, 252n; Lutheran-Protestant, 28, 206–207; positive, 29, 206–207; public, 152–153; Tibetan Buddhism (Lamaism), 31n–32n; universal, 22–24. *See also* Christianity; God; Hinduism; Islam; Jews
Remond, Nicholas, 193n
Representation (*Vorstellung*), 50, 63–65, 86–87, 98, 107–108, 138, 142–143, 170n, 192–193, 220n, 224n, 242, 251, 254, 261; Locke's "ideas" as, 172–178
Resolution (*Auflösung*), 203–205, 236, 272
Resurrection, bodily, 66
Return (*Rückkehr, Zurück-gehen*): of all things, 88–89; into self, 79–80, 102, 125–126; of spirit to God, 164
Reuchlin, Johann, 73–74
Revelation (*Offenbarung*), 29, 126, 143; inward, 139, 251–253
Richter, Gregor, 119n
Right, legal, 69–70, 95, 179, 180–183, 215, 246
Rixner, Thaddä Anselm, 17n, 37n, 56n, 59n, 64n, 67n, 68n, 73n, 75n, 76n, 83n, 84n, 85n, 90n, 91n, 92n, 112n, 124n, 127n, 151n, 209n, 210n, 211n, 212n, 213n
Robinet, Jean-Baptiste, 163n, 258n
Roman world, 40–41, 51–52
Roscelin of Compiègne, 62, 64n
Rousseau, Jean-Jacques, 208

Rückert, Friedrich, 39n
Rüdinger, Andreas Christoph, 211n

Sacrament (Lord's Supper), 47, 96
St. Clair, Arthur, general, 213n
Saint-Martin, Louis Claude de, 118n
Salitter, 119, 120, 123, 124n
Salvation, 98
Sancrucius, 59n
Sanctification, 100–101
Scaliger, Julius Caesar, 72n
Schelling, Friedrich Wilhelm Joseph, 2, 9, 10, 13, 22n, 34n, 108, 109n, 118n, 135, 159n, 234, 235, 253n, 258n, 259–271, 272
Schlegel, Friedrich, 22n, 23n, 118n, 253n
Schleiermacher, Friedrich, 13, 163n, 200n, 252n
Schmidt, Johann Lorenz, 152n
Scholasticism, 40–68, 72, 77, 81, 94, 99, 111, 115n, 190, 202, 263; Scholastic method, 59, 111, 178
Schönborn, Johann Phillip von (elector of Mainz), 186
Schulze, Gottlob Ernst, 234, 235n
Sciences, natural, 71, 111–117, 129, 135, 137, 148–149, 178, 180, 183–184, 264
Secular sphere, 45, 69–71
Self-consciousness (*Selbstbe-wusstsein*), 146, 193, 218, 219–220, 224, 251; transcendental unity of, 221n, 229. *See also* I
Selfhood (*Ichts*) or Separator, 126–130
Selfishness (*Selbstischkeit*), 69
Selflessness (*Selbstlosigkeit*), 69–70, 74
Semler, Johann Salomo, 152n
Sensation (*Empfindung*), 172,

174–176, 214, 222–223, 237.
See also Senses
Senses, sensible, sensibility (*Sinne, Sinnliche, Sinnlichkeit*): inner sensibility, 213, 222; natural sensibility, 205–206, 212, 254; senses, 138; sensible domain, 111, 113, 129, 266; sensible forms, 270; sensibility, 215, 222. *See also* Sensation
Shaftesbury, Anthony Ashley-Cooper (earl of), 170–171
Siger of Brabant, 70n
Simple (*Einfache*), 166, 190, 224
Simson, Frances H., 4
Sin, 24–26, 54, 67, 92–93. *See also* Evil
Singular, singularity (*Einzeln, Einzelheit*), 20–21; divine singularity, 33, 49; singular, 154, 159n, 189; singular things, 146. *See also* Individuality
Skepticism, 73n, 134, 137–138, 212, 213, 215n–216n, 235n
Smith, Adam, 184, 210n
Socinians, 34–35
Socrates, 34n, 62, 112, 208n
Solomon (Hebrew king), 67, 114
Sophie Charlotte (princess and queen of Prussia), 187, 188
Soul (*Seele, Gemüt*): animal, 193n; human, 64–65, 101–102, 122, 131, 148, 166–167, 192n, 211n, 244; immortality of, 72, 91n; soul-body relation, 150–151, 191n, 197. *See also* Heart
Sozzini, Franco, 34n
Sozzini, Lelio, 34n
Space, 172, 176, 222–223
Spalding, Johann Joachim, 24n, 208n
Species (*Gattung*), 113, 116, 146, 172, 177–178. *See also* Genus
Speculative: idea, 100; thought, 49–50, 54, 102, 112, 156, 262
Speusippus, 62

Spinoza, Benedict, 78n, 79n, 108, 109n, 134, 138n, 145, 146, 149, 150, 151–165, 168, 169, 170, 172, 188n, 267, 268n. *See also* Geometrical method; Spinozism
Spinozism, 37–39, 78–80, 154, 162–163, 165, 188, 189, 207–208, 240, 241n. *See also* Pantheism; Spinoza
Spirit (*Geist*), 108, 122, 161, 269; absolute, 272; activity of, 145; as being in and for itself, 17; concrete, 17, 102; definition of, 40, 102; as free, 102–103, 145, 150, 257; Holy Spirit, 29, 31, 47, 118n, 122; idea of, 266; labor of, 271–272; as other than natural, 18–19, 41–43, 161; process of in history, 22–24, 68–71, 113; self-consciousness of, 23; self-realization of, 2, 272; subjective, 42–43, 97–103; substance as, 154–155; witness of, 257. *See also* Mind
Spontaneity, 224n, 244
Stanley, Thomas, 133
Stäudlin, Carl Fridrich, 59n
Steinbart, Gotthilf Samuel, 219n
Steuart, John, 184n
Stewart, Dugald, 116n, 212
Stewart, J. Michael, x, 14
Stoicism, 61–62, 73–74
Subject (*Subjekt*): human, 26, 94–95, 216; individual as, 18, 43; as object of grace, 26; principle of subjectivity (*Subjektivität*), 97–98; subjective domain, 94–95, 228, 263–265; thoughts and representations of, 29
Sublation (*Aufhebung*), 156, 192, 250, 266
Substance (*Substanz*), 37–39, 87, 125, 145–146, 150n, 156–163, 177, 190–193, 208; absolute, 121, 153–155, 159, 195;

bodily, 147; definition of, 145, 156; God as, 145, 156, 195; individual, 189–190; natural, 79n; subsistence (*Bestehen*) as, 177

Sufficient reason, principle of, 194

Superessential, 88–89

Syllogism (*Schluss*), 85n, 115, 139–140, 202–203, 238. *See also* Deduction; Logic

Synthesis, 220, 237

Syrians, 35–36, 60n, 83n

Systema assistentiae, 151, 197, 205

Tartaglia, Niccolò, 76n

Teleology, 116–117, 246–248. *See also* Purpose

Temperamentum, 123, 125

Tennemann, Wilhelm Gottlieb, 17n, 36n, 37n, 52n, 53n, 54n, 55n, 56n, 57n, 58n, 59n, 60n, 61n, 62n, 63n, 64n, 65n, 66n, 67n, 68n, 71n, 72n, 73n, 76n, 77n, 78n, 79n, 80n, 81n, 83n, 84n, 109n, 111n, 117n, 118n, 135n, 136n, 185n, 195n, 209n, 211n, 213n

Tertullian, 20n, 23, 34n

Thales, 17

Theodicy, 23, 188–189

Theology, 65–67, 129, 152, 163, 198–200; relation to philosophy, 49–50, 57, 99–100, 107–108, 251–252; Scholastic, 58–60. *See also* Church fathers; Doctrine

Theoretical domain (*Theoretische*), 233

Theosophy, 119

Thing in itself, 227–228

Thinking (*Denken*), 49, 54–56, 84, 89–90, 101–102, 107, 123, 144, 154–155, 158, 224–225, 254, 256–257, 262; abstract, 42–43; as external, 48–49; form of, 262; free-thinking,

91; infinity in, 235–236; meditative thinking (*Nachdenken*), 133; that proceeds from itself (on its own account), 131–132, 135, 137–141, 146–147; pure, 272; spiritual, 146; subjective, 220; thinking things, 146n, 158n; thoughtful cognition (*denkende Erkennen*), 26, 27

Thomasius, Christian, 201n

Thomas of Strasbourg, 66, 67n

Tiedemann, Dieterich, 52n, 59n, 61n, 63n, 73n, 75n, 78n, 185n, 200n, 213n

Tilly (count Johann Tserclaes von), 136

Time, 176, 214, 222–223

Töllner, Johann Gottlieb, 24n

Torment (*Qual*), 123, 129, 130

Totality (*Totalität*), 146, 158–159, 195–196. *See also* All

"Transcendent," 221, 238

"Transcendental": 221, 223, 224n, 236; philosophy, 261n, 265

Transubstantiation, 77

Trinity (*Dreieinigkeit, Dreiheit*), 19, 20n, 35n, 56, 120, 121–130, 133n, 207n; Father-Son-Spirit, 48, 67; Father, 122–130; son, 126–130; Spirit, 130–131

Truth (*Wahrheit*), 129, 154, 163–164, 168–169, 178, 218, 262; of content, 173; as what is concrete, 17; "eternal truths," 144–145; factual, 194n; fundamental truths, 210–211; highest, 98–100; of idea, 19; necessary, 194; truthfulness of God, 143–144

Tschirnhaus, Walter von, 201n

Turks, 81, 206

Unconditioned (*Unbedingte*), 233n, 236–237, 241–243, 251

Understanding (*Verstand*), 90,

130, 147, 155, 156, 158–159, 175–177, 198, 206–207, 224–227, 236, 247, 253n, 262; categories of, 219; general principles of, 179–180; healthy human, 29–30, 50–51, 205–206, 211; philosophy of, 201; "primordial," 87–89; reflective, 134, 180, 226; subjective, 89; universal, 79

Unity (*Einheit*): absolute, 198; of being and thinking, 107, 139–141, 153–154, 159; determinate, 192; of everything, 78–82, 89–90, 189; of opposites, 122–123, 130; of sensory manifold, 224–228; spiritual, 18–19; of subjective and objective, 260; of thinking with itself, 101

Universality (*Allgemeinheit*), 33, 44, 214–216, 217, 219–221, 222–223; principle of, 121; universal (*Allgemeine*), 63–64, 80n, 113, 140–141, 154–155, 159n, 167–169, 170, 172–173, 177–178, 182, 207, 214, 248, 254

Universe, 79n, 81–82, 88–90, 195–196, 238

Utility (*Nützlichkeit*), 111–112, 185

Valentinus, 34n
Vane, William, 171n
Vanini, Lucilio Cesare, 70n, 72n, 76, 90–93, 94, 188
Vice, 160
Vico, Giambattista, 3
Vitality (*Lebendigkeit*): in nature, 79–81, 247–248; of spirit 102, 161, 256. *See also* Organic life
Vocation (*Bestimmung*): of hu-

manity, 21, 25, 26, 218; of spirit, 25, 165, 272
Voet, Gisbert, 137n
Voltaire (François-Marie Arouet), 208
Vortices, 148

Wagner, Johann Jakob, 85n
Walter, Balthasar, 120n
Wendt, Amadeus, 17n, 195n, 210n, 211n
Wessel, Johann, 73n
Wette, Wilhelm Martin Leberecht de, 252n
Will (*Wille*), 130, 159; of God, 126, 195; human, 95, 143, 160, 169, 181, 199, 244–246; universal, 182. *See also* Freedom
William of Champeaux, 62
William III, of Orange, 171
Wissowatius, Andreas, 35n
Witness of the spirit, 99–100
Wolff, Christian, 108, 135, 150, 162n, 170n, 198–203, 204n, 213n, 218, 239n; Wolffian philosophy, 198, 202n, 218–219
Wollaston, William, 209
Word of God, 126
Worldliness (*Weltlichkeit*), 44–46, 65, 68–69; worldly domain, 110, 112
World-soul, 82n
Worship, 96–97
Wrath of God, 127–128, 130
Wuttke, Heinrich, 198n, 199n, 200n, 202n

Xenophanes, 107n

Zeno, 157n
Zimara, Marcus Antonius, 72n

Designer:	U.C. Press Staff
Compositor:	Prestige Typography
Text:	10/13 Sabon
Display:	Sabon
Printer:	Braun-Brumfield, Inc.
Binder:	Braun-Brumfield, Inc.